In the KITCHEN
with A GOOD APPETITE

Melissa Clark

HYPERION

NEW YORK

In the KITCHEN
with A GOOD APPETITE

150 RECIPES AND STORIES

ABOUT THE FOOD YOU LOVE

Photo credits: pp. xx, 432: Stock.Xchng/Andrzej Pobiedziński; pp. 5, 247, 271, 297, 385, 417: Stock.Xchng; p. 77: Stock.Xchng/Ivan Vicencio; p. 119: Stock.Xchng/Marco Michelini; p. 345: Stock.Xchng/Zsuzsanna Kilian

Library of Congress Cataloging-in-Publication Data

Clark, Melissa.
    In the kitchen with a good appetite : 150 recipes and stories about the food you love / Melissa Clark.—1st ed.
        p. cm.
    ISBN 978-1-4013-2376-9
  1. Cookery, International. I. Title.
    TX725.A1C5585 2010
    641.59—dc22   2010005760

Hyperion books are available for special promotions and premiums. For details contact the HarperCollins Special Markets Department in the New York office at 212-207-7528, fax 212-207-7222, or email spsales@harpercollins.com.

Book design by Shubhani Sarkar

FIRST EDITION

10   9   8   7   6   5   4   3   2   1

SUSTAINABLE FORESTRY INITIATIVE
Certified Fiber Sourcing
www.sfiprogram.org

THIS LABEL APPLIES TO TEXT STOCK

We try to produce the most beautiful books possible, and we are also extremely concerned about the impact of our manufacturing process on the forests of the world and the environment as a whole. Accordingly, we've made sure that all of the paper we use has been certified as coming from forests that are managed, to ensure the protection of the people and wildlife dependent upon them.

TO MY PARENTS,
WHO TAUGHT ME FIRSTHAND
JUST HOW DEEPLY FOOD MEANS LOVE

CONTENTS

3   Learning to Like Fish

4 It Tastes Like Chicken

5 I Never Was a Vegetarian

6 Things with Cheese

12 Lessons in Imbibing

ACKNOWLEDGMENTS

Let's start way back when I was a graduate student–caterer, workshopping my short stories in the Columbia MFA program by day, moonlighting as the de facto in-residence faculty caterer. I knew I wanted to write, and I knew I wanted to cook. But as far as what I wanted to do to make a living? The thought that I could still apply to law school when the MFA was done was never far from my mind.

Then one day Betty Fussell came to teach a class on food writing. Suddenly my obsession with making the best chocolate cake had meaning beyond my sweet tooth. Writing about it made me feel like I had something vital to say, and surprisingly to me, people were nearly as happy to read about my experiments in the kitchen as they were to partake. I'll always remember that class. It gave me the courage to say, "I'm going to be a food writer when I grow up." So I want to thank Betty Fussell for her encouragement and example.

Upon hearing about my food writing career plans, my good friend Josh Mack introduced me to a book packager who needed someone to write a bread machine cookbook in six weeks. It was summer vacation from grad school, and I spent it testing bread recipes, three bread machines humming in my walk-up around the clock. Every four hours, which was how long the cycle took to complete, I'd feed the machines more flour, yeast, flavorings, etc., and continue the testing until I finally had 125 publishable recipes. I loved every minute of it, and the cookbook gave me the credential I needed to get a job as a recipe editor at a food magazine. So thanks to Josh.

I spent several years editing recipes for *Great American Home Cooking*, a test magazine that never launched. But that didn't matter. I had a blast, and learned so much, mostly from Pamela Mitchell and Tracey Seaman (and may I add they baked the cake for my second wedding? It rocked!). Many thanks to both of them.

It was during that time that I also met Rick Flaste, who was then coauthoring a cookbook. Rick had hired my friend Ana Deboo as an editing assistant, and when she went to India for a three-week vacation, I subbed for her. Thanks to dear Ana for taking that vacation, and for years of help and support on almost every book I've worked on.

Meeting Rick was one of the most important events in my career. Rick was a star editor at the *New York Times*, then the head of the Science section. When he helped create the Dining section a few years later, he remembered me, and asked me to write a tiny, weekly Q&A called the "Food Chain." This was in 1998. I've been writing for the *Times* as a freelancer ever since. And Rick has since become a supportive friend and sounding board. Thanks to Rick, to whom I owe a lot more than just the next round.

It was Rick who persuaded Pete Wells to become the current editor of the section, and it was Pete who came up with the idea for "A Good Appetite." When he asked me to write it, I was naturally beyond thrilled and still am. I thank Pete in my head every single week.

And of course, I must thank my other fantastic editors: Nick Fox, Pat Gurosky, and Samantha Storey.

I am exceedingly grateful to my always-on-it agent, Janis Donnaud, who's got my back. She makes it all happen on every project I'm involved in, and I don't often get a chance to say thanks.

I couldn't do a tenth of what I do without my recipe testers and editors: Zoe Singer, Sarah Huck, and Jaimee Young. Nearly every recipe and sentence in this book was improved thanks to their hard work. And even better, they make my workday fun and productive and super special.

The Hyperion team has been a dream to work with. Many thanks to editor Leslie Wells for being so smart and charming, publisher Ellen Archer for being an inspiration, Shubhani Sarkar for the lovely design, and Allison Mc-Geehon for the help getting the word out about the book. Thank you also to Laura Klynstra, Matthew Benson, and Morgan Welebir.

As always, I'm grateful to my family and friends who have helped me bring this book to life, whether they fielded panicked phone calls, tasted countless variations on the same dish, or were the inspiration for many of the recipes and stories within these pages. Thanks to my sister Amy Sara Clark, my aunt Sandy Clark, cousins Laurie Beth Clark and Michael Peterson, friends Robin Aronson, Karen Rush, David Wondrich, Marina Wondrich-Rush, Alice

Feiring, Frank Bruni, Zoe Reiter, Susan Gross and Dan Silverman, Kate Krader, Anya Von Bremzen, Shawn and Steve Kelley, Gabriel and Judith Levitt, Katherine Schulten, Mike Dulchin and the twins Madeleine and Nick Dulchin, Jessica Monaco and Nick Noyes, Bryony Romer, Mary Jones, and John Magazino.

Finally and most important, I want to thank my husband, Daniel, and baby daughter, Dahlia. I get more joy from our little family than from anything else I can think of. You both restore me, and make me more . . . me.

FIRST WE GET LOST,
THEN WE HAVE LUNCH

Driving around and around the traffic circle in southern France, my mother attempted to give my father directions.

"Eleven o'clock, direction Les Baux, eleven o'clock, go, now!" she said, her voice tight and emphatic. She was indicating the turn, not the time. It was nearing 1:00 P.M., and we were late for lunch at Beaumaniere in Provence.

My sister and I, ages nine and eleven, were immersed in our comic books and completely ignoring the magnificent mountain view outside the car window. We were inured to the buzzing front seat tension; we'd heard it before, the familiar prelunch panic of locating the restaurant, or at least trying to find a person out at lunchtime in rural France to ask directions.

On our summer vacations, we were always late for lunch.

My father turned the car as commanded. Finally on the right road, my mother relaxed.

"Girls," she said, peering at us in the rearview mirror while she combed her hair, "this is a very famous restaurant."

"Uh-huh," we replied, eyes glued to Betty and Veronica.

"Missy, you were here before," she added slyly.

"Um," I said.

"You were conceived at the inn. Dad and I stayed here after a dinner of langoustines with Pernod and this wonderful pâté. Our room had an artichoke-shaped shower . . ."

"How many forks?" I yelped, desperate to change the subject. Even though I was curious about how the langoustines were prepared, the idea of my own conception, possibly in an artichoke-shaped shower, was just too noisome to contemplate.

Plus, the number of forks mattered to me. The more forks, the fancier the restaurant (according to our foodie bible, the *Michelin Guide Rouge*), and the fancier the restaurant, the more desserts they usually served—predessert, dessert, petit fours. I loved a multifork restaurant.

"Two stars, four or five forks," my mother said, much to my delight.

IT WAS MY PARENTS' DREAM to eat at every Michelin-starred restaurant in France. Augusts—the traditional month of vacation for psychiatrists (their shared profession)—were spent in this happy pursuit with my sister and me in tow. Fancy restaurants like Beaumaniere were an integral part of the experience. We kids might have missed out on appreciating the more epicurean aspects of such a meal, but there was usually something pretty good to eat.

At Beaumaniere, I had a tentative nibble of tender, gamy veal kidney coated in a creamy mustard sauce—not so bad. And my first ever bite of summer truffle shaved tableside into delicate petals over a fingerling potato tart. Now, that was heaven. I even found out how good eggplant and zucchini could be when braised in olive oil and rosemary until soft and bursting from their skins, served with rare lamb.

We had a family tradition when it came to eating out, whether we were at the most elegant restaurant in France or a diner in Brooklyn. We all ordered different dishes (duplicates were a no-no), ate a precise quarter of what was on our plates, then passed them, "Clark-wise," we joked, to our left. That way we each got to taste everything the table had ordered.

Back home in the United States, our odd behavior warranted a quick shrug from waiters. But in France, they were truly flummoxed and a little horrified (and this was before we even asked for the doggie bag). Crazy Americans, they sniffed behind our backs.

This meant that tasting menus for the whole table were off-limits. Why sample only five or six of the chef's creations when, with all four of us ordering three courses, we could taste twelve?

This doesn't even count the cheese course, like the one at Beaumaniere, where, I happily learned, fromage blanc might be accompanied by lots of sugar for topping, but it still didn't count as dessert.

After the last chocolate truffle was devoured by the kids and espresso sipped by the parents, we all climbed back into the steaming car to reverse the journey to the tiny house we had rented. It was just past 4:00 P.M. We'd left the house at 11:00 A.M.

"So," my mother said, checking her teeth in the mirror, "what shall we have for dinner tonight?"

AND SO IT WENT FROM MORNING TILL NIGHT, with one meal flowing into the next. At breakfast my parents cross-referenced Michelin with another guide called *Gault Millau,* choosing a place for lunch. Then into the car we piled, driving up to two hours to the restaurant of choice. Sometimes we stopped at a town on the way with a pretty church or museum. But the pretty church and museum were beside the point. It was all about lunch—until dinnertime, that is.

Our trips revolved around food: reading about it, buying it, cooking it, ordering it in restaurants. There was one time we even scavenged for it—plucking snails from the garden of our Burgundy house rental—snails that my parents purged, starved, and cooked a few days later. While my sister and I didn't care much for the gritty gastropods, the garlic herb butter surrounding them was magical.

So it was no wonder that when I was a kid, the words *vacation* and *cuisine* were inseparable from my image of France, the idyllic country where even desserts were followed by dessert—trays of colorful macaroons and crumbly sable cookies that were brought to the table after the *mousse au chocolat* was devoured. France was a country where parents were never on diets and schoolchildren ate chocolate sandwiches instead of tuna fish. I could even have chocolate for breakfast—melted bittersweet bars layered into flaky croissant dough.

Back in Brooklyn, it was cereal for breakfast, egg salad sandwiches for school lunch, and fish sticks and flank steak on most nights for dinner. But my culinary education forged on nonetheless.

In Chinatown at dim sum, I learned about chewy, succulent pork tripe and pale dumplings filled with bright green chives. In Little Italy, I'd plead for escarole and spumoni, and Sheepshead Bay meant creamy chowder and biscuits at Lundy's. My favorite uncle, Danny, for whom my daughter Dahlia is named, initiated my love of sushi when I was twelve, teaching me to slurp the raw quail egg off the sea urchin so it wouldn't drip down my chin. Perhaps more traditionally for a Jewish Brooklynite, for Sunday brunch there were bagels and lox, taut sour pickles, and crumbly babka. And once a week on Thursday, my dad cooked something special for the family—perfecting his version of shrimp in lobster sauce or veal scaloppine with wild mushrooms he picked up at Balducci's—back when it was in the Village.

WHETHER EATING AT A RESTAURANT OR AT HOME, my parents had a rule that my sister and I actually followed: Try everything once and if you don't like it, you don't have to try it again. If we refused, punishment was subtle but palpable parental disappointment.

My sister, less susceptible to that kind of guilt trip, was a pickier eater and all-around more normal child when it came to food.

"*Eww!*" she'd exclaim over a piece of stinky vacherin.

I was more afraid of losing my parents' esteem than slipping down a raw oyster or licking a wobbly cube of foie gras aspic. The upside was that most of those things actually tasted good, and it was thrilling, even at age nine, to suck the unctuous marrow prize out of a craggy veal bone.

FLASH FORWARD to my putative adulthood.

Those summer vacations may have gone the way of the French franc, but when it comes to home cooking, I am just as intrepid.

After all, if there's one thing I learned from my parents, it's that getting lost is all part of finding a great meal. For me these days, this means cooking without recipes and creating dishes from my cravings coupled with what's available in the supermarket, seasoned with the mishmash of food memories I've amassed over the decades.

With work and family life ever present, my recent recipes tend to be on the quicker, more straightforward side of gourmet, but no less delectable for that. And as my baby daughter, Dahlia, cuts her first tooth and starts on solids, I look forward to there being one more family member to join in on the passing of the plates, now Clark-Gercke-wise, but still to the left.

1 Waffling toward Dinner

The first best thing about adulthood is being able to order three desserts for two people. The second is having breakfast for dinner whenever the urge for pancakes pulls harder than pork chops.

Breakfast for dinner has a lot of advantages over dinner for dinner. For one, it's relatively quick and easy to make, this being a prerequisite for anyone not fully caffeinated who is playing with fire. For another, you can probably make it with the staples in your fridge and cupboards, so no advance planning is generally necessary. And if you like breakfast and wish you were more awake when you ate it, it's plain ideal.

One thing about breakfast for dinner is that it's best made for an intimate number of people, preferably one. (I'm not talking about brunch, which, as a meal usually made for company or ordered in restaurants, is another matter entirely.) Eating cheese-topped scrambled eggs by yourself with the newspaper and a glass of wine will heal all the evils of your day, and you can assemble it in about six minutes flat. This makes it particularly appropriate for starving people who work late, or at least procrastinate their dinner making until waiting for takeout seems an eternity.

As opposed to dinner, breakfast has fewer moving parts to keep track of. Sure, there's the banana to cut up for the oatmeal, and the maple syrup and butter to slather on top of French toast. But it's nowhere near as complex as mincing garlic, chopping onions and vegetables, and sautéing them all to a perfect gold before adding canned tomatoes or fish or what have you. Like stretch jeans and dim lighting, breakfast is forgiving.

As much as I have the biggest sweet tooth on this side of adulthood, I still prefer savory breakfasts for dinner to sweet ones (this does not apply to morning-time breakfasts—those I prefer sweet). This is because savory foods go better with red wine, and that's what I want to drink with my dinner most of the time (though I can envision bourbon complementing French toast if you go easy on the syrup).

Naturally, of all the savory breakfast foods that are brilliantly adaptable for dinner, eggs top the list, followed closely by bacon and sausage, and rather distantly by bagels and lox (unless you are serving Champagne, in which case they supersede even the eggs). I won't even mention home fries, which I would rather never eat again any time of the day.

Of course the relegating of eggs to breakfast is a uniquely American phenomenon (egg salad and deviled eggs excepted). Some of France's most celebrated dinner dishes involve eggs, perhaps cooked in red wine with mushrooms and bacon (*oeufs en meurette*), dolloped with homemade mayonnaise (a precursor of deviled eggs), made into omelets with cheese and herbs, or any of the other forty-five preparations that *Larousse Gastronomique* puts forth. In Italy, it's the rare and spoiled aficionado who eats scrambled eggs with truffles or a giant, egg-stuffed raviolo in the dawning hours.

And don't forget that the obverse also applies. Dinner for breakfast (as we Americans would see it) is the norm in much of the rest of the world, which happily awakens to grilled salmon, rice and beans, or big bowls of spicy noodle soup with nary an egg, or pancake, or piece of toast in sight.

I suppose my guiding philosophy is to eat what you want when you want it, and if that means dumplings or truffles at 9:00 A.M., and eggs Benedict at midnight, then so be it. After all, isn't that what being an adult is all about?

BUTTERY POLENTA WITH PARMESAN AND OLIVE OIL–FRIED EGGS AND SWISS CHARD

A curious universal that Americans share with one another to the exclusion of the rest of the world is our penchant for cold cereal for dinner.

Even if you haven't doused peanut butter Captain Crunch with milk since college, unless you were brought up in a faraway land like Europe or Mars, chances are you've fixed yourself a nice big bowl of Cheerios, plopped in front of the TV, and eaten a meal that made you happy.

What's odd is, given this predilection for cold cereal, hot cereal never really entered the picture. Rice Krispies with *CSI*? But of course. Farina with *Project Runway*? Maybe not.

The exception is grits and her first cousin on the Italian side, polenta. Served soft and steaming, with plenty of salt and pepper and maybe some grated cheese, a bowl of buttery polenta or grits is exactly what to have for dinner when you're hungry for something more immediate and comforting than takeout, and more filling and savory than Wheaties. It's just right when you want to cook something for yourself and your family that's a little bit special, a lot delicious, but still easy enough to do without pulling down the mandoline/Silpat/juicer from on top of the cabinets.

A dish like buttered, cheesy polenta, perhaps topped with olive oil–fried eggs and served with sautéed Swiss chard, will satisfy your cravings, whether you eat it in front of the TV, or even better at the table, with a loved one and/or a nice glass of blood-warming red wine.

For this dish, you can use either coarsely ground polenta or grits; essentially, they are the same thing, both made from ground dried corn, though some people will tell you polenta is milled finer than grits, or vice versa. Either way, look for stone-ground, which is coarser and more flavorful. Unless you're truly pressed for time, avoid anything labeled "instant," a euphemism for quick and pasty.

Once you've got your ground corn, you can cook it in water, broth, or even—as a hedonistic friend of mine does before grating in at least a pound of Cheddar and a fist-size lump of butter—in whole milk. Recipes will tell you that you need to patiently stand over the pot, dutifully stirring the cornmeal, or it will clump up in protest. I've never found this to be true. A brisk stir with a whisk every couple of minutes will correct any lumpy inclinations and give you freedom to make the rest of the meal.

One caveat: The worst burn I've ever gotten—far more painful than the time I grabbed the handle of the cast-iron pan that had just been taken out of the oven—was from an eruption of molten polenta landing with a splat on my wrist. Stand back, stir thoroughly, then step away from the stove and go do something else in the kitchen. Or partially cover the pot, leaving enough of a gap so the steam can escape.

If you like greens, you could sauté a bunch of Swiss chard with loads of garlic and a jolt of red pepper flakes, which will break up the creamy lusciousness of the polenta.

While the polenta is bubbling and raining yellow on the stovetop, rinse the Swiss chard leaves, gather some into a stack, lop off the stems with a knife, and slice them up. Cook them while the polenta simmers.

If you don't like or have Swiss chard, any green vegetable will do. Broccoli rabe or broccoli, kale, spinach, collards, Brussels sprouts, green beans, or even radicchio—just something to act as a bright-tasting, healthful, guilt-reducing counterpoint to all that melting butter and cheese (you could also cut the amounts of butter and cheese if your guilt runs deep).

As a final garnish, there is the crowning pièce de résistance that in my mind elevates this dish way above Froot Loops. That's the olive oil–fried eggs.

I got the idea to top one breakfast item with another and serve it for supper from the Spanish, who, in their great culinary wisdom, are apt to give you garlicky potatoes with fried eggs at 10:00 P.M. And of course grits with fried eggs and biscuits (and/or ham, bacon, red-eye gravy) might just be one of the great meals of all time no matter when you serve it forth.

Cooked sunny-side up, the runny egg yolk coats the greens and cornmeal mush like a golden, velvety sauce. It picks up and carries the flavors of cheese, garlic, and pepper, imbuing each tender mouthful. If you cook the eggs over high heat, letting the whites get brown and crisp around the edges, they'll shatter when you bite, adding crunch to the sea of softness.

Preparing it isn't at all tricky, but it does take more effort than pouring milk over cold cereal. One undisputable fact: Polenta with sautéed greens and olive oil–fried eggs pairs much, much better with red wine than cornflakes, and to my mind, that's reason enough to make it tonight.

Buttery Polenta with Parmesan and Olive Oil–Fried Eggs

4½ cups water or low-sodium chicken or vegetable broth
1½ cups polenta (not quick cooking), coarse cornmeal, or corn grits
¾ teaspoon salt
2 to 4 tablespoons unsalted butter
¼ teaspoon freshly ground black pepper, plus additional
1-ounce chunk Parmesan cheese (or substitute ¼ cup grated
    Parmesan cheese)
2 tablespoons extra-virgin olive oil
8 large eggs
Coarse sea salt, for garnish

Time: 25 minutes

Serves 4

1. In a large pot, bring the water or broth to a simmer. Stir in the polenta and salt. Simmer the polenta, stirring frequently but not constantly, until thickened to taste, about 10 to 20 minutes. Stir in the butter and pepper and cover the pot to keep warm.
2. Using a vegetable peeler, slice the cheese chunk into slivers. Or grate the cheese on the largest holes of a box grater.
3. In a large skillet, heat 1 tablespoon of the olive oil until very hot. Fry 4 of the eggs until the edges are crispy and the yolks are still runny. Repeat with the remaining oil and eggs.
4. Pile the polenta into bowls, top with the cheese and then the fried eggs. Garnish with sea salt and more pepper, and serve.

Garlicky Swiss Chard

Time: 15 minutes

Serves 4

2 bunches Swiss chard, stems removed
1 tablespoon olive oil
2 garlic cloves, minced
Large pinch crushed red pepper flakes
Salt

1. Stack the chard leaves on top of each other (you can make several piles) and slice them into ¼-inch strips.
2. Heat the oil in a very large skillet (or use a soup pot). Add the garlic and red pepper flakes and sauté for 30 seconds, until the garlic is fragrant. Stir in the chard, coating it in oil. Cover the pan and let cook for about 2 minutes, until wilted. Stir and cook for 2 minutes longer, uncovered. Season with salt. Serve in the same bowl as the polenta, if desired.

VARIATION: BUCKWHEAT POLENTA WITH BACON-SAUTÉED RADICCHIO

I made this variation on my polenta and egg recipe when I spied a package of buckwheat polenta at Bklyn Larder, a gourmet market near my home. I had heard about buckwheat polenta but never tried it, and the jaunty striped package beckoned from its shelf.

The powder inside was golden flecked with brown—a mixture of cornmeal and ground buckwheat, not all buckwheat as I had assumed. The directions were the same as for regular polenta and it cooked up in minutes. Meanwhile, I sliced some radicchio to sauté with garlic in place of Swiss chard.

As I was slicing, the red and white ruffles of radicchio reminded me of red cabbage, which in turn made me think of German food, and naturally conjured bacon. So I decided to add some to the pan and serve the crunchy, salty bits as a garnish. Plus then I could sauté the radicchio in the leftover bacon fat, which, when seasoned with a little red wine vinegar, would be an excellent way to tame the bitter vegetable.

I suppose that to keep faith with my original recipe I could have also cooked an egg in the extra bacon fat. But I literally had other fish to fry, namely two pink-edged little bass fillets. I dusted them with cayenne, fried them in bacon fat, and garnished them with cilantro; that was all they needed.

It made a heartier meal than the egg version, and richer, too, from the bacon and the buckwheat, which added a haunting earthiness to the sweet corn polenta. Regular polenta will work, too, if you don't feel like hunting down the buckwheat kind. You can also serve the bacon-sautéed radicchio on its own as a side dish. Or scramble it into eggs for a meal anyone would be happy to wake up—or wind down—to.

Buckwheat Polenta with Bacon-Sautéed Radicchio

1 cup buckwheat polenta (or substitute regular polenta)
1 teaspoon kosher salt, plus additional
2 tablespoons unsalted butter
Freshly ground black pepper
4 strips bacon, cubed
2 garlic cloves, minced
2 heads radicchio, halved lengthwise and thinly sliced
½ teaspoon red wine vinegar

Time: 20 minutes

Serves 2

1. In a large pot, bring 3 cups of water to a simmer. Stir in the polenta and salt. Simmer, stirring frequently, until the polenta is thickened to taste, about 5 minutes. Stir in the butter and pepper to taste and cover the pot to keep warm.
2. In a large skillet over medium heat, cook the bacon until brown and crisp and transfer to a paper towel–lined plate to drain.

3. Pour off all but 2 tablespoons of the grease from the bacon pan (you can save it to sauté fish or eggs if you like) and add the garlic. Cook for 30 seconds, until fragrant, then add the radicchio. Decrease the heat to low and cook, stirring frequently, until tender and wilted, about 5 minutes. Stir in the vinegar and salt and pepper to taste. Serve the radicchio over the polenta, garnished with the bacon.

PESTO SCRAMBLED EGGS WITH FRESH RICOTTA

In my fantasy life living on a farm, autumn would be dedicated to "putting things up." I'd pickle, can, preserve, dry, and freeze all of the waning garden bounty before it succumbed to the first frost. Then in winter, I'd make entire meals out of the pantry, reveling in the likes of black currant jelly and pickled green tomatoes lined up on neat, well-organized shelves.

In my Brooklyn reality, however, my garden gets just enough sun to nourish the few pots of herbs I try to remember to water. And the pantry is cramped and permanently overflowing with a chaotic assortment of who knows what. But that doesn't stop me from preserving my harvest to the utmost. Which means come October, I make pesto for the freezer.

Over the years, I've played with different kinds of pesto, blending the nuts and herbs into baroque combinations like black mint–pecan, lemon verbena–parsley-cashew, and lovage-pistachio. And year after year, those elaborate concoctions sit in the freezer until I've gone through the entire batch of classic basil and pine nut. Because as good as the more experimental kinds may be, there are few things that brighten up a dreary winter's evening more than the grassy summer scent of basil and garlic emanating from a bowl of steaming-hot pasta.

So this year I decided to dry the lemon verbena and mint for tea, and focus all my pesto energies on basil. And so one recent sunny Sunday morning, I piled the freshly picked sprigs into a satisfying mountain on the counter.

Of all the pesto research I've done, the key, command the books, is to make sure to use Genovese basil (a delicate type with diminutive leaves), Italian pignoli nuts, Ligurian olive oil, Parmigiano-Reggiano or pecorino cheese, and good sea salt. Of the five, I had exactly two on hand, the cheese and the salt. And since I wasn't planning on using cheese (pesto freezes better without it, then you can add some when you defrost if you like), I was down to one. My basil was the regular, floppy-leafed kind that seems to grow well on my deck, my olive oil from Tuscany, and while I wasn't sure of the exact provenance of my pine nuts, for $7 a pound, my guess was somewhere in China rather than the Mediterranean.

Nevertheless, I forged on, using the food processor rather than the mortar and pestle my sources insist on. It wasn't because I was lazy . . . okay, it was because I was lazy. Pounding enough pesto for four by hand is all well and good, but to make enough to last me until spring was a test of endurance I was unwilling to endure.

Once you've decided to forgo a mortar and pestle, making pesto is fast and very simple: You put all your ingredients into a food processor and press Start. About five minutes later, a jumble of bright green leaves, beige nuts, and dark oil becomes an emerald emulsion with a heady, herbal, garlicky fragrance that immediately fills the kitchen and makes your stomach growl, especially if it's around dinnertime.

I thought about boiling up some linguine and making myself a hearty meal of pasta with pesto. But since it was Sunday, brunch seemed more appropriate, even if it was nearing 6:00 P.M. And it would give me an excuse to make another of my pesto staples, softly scrambled eggs with pesto and cheese.

Scrambled eggs with pesto and cheese is a dish I've been making for ages, varying the cheeses to match the contents of my refrigerator. I've used Cheddar, Gruyère, goat cheese, and even cream cheese with great success. On that day, the fridge yielded up some fresh ricotta that I had left over from a cake.

After scrambling the eggs until they were barely set with large, quivering curds, I streaked in some freshly made pesto and dotted the top with ricotta. The ricotta, normally sweet and creamy, tasted even more so next to the salty, pungent pesto, and made a dense, luscious foil for the cloudlike eggs. It was a perfect supper that, thanks to my pesto stash, I'd get to enjoy all winter long.

Last of the Summer Pesto

½ cup pine nuts
¾ cup extra-virgin olive oil
4 ounces basil, stemmed (about 5 cups of leaves)
2 to 3 garlic cloves, coarsely chopped
½ teaspoon salt, or to taste

Time: 15 minutes

Makes about
1 cup

1. Heat a small skillet over medium heat and add the pine nuts. Toast them, shaking the pan and stirring, until golden brown all over, about 3 minutes. Pour the nuts onto a plate to cool.
2. Combine all the ingredients in a food processor or blender and puree until smooth. Use immediately, store in the refrigerator for up to a week, or freeze for up to 6 months.

Soft Scrambled Eggs with Pesto and Fresh Ricotta

1 tablespoon butter
5 large eggs
2 tablespoons grated Parmesan cheese (optional)
Pinch salt
Freshly ground black pepper
2 tablespoons pesto, plus more to taste
⅓ cup fresh ricotta cheese, broken up into clumps

Time: 5 minutes

Serves 2

1. Melt the butter in a medium-size skillet, preferably well seasoned or non-stick.
2. Meanwhile, beat the eggs with Parmesan cheese, if using, salt, and pepper. Pour the eggs into the pan, swirl, and turn the heat to low. Using a heatproof rubber spatula, scramble the eggs until very loosely set and still runnier than you like them. Remove the pan from the heat and drizzle the pesto on

top of the eggs. Give the eggs one more gentle scramble—enough to finish cooking them and to distribute the pesto somewhat. The pesto should still be in dark green streaks, not homogenously combined with the eggs. Scatter the ricotta on top of the eggs and drizzle with more pesto if desired. Serve at once.

DIM SUM EQUALS CHICKEN FEET (AND CHEATERS PORK AND GINGER DUMPLINGS)

I cannot remember the first time I ever ate dim sum, but I can remember the first time I ate chicken feet, boiled in the kosher soup my grandmother made for Friday night dinner. They were spread out on a china plate, pale and bloated next to the border of tiny pink rosebuds. It never occurred to me not to partake. There was no surrounding taboo, no disgust at consuming something so obviously fowl. I just ate them, and they were good: soft, fatty, and salty, as perfect a child's finger food as canned jumbo black olives that fit like snug hats on tiny fingertips.

Eating them was fun. First, I bit off the center pad, which detached in a sinewy lump. That was the prime morsel, the filet mignon of a chicken talon. Then I nibbled the cartilage running up the leg. The toes, which were the most fun, went last, one claw at a time sucked bare and dry. Then, as daintily as an eight-year-old might manage, I spat out the bones. By the time I went through this elaborate technique with each foot (usually two or three), dinner was over, and I was excused from eating stringy pot roast over the protests of my grandmother, who, though legally blind, could somehow still see the uneaten slabs of dry meat on my plate.

Friday night dinners were abandoned when my grandmother died; I was twelve. Since my parents didn't make chicken soup with feet, I didn't have my favorite dish again until college, when my family starting making a habit of going for dim sum.

We started meeting in Chinatown for convenience. It was a perfect halfway point between Flatbush (in Brooklyn), where my parents live, and Morningside Heights (on the Upper West Side of Manhattan), where I went to school. Since as a college student I certainly wasn't going to waste a weekend night having dinner with my parents, a weekend breakfast of dim sum seemed just right.

And thus the ritual began. One Sunday a month, I woke to my alarm at 8:30, and rode the subway down to Canal Street to meet my parents for breakfast. While in China dim sum is mostly thought of as a teatime meal or snack, in New York's Chinatown, the crowds start early. By 11:00 every seat is taken, and restaurants remain teeming and jostling until at least 2:00. My parents insisted that the freshest and best dim sum was to be had early in the morning, so we always met around 10:00, finishing before the legions descended.

Having dim sum became the time I spent with my family, and it remains a cornerstone to this day. It was at dim sum that I introduced my parents to my more serious boyfriends, putting them through what I called "trial by dim sum" to see if they could stomach spicy pork tripe, salt-fried squid, or beef dumplings before noon. I fell in love with my first husband, an otherwise prim Swede, as I watched him gleefully gnaw the web between stewed ducks' feet and bite the heads off shrimp. Years later, I broke the news of the divorce to my parents while poking at fried taro cakes with chopsticks, unable to eat.

Fortunately, a loss of appetite is the exception to my dim sum experiences, which is important since the food never stops. At dim sum, dishes come quickly in what seems like a never-ending succession: deep-fried crab balls, tripe, congee, green scallion dumplings, shrimp rice noodles, fried eggplant, snails in black bean sauce, mussels with chiles, and soft, slightly sweet pork buns—a favorite with friends who would rather be at brunch.

I drag people to dim sum as often as possible. With a crowd, we can sample a wide variety of little dishes as they pass on steel carts, pushed by uniformed women who announce their cargo in Cantonese as they go from table to table. It occasionally surprises them when I call for chicken feet— served not pale and bloated like at my grandmother's house, but rich and brown and braised in a spicy sauce. I still eat them according to the technique I developed as a child, which I hope to be able to teach to my daughter during dim sum one day. Of course when she grows up, she may abandon dim sum in favor of some other ritual—like Friday night dinner. Luckily, the technique will still serve her well.

And in the meantime, there are always dumplings.

Cheaters Pork and Ginger Dumplings

1 tablespoon soy sauce, plus additional, for dipping

1 teaspoon sesame oil

¼ pound shiitake mushrooms, stemmed and caps wiped clean

½ pound ground pork

1 egg white

2 scallions, finely chopped

2 teaspoons cornstarch

1 teaspoon freshly grated gingerroot

1 teaspoon mirin or sherry

Pinch kosher salt

Large pinch ground white pepper

24 (3-inch) round gyoza or wonton wrappers, or (4-inch) square wrappers,
    cut into 3-inch rounds

Bok choy, cabbage, or lettuce leaves, for lining the steamer (optional)

Time: 35 minutes

Makes 24

1. Preheat the broiler. Arrange an oven rack six inches from the heat source.

2. In a bowl, whisk together the soy sauce and sesame oil. Place the mushroom caps on a baking sheet. Brush both sides lightly with the soy sauce mixture (reserve what's left for the pork mixture). Broil the mushrooms, turning once halfway through, until golden brown and almost dry to the touch, about 8 minutes. Let cool slightly; finely chop the mushrooms.

3. In a large bowl, combine the remaining soy mixture, mushrooms, pork, egg white, scallions, cornstarch, ginger, mirin or sherry, salt, and pepper; mix well.

4. Line a baking sheet with parchment. Place a gyoza or wonton wrapper on a clean work surface. Brush the tops of the wrappers lightly with water. Place a scant tablespoon of pork mixture in the center of the wrapper. Pinch the edges up around the filling, leaving the top open. Transfer the finished dumpling to the lined baking sheet; repeat with the remaining dumplings.

5. Fill a large pot with ½ inch water. Place a steamer basket inside the pot (it should just fit); line the basket with bok choy, cabbage, or lettuce leaves, if

desired, to prevent sticking. Arrange the dumplings in a single layer inside the basket (cook the dumplings in batches if they do not all fit). Steam the dumplings, covered, over high heat, until the pork is cooked through, about 15 minutes. Transfer to a platter and serve, with additional soy sauce for dipping.

THE MYSTERIOUS DAVID DARES PANCAKE

Call it a German pancake, a Dutch baby, or clafouti, a puffy baked pancake is a basic foodstuff common to cultures with surfeits of milk and eggs, or at least a taste for sweet, custardy breakfasts.

Our family was of these latter ranks. As I was growing up, my mother made what she called her "David Dares" pancake, and while the name made no sense, in the context of breakfast neither does "Dutch baby."

Whatever the designation, I loved that pancake, with its airy, souffléd custard that browned in the oven and its glazed sugar top drizzled with a zippy burst of lemon. My mother baked it in a gratin dish deep enough for the eggs to set into a wiggly, flanlike layer beneath the buoyant, crunchy crust that deflated dramatically when you dug in. But that certainly didn't stop us.

We didn't eat David Dares pancakes often. Brunch time was usually reserved for bagels and lox, which was sacrosanct in our house. Nearly every Sunday, my father took my sister and me to an appetizing store on Avenue C in Brooklyn, where he ordered the requisite ⅜ pound Nova, sliced thin, and two small and crunchy sour pickles for the girls. We nibbled our pickles on the way home, working up our appetites for warmed (not toasted) poppy seed bagels slathered with scallion cream cheese and daintily draped in the translucent pink sheets of salty lox.

But on certain Sundays, my mother decided that she was in the mood for a David Dares pancake, and so it went.

I never saw a David Dares pancake outside of our house until I grew up and left for college. One weekend I visited my best friend, Mara, in Boston, where she was interning for the summer. For breakfast, she made what she called German pancakes, which closely resembled the David Dares, but with less sugar and no lemon. I told her about my mother's version.

"But why are they called David Dares? Do you think someone dared a guy named David to make them?" she joked.

Actually, that was exactly what I used to think when I was a kid, imagining the airy pancake invented by an intrepid epicure named David, who, upon being dared to create an unusual breakfast, made an ordinary pancake batter rise and puff in the oven like magic.

That Mara could picture the same thing just proved why we were best friends.

Anyway, Mara gave me her recipe, but even so, it just isn't as good as David Dares—or at least my mother's incarnation of it.

When I finally got around to asking my mother for the recipe, she was stymied.

"But I haven't made that pancake in years," she said, adding that even if she could find the original, it wouldn't be the same.

"You know how I love to tweak a recipe, and I know I did a lot of tweaking with that one, but I can't remember how."

She did remember how to correctly spell the name of it, which turned out to be named after David Eyre, a gentleman in Hawaii with whom food editor Craig Claiborne once had brunch. Mr. Eyre got the recipe from a cookbook published in 1919, which recommended serving the pancake for dessert. I found all this out with a few clicks on the *New York Times* Web site.

I liked my childhood narrative better, though I was happy to uncover the original recipe. It was similar to Mara's, but added a confectioners' sugar and lemon juice topping that was responsible for its sweet-tart, refreshing flavor and caramelized crust.

Naturally, when I made the pancake, I could not suppress the urge to tweak. I added a little salt to deepen the flavor, and an extra egg to mimic the thick, flanlike quality of my mother's version. And although she still can't remember, I'll bet back when I was a kid, she did the same.

The Mysterious David Dares Pancake

3 large eggs, lightly beaten

½ cup milk

½ cup all-purpose flour

¼ teaspoon freshly grated nutmeg

Pinch kosher salt

4 tablespoons unsalted butter

2 tablespoons confectioners' sugar

2 tablespoons freshly squeezed lemon juice (about ½ lemon)

Time: 25 minutes

Serves 4

1. Preheat the oven to 425°F. In a medium bowl, whisk together the eggs, milk, flour, nutmeg, and salt until combined. The mixture will still have some lumps.

2. In a 10-inch ovenproof skillet over medium heat, melt the butter. When the butter has melted, carefully pour in the pancake batter and transfer the skillet to the oven. Bake until the pancake is puffy and golden brown around the edges, about 15 minutes.

3. Working quickly, take the skillet out of the oven and, using a fine-mesh sieve, shake the confectioners' sugar over the pancake. Return the skillet to the oven until the butter has been absorbed into the pancake and the sugar is lightly caramelized, an additional 2 to 3 minutes.

4. Splash the lemon juice over the pancake, cut into wedges, and serve immediately.

CRÈME BRÛLÉE FRENCH TOAST WITH ORANGE BLOSSOM WATER

My friend Robin called the other day. "I was making French toast for my kids, and all of a sudden I remembered that amazing French toast you used to make when you lived on Third Street. Do you have the recipe?"

Not only didn't I have the recipe, I had no idea what she was talking about.

It's true, I lived in a fifth-floor walkup on Avenue A and 3rd Street, where Robin and I would hang out before or after eating sushi down the street. But what French toast?

"Really? You don't remember?" she asked, incredulous at my seeming senility. "You were just starting up with Joe and you were working on perfecting French toast, I don't know, maybe to serve to him? Every time I came over—there was a period of about a month there when this was going on—if it was morning, or afternoon, or night, you'd serve me some French toast experiment. You'd use orange blossom water and French bread and soak it for a really long time. Then when you cooked it, the crust got crunchy and delicious."

I could vaguely picture a younger me kneading the bread so it would absorb more of the milk mixture, and debating about whether adding both vanilla and orange blossom water would be overkill (no). And I could even imagine serving such a French toast to my ex, Joe, with him in a vintage shirt covering up his tattoos and a straw fedora tilted toward his chin, which was covered in a hipster manifestation of facial hair growing this way and that. But it was all so vague and hazy.

However, the recipe Robin was talking about sounded tempting enough to re-create whatever the heck it was I did back then.

I waited until the weekend, letting a baguette harden on the counter in the days before. The drier the bread, the more of the custard mixture it would absorb, so old bread is a plus when it comes to the best French toast (though regular bread works nearly as well if that's what you've got).

I stirred together a simple custard of eggs and milk, adding a splash of orange blossom water and some orange juice. As I whisked, the scent of orange blossoms made me think about Moroccan cooking, or at least the recipes I've made from various Moroccan cookbooks over the years. They often seemed to combine orange blossom water with cinnamon, so I sprinkled some in. Who knows if I had the same association back when I lived on 3rd Street, but it was likely.

While the bread soaked up all the custard, I thought about another tasty French toast recipe I used to make, albeit more recently. It called for baking the bread over a brown sugar–butter syrup, which caramelized on the toast, forming a crème brûlée–like topping.

The good thing about baking French toast is that one doesn't need to stand over the stove frying it, leaving a person free to mix mimosas. And I can bake bacon at the same time so brunch will be ready all at once.

So when the bread was well soused, I placed it on top of the brown sugar–butter mixture, and popped it into the oven. It emerged with a crackling, glassy sugar surface over tender slices of bread imbued with the scent of Northern Africa (as I imagined it). It wasn't exactly the French toast I made when I lived on 3rd Street, nor was it something that would necessarily attract Robin's five-year-olds—at least until they're old enough to ironically sport their own fedoras and mutton chops.

Crème Brûlée French Toast
with Orange Blossom Water

Time: 35 minutes

Serves 4 to 6

1 cup packed light brown sugar

8 tablespoons (1 stick) unsalted butter, melted and still warm

2 large eggs, well beaten

1½ cups milk

2 tablespoons freshly squeezed orange juice

2 teaspoons orange blossom (flower) water

1 teaspoon vanilla extract

½ teaspoon ground cinnamon

¼ teaspoon kosher salt

1 (10-ounce) French baguette, sliced diagonally, 1 inch thick
(about 20 slices)

1. Preheat the oven to 375°F. In a medium bowl, whisk together the brown sugar and butter until the sugar is completely dissolved. Pour the mixture into a large rimmed baking sheet (about 11×17 inches).

2. In a pie pan or other shallow dish, combine the eggs, milk, orange juice, orange blossom water, vanilla, cinnamon, and salt. Coat both sides of the bread slices in the egg mixture, letting the bread soak up the custard for at least 15 minutes, then place them on the prepared baking sheet over the brown sugar mixture. Bake for 25 to 30 minutes, or until the tops of the bread are golden brown and the sugar is bubbling.

3. Serve immediately while still hot, with the crunchy brown sugar side up, spooning more of the pan syrup over the tops.

NOTE: To oven-bake your bacon at the same time, place strips of bacon on another large rimmed baking pan (about 11×17 inches) and place it in the oven on the rack below the toast (so none of the bacon grease accidentally splatters on the toast). The bacon will cook in about the same time as the toast (25 minutes or so), though watch it carefully. When it's done to taste, take it out of the oven and drain the strips on a brown paper bag or paper towels. If you like it sweet, you can drizzle a little maple syrup over the bacon before baking.

ANYA'S POTATO AND ONION TORTILLA WITH ALLIOLI

When it comes to entertaining, my friend Anya Von Bremzen goes all out. An invitation to her house for a "simple dinner with a few dear friends" means a buffet table overflowing with hors d'oeuvres—caviar blinis and eggplant salads, home-stuffed grape leaves and fresh tuna empanadas—followed by several sit-down courses of paella or braised baby lamb, then an extravagant dessert, maybe ice cream steeped with the dried rose petals she carted home from Istanbul.

Even something as debilitating as abdominal surgery is no reason for Anya to slacken the offerings. I went to visit her after she had just come home from the hospital, expecting a somber and brief sickroom chat.

But sheathed in a bright silk peignoir and golden slippers, Anya led me to a table filled with pitchers of passion fruit punch and platters of canapés with smoked fish and sliced meats.

"It's nothing, just a little something I threw together in between naps," she said with a sigh before sinking down to the couch to rest.

I always mean to leave her house with recipes. Really, I do. But with the sparkling fruity aperitifs followed by wine followed by a silver tray of after-dinner liqueurs and icy home-flavored vodka, my will to beg is impaired.

Luckily for me, Anya has written several cookbooks. So when I want to re-create a recipe I've had at her house, like the tender, eggy tortilla strewn with potatoes and chorizo and topped with garlic allioli, chances are it's been published.

The recipe was easy to find (open to page 142 of *The New Spanish Table* if you happen to have it in your bookcase). I had all the requisite ingredients on hand except, it turned out, the chorizo. Mine had incubated a strange blue fuzz, so I threw it out.

No matter. The allioli, the Spanish version of aioli or garlic mayonnaise, had enough flavor to carry the dish, especially if I browned the onions until they turned deep mahogany and took on a savory, brawny taste.

I made the allioli first. It seemed like egg overkill to sauce an omelet with mayonnaise, but I had a dozen eggs from the farmers' market and it tasted so good at Anya's . . .

Here's a confession about making allioli, mayonnaise, aioli, or any egg-based emulsion. Every time I attempt to do it in the blender, it breaks apart (the sauce, not the machine). I am sure I could figure out why if I called a few culinary scientist types for explanation. But after so many disappointments, a few years ago I started making the sauce by hand with either a mortar and pestle or bowl and whisk, and it comes out perfectly, never separating. And a small batch (1 yolk, ½ cup oil) whips up in under 2 minutes, way before my arm starts to ache.

It helps to have an extra pair of hands so one person can drizzle in the oil while the other stirs. But as long as you drizzle slowly, letting the drops incorporate without flooding the yolks, the mixture stays tight, shiny, and very thick. (If it's too thick, add a few drops of hot water to thin it.)

I could have added a whole host of things along with the garlic to flavor the allioli, but I was too lazy to chop up herbs or chiles or toast cumin or coriander. So I left it plain but oh so good.

Then I made the tortilla, adding the potatoes and eggs to the pan and letting it cook three-quarters of the way through before sticking it in the oven to finish.

When I turned the tortilla out of the pan, it was just solid enough to slice, but still soft and jiggly on the inside. I spooned a giant glob of allioli on top of my slice and took a bite.

The onions were both sweet and savory, and gave the tortilla a hearty, rich flavor even without the chorizo (which I'll try next time, adding it to the pan with the onions). And the potatoes were tender and toothsome and gave the eggs just enough substance without adding heft.

At Anya's, the tortilla was cut up and served with cocktails as an elegant finger-size tapas. But at home, with a bitter greens salad, I'd call it dinner, or with some hot buttered toast and jam, it could turn into brunch. Or vice versa.

Anya's Potato and Onion Tortilla with Allioli

Time: 20 minutes

Serves 2 to 4
(If you have any
left over, it's great
cold the next day,
eaten as is, or made
into a sandwich
with some of the
allioli smeared
on the bread.)

ALLIOLI

1 garlic clove, minced

Pinch kosher salt

1 teaspoon freshly squeezed lemon juice

1 large egg yolk

½ cup extra-virgin olive oil

TORTILLA

2 tablespoons unsalted butter

1 large Spanish onion, halved and thinly sliced

Kosher salt to taste

Freshly ground black pepper to taste

1 cup cubed potato, cooked

8 large eggs, lightly beaten

2 tablespoons chopped fresh basil

1. First, make the allioli. Using a mortar and pestle, pound the garlic and salt to make a paste. Alternatively, you can use the flat of a knife to mash the garlic and salt on a cutting board until it becomes a paste and add it to a mixing bowl.

2. Whisk in the lemon juice, then the egg yolk until thoroughly combined. While whisking or pounding constantly, slowly drizzle in the olive oil. It's best to have an extra pair of hands here; one person can whisk/pound while the other drizzles in the oil. Continue whisking until the oil is fully emulsified. If it seems too thick, drizzle in a few drops of hot water and mix well.

3. To make the tortilla, melt the butter in a large, preferably nonstick but oven-safe skillet over medium heat. Add the onion, season to taste with the salt and pepper, and sauté until golden brown. Stir in the potato.

4. Reduce the heat to low and preheat the oven to 500°F. Using a heatproof spatula, mix in the eggs and basil. Allow the eggs to cook, stirring with a spatula and pushing in the edges as they become firm so the liquid eggs run underneath the cooked, until the eggs are just set on the bottom but the top is still wet, about 5 minutes.
5. Place the skillet in the oven for about 3 minutes, or until the top of the tortilla is dry (do not overcook). Invert onto a plate and slice into wedges. Serve hot with dollops of the allioli.

BAKED FLOUNDER AND EGGS

On a recent Saturday morning, my friend Judith and I shopped for breakfast at the Greenpoint farmers' market. We bought eggs, butter, cheese, fresh bread, and plenty of apples—the makings of a princely meal—and I chattered enthusiastically about the apple French toast and scrambled eggs with cheese that we could whip up back at Judith's house.

But Judith wasn't listening. She had stopped at the fish stand and was staring bright-eyed at the pale fillets.

"What do you think about that one?" she said, pointing to a thick white slab of flounder with a reddish pink blush.

"It looks good. Is that for tonight?" I asked.

"No, for this morning," she said, adding that her family often had fresh fish for breakfast when they vacationed at the North Sea in Holland (Judith grew up in Germany).

Now, I know perfectly well that fish is a common breakfast staple all over the world, from the grilled fish and rice of Japan, to kippers and eggs in England, to the bagels-and-lox brunches of my own childhood.

But fresh flounder for breakfast seemed exotic, especially when I still had French toast on the brain. But Judith was determined, so flounder for breakfast it was.

Applying a less-is-more, beach-vacation philosophy of cooking, Judith simply swathed the fish in butter, salt, and pepper, and stuck it under the broiler. While it cooked, I scrambled the eggs. There was nothing surprising about the flavors of the meal—the sweet, soft fish with its saline, buttery juices melding with fluffy farm-fresh eggs—but eaten all together, it was divine.

I thought of Judith's flounder breakfast for weeks afterward, every time I passed the fishmonger at the Grand Army Plaza farmers' market near my house. But unlike the Greenpoint market's vendor with nary a crowd, at Grand Army Plaza, the line is notoriously snaking. I rarely have the patience to wait.

But one blustery, frigid morning, the fish stand was blissfully unmobbed, and there were flounder fillets galore. I picked up two, and some free-range eggs from another stand, and all but ran home to make breakfast.

I could have stuck to Judith's original, gorgeously spare recipe. But leaving well enough alone isn't my strong suit; my urge to embellish runs deep.

I kept the backbone of her recipe the same, coating the fish with plenty of butter and seasoning it generously with salt, pepper, and a touch of paprika.

Then, for a garnish, I chopped together parsley, scallions, and capers to add a tangy, bright note and a little bit of color to the ghostly fish.

The other part of the dish I wanted to alter was the eggs. As good as the scrambled were, they required a bowl to whip them and a skillet to scramble them.

A lazier option would be to crack the eggs directly into the roasting pan with the fish and let everything cook together. As a bonus, if I timed it right, the yolks would stay runny and gush all over the flounder, creating a velvety sauce.

I figured it would take the eggs less time to cook than the fish, so I added them after the fillets had been in the oven for a few minutes. By the time the fish turned opaque and tender in the center, the eggs were just set, sunny-side up.

With its pungent green garnish adding verve and the yolks lending creaminess, it was a more complex dish than the original. It was interesting enough, even, to break out for dinner—the perfect end to a day that starts with French toast.

Baked Flounder and Eggs

Time: 20 minutes

Serves 2

3 tablespoons unsalted butter, melted

2 (8-ounce) boneless, skinless flounder fillets, rinsed and patted dry

3/4 teaspoon kosher salt

1/2 teaspoon paprika

Freshly ground black pepper

4 large eggs

3 tablespoons chopped scallions (optional)

3 tablespoons chopped fresh parsley (optional)

1 1/2 tablespoons drained capers, chopped (optional)

1. Preheat the oven to 400°F.
2. Pour the butter in the bottom of a metal 13×9-inch baking pan. Place the fish in the pan and turn to coat with the butter. Season with about half the salt and paprika and plenty of black pepper.
3. Bake for 2 to 4 minutes, then add the eggs (Note: If you like runny eggs, add them after 3 or 4 minutes; for medium-firm but still slightly runny eggs, add them after 2 minutes; and for very firm eggs, you can add them along with the fish at the beginning). Crack the eggs into the bottom of the pan in the corners; the eggs should land next to, not on top of, the fish. Season the eggs with remaining salt, paprika, and more pepper. Continue baking until the fish is just opaque and the eggs are lightly set, 7 to 8 minutes more.
4. Meanwhile, in a small bowl, combine the scallions, parsley, and capers, if using. Transfer the fish and eggs to serving plates; garnish with the caper mixture if you like.

OLIVE OIL GRANOLA
WITH DRIED APRICOTS
AND PISTACHIOS

There was a crowd of shoppers swarming at the back of Bklyn Larder. They hovered around a tray of free samples, gluttonously gobbling the contents of the little (recyclable) plastic cups. I elbowed my way up to the food, wondering what it could be. Morsels of heritage pork cured in Barolo? Preserved duck eggs covered in truffles?

In fact, it was granola. And I never would have bothered trying any if it weren't for the hordes yelping with delight as they swallowed their umpteenth portion.

I stuck my hand into the fray and nabbed a cup. It was filled with copper-colored oats, pecan slivers, and flat chips of coconut. Like most granola, the first bite was sweet and crunchy. But then the salt hit me, followed by something savory and almost bitter. The sweet-salty-bitter combo was addictive, like a Campari soda and a bowl of salted almonds. I just couldn't stop.

There was no way I could leave the shop without my own $9 sack of nutty bliss, which I devoured on the two-block walk back home.

The secret ingredient, said the label, was olive oil.

Although I'm not a granola expert, when I have made the stuff, it's always been slicked with a neutral oil such as safflower, which adds richness and helps crisp the oats but does nothing for the flavor. Using good extra-virgin olive oil, along with a hefty dose of salt, was a brilliant twist.

Since making granola is not hard and since my bag was now empty, I thought it would be more economical to whip up a giant batch to have on hand for incessant munching. Plus, I liked the idea of tailoring the fruits and nuts to whatever I had in the cupboard, in this case Turkish apricots and pistachios.

But first, I called Nekisia Davis, the owner of Early Bird Granola, to see if she'd divulge the recipe. I knew Ms. Davis from when she was a manager at Franny's, a restaurant three blocks from my house, where she used to concoct amaro from roots, stems, and leaves. She gave me the proportions, emphasizing that it's the balance of sweet and salty that makes her granola like health-conscious crack.

"But how did you come up with the idea to use olive oil?" I asked

"I put olive oil in everything," she said. "I make French toast in olive oil, I put it on toast with jelly. Besides, the fat in olive oil is really good for you; it negates itself."

Her recipe was easy. Before baking, I mixed up the ingredients, substituting pistachios for pecans, and nixing the sunflower seeds because I don't like them. I also added dashes of cinnamon and cardamom to complement the apricots, which I tossed with the warm granola when it came out of the oven (adding the fruit before baking dries it out).

Once it had cooled, I mixed the granola into a bowl of ripe berries, dabbing the top with milky ricotta. I lapped it up and yearned for more. But that was no problem. With two quarts in the cupboard and the recipe on hand, I knew I'd be eating granola all summer long—unless the hungry hordes find out where I live.

Olive Oil Granola with Dried Apricots and Pistachios

Time: 50 minutes

Makes about
9 cups

3 cups old-fashioned rolled oats

1 1/2 cups raw pistachios, hulled

1 cup raw pumpkin seeds, hulled

1 cup coconut chips

3/4 cup pure maple syrup (you can use 2/3 cup, but the granola will be drier)

1/2 cup extra-virgin olive oil

1/3 cup packed light brown sugar

1 teaspoon kosher salt

1/2 teaspoon ground cinnamon

1/2 teaspoon ground cardamom or ground ginger

3/4 cup chopped dried apricots

Fresh ricotta, for serving

Fresh berries, for serving

1. Preheat the oven to 300°F.
2. In a large bowl, combine the oats, pistachios, pumpkin seeds, coconut chips, maple syrup, olive oil, brown sugar, salt, cinnamon, and cardamom or ginger. Spread the mixture on a large rimmed baking sheet (about 11×17 inches) in an even layer and bake for 45 minutes, stirring every 10 minutes, until golden brown and well toasted.
3. Transfer the granola to a large bowl and add the apricots, tossing to combine. Serve with ricotta and berries, if desired.

2 The Farmers' Market and Me

It started out casually, my relationship with the farmers' market. In college, I'd traipse through when I was passing by Union Square, maybe buy a few apples or a ripe summer peach to eat over my books, trying not to drip nectar on Carolyn Heilbrun.

Later, when I started catering (an ill-conceived and stressful attempt to support myself as a writer), I'd make a detour for thimble-size chiogga beets, golden raspberries, and pale blue borage flowers, forgetting in those moments of sublime shopping that making a profit was actually the point.

My commitment has steadily grown, to the point that now, at the risk of sounding like the Brooklyn-inhabiting, reusable shopping bag–carrying, *New Yorker*–subscribing cultural cliché I surely am, I'll admit that I've become farmers' market obsessed. If a week goes by without at least a visit or two, I mourn the loss of purslane, unhomogenized whole milk, pastured eggs, and the choice of fifteen kinds of organic potatoes, with anxiety bordering on a Michael Pollan–induced panic. Yes, life will go on and I'll even manage to find what to eat. But considering that I plan my meals around my farmers' market vegetable haul, without it something essential is missing.

My FM routine is as follows: Saturday mornings, when my baby peeps and squawks her way awake just shy of 6:00 A.M., and no number of pillows over my head can muffle the hungry wails emanating from the baby monitor, I give in and get up. Still bleary and without my tea, I load Dahlia into her stroller and set off, making my husband, Daniel, come with me, not just for company, but for another pair of arms to haul the bags.

We go on sunny summer mornings, slathering the baby in SPF 30. We go in the rain, strapping her under a plastic rain guard. We go in the snow, buying wilted, partially frozen collard greens and waxy rutabagas. We go in spring, the hardest season, when the weather turns fine and the trees bud and flower, but the market stalls bear only mealy apples and over-wintered leeks. The sight of those first stalks of rhubarb might be even better than the coffee cake they'll become.

But no matter the season, once home, I revel in my spoils, even if it means eating tomatoes or parsnips every single day when they're around. Granted, I may be an addict, but I'm not a purist. If I get to the market too late for squash blossoms, I'd rather go to the fancy supermarket than miss out entirely.

Like the best of neuroses, my farmers' market obsession most likely stems from my parents, though I can't exactly figure out how. They are farmers' market regulars, to be sure, but being eminently more practical than I, if they skip a week and are forced to consume bagged carrots and salad-in-a-box, it's no big deal.

But there's a piece of my contentment that's dependent on the ritual of bringing everything home, then sorting through the herbs and greens and roots and arranging them like some gorgeous edible work of art in a giant, shallow wooden bowl. An ex-boyfriend taught me this; it's so much more aesthetically pleasing than keeping everything in the fridge, though it won't work for easily wiltable greens like arugula. Plus it helps me remember what I've got, so I'm less likely to let those pears rot behind the yogurt.

I don't usually plan my meals ahead, instead letting my appetite guide me through the week, from the Saturday night bounty to Thursday's meager larder. But that's okay—sometimes the best meals are made from the last of the yellowing kale. And when that doesn't work out, there's always takeout, made with produce whose provenance is simply beside the point.

EXTRA-SHARP LEEKS VINAIGRETTE

Among all the comestibles a person could lug home from a trip to France—the handmade Alsatian quince jam and fancy provençal lavender honey, the walnut oil, freshly pressed at a tiny producer in the Midi, or, say, a big bag of brown-edged butter cookies from Poilâne—my friend Alice always makes room for a few jars of cheap mustard from the supermarket.

This mystified me. Why carry back mustard when so many of the same brands are easily and inexpensively available here?

"They're old by the time they get here and have no bite," she'd say with a shrug as she stuffed yet one more jar into her suitcase.

I chalked it up to eccentricity, until a dinner party she threw last winter. Newly back from a trip to Paris, she made a dish to showcase her spoils: leeks with a mustardy vinaigrette.

I wasn't prepared to be so wrong. One taste of the tender, silky leeks swathed in a zippy, sinus-clearing dressing perfectly tamed by the gentleness of the allium made me apologize for ever doubting her. And beg her for the recipe.

"It's simple," she said. "Make a vinaigrette with plenty of good, fresh, hot mustard that you just brought home from France, toss it with cooked leeks, *et voilà*."

But what if you haven't just gotten home from Paris with a suitcase full of Amora Fine et Forte (Alice's mustard of choice)?

"Look for the brightest yellow Dijon you can find," she instructed. "As the color oxidizes and fades, so does the flavor. And if they have extra-hot, buy that."

Thus enlightened, I hurried to my local Key Food and searched the condiment aisle for daisy yellow in a disappointingly drab field of browns and tans. I eventually settled on some beige Maille extra-hot with a flaming orange accent on the label as proof of its incendiary force. Then I picked up leeks at the farmers' market, and brought my bounty home to try to replicate Alice's recipe.

But before I made the vinaigrette, I had to clean and cook the leeks. There are many ways to clean a leek, and here's mine: First, slice off the hairy bottoms and all of the dark green tops of the leeks, leaving pale green and white cylinders that you should halve lengthwise. Working with a half leek at a time, rinse under cold running water until the translucent layers start to separate. Then flip the leek layers like the pages of a book, letting the water sluice away the nuggets of black earth inevitably hiding within. It's very satisfying, a little like sweeping out the Augean stables.

I cooked the leeks carefully, first reuniting the halves and tying them up with kitchen string to keep them from falling apart in the boiling water. When they were very soft, I sliced them into long strips just like Alice had.

Finally, I made a classic mustard vinaigrette using my flaming Maille. It was good and quite sharp. I tossed it with the leeks, and took a big mouthful, expecting the same vivid, pungent flavors I had at Alice's.

But it was bland and blah. The mellowness of the leeks completely canceled out the mustard's bite. So I added another tablespoon of mustard, effectively doubling my original measure. And it was a little better. But not much.

Undaunted, I continued this way until I had used up half the jar. I also added a squeeze of lemon juice to play up the tartness. Then I put the leeks away for a while because my palate was numb.

A glass of wine and a few hours later, I pulled the leeks out of the fridge and dug my fork in. I don't know if it was the added lemon juice, the resting period, the wine, or the huge quantity of mustard, but they were utterly transformed. Instead of slippery, mild-mannered ribbons, I had a powerful and piquant dish. It was bright and jolting, but still satiny and sweet from the leeks, and I'd say equally good as Alice's with the Parisian dressing.

And I once again learned that good old American lesson in taste: If you can't have old-world authenticity, just add more of what you've got.

Extra-Sharp Leeks Vinaigrette

5 medium leeks, white and light green parts only, halved lengthwise
    and well rinsed
5 tablespoons hot Dijon mustard
1 tablespoon freshly squeezed lemon juice
½ tablespoon red wine vinegar
½ cup extra-virgin olive oil
¼ teaspoon kosher salt
Freshly ground black pepper

Time: 25 minutes

Serves 4

1. Bring a pot of water to a boil. Reunite the leek halves; bundle the leeks and secure with kitchen string. Simmer until fork-tender, about 15 minutes. Drain and unbundle the leeks. Let cool.
2. Whisk together the mustard, lemon juice, and vinegar. Whisking constantly, slowly drizzle in the olive oil. Season with salt and pepper.
3. Slice each leek half lengthwise into thirds. Trim the root ends, if desired. Toss with the vinaigrette to taste. Extra vinaigrette will keep in an airtight container in the fridge for up to 1 week.

PAN-ROASTED ASPARAGUS WITH FRIED EGGS AND ANCHOVY BREAD CRUMBS

David Chang is the last chef on earth you'd think would inspire a vegetarian dish, but so it was with this asparagus dish and me. Famous for being anti-vegetarian, at his restaurant Momofuku he makes sure not to go out of his way to cater to them. Of the twenty or so items on the menu, those herbivorously inclined can order exactly two: the house-made oshinko pickle and the shiitake mushroom steamed buns. Everything else has pork or chicken broth or bacon tucked away inside, even something as seemingly vegetarian-friendly as a dish of pan-roasted asparagus with miso.

I can't remember what the offending meat product is, maybe a little lard in the pan, maybe a soupçon of broth, but whatever it is, I can't really detect it. Instead the dish tastes deeply of green, grassy asparagus, caramelized, softened, and singed from the skillet.

Now, I've made a lot of asparagus over the years. I've steamed it, roasted it, grilled it, sautéed it, butter-braised it. But not until I tried Chang's version did I even think to panfry it.

Once I did, though, I was a convert. All those other methods have their charms, but to me, panfrying combines the best attributes of them all. Like grilled and roasted asparagus, it blisters and chars, giving the stalks a nutty brown flavor. And it's as fast and easy as steaming.

Unlike Chang, I don't add any meat to the pan, just oil (either olive or peanut), asparagus, and a little salt and pepper. The trick is to cover the pan but hover nearby, shaking it every few minutes so the stalks sear on all sides without burning. The cover traps the hot steam, so you can steam and sear at the same time. Come to think of it, steam-sear is a much more accurate description than pan-roast, but not nearly as appetizing.

On its own, pan-roasted asparagus makes a fine and simple side dish to almost any meal in need of a little green. But in the first few weeks of spring when purple-tinged bunches of the stalks are just appearing at farmers' markets, I want them in the center of the plate, not on the sidelines. That's when I made this dish, pan-roasting the asparagus, then topping it with fried eggs and garlicky bread crumbs.

I got the idea from Franny's, where they serve an asparagus salad composed of the wood oven–roasted stalks covered in vinaigrette, bread crumbs, and minced hard-cooked eggs. Since I don't have a wood-burning oven, I pan-roast the stalks, then use the same pan to crisp the bread crumbs with garlic and anchovies for a savory edge, and also to fry a couple of eggs. Hard-cooked are nice, but lack the runny yolk mixing with the bread crumbs and dripping onto the asparagus. Altogether, I think this dish is as close to vegetable heaven as you can get. Without bacon, that is.

Pan-Roasted Asparagus with Fried Eggs and Anchovy Bread Crumbs

3 tablespoons extra-virgin olive oil

3 tablespoons unseasoned, preferably homemade bread crumbs

1 anchovy fillet, minced

1 small garlic clove, minced

Kosher salt to taste

1/4 teaspoon freshly grated lemon zest

1 bunch asparagus, trimmed

Pinch freshly ground black pepper

2 large eggs

Time: 10 minutes

Serves 2
as an appetizer
or side dish

1. Heat 1 tablespoon of the oil in a large skillet over medium heat. Add the bread crumbs and anchovy and cook, stirring occasionally, until the bread crumbs are browned and toasted, about 2 minutes. Stir in the garlic and a large pinch of salt and sauté until fragrant, 1 to 2 minutes longer. Add the lemon zest, then transfer the mixture to a small bowl.

2. Wipe out the skillet with a paper towel and return it to the heat. Add another tablespoon of the oil and then add the asparagus and a pinch of salt and

pepper. Cover and cook, stirring and shaking the pan occasionally, until the asparagus is tender, 5 to 6 minutes. Transfer the asparagus to a serving plate and sprinkle with the bread crumb mixture.

3. Add the remaining tablespoon of the oil to the skillet and return it to the heat. Crack in the eggs and fry until just set but still runny, 2 to 3 minutes. Slide the eggs on top of the asparagus and serve.

HELLO, SALAD (TENDER GREENS WITH HERBS AND HAZELNUTS)

If there was ever a culinary low point in my life, it was when, at the knowing age of about twenty-five, I decided I'd eaten enough salad and I was giving it up.

"I don't even like lettuce," I declared to my then-husband, Max, over dinner one night. He grunted affirmation from behind his *Wall Street Journal*. As long as I'd still make spaghetti carbonara, he was perfectly fine living salad-free.

The truth of it was that for much of my early, fat-phobic adulthood, I nearly subsisted on the stuff, dutifully chomping my way through vast mounds of slightly wilted, prewashed mesclun coated in a nonfat, Caesar-like dressing of my own device. It almost ruined my taste for the stuff.

Thankfully, I didn't remain saladless very long. After a few months, I began to miss it. Even Max started yearning for a crunchy leaf or two with his pasta and potatoes.

So I started experimenting with vegetables and greens other than lettuce, which I considered a heinous weed. This is especially true when it is mixed with other baby greens, put into a bag that encourages the red oak lettuces to rot with alarming speed, and labeled "mesclun," destined to be mispronounced "mescaline" by waiters all over town.

But a bowl of watercress and slivered red peppers tossed with shredded Cheddar cheese and drizzled with olive oil? Now, that makes a tasty lunch. Shredded carrots slathered with mayonnaise and orange juice is lightly sweet and delightfully satisfying. And there is nothing heinous about baby arugula at all, especially when dressed with walnut oil and a few drops of my mother's homemade vinegar.

Little by little, I made my way back to salad, though I admit that I still won't go near bagged mesclun or nonfat dressing of any kind.

But otherwise, the sky's the limit, and now no dinner is complete without a big bowl of some kind of crisp greens gracing the table. Baby arugula is still a favorite, and radicchio is my winter staple since I can always find purple globes of it at the vegetable market down the street. I don't even mind dealing with fresh crinkly spinach that needs to be washed three times because it has the gumption to stand up to my bracing garlic-mustard vinaigrette. In spring, delicate leaves of young lettuces and herbs, perhaps tossed with a nut oil and some chopped toasted nuts, is the veritable antithesis to my fat-free mesclun salads of old. And when I serve it to my husband, Daniel, he greets it like a long-lost friend, even though we eat salad every night.

"Hello, salad," he says affectionately, piling his plate high.

Hello, Salad (Tender Greens with Herbs and Hazelnuts)

Time: 5 minutes

Serves 2 to 4

1 teaspoon sherry, white wine, or Champagne vinegar
1/8 teaspoon kosher salt, more to taste
1 1/2 tablespoons hazelnut or walnut oil
6 cups tender baby greens, loosely packed
Handful soft mixed fresh herbs, such as cilantro, mint, parsley, and/or basil
1/4 cup chopped toasted hazelnuts or walnuts (see Note)

1. Combine the vinegar and salt in a small bowl and mix well to dissolve the salt. Slowly whisk in the oil.
2. Place the greens, herbs, and hazelnuts or walnuts in a large bowl and toss with the vinaigrette. Season with more salt to taste.

NOTE: To toast nuts, spread them on a baking sheet and bake at 325°F, stirring every 5 minutes, until they start to smell nutty, 10 to 20 minutes depending on the type and size of the nut. Cool completely before chopping.

VARIATION: SPINACH AND AVOCADO SALAD WITH GARLIC MUSTARD VINAIGRETTE

1 garlic clove

Pinch kosher salt, more to taste

1 teaspoon freshly squeezed lemon juice, more to taste

½ teaspoon Dijon mustard

2 tablespoons extra-virgin olive oil

6 cups spinach leaves (or other dark greens such as arugula or watercress), loosely packed

½ avocado, cut into cubes

Time: 10 minutes

Serves 2 to 4

1. Using a mortar and pestle or a heavy knife, pound or mince the garlic together with a pinch of salt until a paste forms. (If using a knife, use the side of it to smear and mash the garlic once it's minced.) Scrape the paste into a small bowl and whisk in the lemon juice, mustard, and another pinch of salt, whisking to dissolve the salt. Whisk in the oil.
2. Place the spinach and avocado in a large bowl and gently toss with the dressing. Season with more salt and lemon juice to taste.

VARIATION: SAUSAGE SALAD WITH RADICCHIO AND FRISÉE

This is a takeoff on a bitter greens salad with bacon vinaigrette; I've just substituted one pork product for the other. The nice thing about the sausage is that it's unexpected and has a softer, yet more complex bite than crunchy bacon. It's also more of a complete meal—either a light dinner or a hearty lunch. Good bread and butter, maybe drizzled with a little honey, are all you need alongside.

50

Sausage Salad with Radicchio and Frisée

1 large garlic clove
Pinch kosher salt, more to taste
½ pound Italian sausage, casings removed
1 tablespoon extra-virgin olive oil, more to taste
1 tablespoon red wine vinegar
1 small radicchio, halved, cored, and sliced
1 small frisée, torn into pieces

1. Using a mortar and pestle or a heavy knife, mash together the garlic and salt until a paste forms. (If using a knife, mince the garlic with the salt, then smash with the flat of the blade.)
2. In a skillet over medium-high heat, sauté the sausage in the oil until browned, about 5 minutes. Stir in the garlic paste and vinegar and cook, scraping up any brown bits, until the garlic is fragrant, another 1 to 2 minutes.
3. Place the radicchio and frisée in a large bowl. Add the sausage mixture and pan drippings and toss well. Serve immediately, seasoning with more salt and oil to taste.

BROWN BUTTERED CORN
AND BROILED STRIPED BASS WITH
BROWN BUTTER CORN SAUCE

Corn on the cob. Butter. Dental floss. It's an honored summer trinity that I look forward to every year.

But after two months of boiled corn on the cob and grilled corn on the cob, I decided I was ready for another paradigm. What I wanted was a recipe that called for slicing the kernels off the cob before cooking, which would leave all those tooth-invading fibers behind.

Of course, recipes for this kind of thing abound. There's creamed corn and corn salad, and succotash and corn chowder, not to mention any number of recipes for corn sautéed with this and that. Any would technically fit the bill. Yet none exactly fit my mood.

The thing that makes corn on the cob so compelling, to me at least, is its very simplicity. With freshly picked in-season corn, butter and salt are really all you need.

I thought about this as I sliced the kernels off some ears of corn. I realized that the only other flavor enhancer I really love with fresh corn is the caramelization you get from cooking the ears over the high heat of the grill.

An excellent idea, I thought, would be to grill the corn, let it cool, then cut the kernels off the cob and reheat them in melted butter. Except the kernels were already off the cob, and cut corn kernels are not exactly conducive to grilling.

Plus, since I planned to cook the rest of the meal in the oven (Long Island striped bass fillets), there wasn't any other compelling reason to brave the humidity and vicious mosquitoes to light the grill.

But I liked the idea of heating the kernels in a little pan of melted butter. If I simmered it all for a few minutes, I could cook the raw kernels into a nice dish of buttered corn. It was a possible plan, though it wouldn't give me the nutty, golden-brown flavor of the grill.

Then it hit me. I could brown the butter so it would take on a deep caramelized flavor and cook the kernels in that.

So that's exactly what I did, simmering the butter with a sprig of lemon thyme until the white foam fell to the bottom of the pan and turned hazelnut brown. Then I added the corn and let it bubble until it was tender but still plump. The sweet kernels absorbed the butter and hints of lemon thyme, yet weren't masked or muddied by them.

It was very easy to eat (no dental floss needed) and extremely good. So good, in fact, that I stood over the pot and gobbled about half of its contents before I realized that I was supposed to be serving this for dinner with the fish.

There was about half left, enough for a garnish, but not quite a side dish.

I could have stretched the corn with lots of broth and made soup. But I didn't want soup. I wanted something to go with my fish.

What if, I thought as I preheated the oven for the bass, I added just a little broth, pureed some of the corn, and turned the brown buttered corn into a corn sauce?

I tried it, adding a squeeze of lemon to balance out the richness, and also because I like lemon with fish. Sweet and a little tart, nutty-tasting, and very creamy, it had all the fabulous flavors of the brown buttered corn I had devoured, but was more refined—fancy, even—and perfect for fish.

Fifteen minutes later, my husband and I sat down to a dinner of striped bass fillets with an elegant brown butter corn sauce. You know, just as I had always planned.

Brown Buttered Corn

Time: 15 minutes

Serves 4

3 ears corn, shucked
4 tablespoons butter
4 thyme sprigs, preferably lemon thyme
Coarse sea salt (fleur de sel is good here)
Freshly ground black pepper
Chopped fresh soft herbs (basil, mint, parsley, cilantro), optional

1. Break the ears of corn in half and stand one half vertically on a cutting board. Using a sawing motion, run a knife between the cob and kernels to remove the kernels. Using the back of the knife, scrape the denuded cob to release the corn's juices. Transfer to a bowl. Repeat with the remaining corn halves.

2. Melt the butter in a saucepan along with the thyme. Once the butter is melted, let it continue to cook until you see golden brown specks in the bottom of the pan and the butter smells nutty, about 5 minutes. Add the corn and a large pinch of salt and pepper, stir well, and cover the pot. Let cook until the corn is tender, about 5 minutes longer.

3. Remove the thyme sprigs, add more salt and pepper if desired, and serve hot, garnished with herbs, if desired.

Broiled Striped Bass with Brown Butter Corn Sauce

6 fish fillets such as striped bass, flounder, or red snapper,
    about 6 to 8 ounces each
Kosher salt and freshly ground black pepper
2½ tablespoons butter, softened
3 garlic cloves, minced
1 teaspoon grated lemon zest (optional)
1 recipe Brown Buttered Corn (page 53)
½ cup vegetable broth or water
2 tablespoons extra-virgin olive oil
2 tablespoons freshly squeezed lemon juice,
    or to taste
Chopped fresh soft herbs (basil, mint, parsley, cilantro)

Time: 20 minutes

Serves 6

1. Preheat the oven to 500°F. Season the fish fillets all over with salt and pepper and place in a baking pan, skin side down.

2. In a small bowl, mash together the butter, about two-thirds of the garlic, and the lemon zest, if using. Smear on top of the fish fillets. Roast until

cooked through to taste, 7 to 12 minutes, depending upon the variety of fish and the thickness of the fillets.

3. Meanwhile, in a blender or food processor, puree half the brown buttered corn with the broth or water, oil, lemon juice, and remaining garlic. Stir in the remaining corn. Serve the sauce over the fish, garnished with the herbs.

RICH AND NUTTY BROWN BUTTER CORN BREAD WITH FRESH CORN

Here is yet one more thing to do with brown butter and corn.

This recipe started out as an accident. I was melting butter in a skillet while making corn bread and got distracted. When I came back to the stove the butter was nut brown and fragrant instead of merely liquid, and made one of the richest, most deeply flavored corn breads I'd ever had.

Now it's my go-to corn bread recipe, and it's extremely adaptable. This version has sweet, nubby fresh corn kernels caramelized with the butter and maple syrup, but you can leave them out.

I've also added shredded or crumbled cheeses of all milks, chopped fresh herbs, chili powder, sautéed onions, diced jalapeño, minced roasted bell pepper, and shredded coconut. All work perfectly, though the corn bread doesn't really need them. The caramelized, buttery flavor can stand alone.

In a perfect world, try to time this so you can serve it warm from the oven. But you can also just heat it up by toasting slices before serving. More butter slathered on top doesn't hurt either.

Rich and Nutty Brown Butter Corn Bread with Fresh Corn

Time: 1 hour

Serves 6

8 tablespoons unsalted butter (1 stick)

1 ear corn, kernels removed (about 1 cup), optional

1 tablespoon pure maple syrup

1 cup all-purpose flour

1 cup stone-ground yellow cornmeal

1 tablespoon baking powder

¾ teaspoon kosher salt

1¼ cups whole milk yogurt or sour cream

1 large egg

2 tablespoons sugar

¼ teaspoon baking soda

1. Preheat the oven to 375°F. In a 9-inch oven-safe skillet, melt 4 tablespoons of the butter over medium-high heat. Add the corn and maple syrup and sauté, stirring, until the corn is tender, 10 to 12 minutes. (If not using the corn, just melt together the butter and maple syrup.)

2. In a large bowl, sift together the flour, cornmeal, baking powder, and salt. In a separate bowl, whisk together the yogurt, egg, sugar, and baking soda. Gently fold the wet ingredients into the dry ones until just combined. Fold in the corn-butter mixture.

3. Return the skillet to the heat and melt the remaining 4 tablespoons of butter, tilting the pan to coat the sides completely. Cook the butter 2 to 3 minutes until pale gold with a nutty fragrance, being careful not to let it get too brown. Take the skillet off the heat and scrape in the batter, smoothing the surface with a rubber spatula.

4. Bake until the top is golden and a toothpick inserted into the center comes out clean, 25 to 30 minutes. Cut into wedges and serve.

ZUCCHINI WITH MINT AND GARLIC

Nearly everyone complains about her mother-in-law at least some of the time, and Josephine, my ex-mother-in-law from my second marriage, was no exception.

Josephine's MIL lived on a farm in the South, where she overgrew vegetables in a way that annoyed Josephine.

"She'd leave her zucchinis on the vine until they were as big as my leg. She was a very thrifty woman," Josephine lamented one afternoon. We were slicing skinny zucchini no longer than my index finger and waiting for the grill pan to heat up.

"I'd wander in the garden, looking at all the baby zucchini, wishing I could pick them. But she'd think that was wasteful," Josephine continued with a frown.

Without a vegetable garden of her own, Josephine would buy only the daintiest of zucchini at the market on Arthur Avenue in the Bronx, picking out the slimmest specimens with the tautest, shiniest green skin.

Once home, she'd hunch over the kitchen table, thinly slicing each zucchini by hand with her favorite blunt little paring knife, despite the fact that my father-in-law kept dozens of freshly sharpened knives in the drawer.

Then Josephine would sear the slices on her grill pan. This took a long time because her grill pan was narrow and the flame on her old stove was low in the BTU department. But she'd stand there for almost an hour, turning the neat slices over and over until they were soft and browned, drizzling them with a little olive oil, then scattering the cooked ones with pungent minced garlic and fresh chopped mint.

Actually, "stand there" is the wrong description for how Josephine cooked. The master of culinary multitasking, Josephine could tend the zucchini, stir the Sunday sauce, and bake pizzelle cookies in an electric press simultaneously, flitting from one task to the next as each needed attention. She had it down to a birdlike little kitchen dance: flipping the zucchini; tasting the sauce, adding more oregano; spooning batter into the pizzelle press, letting it bake while she flipped the zucchini; and so on, all the while telling stories about her favorite aunt, who hand-formed orecchiette for Christmas dinner for forty people as a matter of course.

Josephine served the zucchini cold as part of her copious antipasti selection that always preceded those belt-unbuckling, multicourse, Italian-American feasts she modestly referred to as Sunday dinner.

Her antipasti were wonderful (and probably still are, although I haven't seen her in years). Along with the things she brought in from Arthur Avenue—the soft and milky mozzarella that had never seen a refrigerator, loaves of crunchy semolina bread, bright green cured olives, and the special aged pork sausage that you had to be grandfathered into the good graces of the butcher to procure—there were the vegetables she made. Although the zucchini was my favorite dish, she'd also put out fat bell peppers that she had roasted, peeled, and marinated in red wine vinegar. There might be sweet-and-sour eggplant salad with salted capers, and sweet pickled carrots with chopped parsley. She and my father-in-law ate the leftovers all week long.

Of all her recipes, the zucchini is the one I make most often. Although I'm nearly as good at the multitasking kitchen dance as Josephine, I've adapted the technique so it doesn't need quite as much fawning over. Instead of a grill pan, I use the broiler, turning the zucchini only once. In summer, I'll use the grill, laying the zucchini slices in a grill basket and taking great care when I flip it, since the oil-slicked slivers tend to slip when moved.

Then I serve it cold or warm, usually as a side dish to a meal that is, sadly, not usually as bountiful as at Josephine's.

Zucchini with Mint and Garlic

Time: 10 minutes

Serves 4

1¼ pounds zucchini (about 4 small), scrubbed, trimmed,
    and sliced ⅛ inch thick
2 tablespoons extra-virgin olive oil, plus additional for drizzling
¾ teaspoon kosher salt, plus additional to taste

1 garlic clove, minced

1 tablespoon chopped fresh mint or basil

1. Preheat the broiler. In a bowl, toss the zucchini with the oil and salt. Arrange the slices on two baking sheets in an even layer.

2. Broil until the slices begin to brown, about 5 minutes. Flip the slices and broil for about 5 minutes more. Transfer the zucchini to a bowl and toss with the garlic and mint. Drizzle with additional oil and salt to taste.

RAW TUSCAN KALE SALAD WITH CHILES AND PECORINO

There are some dishes I order off restaurant menus because they sound better than everything else, and there are some dishes I order because they sound worse. My reasoning goes like this: If a chef dares to offer something as unappealing as, say, a raw kale salad, chances are it's because it's fantastic.

I've played this game at restaurants all over the world to very mixed results. But when I score, I score big, having a perspective-changing moment that can inspire pure glee.

And such was what I was hoping for with the raw kale salad at Franny's in Brooklyn.

I'll admit that having ordered and adored a raw Brussels sprouts salad at Franny's the year before, the risk factor skewed pretty low. In that salad, chef Andrew Feinberg doused the shredded crucifers with so much olive oil, lemon juice, salt, toasted walnuts, and pecorino cheese that their sulfurous and often harsh disposition had no choice but to mellow and sweeten under such lush treatment.

Even so, raw kale sounded more challenging, but still I ordered the salad. It arrived as a shadowy green mountain under a blizzard of grated Pecorino Rossellino cheese (a nutty Italian sheep's milk cheese with a ruddy rind) and bread crumbs, flavored with lemon and chile. Tangy, spicy, slick with good oil, and crunchy from the earthy-flavored kale, it was as pungent and rich as it was fresh and clean tasting, a veritable raw foods epiphany. The minute I left Franny's, I immediately craved another.

Having made Franny's Brussels sprouts salad many times since I first tried it, I figured I could easily reproduce the kale at home as well. So the next time I saw nice-looking kale, I bought some. I chopped it up, tossed it with all the requisite ingredients, including the Pecorino Rossellino I had managed to track down at Blue Apron in Brooklyn, and bit into a huge forkful. Then I chewed. And chewed, and chewed, until eventually it was either swallow or spit. I'll spare you the details.

That's when I realized that not all kale is created equal. At Franny's, they use inky Tuscan kale. Up until that moment, I had thought the various kales were pretty interchangeable, a quality I now know they possess only when cooked.

Tuscan kale, also called black and lacinato kale, has a more delicate leaf and softer stem than the sturdier, bright green, curly stuff, and the differences are glaringly apparent when munched raw.

I ended up sautéing my failed salad and enjoying it just fine. But it didn't satisfy the craving.

Since Tuscan kale isn't nearly as easy to track down as regular kale, it took several weeks of farmers' market trolling to spot some (gourmet markets also stock it). I brought it home and immediately sliced it into ribbons. Once again, I tossed it with olive oil, lemon, salt, chile, homemade bread crumbs, and garlic.

Then I poked around my cheese drawer for the rest of the Pecorino Rossellino, but remembered I had finished it several cheese sandwiches ago. The only other candidate was a half-empty container of grated Pecorino Romano of rather questionable age and origin. But it smelled and tasted fine, so I showered it over the salad.

Then I tossed and dug in, forking up a much smaller bite this time just in case. But my salad was everything I had hoped for—with a thick, garlicky, almost Caesar-like dressing coating the succulently crenulated leaves. Plus, the kale held up without wilting much all afternoon, which makes it a perfect dish to bring to a party. Where I'm sure it would be a hit, at least with anyone willing to try it.

Raw Tuscan Kale Salad with Chiles and Pecorino

Time: 20 minutes

Serves 2 to 4

1 bunch Tuscan kale (aka black or lacinato)

1 thin slice country bread (part whole wheat or rye is nice), or ¼ cup good, homemade coarse bread crumbs

½ garlic clove

¼ teaspoon kosher salt, plus a pinch

¼ cup finely grated pecorino cheese, plus additional for garnish

3 tablespoons extra-virgin olive oil, plus additional for garnish

Freshly squeezed juice of 1 lemon

⅛ teaspoon red pepper flakes

Freshly ground black pepper to taste

1. Trim the bottom 2 inches off the kale stems and discard. Slice the kale into ¾-inch ribbons. You should have 4 to 5 cups. Place the kale in a large bowl.
2. If using the bread, toast it until golden on both sides. Tear it into small pieces and grind in a food processor until the mixture forms coarse crumbs.
3. Using a mortar and pestle or a heavy knife, pound or mince the garlic and ¼ teaspoon salt into a paste (if using a knife, use the side to smear and smush the garlic once it's minced). Transfer the garlic to a small bowl. Add ¼ cup cheese, 3 tablespoons oil, lemon juice, pinch of salt, pepper flakes, and black pepper and whisk to combine. Pour the dressing over the kale and toss very well to combine thoroughly (the dressing will be thick and need lots of tossing to coat the leaves). Let the salad sit for 5 minutes, then serve topped with the bread crumbs, additional cheese, and a drizzle of oil.

VARIATION: RAW BRUSSELS SPROUTS SALAD WITH MANCHEGO AND TOASTED WALNUTS

This is based on Andrew Feinberg of Franny's original recipe. Like its cruciferous sister, the raw kale salad, this can be made hours ahead and will just get better as it sits. If you think your friends might be a little put off by the image of raw Brussels sprouts, call this Brussels sprouts cole slaw with walnuts and watch them fill their plates.

Raw Brussels Sprouts Salad with Manchego and Toasted Walnuts

10 ounces Brussels sprouts (1 container), trimmed
Juice of ½ lemon
Coarse sea salt or kosher salt and freshly ground black pepper to taste
½ cup extra-virgin olive oil, or more to taste
1 cup chopped toasted walnuts (see Note, page 49)
¾ cup grated Manchego or young pecorino cheese (or even aged Gruyère)

Time: 15 minutes

Serves 6

1. In a food processor using the thinnest slicing disk, slice the Brussels sprouts (they will fall apart into shreds). Or, using a knife, slice the sprouts as thinly as possible. Put the sprouts in a bowl and toss with the lemon juice and a generous pinch of salt and pepper. Let rest for 5 minutes.
2. Add the olive oil and toss well. Add the walnuts and cheese and toss gently. Taste and adjust the seasonings. You can serve this immediately, but it gets better after an hour or so.

GARLICKY SESAME-CURED BROCCOLI SALAD

"How about Sexy, Spicy Broccoli?" a friend suggested.

I had asked her to help me rename one of my favorite dishes, marinated raw broccoli salad. After years of rejection on the potluck circuit, I decided it was time for a rechristening.

It's made from uncooked broccoli tossed with an assertive garlic, sesame, chile, and cumin-seed vinaigrette slicked with good extra-virgin olive oil and red wine vinegar. The acid "cooks" the florets a little, like ceviche. After an hour, the broccoli softens as if blanched, turning bright emerald and soaking up all the intense flavors of the dressing. Fresh, crunchy, and deeply garlicky, it's easily the most addictive vegetable in my repertory.

Plus, I can make it in minutes and it keeps for days, becoming even tangier as it sits. So why was it such a hard sell?

"Marinated raw broccoli just doesn't sound, you know, yummy," my well-meaning friend said.

It's true that I did swipe the original recipe from some frighteningly health-oriented cookbook, the title of which I've since blocked out after a certain vile tempeh episode. But over the years I've veered the proportions away from the abstemious, tripling the olive oil, doubling the salt and garlic, and adding cumin and sesame oil to make it even more compelling.

It's the kind of recipe that's ripe for substitutions, too. I've used fennel and caraway in place of cumin seeds, left out the sesame oil, exchanged vinegar for citrus juice. I've even increased the dressing and added cubed tofu or cooked shrimp to turn the salad into a main course.

At cocktail parties, I've positioned a bowl of marinated raw broccoli next to the nuts, and watched my guests munch the pungent florets like olives.

The name is probably the only one of its original features I didn't monkey around with. And it was high time, though sexy broccoli wasn't exactly what I was looking for.

The next time I was invited to a potluck, I tried a new tack, unveiling a shiny new title that highlighted the broccoli's best attributes. How about a garlicky sesame-cured broccoli salad, I offered. It was instantly accepted.

The afternoon of the party, I assembled the salad as usual, making one tiny tweak. Instead of just tossing all the ingredients together in a bowl, I sautéed the garlic in the olive oil for a few seconds before pouring it over the florets. I figured the cooked garlic would be slightly more mellow and refined, so I could use even more of it. Plus, the warm oil would spark the flavors of the chile flakes, giving the dish a more profound spicy bite.

I took it to my friend's apartment, letting it marinate on the subway. Then I put it on the buffet and plunged into the crowd. Later that night, I overheard two guests talk about the broccoli salad.

"I don't know what it's called," one of them said, "but it's terrific."

I didn't bother chiming in with the new name. Terrific broccoli salad was just fine by me.

Garlicky Sesame-Cured Broccoli Salad

1½ teaspoons red wine vinegar
1 teaspoon kosher salt, more to taste
2 heads broccoli, 1 pound each, cut into bite-size florets
¾ cup extra-virgin olive oil
4 fat garlic cloves, minced
2 teaspoons cumin seeds
2 teaspoons roasted (Asian) sesame oil
Large pinch crushed red pepper flakes

Time: 10 minutes,
plus 1 hour
marinating

Serves 6 to 8
as a side dish
or more as an
hors d'oeuvre

1. In a large bowl, stir together the vinegar and salt. Add the broccoli and toss to combine.

2. In a large skillet, heat the olive oil until hot but not smoking. Add the garlic and cumin and cook until fragrant, about 1 minute. Stir in the sesame oil and pepper flakes. Pour the mixture over the broccoli and toss well. Let sit for at least 1 hour at room temperature, or chilled, up to 48 hours (chill it if you want to keep it for more than 2 hours). Adjust the seasonings (it may need more salt) and serve.

ROASTED SPICED CAULIFLOWER WITH ALMONDS

More than braising, baking, sautéing, and even simmering, if there is one fall-back technique that I use on a near daily basis in my kitchen, it's roasting.

You can roast almost anything to delectable results. Just take whatever it is that you want to eat, toss it with loads of olive oil and more salt than you think you need, and put it in a low-sided pan in a hot oven. While you unload the dishwasher or mash some garlic for a vinaigrette, your dinner will soften on the inside and caramelize on the surface, taking on that characteristic roasted, sweet flavor. It will condense and deepen in the heat, becoming more intensely *itself* in taste. Beets get beetier, broccoli gets broccolier.

Because the process is the same for nearly every vegetable, meat, fish, or fowl, you can set your brain on automatic when you roast; all you need to do is watch carefully so you can judge when dinner is done. It helps if all the ingredients are cut into the same-size pieces so they cook at the same rate, though if some end up darker brown veering on black and some more golden, that's okay too—especially if you adore the burned ends of roasted carrots, potatoes, and Brussels sprouts as much as I do.

One thing I've learned through trial and error is not to crowd the pan. Leaving space between all the chunks is what gives the heat a chance to envelop and brown them. Squishing them all together will steam them and make everything mushy, which is not terrible, but probably not what you wanted when you decided to roast. I use large, industrial baking pans (called sheet pans) that I picked up at a kitchen supply store. Jelly roll pans work well too, but are a little smaller.

When I'm feeling completely sapped of all my creative juices, I roast. As long as you start out with something fresh and preferably seasonal, it won't need any bells and whistles to make it taste good. Sure, you can do things like substitute nuggets of butter for the olive oil, though I don't usually bother, since cutting butter into bits is more fidgety work than overturning a bottle of oil. But swapping in smoked salt for plain sea salt will give your food a hot-off-the-grill flavor without having to go outside and battle mosquitoes.

If you happen to be feeling creative, you could sprinkle on spices and nuts, as I do here. They turn plain-Jane cauliflower into a kicky dish suitable for company, though for a marvelous, minimalist version, stick to the basic trio of cauliflower, oil, and salt. The nutty browned flavor of the heat commingling with the sweet earthy essence of vegetable is all you really need. Ditto the carrots and eggplant variations, though the green goddess dressing on the eggplant is a gem of a recipe in its own right, and worth the five minutes it takes to whirl in the blender. Make it even if you skip the eggplant; it will be terrific as a dip for chips, carrots sticks, your fingers.

But back to roasting. I learned about roasting from chef Waldy Malouf, with whom I wrote a cookbook called *High Heat*. The trope was that every recipe could either be grilled or roasted depending on the season and your mood, and that application of high heat brought out the best flavors in nearly every ingredient.

After testing my way through 125 recipes both in the oven and on the grill, I can positively say that I prefer the oven. It's not just because I find roasted foods slightly more delicate and compelling than the brawniness of grilled foods. It's because I like keeping busy inside the kitchen, washing the salad greens or opening the wine while the fish roasts, rather than standing around outside just waiting for it to cook but doing nothing else besides (though I suppose I could weed the garden). Unitasking, my husband calls it. And he is the champion of it. Which is why, when it comes to the few things that are better grilled than roasted—burgers, ribs, steak—he mans the grill. And I roast the side dishes, happily ensconced inside.

Roasted Spiced Cauliflower with Almonds

¾ teaspoon whole cumin

¾ teaspoon whole coriander seed

½ teaspoon whole brown mustard seed

1 large cauliflower, trimmed and cut into 1-inch florets

2 tablespoons extra-virgin olive oil

½ teaspoon kosher salt, plus additional to taste

¼ teaspoon freshly ground black pepper

2 tablespoons sliced almonds

Time: 40 minutes

Serves 4

1. Preheat the oven to 425°F. Using the flat side of a knife or a mortar and pestle, lightly crush the cumin, coriander, and mustard.

2. On a rimmed baking sheet, toss the cauliflower with the oil, salt, pepper, and spice mixture, then spread out into an even layer. Roast for 15 minutes, then stir the cauliflower and cook for 10 more minutes. Sprinkle on the almonds, stir again, and cook for an additional 5 minutes, until browned and softened. Serve hot, warm, or cold.

VARIATION: POMEGRANATE ROASTED CARROTS

Pomegranate molasses tastes nothing like either pomegranate or molasses, but has a puckery, caramel, almost SweeTarts candy flavor that perks up just about anything you drizzle it on. I bought a bottle several years ago to make a North African meal, and have since gone through phases of sprinkling it obsessively on anything that stands still long enough, then letting it languish for months, only to gleefully rediscover the sticky bottle wedged behind the pumpkin seed oil.

For a while, I used it to dress my nightly salads, tossing in a few drops along with olive oil and salt (no vinegar needed). But after a few months, my husband rebelled ("Did you have a falling out with vinegar?"), so I moved on to roasted vegetables, stirring the molasses in at the end of the roasting time to prevent baked-on, black scorches (one nasty cleanup was plenty).

Of all the vegetables that have met its tart tang, sweet roasted carrots, seasoned with a little chile for spice, make the best partner. Don't try to substitute regular molasses here, the flavor is too strong. If you don't have pomegranate molasses (available in Middle Eastern and gourmet food shops), use 2 teaspoons of balsamic vinegar instead, adding it halfway through the cooking time. Mint and parsley make fine stand-ins for cilantro.

Pomegranate Roasted Carrots

Time: 40 minutes

Serves 4

1 pound carrots, peeled, trimmed, and halved or quartered lengthwise
   (halve the thin carrots, quarter the fat ones)
1 tablespoon extra-virgin olive oil
¼ teaspoon kosher salt
Pinch Turkish or Syrian red pepper (such as Aleppo pepper) or cayenne
1 teaspoon pomegranate molasses or 2 teaspoons balsamic vinegar
2 tablespoons chopped fresh cilantro, basil, or parsley

1. Preheat the oven to 425°F. On a rimmed baking sheet, toss the carrots with the oil, salt, and red pepper or cayenne. Spread them out in a single layer.
2. Roast for 15 minutes, stir well, and roast for 10 more minutes. Then remove from the oven and drizzle with the pomegranate molasses; toss gently to coat the carrots with the molasses. Roast until the carrots are golden and soft, about 5 more minutes. Serve garnished with cilantro.

VARIATION: ROASTED EGGPLANT WITH BASIL GREEN GODDESS DRESSING

These salty, browned chunks of eggplant are as addictive as potato chips, though what they lack in crunch they make up for in sweetness. The snappy green goddess dressing isn't strictly necessary, though it is very nice, adding a creamy, herbal character that goes well with the buttery texture of the eggplant. But if you'd rather leave it out, just sprinkle the eggplant with a little red wine vinegar and herbs—or Thai fish sauce if you've got it—before serving. Or toss it with cherry tomatoes, diced bell peppers, crumbled feta, and vinaigrette for a tasty eggplant salad that holds up well at a summer barbecue.

Roasted Eggplant with Basil Green Goddess Dressing

1 large eggplant (about 1 pound), scrubbed, trimmed, and cut into
    1-inch cubes
5 tablespoons extra-virgin olive oil
1¼ teaspoons kosher salt
¼ cup crème fraîche or sour cream
2 tablespoons mayonnaise
2 anchovy fillets, chopped
2 garlic cloves, chopped
1 tablespoon chopped fresh chives
1 tablespoon chopped fresh parsley
1 tablespoon chopped fresh basil
1½ teaspoons freshly squeezed lemon juice
¼ teaspoon freshly ground black pepper

Time: 30 minutes

Serves 4

1. Preheat the oven to 400°F. In a rimmed baking sheet, toss the eggplant with the oil and ¾ teaspoon kosher salt. Arrange the cubes in a single layer and roast for 30 minutes, stirring once or twice.
2. While the eggplant is roasting, make the dressing. In the bowl of a food processor, place the crème fraîche, mayonnaise, anchovies, garlic, chives, parsley, basil, lemon juice, pepper, and the remaining ½ teaspoon salt. Run the motor until the mixture is fully combined and bright green. Serve the dressing alongside or drizzled over the eggplant.

RED LENTIL SOUP WITH LEMON

For years it seemed that everyone I knew had a special lentil soup recipe in their lives, one that sustained them and kept them warm all winter long. I'd flirted with countless incarnations in my time, and most tasted reasonably good. They were brawny, solid, and predictable, and I liked them in varying degrees, but never quite enough to take home to my soup pot. But recently I fell head over heels. Could this be the one?

It was so unexpected. At my friend Anya's dinner party, little white espresso cups filled with some kind of steaming liquid were passed around as hors d'oeuvres. Deep in conversation, I took an absent-minded sip that instantly dazzled, yet mystified me. A gorgeous soup, it was warming and hearty, and possessed a velvety texture that recalled some kind of pureed legume. But it had a zesty, spicy flavor that was more ethereal and sunny than any earth-bound wintry bean.

"It's nothing, just a little lentil soup," said my hostess nonchalantly when I cornered her in the kitchen.

Lentil? It didn't taste like lentils. And with its muted golden color, it didn't look like them either.

"Red lentils, sweetie, with chili powder and a little lemon. I'll e-mail you tomorrow with the recipe," she promised.

In fervid anticipation, I picked up some red lentils the very next morning. Unlike their more familiar green and brown cousins, red lentils are hulled and split when you buy them. This lets them cook much faster than their relatives, though they don't hold their shape as well, making them problematic for salads and ideal for soup.

Such was what I found out with a little Googling.

Finally, the e-mail appeared. I wasn't playing coy; I had already pulled out the soup pot.

As I figured, the ingredient list called for red lentils (check), broth (check), onion (check), cumin (check), garlic, lemons, and chili powder (of course).

Then came some surprises: dried mint, fresh tomatoes, and bulgur—none of which were in the cupboard.

As determined as I was to make the soup, I was equally determined not to leave the house. It was cold and rainy outside, and there was only so much I was willing to sacrifice for such a nascent crush.

Still, I had my heart set on lentils. Clearly, there would need to be some compromises if this was going to work out.

The tomatoes were easy to get around. I used a fat dollop of tomato paste instead, sautéing it with the onions and garlic to give it a sweeter and more intense flavor. I also added a chopped carrot to compensate for the lost vegetable matter and ruddy color.

The bulgur was a harder swap out. I considered rice, buckwheat groats, even steel-cut oats, before deciding to leave it out altogether and double the lentils. Of those, I had plenty, and weren't they the point?

Then I added some broth to the pot and set it all to simmer. Half an hour later, my lentil soup was bubbling hot and ready. I squeezed in some lemon for vibrancy, drizzled on some good olive oil for richness, and to substitute for the mint, floated a handful of chopped cilantro over the surface.

I was a little nervous about digging in. With all my changes, would the soup live up to my memory and expectations?

In fact, it was even better. Lighter and more brothy than the bulgur original, it had a buoyant, lemony disposition grounded by a profound cumin and chili backbone. It was the perfect lentil soup, at least for me. Bright, deep, compelling, and easily accessible if I kept a supply of red lentils around, I could make the soup in under an hour whenever my heart desired.

And I've been making it ever since.

Red Lentil Soup with Lemon

Time: 45 minutes

Serves 6

4 tablespoons olive oil, plus additional good oil for drizzling

2 large onions, chopped

4 garlic cloves, minced

2 tablespoons tomato paste

2 teaspoons ground cumin

½ teaspoon kosher salt, plus additional to taste

½ teaspoon freshly ground black pepper

Pinch ground chili powder or cayenne, plus additional to taste

2 quarts chicken or vegetable broth

2 cups red lentils

2 large carrots, peeled and diced

Juice of 1 lemon, or more to taste

⅓ cup chopped fresh cilantro, mint, or parsley

1. In a large pot, heat the oil over high heat until hot and shimmering. Add the onions and garlic and sauté until golden, about 4 minutes.

2. Stir in the tomato paste, cumin, salt, pepper, and chili powder or cayenne, and sauté for 2 minutes longer.

3. Add the broth, 2 cups water, the lentils, and the carrots. Bring to a simmer, then partially cover the pot and turn the heat to medium-low. Simmer until the lentils are soft, about 30 minutes. Taste and add more salt if necessary.

4. Using an immersion or regular blender or a food processor, puree half the soup (it should be somewhat chunky, not smooth).

5. Reheat the soup if necessary, then stir in the lemon juice and cilantro, mint, or parsley. Serve the soup drizzled with good olive oil and dusted very lightly with chili powder, if desired.

VARIATION: ANYA'S ORIGINAL LENTIL SOUP WITH DRIED MINT AND TOMATO

Anya's original soup is thicker and heartier than my version, thanks to the bulgur.

Anya's Original Lentil Soup with Dried Mint and Tomato

2 tablespoons unsalted butter

1 medium onion, chopped

2 garlic cloves, chopped

¾ teaspoon kosher salt

½ teaspoon red (Aleppo) pepper, plus additional for serving

1 medium tomato, chopped

1 tablespoon tomato paste

1 teaspoon dried mint, plus additional for serving

1 cup red lentils

¼ cup coarse bulgur wheat

4 cups chicken stock

Butter, for serving

Lemon wedges, for serving

Time: 1¼ hours

Serves 6 to 8

1. In a large pot over medium heat, melt the butter. Add the onion, garlic, salt, and pepper, and cook until the onion is soft and the garlic is fragrant, 4 to 5 minutes.

2. Stir in the tomato, tomato paste, and mint, and cook for an additional 1 to 2 minutes. Stir in the lentils and bulgur wheat, and cover with the chicken stock and 2 cups water. Cover and simmer for 45 minutes to 1 hour, until the lentils are tender. Serve each bowl with a little pat of butter on top, letting it melt, along with a sprinkle of mint, red pepper, and the lemon wedges.

3 Learning to Like Fish

At a fancy seafood restaurant in the South of France, my sister and I rebelled over our umpteenth plates of roast chicken and frites.

"You like fish, but we don't like fish," we cried to our startled parents, "and we are sick of fish restaurants with nothing but chicken to eat!"

We were brimming with indignity at ages seven and eight. Tired of having no choices, it would have been mutiny had we been strong enough to overtake the ship.

I don't remember how that outburst was resolved, though decades into my putative adulthood, I can sympathize with my parents' immersion in the pristine seafood of Southern France, the likes of which we didn't see in Brooklyn. I'm sure they figured that eventually we kids would come around and abandon chicken in favor of squid.

But no matter how many times we were offered tastes of briny mussels and oysters and grilled sardines, even bites of mild fillet of sole and pink shrimp with their heads still attached, beady eyes staring, we never partook. It all seemed as appealing as sand. So I categorically avoided anything that wore fins, tentacles, or shells.

There were the few childhood exceptions. I ate tuna because I never accepted that the benign stuff out of a can was really fish. Lox and whitefish salad were grandfathered in; after all, I'd been eating them on bagels since before I had teeth. But otherwise, it was a long while before I learned to love the likes of seafood beyond fish sticks.

Slowly, my tastes evolved. Crab cakes, shredded crustacean hidden within the crunchy exterior, came first. I ate them once at a Christmas party when I was twelve and was hooked. Then I cozied up to shrimp (peeled, no head, please) before discovering the sweet, saline juice sucked out from a lobster's legs. Fried calamari, dunked in tomato sauce, followed fast and hard.

By the time I went to college, I was eating pretty much anything the seas, lakes, and streams could serve forth—frogs and sea snails included—and now

I'm the kind of extreme seafood eater who likes nothing more than chewing on the very shrimp heads that used to make me blanch (okay, not the very ones, but very similar ones). Whatever it is a shrimp has up in its noggin tastes like the essence of the sea seasoned with funk and butter, and I love mopping it up with bread.

In fact, I was so crazy about shrimp heads that the feelings overflowed onto my boyfriend Max, a Swedish graduate student who shared a penchant for crunching on crustaceans. I married him, and we spent a blissful year savoring herrings, salmon roe, smoked eel, and other traditional Scandinavian sea fare. Then I realized that good marriages are built on things deeper than a shared love of seafood and more powerful than even surströmming, the odoriferous fermented fish that I never did work up the nerve to sample despite his many urgings. The problem was, he didn't agree. Mutiny was inevitable.

MAX'S ARCTIC CHAR WITH
EGG LEMON DRAGON SAUCE

I knew that my first husband, Max, was a seafood lover beyond the likes I'd seen in the other men I'd dated. He noshed on gravlax and pickled herring like potato chips, spooned up salmon roe from the jar, sucked Swedish caviar spread out of a tube—for breakfast, with coffee.

But it wasn't until he took me to visit his family in Sweden that I realized the depths of his fishy obsession.

Then it hit me like a three-pound pike flung onto the bottom of our little motorboat anchored in the Stockholm archipelago. There were four of us in the boat if you didn't count the growing pile of pike: Max, myself, Max's best friend, Lars, and Lars's stunningly blond girlfriend, Tova.

The plan was to tour the little granite islets that dot the calm waters, stopping for a picnic lunch and maybe casting a line or two to fish for pike.

The reality was a driving, merciless rain that made the islets too slick to walk upon. We only stopped once so Tova and I could pee, but there was no cover on the pink granite. The only way to hide our bare bottoms was to scamper over the slippery surface to the other side of the rock. Tova skipped gracefully up the hill in all her honey-colored, Scandinavian glory, while I trudged behind on all fours, desperate not to slide into the water and have to be rescued by Max, who was pissy enough as it was about having to stop at all.

Finally Tova and I found a place to drop our rubber rain pants. There was shelter next to a crater that held a dead swan floating in a pool of bottle-green water. Its feathery white wings were outspread, as if it were flying off to some other, more pleasant reality.

Back on the boat, the rain came down harder and we ate our soggy sandwiches of brown bread and caviar spread while Max and Lars cast line after line, reeling in silvery pikes.

The afternoon dwindled. The rain fell. The boys fished competitively, neither willing to call it quits while the other was ahead by a fish.

To pass the time, Tova sang Nordic folk songs in her honey-coated voice and I sat hunched and miserable and soaked to the skin, attempting to focus on the nineteenth-century novel I stuck in my oversize slicker pocket as we left the summer house that morning. I'd hoped to read it lying on sun-warmed rocks while Tova swam and the boys fished. I can't remember what book it was other than that it was the Penguin edition of something or other, which should have, I thought, withstood the rain a little better than it did.

Finally, dusk dimmed the overcast sky and we had to go back. Lars had beat Max by one pike, and Max fumed all the way home.

When we got there, Max and Lars cooked a feast. They baked several of the fish, slathering them in a melted butter and hard-cooked egg sauce scented with tarragon, called "dragon" in Swedish. Naturally, it was Max's favorite herb.

By the time we returned to New York a few weeks later, I knew our relationship had sunk, and that my soul mate was an unbearable grouch. I was ready to fly away to some other, more pleasant reality.

But even after Max had moved out, taking all the tubes of caviar spread with him, I still kept his butter, egg, and tarragon sauce for fish and gave it an honored place in my repertoire. I can't usually find pike, but find the sauce works well on almost anything aquatic, especially red-fleshed, sweet arctic char. And the best part? I don't have to go on a fishing trip to procure it. In fact, I haven't been fishing since.

Max's Arctic Char with Egg Lemon Dragon Sauce

Time: 10 minutes

Serves 2

2 arctic char fillets, 8 ounces each
3 tablespoons unsalted butter, melted
Kosher salt and freshly ground black pepper
1 large egg, hard-cooked, peeled, and diced
1 teaspoon chopped fresh tarragon
1 teaspoon freshly squeezed lemon juice

1. Preheat the oven to 400°F. Line a rimmed baking sheet with foil and place the fish on it, skin side down. Brush the fillets with some of the melted butter. Season with salt and pepper. Bake until just cooked through, 7 to 8 minutes.
2. While the fish is baking, stir the egg, tarragon, and lemon juice into the remaining butter.
3. Transfer the fish to a platter and pour on the butter mixture to serve.

STEAMED WILD SALMON WITH MUSTARD GREENS, SOY SAUCE, AND GINGER

Of all the fish I've come to love after a childhood of avoidance, cooked salmon was late to the table. I'd been eating bagels and lox for so long that when I thought of salmon, I pictured the silky, supple, smoked stuff and not its fully cooked cousin.

It might have been because most of the cooked salmon I had been eating was overcooked and chalky. Even when it was still rare in the middle, the exterior was usually seared to a hard crisp, which dried out the crust in an unpleasant way. So for years I more or less restricted my salmon intake to smoked on bagels, cured as gravlax, or raw as sashimi or sushi.

But then one night at a fancy restaurant I tasted a cooked salmon so moist and velvety it flaked into large, soft chunks that melted like fish-flavored butter on the tongue. Not only was there nary a brown sear mark on the pink flesh, the color was deep coral all the way through.

"Gently cooked wild salmon. Chef *sous-vides* it at a very low temperature," the waiter told me.

The chef in question is David Bouley. And I wanted the recipe badly enough that I agreed to work on a cookbook with Mr. Bouley several years later.

Although I thought I'd need special vacuum-sealing equipment, his recipe didn't call for any. Just wrap a heatproof plate of buttered salmon in plastic film, then let it cook in a 250°F oven (the plastic won't melt in such a low oven).

It couldn't be any simpler, and I spent a good year making David Bouley's salmon as a regular part of my dinner party rotation, changing the sauce to fit the seasons. I'd make it with sorrel sauce in spring, tomato water in summer (remember tomato water, made from hanging ripe tomatoes in cheesecloth and letting them drip, another David Bouley conceit?). Sautéed cabbage was nice in winter, and rosemary and mushrooms filled the bill in fall.

But over the last couple of years, I've become far less enthused about the idea of cooking my fish wrapped in potentially BPA-laden plastic. So I put that recipe on hiatus, and went back to eating my salmon raw, cured, and smoked.

I might not have gone back to cooking the fish at all if it weren't for getting pregnant. All of a sudden, raw, smoked, and cured salmon were on the no-no list, along with wine, hot tubs, and softly scrambled eggs. I can't say I stuck to this list very faithfully, but I did cut down drastically on my uncooked fish consumption.

But my body and my baby still needed all those good oils found in low-mercury fish such as salmon, so it was time to take my fish to the fire.

I went out and bought the most beautiful piece of wild Alaskan salmon I could find (paying $20 a pound for the privilege). And then I thought about how to cook it.

Searing obviously was out of the question, which eliminated broiling, grilling, and panfrying.

I could have butter braised it, one of my favorite ways to cook fish. But being pregnant, I decided I wanted lighter, more healthful fare than eating a pan full of butter. Which is how I got to steaming.

Steaming is not my favorite way to cook anything other than pudding and dumplings. I'm a fast friend of fat, and tend to find steaming stingy and lean. But I'd had good success with a steamed flounder recipe once, and was open to trying out the technique with my salmon.

In the flounder recipe, I steamed the fish on a bed of mustard greens seasoned with soy sauce, garlic, and ginger, and it was so easy and so good that if it weren't for the fact that flounder is on the endangered fish list, it would have become a weeknight staple.

I hoped all I had to do was to swap in salmon for the flounder and the flavors would meld.

For once I followed my own recipe, sautéing the mustard greens with the garlic and ginger, and adding soy sauce and sesame oil for a nutty, salty tang. Then I spread the greens out in the pan and plopped the salmon on top, covering the skillet to trap the steam. A few minutes later, I had soft, sweet just-cooked fish on top of pungent greens.

It was a resounding success. Almost as good as bagels and lox, but a whole lot more salubrious, at that moment, for baby and me.

Steamed Wild Salmon with
Mustard Greens, Soy Sauce, and Ginger

Time: 15 minutes

Serves 2

1 tablespoon vegetable or peanut oil

1 teaspoon toasted sesame oil, plus additional for drizzling

3 garlic cloves, minced

1-inch-thick slice peeled fresh gingerroot, minced

1 very large or 2 small bunches mustard greens, cleaned, stemmed, and torn into pieces

1 tablespoon soy sauce, plus additional for drizzling (if using tamari or double soy sauce, use a little less)

2 wild salmon fillets, 6 to 8 ounces each

Kosher salt and freshly ground black pepper

1. Heat the oils in a very large skillet. Add the garlic and ginger and sauté until fragrant and translucent, about 2 minutes. Add the mustard greens, soy sauce, and 3 tablespoons water, and sauté until the greens start to wilt, 2 minutes longer.

2. Spread the greens out in the bottom of the pan. Season the salmon with the salt and pepper, and place on top of the greens. Cover the pan, reduce the heat to medium, and let the fish steam until just cooked through, about 6 minutes. If the pan dries out before the fish is cooked through, add a little more water, a teaspoon at a time.

3. Uncover the pan and transfer the fish to serving plates. If the greens seem wet, turn the heat to high to cook off any excess moisture. Serve the greens on top of the fish, drizzled with a little more sesame oil and soy sauce, if desired.

PORGY WITH FENNEL
FROND PESTO

I'm almost embarrassed to admit that for years when I thought of Porgy, my mind jumped to Bess and not dinner.

It's not to say I didn't know that Porgy, the opera character, was named after porgy, the fish. It's just that I had seen the show three times—more often than I'd seen the fish sold in my local seafood shop, which was zero times.

I never saw it on restaurant menus either. Or read recipes for it in books or magazines. As far as dinner was concerned, porgy might as well have been unicorn tail for all that I've come into contact with it.

This all changed when my fish market stopped being my primary source of seafood, and the farmers' market took over. Trying to eat more locally, I wanted fish that were abundant in the waters near Brooklyn. And it turns out porgy is one of them.

In terms of sustainability, porgy gets a green light from the Monterey Bay Aquarium's fish chart, meaning I can go ahead and eat it without worrying too much about species extinction. This is probably because the porgies that frequent the waters around New York are small fish with a goodly number of bones, not something that most people want to deal with (a clean pair of needle-nose pliers works nicely on the pinbones).

The upside is that porgies are sweet and tasty, with a loose-textured white flesh that flakes into large pieces when properly cooked. And they're cheap, at around $7 per pound compared with $12 for striped bass. I know a lot about porgies now; their price point and eco-friendliness have made them my go-to farmers' market seafood buy, along with the other sustainable, cheap seafood on offer—mussels, clams, squid, and mackerel.

Sure, there are days when I ache for some pillowy scallops or a succulent, endangered piece of skate. And sometimes I indulge. But more and more often, I'll slap my hand away and point to the porgy.

Porgy's sweet, ocean character can stand up to assertive flavors, which gives the cook lots of latitude in terms of sauces. The easiest thing to do is to rely on sauces that you can make ahead and will be ready before you sauté the fish. That way, once it's done, so are you.

And this is why pesto is perfect with porgy (better than cheating, weak-willed Bess, even if she does sing like an angel).

Actually, pesto is pretty much the perfect partner for almost anything, if you ask me. And I could have just stuck with the always delightful and classic basil version. But I had another thought: fennel fronds. I came up with the idea while walking around the farmers' market with a tall, bushy fennel bulb in my tote bag. The fronds escaped everywhere, tickling passersby. I should have cut them off, but I liked their exuberance. So I needed a reason to keep them intact. That's when it came to me. I'd make fennel frond pesto to serve with my porgy.

When I got home, I started cooking. It made sense to me to include the fennel in my porgy dish as well as the fronds, so I sautéed thin slices of it with onions until everything was soft and caramelized.

Meanwhile, I pulsed together a minimalist pesto using fennel fronds, garlic, and pine nuts, skipping the cheese, since my husband doesn't eat it.

Then I quickly sautéed the porgy, and served it on top of the onion-fennel mixture dotted with blobs of the slick, verdant pesto. The fresh green anise from the fronds made a lovely contrast to both the deep-sea nuance of the porgy and the jammy sweetness of the onions and fennel mush underneath. I'd say the flavors were in perfect harmony, perhaps even more so than Porgy and Bess.

Porgy with Fennel Frond Pesto

1 small fennel bulb with lots of bushy fronds
6 tablespoons extra-virgin olive oil
1 small onion, halved and thinly sliced
Kosher salt and freshly ground black pepper
2 garlic cloves, minced
2 tablespoons pine nuts or sliced or slivered almonds
4 porgy fillets, 3 ounces each
Lemon wedges, for serving
Cooked potatoes of some kind, for serving (optional)

1. Chop off the fennel fronds and coarsely chop enough to measure 1 cup (discard the rest). Put the chopped fronds in a food processor or blender and set aside.
2. Halve the fennel bulb and pull off any browned outer layers. Using a small knife, cut the core out of the bulb, then slice the bulb as thinly as you can (if you have a mandoline and want to use it, feel free).
3. In a large skillet, heat 1 tablespoon of the oil over medium heat. Add the fennel slices, onion, and a large pinch of salt and pepper. Sauté the vegetables until caramelized and softened, about 20 minutes.
4. Meanwhile, prepare the pesto by adding the garlic, nuts, 1/2 teaspoon salt, and a generous pinch of pepper to the food processor, and process until finely chopped. Add 4 tablespoons of the oil and continue to process until the mixture looks like pesto.
5. Season the fish all over with salt and pepper. When the fennel and onion are marmalade-like, transfer to serving plates. Add the remaining tablespoon of oil to the pan and, when hot, add the fish. Cook, turning once, until just cooked through, 2 to 3 minutes per side. Place the fish on top of the fennel, then top the fish with dabs of the fennel pesto. Serve with lemon wedges. Leftover pesto is divine on potatoes—or serve some along with the fish.

OLIVE OIL–POACHED HALIBUT NUGGETS WITH GARLIC AND MINT

Eons ago, I went out with a man who lived near South Street Seaport. His address was part of his appeal. After the requisite wine drinking and some half-hearted (at least for me) clubbing, we'd get to the part of the date I was really looking forward to: a wee-hours trip to the Fulton Fish Market. There we'd buy ultra-fresh slabs of slippery seafood for our late-night suppers.

Carl was an adventuresome cook. He introduced me to steamed fiddle-head ferns and a salad of sea vegetables. He could make sushi from scratch. But when it came to the fish fillets and steaks we brought back to his place after the market, simplicity reigned.

Regardless of aquatic variety, he used the same cooking technique. He'd melt several knobs of sweet butter in his old, well-seasoned cast-iron pan, then add the fish, cut into cubes. He'd let the fish cook slowly over low heat until the flesh went from translucent and quivering to opaque and firm, but not brown at the edges. Then we'd eat it, melted butter and all, on egg noodles or thick slices of bread to soak up the juices.

The trick, Carl told me, is to keep the heat low enough so you don't fry the fish. Instead, the cubes poach gently in fat that keeps their flesh moist and velvety. And because the heat is so low, cutting the fish into cubes quickens the cooking time.

My love affair with Carl's fish recipe far outlasted that with the man, and I've adapted it widely over the years.

I've swapped out olive oil, peanut oil, and even duck fat for the butter, and whole scallops and shrimp for the chunks of fish. In those rare calorie-conscious moments, I'll pluck the fish from the pan with tongs, leaving behind the fragrant fat.

But no matter how much I muck with the components, as long as I hold fast to the cooking technique, it always seems to work.

I especially like it with delicate white fish that are prone to overcooking. For example, a nice piece of halibut. To successfully sear a halibut fillet without drying it out requires the kind of focus I don't possess on a typical weeknight. But slow poaching in lots of fat is forgiving. Even if it does go a minute longer than it should while I'm multitasking, it will stay supple.

The last time I made halibut, I chose olive oil as the cooking medium because I had rosemary in the fridge and pairing the two is a classic. There was also fresh mint, which made me remember the potent Turkish dried mint I had stockpiled in the cupboard. I sprinkled some into the fish pan, along with garlic.

The halibut came out soft and juicy and infused with the heady flavors of olive oil, garlic, rosemary, and mint. A squeeze of lemon and a garnish of chopped fresh mint added brightness to a delightful meal—the late-night-supper-turned-after-work meal, happily no clubbing required.

Olive Oil–Poached Halibut Nuggets with Garlic and Mint

1 pound halibut fillet, cut into 1 1/4-inch cubes
1/4 teaspoon fine sea salt, plus additional
1/4 teaspoon freshly ground black pepper, plus additional
4 tablespoons extra-virgin olive oil
1 small rosemary sprig
1/2 teaspoon dried mint
2 garlic cloves, minced
Fresh lemon juice, to taste (optional)
Chopped fresh mint, for garnish

Time: 15 minutes

Serves 2

1. Season the halibut all over with a generous pinch of salt and pepper.
2. In a medium-size skillet just large enough to hold the fish cubes in one layer but not much bigger, heat the oil over low heat. Add the fish, rosemary sprig, and dried mint, and let cook slowly until the fish begins to turn opaque, about 3 minutes. Stir in the garlic and remaining 1/4 teaspoon each of salt

and pepper, and cook until the garlic is fragrant and the fish just cooked through, another 3 minutes or so (the heat should be low enough so as not to brown the garlic or fish, but high enough to gently cook everything; the cooking time will vary widely with your stove).

3. Taste and add more salt and pepper and a few drops of lemon juice, if desired. Stir in the fresh mint and serve, using a slotted spoon if you want to leave the poaching oil in the pan. But it's delicious over couscous or potatoes.

VARIATION: BROWN BUTTER SWORDFISH WITH TURKISH CHILI AND MINT

Combining plenty of sweet butter and chunks of succulent swordfish, this recipe is more faithful to Carl's original late-night dish than the halibut with olive oil. I once served it to my friends Roger and Sonia, spicing up the butter with the sweet and smoky chili powder and pungent dried mint that I brought back from Istanbul. Although Sonia is Greek to the core, she doesn't mind a little Turkish spicing every now and again, and in this dish the flavors really shine.

If you don't have Turkish chili, Aleppo chili from nearby Syria is a good bet. Or use a mild American chili powder such as New Mexican or ancho.

Brown Butter Swordfish with Turkish Chili and Mint

Time: 15 minutes

Serves 4

1½ pounds swordfish steaks, about 1 inch thick

Kosher salt and freshly ground black pepper

4 tablespoons unsalted butter

2 garlic cloves, minced

½ teaspoon dried mint

¼ teaspoon Turkish chili flakes, more to taste
    (or Aleppo or ancho chili powder)

2 teaspoons chopped fresh mint

Lemon wedges, for serving

1. Using a sharp knife, cut the skin off the swordfish, then cut the fish into 1-inch cubes. Season the fish cubes generously with salt and pepper.

2. In a skillet large enough to hold all the fish cubes in one layer, melt the butter over medium heat. Let the butter cook until the foam falls to the bottom of the pan and the butter turns golden brown, about 3 minutes. The butter should smell nutty.

3. Add the fish to the pan and let cook, turning the fish and basting with the butter, for 3 minutes. Stir in the garlic, dried mint, and chili flakes or powder, and continue to cook, stirring gently so as not to break up the fish cubes, until the fish is just cooked through, about 2 minutes longer. Taste and add more salt and chili if desired. Serve garnished with the fresh mint and lemon wedges.

SPAGHETTI WITH SPICY
TOMATO, CLAMS, AND BACON

Most midlife crises hit a family at its core, and in our case that meant the kitchen.

A few weeks after the birth of our daughter, my husband went out for an innocent morning run in Prospect Park, and came back seven miles later, head over heels. Distance running was his newfound passion, and if we wanted happiness within the family, we would all have to accept Daniel's training regime of twenty-mile practice runs culminating in soaks in an ice-filled bathtub, weeknight tempo workouts in Central Park, crack-of-dawn races after up-all-night teething episodes.

In the kitchen, new space-age foods started appearing in the cupboards, things in shiny packets with names like Chocolate Outrage Gu Gel and Nuun portable electrolyte hydration tabs. Our fridge began overflowing with organic fruit for Daniel's daily smoothie, to which he adds fresh gingerroot and coconut water. I did put my foot down at the gallon tub of dehydrated egg protein concentrate he tried to stash next to the blender, explaining that real free-range eggs from the farmers' market that hadn't been processed were far more healthful and took up less space. And they make his smoothies froth like mousse.

Given all this, I shouldn't have been surprised when, the week before his first half-marathon, Daniel began asking for pasta.

"I'm carbo-loading," he said, munching on a Clif bar.

He wanted pasta, lots of it, the night leading up to the race. And when the New York City marathon came around, he'd want even more pasta in the days before.

While I have nothing against the stuff, pasta wasn't high on my list of things to make for dinner. I'd cook up a batch every few weeks, but not several days in a row. I was still recovering from my six-year marriage into an Italian-American family. Pasta with red sauce was a staple I'd only recently unstapled myself from.

But there were plenty of pasta recipes that did not include simmering canned tomatoes, meatballs, and sausages at my ex-in-laws' house.

I needed to come up with a few distinct sauce recipes that could be whipped up in the amount of time it would take for the pasta to cook. Then I could rotate them in and out when a race approached, making easy substitutions so we wouldn't get bored.

I started with pasta with clam sauce.

This was not the fastest or easiest place to begin, but it was what Daniel and I were most in the mood for on the night before the big race.

I picked up some nice littleneck clams at the fish store, then thought about what kind of sauce to put them into, red or white?

I liked the intense, all-out nature of a white clam sauce. But clams and tomatoes are such a great combination, it would be a shame to leave them out of the pan.

I decided to compromise and use plenty of garlic along with a few fresh plum tomatoes, which would add some color and flavor, but not take over the sauce the way canned plum tomatoes can.

I also wanted to add some bacon because my favorite kind of clams are grilled, and since I wasn't planning on firing up the grill to make pasta, the bacon would add a nice smoky flavor right in the pan.

When I got home, I scrubbed the clams and put them in a bowl of cold water with a bit of cornmeal sprinkled over the top. I've heard this helps the clams expel any sand in their shells. Actually, I've also heard that in fact the cornmeal doesn't do a darn thing, but just to be on the safe side, I usually add it.

A few hours later, I rinsed off the clams and steamed them in my pasta pot. The easy thing about steaming bivalves is that you don't need to use a steamer basket. Just drop them into the inch or so of water on the bottom of the cooking vessel and give them a stir every now and again. As long as you remove them as they cook, they won't toughen.

As the clams open, you can shuck them—or not. There are two schools of thought when it comes to pasta with clams. Leaving them in the shell is perky and festive and proves you didn't wimp out and use canned. But removing the meat makes dining easier, allowing people to focus on other things, like drinking lots of really good wine. You can also split the difference, shucking most of them but leaving a few intact as a kind of 3-D garnish.

While the pasta boiled, I made a quick pan sauce with the garlic, tomatoes, and bacon, adding the cooked spaghetti when it was al dente. Finally, I stirred in the clams and a little bit of the clam cooking water to intensify the ocean flavor.

Then Daniel and I sat down to a tasty meal certain to load his muscles with plenty of glycogen before the big race—which, I'm happy to report, he sped through at his fastest time yet.

Spaghetti with Spicy Tomato, Clams, and Bacon

Time: 30 minutes

Serves 2 to 3

3 dozen littleneck clams, scrubbed

Kosher salt

8 ounces whole wheat or regular spaghetti

2 thick-cut strips bacon (about 2 ounces), cubed

1 to 3 tablespoons extra-virgin olive oil, as needed

1 leek (or 6 scallions), white and light green parts only, cleaned and diced

3 garlic cloves, minced

Pinch red pepper flakes, plus additional

6 plum tomatoes, diced (about 3 cups)

5 thyme sprigs

3 tablespoons chopped fresh parsley or basil

1. In a large pasta pot over medium heat, place the clams and cover with 1 inch of water. Cover and cook for 5 minutes, then uncover and transfer the opened clams to a bowl. Cover the pot and check every 1 to 2 minutes, removing any opened clams. After 15 minutes, discard any clams that don't open. Remove the opened clams from their shells and reserve. Skim off 2 tablespoons of clam juice from the top of the pot (the grit will have settled to the bottom), and reserve.

2. Bring a large pot of salted water to a boil and cook the spaghetti until al dente.

3. While the water for the pasta is boiling, make the sauce. In a large skillet over medium-high heat, cook the bacon until brown and slightly crispy, about 5 minutes. If the bacon was lean, add 1 to 2 tablespoons of oil to sauté the leek. Cook the leek with a pinch of salt until tender, 4 to 5 minutes. Add the remaining tablespoon(s) of oil, if necessary, and sauté the garlic and pepper flakes, stirring, until the garlic is golden and fragrant, about 2 minutes. Stir in the tomatoes, thyme, parsley or basil, a large pinch of salt, and red pepper, and cook until the tomatoes begin to break down and release their juice, about 8 minutes. Reduce the heat to low, just enough to keep the sauce warm while the pasta finishes cooking.

4. Drain the spaghetti and return it to the pot. Stir in the clams, reserved clam juice, and sauce, and serve immediately.

GRILLED CLAMS WITH LEMON-CAYENNE-GARLIC BUTTER

Of all the grilling gurus in my life, from my fire-happy mother (who thinks nothing of grilling lamb chops in January) to big-time grilling mavens such as Waldy Malouf (with whom I wrote a grilling cookbook), the griller who made the deepest impression was my childhood pediatrician, Dr. Arthur Ruby.

Dr. Ruby was a close family friend and partner in gustatory delights. In winter he brought over pots of gelatinous p'tcha (stewed calves' feet) that we ate with challah to sop up the shimmering, garlicky broth. Summertime meant weekends at the Rubys' second home in Cold Spring, New York, where, sometime in the 1950s, Dr. Ruby had a custom-made stone grill built into the patio of the historic clapboard house.

Our Saturday night dinner ritual never varied. Cocktails commenced at 6:00 P.M.; gin martinis for the adults, root beer for the kids, all served in glasses that were stored in the freezer for a permanent frost.

Hors d'oeuvres consisted of baked Brie strewn with canned fried onions, and clams, grilled until their pink bellies were steaming hot and slightly smoky, but still raw, with a crisp bite and soft center.

Then, for a main course, Dr. Ruby artfully grilled a two-inch-thick porterhouse steak that, even when he and Mrs. Ruby moved to Manhattan, still came from a special butcher on Avenue M in Brooklyn. Fresh boiled corn, tomato salad with basil, and hot bread and butter rounded out the offerings.

Naturally, the star of the meal was the steak, which Dr. Ruby managed to grill so that it was perfectly charred on the outside, but still bloody within (pity you if you liked your steak cooked past rare; Dr. Ruby would direct you to the nearest McDonald's thirty miles away).

But the flavor I most associate with those steaming, lazy, hammock-swinging days is briny, smoky clams.

In keeping with his meticulous personality, Dr. Ruby had a particular way of preparing the bivalves. He'd scrub them well, then carefully shuck each one, enlisting my father to help while the coals heated to an ash gray and my mother and Mrs. Ruby sliced fat red tomatoes in the kitchen.

Then he'd carefully lay the clams directly on the grill, taking care not to spill one precious drop of the clam juice into the fiery grate. Exactly one minute later, the clams were ready to be carried on a flowered tray onto the screened-in porch, where we slurped them down, burning our fingers on the hot shells.

Although I've craved grilled clams every time I think about the Rubys', I never did try to make them at home. The idea of shucking the clams, then transferring them to the grill, always seemed like one step too many. And as far as recipes that called for putting the unshucked clams in a pot and placing that on the grill, at that point I might as well just turn on the stove.

Still, I thought as I waited on the fish line at the farmers' market, there's got to be an easier way to grill a clam.

That's when the idea for a compromise hit me. If I didn't shuck the clams but just threw them on the grill grate and let them open as they cooked, would I lose all the clam juice, yielding dry, rubbery morsels? Or if I grabbed them as they opened and quickly tossed them into a bowl, would I be able to preserve some, if not all, of their tasty liquor?

It was certainly worth trying at least once.

As the grill preheated, I stirred together a quick garlic-cayenne-lemon butter—the kind of savory, salty, creamy sauce that would make a two-by-four delectable, let alone an overcooked clam.

Then I stood by the grill, tongs in one hand, bowl in the other, carefully removing the just-opened clams. It took all of five minutes, less time than it took the mosquitoes to find me.

I poured the butter over the clams and sprinkled on some chopped chives, and my husband and I immediately dove in.

The clams were tender and plump, and there was enough clam juice in the bottom of the bowl to meld with the seasoned butter, creating a briny, buttery sauce. They were nothing like what we had at the Rubys', with one tactile exception. The shells still burned our fingers as we scooped them up, but caught up in the whirl of such deliciousness, we couldn't have cared less.

Grilled Clams with
Lemon-Cayenne-Garlic Butter

Time: 10 minutes

Serves 2

1 large garlic clove, minced
Large pinch kosher salt, more to taste
4 tablespoons unsalted butter, melted
2 teaspoons freshly squeezed lemon juice, more to taste
Pinch cayenne
2 dozen littleneck clams, scrubbed
Chopped fresh chives, for serving

1. Using a mortar and pestle or using the flat part of a knife on a cutting board, mash together the garlic and salt until a paste forms. Scrape the paste into a small bowl and stir in the melted butter, lemon juice, and cayenne. Taste to make sure the salt and lemon are balanced.

2. Preheat the grill. Place the clams directly on the grill grate or on a large baking pan in a single layer. Cover the grill and let the clams cook for 2 minutes. Open the grill and check the clams, using tongs to remove any that have opened, and transfer them to a large bowl. Be careful not to spill the clams' juices when transferring them. Close the grill lid and check every 30 seconds, removing the clams as they open.

3. Pour the lemon-cayenne-garlic butter over the clam bowl and toss lightly. Serve hot, garnished with chives.

ALE-STEAMED MUSSELS WITH GARLIC AND MUSTARD

It used to be, when I wanted seafood, I'd go the fish store. I'd eye the briny offerings and choose the critter with the glossiest skin or perkiest gills—whatever looked good and made me hungry when I imagined it on a plate.

These days, when I want seafood, I go to the Internet. I type the variety I'm considering and call up all the pertinent information. Is it overfished and near extinction? Responsibly and locally farmed? High in mercury or otherwise contaminated? The whole endeavor makes me want to defrost some pork chops and call it a day.

But recently I decided to work in reverse. Instead of looking up species after species trying to find something suitable, I'd start with the list of "best choices" (environmentally sustainable) put out by Seafood Watch, and choose something from there.

It was this rather convoluted process that caused me to purchase a sack of Prince Edward Island mussels. Not only are they ocean-friendly, they're wallet-friendly. Two pounds cost me $3.98.

Since mussels are the national dish of Belgium, I decided to steam them with ale, the country's other collective obsession. I picked up a bottle of that, along with some garlic (my personal obsession), sharp mustard, and tarragon (two other Northern European associations I thought would work well together). I also nabbed a crusty baguette so I'd have something to sop up all the savory juices that inevitably accompany a big bowl of garlicky steamed mussels.

My ingredients assembled, I headed to the kitchen.

Truth be told, I was a little worried about the bivalve preparation. The last time I cooked mussels they needed vigorous scrubbing to clean away the mud, followed by a thorough scraping with a paring knife to remove the tenacious hairy byssal threads, aka the beard.

But these mussels arrived prescrubbed and clean shaven, with nary a hair on their pretty blue-black shells.

I had always been schooled not to remove the beards until moments before cooking in order not to stress the mollusks and cause their untimely death. I wondered, shouldn't my mussels be well on their way to spoiling after what was at least a day or two of beardlessness?

They smelled and looked fine.

Just to be safe, I made some phone calls.

Len Currie, the general manager of Confederacy Cove Mussel Company, explained that farmed mussels are routinely cleaned and "debyssed" before being scooped into their plastic net packages.

But doesn't that compromise their shelf life?

"It does, but only by a few hours or maybe a day. You can get a shelf life of ten days or more if you handle them carefully," he explained.

This meant that my mussels needed nothing more than a good rinse before hitting their garlicky bath, which had, thanks to the complexity and bitterness of the ale, simmered into a heady pan sauce.

Once cooked, the mussels themselves were tender, meaty, and succulent. We ate every one, greedily pulling them from their shells and swishing them in the sauce.

It was an easy, inexpensive, and—once I solved the byssal conundrum—stress-free meal. Both for the ecosystem and me.

Ale-Steamed Mussels with Garlic and Mustard

2 pounds mussels
1 tablespoon olive oil
4 full thyme sprigs
3 garlic cloves, minced
2 large shallots, chopped
Kosher salt and freshly ground black pepper
¾ cup good ale
1 to 3 tablespoons butter to taste
1 tablespoon chopped fresh tarragon or parsley
1 teaspoon Dijon mustard
Crusty bread, for serving

Time: 15 minutes

Serves 2

1. If your mussels are farmed (and they probably are), all you need to do is rinse them under cold running water. Otherwise, if you see hairy clumps around the shell (called beards), use a sharp knife or your fingers to pull off the beards, then scrub the shells well with a vegetable brush.

2. In a soup pot with a tight-fitting cover, heat the olive oil, then add the thyme, garlic, shallots, and a pinch of salt and pepper. Sauté until the shallots and garlic are softened, 3 minutes. Pour in the ale and bring to a simmer. Add the mussels and cover the pot. Let the mussels steam, stirring them once or twice, until they all open, 5 to 10 minutes.

3. Use a slotted spoon to transfer the mussels to serving bowls, discarding any that haven't opened.

4. Add the butter, tarragon or parsley, and mustard to the pan juices, and bring to a boil, whisking well. Whisk until the butter melts, then taste and correct the seasonings (adding more butter if the liquid tastes bitter). Pour over the mussels and serve with good bread to sop up the juices.

VARIATION: GARLICKY STEAMED MUSSELS WITH CORN AND SHERRY

I came up with this variation on a mussel theme in summertime, when there was plenty of good, sweet corn at the farmers' market. Since I wanted the corn to shine, I substituted a light, dry fino sherry for the ale and left out the mustard entirely. It's a more buoyant and sprightly dish than its wintry iteration, perfect with a crisp rosé wine—or more fino sherry—alongside.

Garlicky Steamed Mussels with Corn and Sherry

Time: 15 minutes

Serves 2

2 pounds mussels

1 tablespoon extra-virgin olive oil

4 garlic cloves, minced

2 scallions, white and green parts, thinly sliced

1 shallot, finely chopped

Kosher salt to taste

2 ears corn, kernels scraped from the cob

1/3 cup dry (fino) sherry

2 tablespoons unsalted butter

1. Rinse the mussels under cold running water. If you see hairy clumps around the shell (called beards), use a sharp knife or your fingers to pull them off, then scrub the shells well with a vegetable brush.
2. In a soup pot with a tight-fitting cover, heat the olive oil, then add the garlic, scallions, shallot, and a pinch of salt. Sauté until the shallots and garlic are softened, 3 minutes. Add the corn and continue to sauté until it begins to soften, about 3 minutes longer.
3. Pour in the sherry and bring to a simmer. Let simmer until the corn is cooked through, about 5 minutes. Add the mussels and cover the pot. Let the mussels steam, stirring once or twice, until they open, 5 to 10 minutes.

Use a slotted spoon to transfer the mussels to bowls. Discard any that have not opened.

4. Add the butter to the pan juices and simmer until the butter is melted and the sauce is slightly thickened, about 2 minutes. Pour the mixture over the mussels and serve immediately.

ROASTED SHRIMP
AND BROCCOLI

When cooking seasonally, it's not just the ingredients that follow the weather. Techniques do, too. Speedy methods such as steaming, searing, and blanching seem too fleeting and insubstantial for the heft of dense winter turnips and compact Brussels spouts. Instead, come December, I crank up the oven and hardly turn it off until March, roasting everything that can't protest.

My foolproof, basic roasting recipe—which works with nearly every vegetable I've tried—involves nothing more than coating an ingredient with a generous gloss of olive oil, seasoning it well with kosher salt, freshly ground black pepper, and whatever other spices are within arm's reach, and subjecting it to my oven's high heat (generally set between 400 and 450°F, depending on the density of the vegetable and my hunger level). (For more about roasting, see page 68.)

Broccoli works stunningly well. In warmer months I'll savor it raw in salads or steam it lightly to accentuate its grassy green flavor. But in winter, I want it slow-cooked, caramelized, and thoroughly soft. Roasting gets me there with a minimum of fuss.

I've served roasted broccoli florets, strewn with whole coriander and cumin and maybe a pinch of chili, as finger food at fancy parties. I've eaten heaps of it for supper with nothing more than some bread and cheese on the side. I've pureed it into soup thinned down with chicken broth.

But one recent evening, I was itching to try something a little different, and hungered for a meal more substantial than just a bowl of vegetables, no matter how savory.

I wanted to add protein, some quick-cooking ingredient I could roast along with the broccoli, preferably in the same pan.

Tofu would work. But even the firmest of the firm would need pressing and draining before it could be roasted, and I didn't want to wait that long.

Boneless chicken thigh meat was another possibility. Cut into bite-size pieces, it would roast in about the same time as broccoli florets (breast meat would also work, but I don't like it as much). But roasted chicken is always tastier after even a very brief stint in an intense marinade or spice-and-garlic rub. And I was after instant post-supermarket gratification.

So in the end I chose plump pink shrimp. They required no advance preparation, and the color would be gorgeous with the broccoli.

Having roasted shrimp on their own before, I knew their cooking time would be about half that of the broccoli, especially if I wanted supple florets.

So I slicked the broccoli with oil and seasonings and set it to roast. Ten minutes later, I tossed in the shrimp. After twenty minutes altogether, I ended up with juicy, meaty shrimp tinged with lemon zest, and spice-infused, tender, golden-edged broccoli. Perhaps best of all, there was only one dirty pan; easy cleanup is welcome in any season.

Roasted Shrimp and Broccoli

2 pounds broccoli, cut into bite-size florets
1/4 cup extra-virgin olive oil
1 teaspoon whole coriander seeds
1 teaspoon whole cumin seeds
1 1/2 teaspoons kosher salt
1 teaspoon freshly ground black pepper
1/8 teaspoon hot chili powder
1 pound large shrimp, shelled and deveined
1 1/4 teaspoons lemon zest (from 1 large lemon)
Lemon wedges, for serving

Time: 30 minutes

Serves 4

1. Preheat the oven to 425°F. In a large bowl, toss the broccoli with 2 tablespoons oil, the coriander, cumin, 1 teaspoon salt, 1/2 teaspoon pepper, and the chili powder. In a separate bowl, combine the shrimp, remaining 2 tablespoons oil, lemon zest, and remaining 1/2 teaspoon salt and 1/2 teaspoon pepper.

2. Spread the broccoli in a single layer on a baking sheet. Roast for 10 minutes. Add the shrimp to the baking sheet and toss with the broccoli. Roast, tossing once halfway through, until the shrimp are just opaque and the broccoli is tender and golden around the edges, about 10 minutes more. Serve with lemon wedges, or squeeze the lemon juice all over the shrimp and broccoli just before serving.

SHRIMP FOR A SMALL KITCHEN (SHRIMP WITH CAPERS, LEMON, AND FETA)

I've lived in New York City nearly my entire life, which means having grown accustomed to apartment kitchens smaller than the average suburban shower stall. But for the tiniest kitchen of all, my apartment on 27th Street and Lexington Avenue takes the thimble-size cake.

That kitchen was so minuscule that it could hold two bodies only if one of them happened to be feline, like my old cat Harry, for example, who liked to weave in between my legs while I was stirring my morning oatmeal. Granted, I couldn't really separate my legs quite enough to give him a pass through unless one of my feet was planted out the doorway. But Harry didn't mind my half-in, half-out status as long as I let him lick the milky oatmeal pot.

I could make an entire meal without moving the bottom half of my body, just reaching my arms from stove to fridge to the cutting board I positioned over the sink. This arrangement gave me what had to pass for counter space, otherwise I'd be chopping on the floor or on the dining table in my living room.

I suppose I could have used the top of my mini-fridge as a counter, but that was the only place to put the microwave.

Now, the unusual thing about my relationship with my teeny, tiny kitchen was not that I would cook full meals for several guests in it. It's that I also used it as the base for a very small, highly illegal catering company.

Somehow within its confines, I could whip up tandoori chicken skewers, shrimp dip, caviar canapés, and miniature quiches with homemade pastry for forty. To make the pastry, I stood on a step stool to reach the food processor I stashed on top of the microwave. I kept my stockpot under my bed, filled with sweaters that were easily dumped out when the soup siren sang.

Although I lived there for only a year, I developed several go-to dishes that I could pull together in one pan, with minimal chopping and cleanup. This shrimp dish was my favorite. The lemon, garlic, and capers gave it a zesty pungency without much work, while the feta melted into a creamy pan sauce, luxuriously coating the shrimp.

It was, it should be noted, Harry's favorite, too. For obvious reasons.

Shrimp for a Small Kitchen (Shrimp with Capers, Lemon, and Feta)

Time: 10 minutes

Serves 2 to 3

2 tablespoons extra-virgin olive oil

3 garlic cloves, minced

1 pound large shrimp, shelled and cleaned

1/3 cup crumbled feta

Juice of 1/2 lemon

1 to 2 tablespoons capers to taste

Kosher salt and freshly ground pepper to taste

2 tablespoons chopped fresh cilantro or basil, plus additional for garnish

1. Heat the olive oil in a large skillet over medium heat. Add the garlic, stirring, and cook until fragrant but not browned, about 1 minute. Stir in the shrimp, then add the feta, lemon juice, capers, and salt and pepper.

2. Continue stirring over the heat until the shrimp become just opaque and the sauce begins to thicken, about 2 minutes. Add the cilantro or basil and stir to combine. Serve garnished with additional herbs, if desired.

GRILLED SQUID WITH
SNAIL BUTTER

When I was growing up, my parents were so obsessed with eating snails à la bourguignon that, one summer while vacationing in Burgundy, they paid my sister and me five centimes per to collect snails from the garden of the little house we were staying in. Gathered into a bucket secured with a screen top, the grown-ups starved and purged the gastropods according to the traditional recipe before cooking them a few days later—drowned in garlic parsley snail butter, of course.

As much as my sister and I hated the idea of the poor critters starving to death on our patio, we did relish dipping nuggets of crusty baguette into the molten, garlicky, green-flecked snail butter, which we vastly preferred to the chewy snail bodies themselves.

Years later, I feel the same, and am convinced that the only reason to order snails à la bourguignon is to sop up the butter surrounding them, then unload the snails to your tablemates, passing them off as delicacies.

After years of doing just this, it occurred to me that maybe I should give up ordering snails entirely and just make the butter at home. Comprised of garlic, parsley, shallot, and butter, it's a simple matter of mashing everything up in the food processor, then slathering it over anything that stands still.

I've smeared it on bread, radishes, hot grilled steak (where it dribbles delectably down the sides), sautéed shrimp, broiled mushrooms, and even crispy fried tofu, which sounds odd until you taste it.

Given this predilection, it's not a huge surprise that recently, after picking up some squid at the fish store, I decided to stop and buy ingredients for snail butter, too. After all, with a chewy-tender texture and relatively bland flavor, squid are like the snails of the sea, but with a saline rather than earthy taste.

Although I could have sautéed the squid directly in the butter as I do with shrimp, the weather was balmy and I was in the mood to grill.

While the grill preheated, I made the snail butter, combining garlic, the last of a wilting shallot, lots of parsley, and butter in the food processor. But because I hadn't softened the butter enough, the mixture remained in distinct chunks instead of melding. Remembering that many recipes also call for a few drops of liquid like white wine, both for flavor and to help everything emulsify, I decided to dribble in some Pernod from the bottle that lives out on our counter in summer, waiting for the aperitif hour. It added a full, licorice note that was perfect with the green flavor of the parsley.

Butter completed, I debated melting some and tossing it with the squid before grilling to keep their floppy bodies from sticking to the grate. But fearing a grease fire, I ended up tossing the squid with just a touch of olive oil, which is less slippery than butter. When both the bodies and tentacles were lightly golden in spots, I added them to a bowl along with a dollop of pea-green snail butter.

Expecting garlicky squid nirvana, I popped a mound of purple tentacles into my mouth.

Strangely, instead of packing the garlic-and-herb wallop I expected, the flavors were weak, even though the snail butter tasted perfectly spunky when I spread it on grilled bread.

I added another spoonful of butter to the squid anyway, hoping more would help. It didn't. Neither did more salt nor another splash of Pernod. By this time, the squid were doused in enough snail butter to leave a pool at the bottom of the bowl, which even to me seemed unnecessarily decadent.

As I licked my fingers, I thought about another of my favorite pungent parsley and garlic combinations: an Italian gremolata. Sprinkled raw on top of veal osso buco, it gives a jolt of piquancy to the rich and fatty meat.

If I chopped up more garlic, parsley, and shallot and sprinkled that on top of the squid, would it help focus and intensify all the fleeting nuances?

Eureka! It did, complementing the soft, ocean flavor of the squid and underscoring the notes of garlic, parsley, and shallot in the butter itself. My husband Daniel and I gobbled every last tentacle, then sopped up the butter in the bottom. It was better than snails, even without the five centimes cash back.

Grilled Squid with Snail Butter

¼ cup packed fresh parsley leaves

4 garlic cloves, sliced

2 tablespoons pastis, such as Pernod

2 teaspoons chopped shallot (optional)

¾ teaspoon kosher or coarse sea salt, plus additional

¼ teaspoon freshly ground black pepper

½ cup (1 stick) unsalted butter, softened

2 pounds cleaned squid

2 tablespoons extra-virgin olive oil

4 large slices crusty country bread

Time: 20 minutes

Serves 4

1. Preheat or light the grill. In a food processor, combine the parsley, garlic, pastis, shallot (if using), salt, and pepper; pulse until finely minced. Remove half the mixture and reserve for the garnish.

2. Add the softened butter to the food processor and pulse until the mixture is smooth and tinged with green. (You can make the butter a few days ahead and store it in the refrigerator.)

3. Rinse the squid with cold water and pat dry with a paper towel. Cut the squid bodies lengthwise to make flat pieces. Season with a large pinch of salt and toss in the olive oil.

4. Grill the squid over high heat, turning once, until just opaque, about 2 to 3 minutes. Spread some of the snail butter on thick slices of bread and grill along with the squid. While the squid is still hot from the grill, toss it with a generous lump of the snail butter and another fat pinch of salt. Sprinkle the squid with the reserved parsley-garlic garnish and serve with bread while hot.

SCALLOP PAN ROAST

A pan roast at the Oyster Bar, like cheesecake at Junior's and frozen hot chocolate at Serendipity 3, is one of those iconic dishes New Yorkers love to champion—even if we haven't tasted them in decades.

Such was the case at a recent gathering, when I nostalgically waxed on about bowls of ruddy-hued, creamy pan roasts brimming with plump oysters, clams, lobster, and scallops that were worth fighting the crowds at Grand Central Station for.

"Really? When was the last time you ordered one?" a friend demanded. "Because the last one I had tasted like creamy ketchup," he said, wrinkling his nose.

He had a point. Although I eat at the Oyster Bar at least twice a year, I couldn't remember the last time I got the pan roast. I inevitably consider it, but the reality of lunching on an entire cup of heavy cream garnished with butter always causes me to muster some latent common sense. So I end up with something lighter: you know, fried oysters with tartar sauce.

Still, I couldn't imagine that my pan roast memories—even if the most current might date back to graduate school—could be so rose-colored. Maybe my friend had visited on an off day. Or perhaps the pan roaster, a white-clad chef manning the four steam-heated cauldrons where stews and pan roasts are concocted, was new and hadn't yet mastered the finer points of his trade.

Clearly, it was time for me to sample another pan roast. But instead of chancing an ill-made version at the restaurant, I decided to make a pan roast at home. Besides, my parents, food-obsessed native New Yorkers in their own right, were coming over, and I thought they would appreciate a taste of nostalgia, too.

Getting the recipe was easy. I simply pulled down my copy of the Oyster Bar's cookbook and opened it up. It called for simmering oysters (or clams, lobster, shrimp, scallops, or a combination) in heavy cream and butter flavored with clam juice, Worcestershire sauce, celery salt, and, to give it that reddish color and sweet tomato *je ne sais quoi*, Heinz chili sauce, which is basically ketchup with spices.

A quick trip to the supermarket and fish store yielded all the necessary ingredients, including tiny bay scallops that I couldn't resist. As I was unpacking them, my parents arrived, cold and hungry. I explained my pan roast plan and they smiled.

"We haven't had one of those in years," my father said as he mixed himself a martini from the gin and vermouth sitting on the counter.

Meanwhile, my mother read the recipe lying open on the table.

"Oh, no, a whole tablespoon is much too much Worcestershire sauce; it will ruin those nice scallops. I would use half that," she said emphatically, adding that I might want to cut the cream with some milk, too, for a slightly lighter, less diet-busting stew. My father nodded in agreement.

Since I learned much of what I know about cooking from them, I took their advice and made a thus modified pan roast. It took all of six minutes, and emerged characteristically rosy and lush, with pillow-like scallops bobbing on the surface. We dipped spoons into the pot for a sample, and pronounced it very good—rich enough without being overly decadent, tart but not too sharply Worcestershire-laced (thanks, Mom), and vaguely sweet from the combinations of scallops and chili sauce.

But still, it was lacking a certain complexity. Was it better at the Oyster Bar? None of us could remember.

"Maybe we should add a squeeze of lemon," I suggested.

My father shook his head. "It will curdle the cream," he rightly observed. Instead, he reached for the bottle of gin and dribbled a little into the pot.

The aromatic, herbal alcohol was exactly what the pan roast needed, somehow lifting all the flavors and melding them, too. It was a brilliant and unorthodox addition that elevated the pan roast to greatness.

But what made him think of adding gin?

He shrugged his shoulders and scraped the last bit of milky broth from his bowl.

"Everything tastes better with a little gin," he said.

Scallop Pan Roast

Time: 10 minutes

Serves 2

$\frac{1}{3}$ cup bottled clam juice

3 tablespoons unsalted butter

2 tablespoons chili sauce, preferably Heinz

1 tablespoon Worcestershire sauce

4 teaspoons gin

$\frac{1}{2}$ teaspoon sweet paprika

2 dashes celery salt

Dash Tabasco sauce

$\frac{1}{2}$ pound bay scallops, or sea scallops cut up if large

$\frac{1}{2}$ cup heavy cream

$\frac{3}{4}$ cup whole milk

2 slices toast

1. In a heavy saucepan over low heat, combine the clam juice, 2 tablespoons butter, chili sauce, Worcestershire sauce, gin, paprika, celery salt, and Tabasco; bring just to a simmer.
2. Add the scallops and let cook for 30 seconds without simmering (if you see a bubble, pull the pan off the heat for a few seconds). Add the cream and milk and continue to heat without simmering until the mixture is steaming hot and the scallops are opaque, about 2 minutes longer.
3. Place a piece of toast in each of two bowls and then add the pan roast, dividing the scallops evenly. Float the remaining butter on top, $\frac{1}{2}$ tablespoon per bowl. Eat immediately.

COCONUT FISH STEW WITH BASIL AND LEMONGRASS

My mother is the queen of doggie bags. I spent a mortified childhood cringing in fancy restaurants as she smiled sweetly and asked for every leftover morsel to be wrapped up.

"The chef takes it as a compliment," she said as foil swans with slivers of duck magret in their bellies swam across the dining room to our table.

At home, the leftovers became fodder for new dishes. Those bits of duck magret got tossed with tomatoes and pasta; osso buco was whisked into eggs for frittata; soft-shell crabs were nestled in toasted English muffins.

Naturally, I've inherited some of the same urges. And this is probably why, one recent evening, I found myself staring into a partially consumed container of Thai takeout, wondering how I could metamorphose it into dinner.

There wasn't much left: a half quart of tom yum—the famous Thai hot and sour soup—with a few floating shrimp and some plain white rice. How to stretch that into a meal for two?

I dug deeper into the fridge and unearthed some leftover roasted chicken.

What if I added the chicken to the soup and served it over rice? While that sounded filling enough for dinner, it wasn't appealing enough. What else could I add?

Tomatoes or avocado might have lent a meaty textural contrast, but I didn't have any. Nor, surprisingly, were there any canned tomatoes in the pantry, which I thought I might have simmered into the soup to make it richer.

But there was a can of coconut milk. Wouldn't that serve the same enriching purpose?

I gave it a try, simmering the tom yum broth with the coconut milk until silky, then mixing in the shrimp, chicken, and rice. As a final touch, I squeezed on some lime juice and dusted the top with chopped parsley, the only green herb at hand.

To my astonishment, my improvised little stew—sweet, sour, and very savory—was delightful, even better than that original Thai meal and not much harder than ordering in.

Of course I realized, as my husband and I spooned up the heady broth, that the reason it was so easy was because the premade tom yum provided most of the complex flavor. But was there a way to re-create a version of this stew without having to call up my local Taste of Thai?

A few weeks later, I decided to find out.

First, I found a simple version of tom yum online. Then I trotted over to my local market.

Although the store, a one-stop greengrocer and fishmonger, is generally well stocked with Asian ingredients, my recipe called for things far too exotic for the likes of Park Slope, including galangal and fresh kaffir lime.

I was able to find lemongrass, though, and figured I'd use lime zest in place of kaffir lime. I wanted to buy ginger to substitute for galangal, but the roots on offer were so shriveled that I decided on nice plump shallots instead, figuring they would add a different but just as welcome aromatic touch. I also picked up some fresh cilantro and basil as more authentically Southeast Asian herbs than parsley.

Last, instead of chicken, I went for a combination of red snapper and shrimp since both looked good and fresh, glistening on ice.

Once home, I made a quick broth using all my groceries plus fish sauce for a salty depth, and touches of brown sugar and rice vinegar to accentuate the sweet-tart flavors I was after.

Then I threw in the fish, shrimp, and herbs, and let the flavors meld while the seafood cooked.

A few minutes later, my husband and I sat down to what turned out to be my favorite incarnation of my Thai food experiments. Although it wasn't authentic, my latest stew was profoundly flavored and nuanced, with pungent notes of herbs, lime, and saline fish sauce, softened by the creamy coconut milk, supple seafood, and rice.

At the end of the meal, there was a small amount left over. And I couldn't help but imagine, as I crammed the container into the fridge, just how I'd reinvent it the next time.

Or maybe, for once, I'd leave well enough alone.

Coconut Fish Stew with Basil and Lemongrass

1 tablespoon vegetable oil

2 shallots, thinly sliced

1 small garlic clove, minced

2½ cups chicken stock

1 (13.5-ounce) can coconut milk

1 lemongrass stalk, finely chopped

1 jalapeño pepper, seeded, if desired, and thinly sliced

2 tablespoons rice vinegar

1 tablespoon fish sauce

1 tablespoon light brown sugar

¾ teaspoon salt

Finely grated zest of 1 lime

¾ pound seafood, such as snapper or other firm fish (cut into 1½-inch chunks), peeled shrimp, and/or scallops, or a combination

2 tablespoons chopped fresh cilantro

2 tablespoons chopped fresh basil

Freshly squeezed lime juice to taste

Cooked rice, for serving (optional)

Time: 20 minutes

Serves 2

1. Heat the oil in a medium pot over medium heat. Add the shallots and garlic and cook, stirring, until the shallots are softened, 3 to 5 minutes. Stir in the stock, coconut milk, lemongrass, jalapeño pepper, vinegar, fish sauce, sugar, salt, and lime zest. Simmer for 10 minutes.

2. Stir in the seafood and herbs. Cook 2 to 3 minutes. Stir in the lime juice and serve with rice, if desired. (Note: Without rice, it's more of a soup than a stew.)

4 It Tastes Like Chicken

It all started with that first childhood betrayal, discovered on the sly.

There I was, nine years old and at the height of my eavesdropping-on-the-telephone phase, back when everyone had landlines. My parents were hosting a dinner party and one of their guests was summoned to a call. From my parents' bedroom, I silently picked up the receiver: It was the guest's teenage son. The conversation proceeded dully, followed by this juicy tidbit:

The son: "So, how's dinner?"

The dad: "It's nice. It's rabbit ragout."

That's funny, I thought, what my parents served me from that very same stew pot before the guests arrived was chicken.

Then I put it together.

No! Not a bunny, I thought, as I pictured poor Bugs Bunny, carrot in hand, being dismembered and sautéed—a cartoon assemblage of pink rabbit ears, fluffy white cottontail, and bright orange carrot swirling in a pot.

From that point forward, I was on my guard; in the Clark household, chicken might not really be chicken.

Frogs' legs, for example, might be chicken if we happened to be on vacation in France at a restaurant with a limited menu. I vaguely remember one such dish with small pieces of chicken-like meat covered in a garlicky, tomato-based sauce.

"Chicken in France is bonier and more slippery than at home," I observed to my parents, who smiled with a strange look in their eyes that I have since found out was guilt.

Steak wasn't always beef steak either, such as the time on vacation in France one summer, when my mother served us tough and gray slabs of meat in a vinegar sauce.

"Steak's ready," she said, calling us to dinner.

What she didn't say was "horse meat steak."

I found out a few days later when, still smarting from the vinegar-laced meat, I rejected real beef steaks, rubbed with garlic and herbs and grilled until rare.

She confessed so I wouldn't miss out on the good stuff ("We passed a horse meat butcher and I couldn't resist trying it," she said). Looking back, I appreciate her coming clean, though I was furious at the time.

But nonetheless, the deceptions continued. The pearl they found in some oysters, as a way to tempt my sister and me into bivalve eating, turned out to be a plastic bauble from our Barbie doll accessories.

And that plate of al dente sesame noodles at a Chinese restaurant? It was julienned jellyfish. Likewise at the same restaurant, the cold and chewy chicken salad with celery was marinated squid.

The thing about all this chicken trickery is also what makes the fowl the great culinary unifier among omnivores. It's got just enough flavor on its own when roasted simply, say, with a little garlic and lemon. But it also takes on the taste of whatever potent sauce you cook it with. And if you cooked something else in that same potent sauce, well, that's why a spicy conch stew, to an eight-year-old who wasn't really paying attention, could easily pass for really tough chicken.

Naturally by the time I was in junior high school, I was used to this ruse. And soon enough my parents were telling me the truth. It was deeply gratifying to all of us when I became excited instead of horrified by the deep-fried sweet-breads my mother considered calling chicken nuggets.

By the time my parents and I went to Hong Kong when I was in college (my sister skipped this trip, though I can't remember why), we were all on the same page. So when the waiter at a fancy restaurant offered us the house special snake soup, I didn't even blink when my mother said, "Of course."

He brought three steaming bowls to the table, a deep golden broth strewn with herbs and mounded with shredded pale meat.

My parents dug right in. I hesitated for a moment, working up the nerve.

The waiter noticed my reticence and came over to ask if everything was okay with the soup. I said it was fine. I'd just never had snake before.

"It tastes like chicken," he said reassuringly. And I had no doubt that he was right.

SPICY, GARLICKY CASHEW CHICKEN

It's not often that a peanut butter and banana sandwich will inspire a spicy grilled chicken dinner. But such was the case one recent afternoon, when I was simultaneously preparing one meal and daydreaming about the next.

I had just lugged home a brand-new cast-iron grill, so naturally, as I smeared peanut butter onto seven-grain for lunch, I was also contemplating grilled chicken legs for dinner.

I could just picture myself standing on the deck at dusk, gin gimlet in one hand, oversize tongs in the other, flipping drumsticks cloaked in crisp skin that was ever so slightly, seductively, charred around the edges. Fragrant smoke wafted around me in my mind, and I inhaled the aromas of sizzling chicken. And garlic. And . . . um . . .

The shimmering fantasy faded. What else besides the garlic could I massage all over those fleshy legs?

That's when I noticed the recipe on the cap of extra-crunchy. Peanut sauce, it read, good for noodles and chicken. The ingredient list contained garlic powder, soy sauce, cayenne, and granulated sugar. I could practically taste it—a cloying, stick-to-the-roof-of-the-mouth paste. But it did spark more delectable memories, like a peanut satay sauce for chicken.

Indeed, a spicy, chile-flecked peanut concoction slathered over the chicken legs was starting to sound mighty appealing. Except that I had finished the last of the peanut butter and there weren't any peanuts in the house for me to grind up. But an excavation of the cupboard revealed a jar of cashews. Why not use those instead? It was easier than going to the store.

The dish was starting to take shape. Since I had to dirty the blender by grinding the nuts, I figured I'd grind up the rest of the ingredients, too, which would save me the trouble of mincing and mixing.

Then I poked around the kitchen for other things to add. Garlic was a must and in plentiful supply, so I tossed in four fat cloves, along with some jalapeños I keep around in the summer for emergency guacamole.

Here's something I've learned about jalapeños: These days, most are bred as bland as bell peppers. So I never automatically seed them, because the seeds and veins contain most of their heat. But occasionally, you encounter a really fiery specimen. My rule of thumb is to halve a pepper and lick the guts. If there is a mild sting, I leave in the seeds. If I leap up screaming, I consider deseeding.

Also in the fridge for guacamole-making was the end of a bunch of cilantro. There weren't enough leaves left to make an impact, so I threw in some of the stems as well, which have an intense flavor of their own.

I needed to add some liquid, too, for a proper consistency. Soy sauce was a good idea (thanks, Smucker's) and so was fresh lime juice, which would pair well with my gimlet. I also added some oil to help distribute the flavors and keep the chicken skin from sticking to the new grill grate.

I whirled it all together and applied half to the chicken, leaving half to serve as a sauce alongside. When the sun started to set, I lit the charcoal and waited for it to glow. Then I added the chicken, carefully tending it while gimlet sipping, just as I imagined.

Those drumsticks rolled off the grill as juicy, tender, and burnished as I could have hoped for, and the cashew sauce was even more marvelous than most peanut satays. It had a salty, buttery richness that tamed the intense heat from the chile, and a touch of sweetness from a dash of brown sugar that I added at the last minute.

It all got me thinking about my next meal, breakfast. Maybe a berry-yogurt-banana parfait with chopped toasted cashews? Thus the happy cycle continues, one meal into the next.

Spicy, Garlicky Cashew Chicken

1 cup roasted salted cashew nuts
6 tablespoons chopped fresh cilantro, with some stems
¼ cup safflower or olive oil
4 garlic cloves, roughly chopped
2 tablespoons soy sauce
2 teaspoons brown sugar
Juice of 1 lime, plus lime wedges for garnish
1 to 2 jalapeño peppers, seeded or not, to taste
Kosher salt and freshly ground black pepper
3 pounds chicken thighs and/or drumsticks

Time: 45 minutes,
plus optional
marinating

Serves 4

1. In a blender or food processor, combine the nuts, 2 tablespoons cilantro, the oil, garlic, soy sauce, sugar, lime juice, jalapeño, and 2 tablespoons water. Blend until smooth, scraping down the sides as necessary. Taste and season with salt and pepper if desired.

2. Season the chicken all over with salt and pepper. Smear on enough cashew mixture to coat the pieces thoroughly, but don't make it too thick or the sauce will fall off into your grill. (Set aside any remaining mixture.) Let marinate at room temperature while you heat the grill or broiler. Or refrigerate for up to 12 hours before cooking.

3. Preheat the broiler or grill. Grill or broil the chicken, turning frequently, until it is crisp and golden on the outside and done on the inside (cut a small nick to check), 20 to 30 minutes.

4. Sprinkle the chicken with the remaining 4 tablespoons cilantro and serve with lime wedges and the remaining cashew mixture.

VARIATION: GARLICKY CASHEW PORK AND PINEAPPLE SKEWERS

Being a lover of all things porcine, it was not a very far leap for me to think about converting the cashew chicken recipe into a cashew pork recipe, especially when I'm in freezer-cleaning mode.

The freezer had become unruly, teeming with the likes of a rainbow of baby food cubes, the skin-on tuna steaks our babysitter's mother carried over from St. Lucia, a friend's friend's house-smoked pheasant—not to mention all the unlabeled containers that I was sure I'd remember the contents of when I stuck them in there.

As I excavated, I found other forgotten bits, too, including a pork tenderloin, vintage unknown. I vaguely remembered buying it on sale last winter (or was it the winter before?), after which it migrated under the bacon and behind the squishy blue ice pack that my husband uses to cool down his sore legs after long runs.

Pork tenderloin, I thought as it defrosted on the counter, is lean and meaty, exactly what the National Pork Board was talking about in their old "other white meat" campaign.

Like the original white meat, chicken, it carries the flavors of robust sauces and marinades beautifully, which made me think of the spicy garlicky sauce from the cashew chicken recipe. That sauce would work particularly well if I cut the pork into pieces and skewered it, satay style.

As I threaded the pork onto skewers, I remembered that there were pineapple chunks in the fridge, rejected by the baby, I think, for being too fibrous for her one tiny bottom tooth. I had planned to puree the chunks with tofu for her lunch. But surely she could spare a few for me to slip onto the skewers with the pork?

Pork and pineapple is a classic (and delectable) combination. And slathered with spicy cashew sauce, it sounded like the ideal way to perk up this cloudy, dreary day.

I had nearly everything on hand to make the sauce except the fresh jalapeños and lime, so I substituted crushed red pepper flakes and lemon.

Then I brushed it all over the pork and pineapple chunks and preheated the broiler (the grill was closed up for the winter).

Broiling pineapple coated in brown sugar and spices has a smoky, juicy, caramelized scent that quickly filled the kitchen, mingled with the aroma of pig and garlic. My husband and I happily ate it for dinner, dipped in more of the pungent sauce.

But even so, there was still some sauce left over. I spooned it into a little container and stored it (labeled!) in the freezer that for now, one pork tenderloin down, seemed to have plenty of space.

Garlicky Cashew Pork and Pineapple Skewers

1 cup roasted salted cashew nuts
6 tablespoons chopped fresh cilantro, with some stems
¼ cup safflower or olive oil
4 garlic cloves, roughly chopped
2 tablespoons soy sauce
2 teaspoons brown sugar
¼ teaspoon crushed red pepper flakes
Juice of 1 lemon, plus lemon wedges for garnish
Kosher salt and freshly ground black pepper
1 pork tenderloin (about 1½ pounds), cut into 1¼-inch chunks
2 cups fresh pineapple chunks

Time: 45 minutes, plus optional marinating

Serves 4 to 6

1. In a blender or food processor, combine the nuts, 2 tablespoons cilantro, the oil, garlic, soy sauce, sugar, red pepper flakes, lemon juice, and 2 tablespoons water. Blend until smooth, scraping down the sides as necessary. Taste and season with salt and pepper if desired.

2. Season the pork all over with salt and pepper. Smear on enough cashew mixture to coat the pieces thoroughly (use about half of the mixture), and reserve the remaining cashew sauce. Let the pork marinate at room temperature while you preheat the broiler. Or refrigerate for up to 12 hours before cooking.

3. Preheat the broiler. Thread the pork and pineapple chunks onto metal skewers, alternating the two. Broil the skewers, turning once, until the pork is singed in parts and the center is cooked through, about 12 minutes.

4. Sprinkle the pork skewers with the remaining 4 tablespoons cilantro and serve with lemon wedges and the remaining cashew sauce.

VARIATION: CRISPY TOFU WITH GARLICKY PEANUT SAUCE

Tofu doesn't taste like chicken, but it acts as a canvas for flavors in a similar way. In this case, it functions as a neutral-tasting, high-protein vehicle whose real purpose is to enable gorging on the luscious, spicy peanut sauce. I panfry the tofu here, which gives it a crispy exterior that mimics the crunch of the peanuts and a soft, pillowy center. The sauce is similar to that of the garlicky cashew chicken but uses peanut butter and coconut milk instead of cashew nuts, which gives it a runnier and silkier texture. It's lightly sweet, very spicy, and utterly divine. Leftover sauce is great thinned down with water to make a salad dressing for cucumbers or crisp greens.

Crispy Tofu with Peanut Sauce

1/3 cup peanut butter, preferably natural

2 tablespoons unsweetened coconut milk

1 garlic clove, chopped

1/2-inch-thick coin fresh gingerroot, chopped

1 1/2 tablespoons freshly squeezed lime juice, or to taste

1 tablespoon light brown sugar

1 tablespoon chopped fresh cilantro, plus additional for garnish

2 teaspoons soy sauce

1/4 teaspoon hot sauce

1 pound extra-firm tofu, drained and cut into 3/4-inch cubes

2 tablespoons peanut oil

Kosher salt and freshly ground black pepper, for seasoning

Rice, for serving (optional)

Sliced scallions, for garnish

Time: 20 minutes

Serves 2

1. In a food processor or blender, pulse together the peanut butter, coconut milk, garlic, ginger, lime juice, brown sugar, cilantro, soy sauce, and hot sauce until smooth. Blend in warm water, 1 tablespoon at a time, until the desired consistency is reached (I use about 2 tablespoons).

2. Pat the tofu cubes dry with a clean dishtowel or several paper towels. Heat the oil in a large skillet over medium-high heat.

3. Place the tofu cubes in the skillet and cook, touching them as little as possible, until golden on the bottom, about 3 minutes. Turn and cook the other side, 2 to 3 minutes more. Drain the cubes on a paper towel–lined plate and blot the tops with a paper towel to remove any excess oil. Season with salt and pepper. Serve the tofu over rice, if desired, drizzled with the peanut sauce and garnished with the scallions and cilantro.

ROASTED CHICKEN THIGHS WITH GREEN PEACHES, BASIL, AND GINGER

My friend practically swooned as she described a salad she'd tasted the week before.

"It had green peaches, sliced thin, seasoned with sugar and salt, and then there was mint. It was so simple, but salty, sweet, juicy, savory . . . I am absolutely dying to have it again," she said. As she spoke, her eyes rolled back in her head voluptuously, the kind of look someone gets when thinking about molten chocolate cake or crème brûlée. It seemed a little extreme for salad.

And besides, what exactly was a green peach?

"Unripe peaches. They're hard and a little greenish and sometimes they never ripen," she explained, going on to say she got the recipe from a cookbook called *Seasoned in the South* by Bill Smith (Algonquin Books of Chapel Hill, 2005).

Since that conversation, I've become obsessed with green peaches. I've imagined them countless ways—chopped up with vinegar and brown sugar and layered on ricotta crostini, pureed into a savory sauce with almonds and tossed with pasta, and most recently, roasted with chicken and garlic. Although I'd never even tasted a green peach, I felt I knew exactly how each recipe would turn out. I couldn't wait to actually try them.

The question was, without an orchard on hand, where could I find green peaches?

The farmers' market seemed likely. But all the peach bins I picked through held only yellow-gold fruit.

I decided to forge ahead with a recipe anyway, and stuck several rock-hard specimens into my bag.

I also bought some boneless chicken thighs, figuring that since chicken and fruit is a classic combination, I'd start my experimentation there.

Once home, I examined my peach haul more carefully. None were green, but some were firm and unyielding, some a bit softer, and some were bursting with nectar, ready to eat. I sliced up a selection and tossed them with finger-size slivers of chicken, hoping everything would roast at the same rate.

Then I tossed the peaches and chicken in a pan with my mainstay seasonings of salt, pepper, olive oil, and garlic, and considered what else to stir into the pot.

A fresh, green-flavored herb seemed imperative in summer. I could have used almost any—mint, thyme, dill—but in the end snipped some basil leaves from the deck. I also mixed in a spoonful of grated ginger because I love the combination of peaches and ginger in just about anything. Lastly, I drizzled in dry sherry for acidity and verve.

My kitchen took on the heady, savory aroma of simmering garlic, herbs, and wine. In the oven, the tender, garlicky snippets of chicken melded with the gingery fruit, which ranged in texture from firm to jammy depending upon ripeness, and imbued the meat with an intense peach taste. We gobbled the dish right up, dipping slices of crusty bread into the copious pan juices.

I don't know if it would have been any better with green peaches, but I'd happily make it again with peaches of any hue.

Roasted Chicken Thighs with Peaches, Basil, and Ginger

½ pound hard peaches (about 1 large or 2 to 3 small ones, see Note)
1 pound boneless, skinless chicken thighs, cut into 1-inch strips
2 tablespoons extra-virgin olive oil
2 tablespoons dry (fino) sherry
2 tablespoons chopped fresh basil
2 garlic cloves, minced
1-inch piece fresh gingerroot, grated
½ teaspoon each kosher salt and freshly ground black pepper
Crusty bread or rice, for serving

Time: 30 minutes

Serves 2 to 3

1. Preheat the oven to 400°F. Halve the peaches, remove the pits, and slice the fruit ½ inch thick.
2. In a 9×13-inch pan, toss all the ingredients except 1 tablespoon of the basil. Roast until the chicken is cooked through and the peaches are softened, about 20 minutes. Garnish with the remaining tablespoon basil. The sauce will be thin and brothy, so serve with crusty bread for sopping or over rice.

NOTE: The peaches can be any stage of ripeness, but firmer ones are easiest to work with.

VARIATION: ROASTED CHICKEN THIGHS WITH APPLES, GIN, AND CORIANDER SEEDS

When peach season ended, I was almost more upset about losing one of the easiest and tastiest chicken dishes in my repertory—the Roasted Chicken Thighs with Green Peaches, Basil, and Ginger—than about the lack of the ripe fruit for eating out of hand. The beauty of that recipe is not just the gorgeous melding of flavors, but how quickly and easily I can throw it together. Cut into finger-size strips, the chicken and fruit cook in only twenty minutes, during which they miraculously produce a pan sauce that is fragrant and heady with garlic, wine, and herbs.

I knew there had to be a way to reinvent the recipe so it could be made all year round, not just in peach season.

Substituting apples was a possibility. I rely heavily on them when other fruits are scarce or imported from thousands of miles away.

With my basil plant long since defunct as the wintry winds blow, I also needed a substitute for that as well—or to stop at the supermarket and pick up some hothouse stuff. But I wanted a cozier, colder weather flavor, and to me basil smacks of sunshine, ripe tomatoes, and Southern Italian beach vacations that I never seem to be able to take.

I decided on cilantro. It's an herb that I adore year in and out, with avocados and without. There are some people who can't stand the flavor of cilantro; to them, it tastes like soap. My brother-in-law, in fact, is one of them, and if he were coming to dinner, I might have used dill or parsley. But since he wasn't, I proceeded as planned.

Because apples are denser and slower cooking than peaches, I made sure to slice them very thin before adding them to the pan. Then I tossed everything with the requisite garlic, olive oil, salt, and pepper, and thought about what to add next.

I didn't want to simply repeat the same sherry-ginger flavors. I was branching out with the apples and cilantro, so it seemed right to change the other aromatics as well. I took a quick survey of my spice cabinet and my eyes settled on the coriander seeds, which I had no doubt would go perfectly well with the cilantro.

Then instead of sherry, I tipped some vermouth from the too-tall bottle in the fridge into the pan, and was about to stick everything in the oven when I started to worry that the subtle flavor of vermouth wouldn't be lively enough to lift the dish the way the sherry had.

What else could I add?

I remembered the words of my father when he counseled me on zipping up a scallop pan roast.

"Gin," he said, "makes everything taste better."

And it is certainly on friendly terms with vermouth. So I added a few drops and hoped for a martini-like alchemy in the pan.

Twenty minutes later, the kitchen was enveloped in an apple and curry spice perfume, which carried through to the taste of the dish as well. It was less juicy and fresh tasting than the peach version, but more exotic and fragrant, and heartier, too, with the coriander seeds adding a pleasing crunch against the tender apples. And it will help me and all my wintry chicken thigh dinners bide the time until the peaches ripen again in June—when I'll make my martinis with olives, hold the poultry.

Roasted Chicken Thighs with Apples, Gin, and Coriander Seeds

1 large or 2 small apples

1 pound boneless, skinless chicken thighs, cut into 1-inch strips

2 tablespoons extra-virgin olive oil

1 tablespoon white vermouth

1½ teaspoons gin

2 tablespoons chopped fresh cilantro, dill, or parsley

2 garlic cloves, minced

1 teaspoon whole coriander seeds

½ teaspoon kosher salt

½ teaspoon freshly ground black pepper

Crusty bread or rice, for serving

1. Preheat the oven to 400°F. Core the apples and slice as thinly as you can without getting out (or buying!) a mandoline (between ⅛ and ¼ inch is fine).

2. In a 9×13-inch pan, toss all the ingredients except 1 tablespoon cilantro (or dill or parsley). Spread the ingredients out into one layer in the pan. Roast until the chicken is cooked through and the apples are softened, about 20 minutes. Garnish with the remaining tablespoon cilantro, dill, or parsley. The sauce will be thin, so serve with crusty bread for sopping up the sauce or over rice.

VARIATION: ROASTED CHICKEN THIGHS WITH GREEN TOMATOES, BASIL, AND GINGER

Yet another variation on my chicken thighs with green peaches, this one uses that other underripe fruit usually available at the farmers' market: green to-matoes. When roasted, they get juicy and sweet, and exude a fragrant, herby liquid that is less sweet than the peaches, but earthy and robust. And when you can't get green tomatoes, this recipe works with those pasty-colored, underripe supermarket tomatoes, too. Though the flavor is slightly less complex, it's still a tasty meal served over polenta.

Roasted Chicken Thighs with Green Tomatoes, Basil, and Ginger

1 large green tomato (about ½ pound, see Note)

1 pound boneless, skinless chicken thighs, cut into 1-inch strips

2 tablespoons extra-virgin olive oil

2 tablespoons dry (fino) sherry

2 tablespoons chopped fresh basil

2 garlic cloves, minced

1-inch-long piece fresh gingerroot, grated

½ teaspoon kosher salt

½ teaspoon freshly ground black pepper

Crusty bread or rice, for serving

Time: 30 minutes

Serves 2 to 3

1. Preheat the oven to 400°F. Core the tomato and halve it lengthwise; slice ½ inch thick.
2. In a 9×13-inch pan, toss all the ingredients except 1 tablespoon basil. Roast until the chicken is cooked through and the tomato is softened, about 20 minutes. Garnish with the remaining tablespoon basil. The sauce will be thin, so serve with crusty bread for sopping or over rice.

NOTE: Green tomatoes are available in farmers' markets in the early fall months; if you can't find them, you can also substitute the same quantity of plum tomatoes.

NOT-MY-GRANDMA'S CHICKEN
WITH LEMON, GARLIC,
AND OREGANO

It took a while before my ex-mother-in-law Josephine warmed to me enough to let me cook in her kitchen.

At the beginning of my relationship with her son Joe, I'd play prep cook for the family Sunday suppers in the suburbs. Scurrying around the kitchen doing ten things at once, at first Josephine would grant me only the easy jobs. At the old oak table, I'd slice the eggplant or trim the fennel, then hang around and wait for the next small task while she juggled everything else. Little by little, though, I was allowed to chop the onions and eventually mind the bubbling sauce on the stove.

But it wasn't until Joe and I got engaged two years later that Josephine finally opened her hearth to me. It was at the Christmas before our January wedding that she asked me to take charge of Grandma's chicken.

Making Grandma's chicken for the entire clan's Christmas dinner was no small thing. Along with Josephine's homemade manicotti and Aunt Marie's marvelous scungilli salad, Grandma's chicken was the star of the show. (Of course, this does not count the twenty or so desserts—almost one for each relative at the table—that made their appearance a few hours after the main meal was digested, but that's another stomach entirely.)

I had helped Josephine make Grandma's chicken in the past, and it was a fairly straightforward recipe.

The first step is to heavily salt the bird and let it sit before cutting it into pieces. Josephine told me that Grandma called this "koshering" the meat, though why a Southern Italian family from the Bronx would want to kosher anything was a mystery.

Once the chicken was dismembered, it was anointed with olive oil, dried oregano, chopped garlic, and lemon juice, and put in the oven at 350°F to roast. Every ten minutes, Josephine tended the chicken, turning it, patting it, showering it with more oil, salt, pepper, garlic, and lemon juice. This went on for a long, long time, until the dark meat was cooked through and through and the white meat was—well, let's just say I always ate the dark meat.

The best part of the dish was what Josephine called the "juice," the drippings that she decanted straight from the pan into a little pitcher and passed around at the table, glorious golden chicken fat and all. I loved the juice more than the actual chicken, and would pour it directly onto the crusty slices of bread from Arthur Avenue that I stacked on my plate.

The first year I was put on chicken duty, I followed the recipe nearly as instructed, though I admit to surreptitiously dividing the white and dark meat into separate pans, adding the white meat to the oven fifteen minutes after the dark so it wouldn't dry out.

My change was noticed and endorsed by the relatives, especially by Uncle Gino, who, after correcting my pronunciation of ricotta ("It's ri-GOT," he insisted, waving his arms), told me the chicken breast tasted pretty good.

Thus emboldened, at Easter as a newlywed, I raised the oven temperature to 425°F in an attempt to crisp up the skin. While this worked, it also burned the garlic.

"What'd she do to Grandma's chicken?" complained Uncle Gino, shaking his head and reminding me that in this family, we don't say "ricotta." He intoned the word in a squeaky falsetto meant to imitate my voice. Everyone laughed except Joe and Josephine, who cringed alongside me.

The following Christmas, I added the garlic later into the cooking and it didn't burn, and Uncle Gino laid off the diction lessons. (I had also made a mental vow never to mention a certain creamy, white cheese in the company of Joe's family ever again.)

Over the six years of our marriage, I tweaked and retweaked the chicken until I had it almost where I wanted it but within the bounds of what the family would still recognize.

Then Joe and I split up.

It took me years to want to eat that chicken again. When I did, I knew his Grandma's recipe was in for a makeover. Not full-on plastic surgery—I wanted to keep its garlicky, puckery, oregano-scented bone structure intact—but I wanted to play around a bit more than I would have been comfortable doing at Josephine's.

The first thing I did was to expunge the white meat entirely and use all drumsticks. They were always the best part, and there were never enough of them to go around.

Then I made a paste of the garlic, lemon juice, and salt, so I could brush it on the chicken rather than trying to sprinkle minced garlic cloves all over the tops with my inevitably wet fingers (very hard to distribute the pieces evenly).

Finally, I broiled the chicken a little first to get the skin nice and brown, after which I lowered the oven temperature and painted on the garlic paste mixture, eliminating any problems with burning.

The one thing I didn't and wouldn't change was the juice. When the chicken was golden, juicy, and redolent with garlic and oregano, I distributed it on plates, spooning the drippings all over the drumsticks and some nice crusty bread. It was better than I remembered it, for a whole mess of reasons, but most important that I was eating it in my own home—though I'll admit to missing at least some of those twenty desserts at Josephine's.

Not-My-Grandma's Chicken with Lemon, Garlic, and Oregano

Time: 40 minutes

Serves 2

1½ pounds chicken drumsticks
1 teaspoon kosher salt, plus additional for seasoning
½ teaspoon freshly ground black pepper, plus additional for seasoning
Extra-virgin olive oil, as needed (but use a lot)
5 garlic cloves
Freshly squeezed juice of 1 large lemon
2 teaspoons dried oregano

1. Preheat the broiler. Rinse the chicken, pat dry with a paper towel, and place in a 9×13-inch pan. Season the chicken with salt and pepper and drizzle with

olive oil. Broil the chicken, turning once, until light golden brown, about 3 minutes per side.

2. While the chicken is broiling, make a garlic paste by either using a mortar and pestle to pound the garlic with 1 teaspoon kosher salt or mincing the garlic with a heavy knife, then using the flat side to smear and mash the garlic and salt into a paste. Alternatively, you can make the paste in a blender, if your blender can handle such a small amount. Stir the lemon juice and the remaining 1/2 teaspoon pepper into the garlic paste.

3. Lower the oven temperature to 425°F. Using a pastry brush or spoon, slather the chicken on all sides with one-third of the garlic mixture, a sprinkling of the oregano, and a drizzle of oil. Bake for 25 to 30 minutes, slathering on more of the garlic mixture, oil, and oregano in two more additions (approximately every 7 to 10 minutes). The chicken is done when it's golden brown and cooked through. Serve with the pan juices or the tasty sludge on the bottom of the pan.

GARLIC AND THYME–ROASTED CHICKEN WITH CRISPY DRIPPINGS CROUTONS

When it comes to roast chicken, some people like the breast meat. Others prefer the drumsticks and thighs, and there are those who grab the wings.

Me, I'm a neck and tail girl, but I'd trade them both in for the crispy browned scraps and fatty slick clinging to the bottom of the pan, which I love to mop up with a heel of bread.

So when my friend Susan called to crow about the phenomenal fowl her husband had roasted, cooked right on top of a bed of bread to absorb all those glorious juices, I paid attention.

But my reaction was not without some skepticism. "Doesn't the bread get soggy from being soaked by the chicken juices?" I asked.

"Maybe it's a little soft in spots, but mostly it crisps up like a crouton," Susan said. "It's the best roast chicken I've ever eaten. You've got to try it."

If it had been anyone else on the other end of the line, I would have raised an eyebrow. But Susan's husband, Dan Silverman, is a noted chef (currently at the Standard Grill). He knows what he's doing.

Still, it took me a few months to try the recipe. The presence of a leftover crusty loaf, along with a chicken craving, made it happen one recent Friday.

But first I called Dan just to make sure I had the correct technique. He walked me through the steps, noting that he's laid the chicken on all different kinds of breads, including baguettes, country loaves, and even pita.

"Stale bread is best, but anything will work," he said, adding that his muse for this creation was indolence. "Originally I used the bread just to keep the chicken from sticking to the bottom of the pan. A rack is one more thing to clean, and I'm a lazy cook. Plus we always have stale bread lying around the house."

Uncharacteristically, I followed Dan's simple instructions to the letter, drizzling the bread slices with good olive oil and seasoning them well with salt and pepper before adding the bird, stuffed with garlic, lemon, and herbs. The whole operation took under ten minutes—far less than my usual roast chicken recipe, which calls for rubbing herb butter under the skin. Another lazy chef bonus: Since Dan doesn't baste, I didn't either.

An hour and change later, the chicken was burnished, juicy, and fragrant with lemon and thyme. The bread was golden and crunchy in some spots and moist and chewy in others, but savory, meaty, and salty all over. Although I preferred the crispy bits, the soft ones were nice, too, a little like the bread stuffing you might pair with poultry but with a caramelized flavor.

Dan had suggested making a bread salad with the toasts. But in keeping with the slothful spirit of the dish, I simply served them alongside the bird.

"You see, isn't that the best roast chicken ever?" Susan asked me.

Best roast chicken? Perhaps. But thanks to the bread, I got the tastiest and most easily accessible roast chicken drippings ever. For a pan swabber like me, there's nothing better than that.

Garlic and Thyme–Roasted Chicken with Crispy Drippings Croutons

Country bread, ciabatta, or other sturdy bread, preferably stale, sliced
    ½ inch thick

1 tablespoon extra-virgin olive oil, more as needed

2 teaspoons kosher salt, more as needed

½ teaspoon freshly ground black pepper, more as needed

1 (4- to 5-pound) chicken, patted dry

1 garlic head, sliced in half through the cloves

1 bay leaf

½ lemon

½ bunch thyme sprigs

Time: 1 hour and 25 minutes, plus 10 minutes' resting

Serves 4

1.   Preheat the oven to 425°F. Lay the bread slices in the bottom of a heavy-duty roasting pan in one layer. (If you don't have a heavy-duty roasting pan

or are using a glass pan, please see the Tips section below.) Drizzle liberally with olive oil and sprinkle with salt and pepper.

2. Rub 1 teaspoon salt and ¼ teaspoon pepper inside the cavity of the chicken. Stuff the cavity with the garlic, bay leaf, lemon, and thyme. Rub the outside of the chicken with a tablespoon of olive oil and sprinkle all over with the remaining salt and pepper. Place it, breast side up, on the bread.

3. Roast the chicken until it's deeply browned and the thigh juices run clear when pricked with a knife, about 1 hour and 15 minutes. If at any time while the chicken is roasting the bread starts to smell burned or begins to smoke, use tongs to pull it out of the pan and discard; let the chicken continue to cook. When the chicken is done, let it rest for 10 minutes before carving. Serve the chicken with pieces of bread from the pan.

TIPS: After I published this recipe, several people wrote to me with problems about the bread burning to bits and setting off their smoke alarms (not the desired results). Here are some pointers:

• The first is the thickness of the roasting pan. I use a heavy-duty one with a shiny stainless steel surface. The thickness keeps the heat steady, without hot spots, and the shininess helps reflect the heat. Thin dark pans are more likely to result in burned bread.

• If you have a thin dark pan, lower the oven temperature to 375°F from 425°F. The chicken might take a little longer to roast, but this should keep the bread from burning. You could also try putting the roasting pan on top of a baking sheet before putting it in the oven. That will help insulate it (the thicker the baking sheet, the better).

• Another problem might be the oven temperature. Ovens are notoriously finicky and inexact, and many run hot. I keep two oven thermometers in mine just to make sure it's well calibrated on both sides. (And I happen to have two thermometers—one was my husband's before we moved in together.)

• If you have an electric oven with the heating element on the bottom, the bread might burn if the pan is too close to the heating element.

- It's also important not to slice the bread any thinner than half an inch thick or it could get too dark.

- If the bread starts to smoke or smell burned at any time while the chicken is roasting, just use a pair of tongs to pull the slices out from under the chicken. If you do have to pull the bread out before the chicken is done, discard the bread just to make sure that you don't unintentionally eat any undercooked chicken juices.

VARIATION: MY MOTHER'S GARLIC AND THYME–ROASTED CHICKEN PARTS WITH MUSTARD CROUTONS

Every once in a while, my mother follows one of my recipes.

Actually, *follows* is too exacting a word for what goes on. Let's just say, every once in a while, my mother decides to cook something of mine she's seen in the *New York Times*.

She always calls to tell me.

"I made your pork chops with plum sauce," she says excitedly. "Except that I didn't have pork chops, so I used lamb chops. And I didn't have plums, so I used a combination of prunes and nectarines. Then your father came in as I was making the sauce and added a little ground Szechwan pepper. It was delicious!"

While I'm happy to be her inspiration for dinner, I don't consider it my recipe anymore—it's become hers as much as anything I ever cook is "mine."

Such was the case recently with "my" roasted chicken recipe cooked on a pan full of croutons. She couldn't wait to try it, and was especially drawn to the idea of using up old, stale bread. A child of the Depression, she still re-members her mother, my grandma Lilly, serving sandwiches to unemployed men on the porch. My mother just loves to be thrifty.

Still, she can't help but tweak the recipe.

"I made that roasted chicken on bread. It was terrific!" began the phone call.

So what were her changes? Did she perhaps use turkey instead of chicken, leftover bagel halves instead of bread?

"No, I followed the recipe exactly," she insisted.

I pressed on.

"Really, you used a whole chicken and day-old bread and garlic and thyme, and roasted it at the same oven temperature I called for and everything?"

"Well . . . almost."

In fact, she followed the recipe pretty closely, for her. But she used a cut-up chicken instead of a whole bird and stale whole wheat bread (though she did consider dipping into the stash of bagels she keeps in the freezer along with lox and cream cheese for spontaneous brunches).

Her only profound deviation was to spread the bread with mustard.

Mustard!

It was a brilliant idea. Mustard would add a slight spicy jolt to the croutons, and probably help flavor the chicken pieces as well. I couldn't wait to try it. Plus, chicken parts cook faster than a whole bird, and there would be less of a chance for the bread to burn.

"But wait," I asked my mother, "what did you do about stuffing the cavity with garlic, lemon, and bay leaf, since cut-up chickens have no cavities?"

"I used minced garlic, and then just scattered everything on top. It was easy," she said.

Next time I wanted roasted chicken, I followed her recipe—well, as close to the letter as is humanly possible, given my genetic makeup. I bought a cut-up chicken and some good, pungent Dijon mustard, which I smeared all over the bread.

But I didn't want to bother chopping up all that garlic. So I just broke apart the head into cloves and added those to the pan, drizzling them copiously with oil so they'd soften and caramelize while the chicken roasted.

The roasting took half an hour less then my original recipe, and as I had hoped, the mustard added a tart kick that played well with the sweet, soft cloves of garlic that we squeezed out of their skins and onto the croutons. And the chicken was as juicy and crisp as could be.

Immediately after dinner, I called my mother and told her that I'd made her recipe—albeit with a few tiny changes. Now I'm waiting for her call with a recipe in reply.

My Mother's Garlic and Thyme–Roasted Chicken Parts with Mustard Croutons

Country bread, ciabatta, or other sturdy bread, preferably stale,
   sliced ½ inch thick
Mustard, as needed
Extra-virgin olive oil, as needed
1½ teaspoons kosher salt, more as needed
½ teaspoon freshly ground black pepper, more as needed
1 (4- to 5-pound) chicken, cut into 8 serving pieces, rinsed and patted dry
1 head garlic, separated into cloves
1 bay leaf, torn into pieces
½ bunch thyme sprigs

Time: 1 hour and
10 minutes

Serves 4

1. Preheat the oven to 425°F. Lay the bread slices in the bottom of a heavy-duty roasting pan (see page 141) in one layer. Brush with mustard, drizzle liberally with olive oil, and sprinkle with salt and pepper.

2. Season the chicken all over with salt and pepper and place the pieces on the bread, arranging the white meat in the center and the dark meat and wings around the sides. Scatter the garlic cloves, bay leaf, and thyme over the chicken and drizzle everything with more oil (take care to drizzle the garlic cloves).

3. Roast the chicken until it's lightly browned and the thigh juices run clear when pricked with a knife, about 50 minutes. If you like, you can crisp the skin by running the pan under the broiler for a minute, though you might want to rescue the garlic cloves before you do so they don't burn (if you don't plan to eat them, it doesn't matter so much). Serve the chicken with pieces of the bread from the pan.

SPICED CHIPOTLE HONEY CHICKEN BREASTS WITH SWEET POTATOES

Every Thanksgiving when I was a kid, my uncle Danny used to say, "I like my turkeys built like Jane Fonda, with small tits and a big ass."

Uncle Danny was never one to mince words. When I was sixteen, he took me aside at a family gathering where I was sneakily sampling my way through the open bottles at the bar, and told me that if I was going to booze it up, I should lay off the Scotch and stick to the vodka. It wouldn't be as obvious on my breath and the hangover was easier to bear.

While I disagree with Uncle Danny about the vodka (I prefer brown spirits), I stand with him when it comes to Jane Fonda turkeys. Or at least, I, too, like the dark meat.

I like the gristly, fatty, sinewy bits. I like the deep flavor and moist texture. I like that dark meat doesn't dry out as quickly as white meat, and has more *oomph* and personality.

And this is why, you may have noticed, this chicken chapter has exactly one recipe for the pillar of so many American kitchens, the boneless, skinless chicken breast. And here it is.

I probably wouldn't have made this dish at all, but my arm was twisted by a magazine assignment. I had pitched a chipotle-roasted chicken, and my editor jumped at the idea.

I could see the finished dish so clearly in my head: a whole chicken massaged with an unguent made from chipotle chiles in adobo sauce (possibly my favorite pantry item), honey, and spices, then set over a pan of cubed sweet potatoes that would soften and caramelize as the chicken roasts.

Then my editor burst my tasty bubble.

"It sounds great, but can you do it with boneless, skinless chicken breasts?"

My heart sank a little as I said of course, and hung up the phone.

Sure, I knew I could do it. But what I didn't know was how much I would end up liking what I did.

I kept the recipe as close to my original intent as possible, rubbing a cumin and cinnamon–spiked chile paste all over the chicken breasts. The only major change was to start roasting the sweet potatoes first and then add the chicken later, because the potatoes would need more oven time to soften properly.

The kitchen took on a spicy, autumnal scent from the roasting of cinnamon and sweet potatoes. I stayed close by, checking the chicken carefully to make sure it didn't overcook.

Despite my careful ministrations, I doubted that the chicken breasts would turn out as well as the whole roasted chicken I'd envisioned in my head.

But to my great shock, they were even better.

The dish was so succulent and rich tasting, with an almost mole-like flavor thanks to the chile, cumin, and cinnamon, that I haven't been remotely tempted to try the recipe with the whole bird. And the breasts themselves were juicy and tender enough to make me forget about their lack of sinew and gristle.

In fact, the flavor combination was so good that year I'm even contemplating attempting it at Thanksgiving. I can see patting it onto a nice heritage turkey—the Jane Fonda kind with more dark meat than white—with a nice rye Manhattan in the other hand.

Spiced Chipotle Honey Chicken Breasts with Sweet Potatoes

Time: 15 minutes, plus 35 to 40 minutes' roasting

Serves 6

4 sweet potatoes (10 ounces each), peeled and cut into 1-inch pieces

3 tablespoons olive oil

4 chipotle chiles in adobo sauce, minced

3 garlic cloves, minced

2 tablespoons honey

2 teaspoons cider vinegar

1¼ teaspoons kosher salt, plus additional to taste

1 teaspoon ground cumin

½ teaspoon ground cinnamon

6 boneless, skinless chicken breasts (2 pounds), rinsed and patted dry

Chopped cilantro or basil, for garnish

1. Preheat the oven to 400°F. In a medium bowl, toss the sweet potatoes in 2 tablespoons of the olive oil and scatter on the bottom of a roasting pan. Roast for 15 minutes.

2. Meanwhile, in a small bowl, mix together the remaining tablespoon of olive oil, chipotles, garlic, honey, vinegar, salt, cumin, and cinnamon to make a paste. Rub the paste all over the chicken. Carefully place the chicken on top of the sweet potatoes and continue to roast until the chicken is just cooked through, about 25 minutes longer. Serve garnished with cilantro or basil.

FIGGY, PIGGY DRUMSTICKS AND THIGHS

There it was in the now defunct *Gourmet* magazine, a glossy, sexy photograph of Figgy, Piggy Cornish Hens. Who could resist a recipe with a name like that one? Especially when it involves copious amounts of fresh figs, bacon, and garlic?

Not me.

Even though I never follow recipes, even though I don't usually cook with ripe figs (I gobble them up before they make it to the stove), even though I hadn't thought about cooking with a Cornish game hen in years, this time, I thought to myself as I drooled over the photo, I will follow through.

I copied down the ingredient list and headed to the supermarket. Figs and bacon and garlic were all available aplenty—a good thing since I had already eaten all the figs off the little tree in the backyard.

The meat case, however, was distinctly lacking in Cornish game hens. I picked up a package of chicken drumsticks and thighs instead.

Then I went home and followed the recipe—to the best of my ability.

I started with step one: Cook the bacon in a large skillet.

While it sizzled, I read through the rest of the directions. I was supposed to cook the garlic next, spoon it out of the pan, and then brown the hens (chicken, in my case) in the same fat. Then everything would be transferred to a baking pan along with figs and thyme, and set to roast. Meanwhile, I'd make a sauce with the drippings in the skillet.

Hmm. That meant dirtying and then washing two pans. Why not just roast everything in the skillet and make a sauce afterward?

I decided to try it my way. When the bacon was crisp, I sautéed the garlic in the bacon fat. Then I browned the chicken in the same pan before scattering on the figs and thyme and transferring the skillet to the oven.

I was supposed to use twelve figs, but after all my nibbling was done and I counted up, I was left with eleven in the bag. It would just have to do.

While the chicken and figs roasted, I searched through the fridge for a couple of lemons to make three tablespoons of freshly squeezed juice. I always keep lemons on hand; they are indispensable for salad dressings and sauces, and any time a dish just needs a little jolt. I'm never without one.

But on this day, I was without two. And the one I did find was shriveled and sad looking. I could get maybe one tablespoon of juice out of it, but certainly not three.

I stared at the open fridge, debating what to substitute for the missing lemon juice when I noticed the near-empty liter bottle of vermouth banging against the side of the door. I had a shorter bottle waiting to take its place once I had drained the contents, and this seemed like the ideal opportunity. I mixed it with the lemon juice and, when the chicken was roasted, used the liquid to deglaze the skillet and scrape up all the tasty brown bits stuck to the bottom.

Then I scattered the bacon and garlic on top of the dish and took a bite. The first note to hit was the brawniness of the bacon, followed by the jamlike figs softening the pungent, crisp garlic and meaty chicken. As *Gourmet* promised, it was a figgy, piggy delight—slightly streamlined according to me.

Figgy, Piggy Drumsticks and Thighs

Time: 40 minutes

Serves 4

8 strips bacon (8 ounces), halved

4 garlic cloves, thinly sliced

3 chicken legs, drumsticks and thighs (about 2½ pounds total)

1 teaspoon kosher salt

Freshly ground black pepper

11 or 12 figs, halved or quartered if large

12 thyme sprigs

2 tablespoons vermouth

1 tablespoon fresh lemon juice

1. Preheat the oven to 500°F. In a large ovenproof skillet over medium heat, cook the bacon until crisp. Transfer the bacon to a paper towel–lined plate to drain, but don't drain the fat from the skillet. Add the garlic to the skillet

and sauté for 1 minute or so, until the slices are pale golden. Transfer them to the plate along with the bacon.

2. Rinse the chicken legs and pat them dry with a paper towel. Season the chicken with the salt and pepper. Raise the heat under the skillet to medium-high until the fat begins to smoke, and cook the chicken until browned, 5 to 6 minutes. Flip the chicken and brown the other side, about 3 minutes.

3. Scatter the figs and thyme over the chicken and transfer the skillet to the oven. Roast until the chicken is cooked through, about 20 minutes. Transfer the chicken to a serving platter, and stir the vermouth and lemon juice into the skillet, scraping up any brown bits on the bottom (be careful when touching the skillet handle; it will be hot). Place the skillet over medium heat until the juices thicken, about 3 minutes. Pour the juices over the chicken, garnish with the bacon and garlic, and serve.

QUICK-BRAISED CHICKEN
WITH MOROCCAN SPICES,
LEMON, AND OLIVES

In the beginning of our courtship, I opened my future husband Daniel's refrigerator to snoop. It contained a jar of peanut butter, a bottle of Champagne, and a fancy glass crock half-filled with pale liquid with a bright yellow object bobbing around in it.

"It's a preserved lemon," he said. "I made a batch and that's the last one left."

He was very proud, and went on to describe the Moroccan meal he concocted to go alongside the lemons, including a tagine redolent of spices.

Naturally, when we moved in together, the lemon came along, too. And it stayed in our fridge for three more years. Occasionally we'd talk about using it (in soups or stews, or with beans). But not wanting to use up the last one, we never did.

Eventually, being in need of the refrigerator real estate and because by now the lemon was five years old, we decided to chuck it.

And within a month, I regretted it immensely.

There, on one of my favorite food Web sites, Food52, was a recipe for Moroccan braised chicken with briny green olives and pungent preserved lemon. I had neither.

I could buy the olives at my local market. But preserved lemons are specialty food shop fare, and I didn't want to take the subway in search of them.

Nor did I want to try my hand at preserving lemons at home, which, though easy, takes a week. I wanted the chicken for dinner that night.

Although it would lack the punch of a preserved lemon, I thought maybe I could substitute regular lemon. The only thing that worried me was the bitter, white lemon pith, which would not have been mellowed by salt and time the way preserved lemons are.

I supposed I could have grated the lemon zest, added that to the pan, and then squeezed in the juice. This would avoid the pithy issue altogether. But I liked the idea of lemon slices that kept a little of their texture and "integrity," as the headnote put it.

Thinking about it, I remembered that repeated boiling tames the harshness of citrus fruit peel. One of my best candy recipes involves blanching grapefruit peel, then cooking it in sugar syrup until it crystallizes. It used to be my father's favorite snack until he became diabetic and his doctor told him to nix the sweets.

So I decided to try blanching the lemon pieces in salted water to see if that would mitigate their bitterness and add a salty, cured flavor at the same time. It would not be nearly as nuanced and complex as a properly preserved lemon, but it also would take about seven minutes instead of seven days.

I tried it, adding the blanched lemon slices to the chicken legs that had been simmering in a bazaar of Moroccan spices including saffron, cumin, paprika, and ginger.

It was a quick braise, ready in under an hour, but when I tasted it, the flavors seemed far more layered, as if the bird had stewed all day. The olives and lemon had brightened the sauce, which in turn infused the fruit with a tingling jolt of spice. And the chicken was lusty and falling off the bones.

I'm sure it would also be terrific with preserved lemon, and next time Daniel makes a batch, I'll make sure to try it that way—even if it means using the last one.

Quick-Braised Chicken with Moroccan Spices, Lemon, and Olives

Time: 1 hour

Serves 3 to 4

1 lemon, ends trimmed (see Note)

1 tablespoon plus 1½ teaspoons kosher salt

3 pounds chicken thighs and drumsticks, rinsed and patted dry

1½ teaspoons freshly ground black pepper

3 to 4 tablespoons extra-virgin olive oil

1 large onion, chopped (about 1½ cups)

1 fat garlic clove, minced

1 teaspoon grated fresh gingerroot

1 tablespoon ground coriander

1 tablespoon ground cumin

1½ teaspoons sweet paprika

½ teaspoon ground turmeric

½ teaspoon ground cayenne

2 to 3 cups chicken stock

¼ teaspoon crumbled saffron

½ cup good-quality green olives, pitted if desired (I used pitted picholines)

3 tablespoons dried currants or diced dried apricots (optional)

2 tablespoons chopped fresh cilantro or mint

1. Thinly slice the lemon crosswise into rounds. Cut the rounds into quarters. Place the lemon in a small saucepan with water just to cover and stir in 1 tablespoon kosher salt. Bring the mixture to a boil, then reduce the heat and simmer for 5 minutes. Drain well and rinse the lemon under cold water.

2. Season the chicken with the remaining 1½ teaspoons kosher salt and the pepper. In a large, deep skillet, heat 3 tablespoons of the oil over medium-high heat. Place the chicken in an even layer in the skillet (do this in batches, if necessary) and brown on both sides, about 10 minutes. Transfer the chicken to a paper towel–lined plate to drain.

3. If the skillet looks dry, add the remaining tablespoon of oil. Add the onion and sauté until soft, about 5 minutes. Stir in the garlic, ginger, coriander, cumin, paprika, turmeric, and cayenne, and cook for 1 minute more.

4. Add the chicken and stir to coat with the spice mixture. Pour the stock into the skillet until two-thirds of the chicken is covered. Stir in the saffron and bring to a boil. Reduce the heat to medium-low, cover, and let simmer for about 25 minutes.

5. Uncover and add the lemon slices, olives, and dried fruit, if desired, stirring to combine. Cover and return to a simmer until the chicken is cooked through, about 10 minutes.

6. Transfer the chicken to a serving platter. Raise the heat to high and boil the sauce, uncovered, until it has thickened, about 10 minutes. Stir in the cilantro or mint. Spoon the sauce over the chicken to serve.

NOTE: If you have a large preserved lemon (or 2 small ones) on hand, feel free to skip the blanching step and use that instead.

DAHLIA'S FRAGRANT CHICKEN FINGERS

"That girl sure likes things with flavor," said my daughter's babysitter, biting into a piece of toast slathered with the spicy, garlic-laden hummus I had made for the baby's lunch.

While the toddlerish reign of white foods and grilled cheese is likely nigh, in the meantime, I'm tickled to be feeding my one-year-old almost anything with a kick. Chili, bratwurst, risotto, short ribs, gazpacho, and that pungent hummus are all on her regular dinner rotation, and she eats them with gusto.

So when my babysitter suggested adding chicken fingers into the mix, we both knew she didn't mean the usual bland breast meat coated in crumbs.

No, Dahlia's chicken fingers would have to have verve.

I decided to model the recipe on Naked Nuggets, chicken nuggets created by my friends Eric and Bruce Bromberg, the owners of Blue Ribbon restaurants in New York City (full disclosure: I helped them write their cookbook). I knew that instead of chunks of deep-fried chicken, their recipe, based on the chicken burger they serve at their restaurants, uses ground chicken.

Ground chicken has the distinct advantage of being easy to season. You can mix almost anything into it and it will vigorously absorb those flavors. At Blue Ribbon, the Brombergs keep it simple, sticking mostly to salt, pepper, and garlic. But looking at the pale mound of ground chicken in my mixing bowl, I decided to go for more intensity, knowing that my daughter would probably prefer it. And so would I, the person who ends up eating the bits she feeds me while I'm trying to feed her, not to mention the leftovers on her tray.

But what, exactly, to season the chicken with? As I was thinking about it, I started picturing the chicken fingers in my head. The image reminded me of another, similarly shaped, aromatic ground meat dish that I love to make: lamb kibbe, shot through with cumin, onion, cinnamon, and allspice, plus a healthy dose of chile. Those flavors would work well with the blank culinary canvas that is chicken.

So I went with it, cutting back on the chile somewhat but not entirely, and adding garlic, which was not in the kibbe recipe.

As a binder, the kibbe recipe used soaked bulgur, which I didn't feel like dealing with. I stirred in some bread crumbs instead. Then I formed the meat into fingers, brushed on some olive oil, and put the pan in the broiler.

As they cooked, the scent of spice filled the kitchen. Since I made them small enough for baby hands to maneuver, they were done in minutes, and I set the pan to cool while I waited for Dahlia to return from her day's work at the playground.

In the meantime, though, I sampled a chicken finger—for, you know, parental quality control, the same reason I need to constantly be sampling her mac and cheese just in case Annie decides to change the recipe. The chicken was fragrant, garlicky, and tinged with spice, and altogether addictive, I discovered, as I munched my way through nearly half a dozen (really small!) pieces by the time I heard my babysitter's keys in the door.

I hurried Dahlia into her high chair, excited to see if she'd like the chicken fingers as much as I did.

Before I handed her one, though, I braced myself for a possible rejection. Although Dahlia likes things with flavor, she doesn't like *every* thing with flavor, and I've disappointedly watched her spit out a host of mom-endorsed morsels, including a grilled Cheddar sandwich, ripe pineapple, lentil soup, and salmon caviar (okay, I admit this last one was not a surprise).

I handed her a finger, still slightly warm from the oven. She inspected it, then waved it around like a baton before opening her hand and letting it fall . . . into my waiting hand beneath her high chair (I'd learned a thing or two about mealtimes). I wasn't about to waste a single finger. If Dahlia didn't want them, I most certainly did.

I tried again. This time Dahlia stuck it in her mouth and tore off a chunk with her three sharp little teeth. Then she gummed it around, puffing out her cheeks and shaking her head in delight, and proceeded to eat two more.

The chicken fingers had passed muster, and the mom side of my being was mighty satisfied. The reptile side of my brain, however, was also a little sad not to continue my chicken finger pig-out. But that's okay; I'll just double the recipe next time and make all of us happy.

Dahlia's Fragrant Chicken Fingers

Time: 10 minutes

Serves 4 adults or
8 small children

1 pound ground chicken (or turkey)

½ cup plain bread crumbs

2 scallions, chopped

2 tablespoons chopped fresh cilantro, basil, or parsley,
   plus additional for garnish

1 fat garlic clove, minced

½ teaspoon kosher salt, plus additional

½ teaspoon ground cumin

¼ teaspoon ground allspice

¼ teaspoon ground cinnamon

¼ teaspoon freshly ground black pepper

Pinch Aleppo pepper or cayenne

1 tablespoon extra-virgin olive oil

1. Preheat the oven to 375°F. In a large bowl, combine the chicken, bread crumbs, scallions, cilantro (or basil or parsley), garlic, salt, cumin, allspice, cinnamon, black pepper, and Aleppo or cayenne.

2. Put half the oil into a rimmed baking sheet. Using your hands, form the chicken mixture into ¾-inch fingers and rest each one on the baking sheet. When all the fingers are formed, brush them in the remaining oil.

3. Bake the fingers until just cooked through, 5 to 10 minutes (check them carefully; the baking time will vary a lot depending upon how thick they are). Garnish with additional herbs, if desired.

CRISP CHICKEN SCHNITZEL WITH LEMONY SPRING HERB SALAD

The hallmark of a perfect wiener schnitzel, opined the eminent epicure Joseph Wechsberg, is a slice of veal "tender and so dry you could sit on it without having a fat stain on your pants."

I've clung to this image ever since I first read it in Mr. Wechsberg's classic 1953 book, *Blue Trout and Black Truffles*. Why anyone would ever sit on a schnitzel to test it in the first place wasn't clear, but I liked the notion of such a greaseless fried morsel of meat.

Several years later, when an Austrian chef gave me a schnitzel-making lesson, I thought I knew what was what.

"In Austria they say you should be able to sit on a schnitzel without getting grease on your pants, right?" I said with authority.

The chef raised an eyebrow, then replied, "Maybe they sit on schnitzel in Vienna. Where I come from we prefer a crisp, light schnitzel with a crust that rises like a soufflé."

The secret, he went on to demonstrate, is to trap air in the crust by moving and shaking the pan when you cook the meat.

After dipping the veal in flour, egg, and bread crumbs, the chef put a cutlet in the skillet, swirling it so the hot oil undulated over the top of the cutlet in waves. This motion creates steam that lifts the crust away from the meat, allowing the bread crumbs to crisp without sticking to the veal in a gummy mass.

Indeed, his schnitzel was a golden, gorgeous thing, with a puffy crust that shattered at the touch of a fork and tender, milky meat within. He served it with the traditional garnishes, a sprightly cucumber salad for contrast and a dollop of sweet lingonberry jam.

I took all this in and filed it in my brain for the next time a schnitzel craving hit. Years went by, but when it hit, it hit hard. I wanted a slab of crumby, crisp, fried meat for dinner, and would not be denied.

What I didn't want, however, was mistreated factory farm veal. I know there is responsibly raised veal available in New York, but not at my local supermarket. I chose free-range chicken cutlets instead.

Since the cutlets were not quite $\frac{1}{8}$ inch thick—the proper thickness for schnitzel, according to the Austrian chef—I pounded them a little with a rolling pin. Then, without handling them too much as instructed, I gently dipped them in flour, egg, and bread crumbs.

When they were all nicely coated, I dropped a cutlet in hot oil, swirling the pan and watching the oil ripple over the meat. It puffed slightly and browned beautifully. Inside, the chicken was soft and savory (thanks to a pinch of cayenne and nutmeg) beneath the ultra-crisp crust. I served it with a bright herbladen salad, and my husband and I gobbled up the chicken schnitzel. It passed the Austrian chef's soufflé test easily, and you don't have to sit on any cutlets—unless that's what you're into.

Crisp Chicken Schnitzel with Lemony Spring Herb Salad

Time: 25 minutes

Serves 3 to 4

6 anchovy fillets

1 small garlic clove

Kosher salt and freshly ground black pepper

Finely grated zest of 1 lemon

2½ tablespoons fresh lemon juice

7 to 8 tablespoons extra-virgin olive oil, to taste

2 eggs, beaten

1½ cups panko or other unseasoned bread crumbs

½ cup all-purpose flour

⅛ teaspoon cayenne

⅛ teaspoon freshly grated nutmeg

1¼ pounds chicken cutlets, pounded to ⅛-inch thickness (see Note)

Safflower, peanut, or vegetable oil, for frying

2 quarts mixed baby greens

2 cups fresh soft herb leaves, such as a combination of mint, tarragon, basil,
    parsley, cilantro, chervil, or chives (try to use at least three kinds)

1 scallion, thinly sliced, including greens

1. Mince the anchovies and garlic with a large pinch of salt until you get a rough paste. Put it in a bowl and whisk in the lemon zest, juice, and another pinch of salt and some pepper. Slowly drizzle in the olive oil.

2. Place the eggs in one shallow dish, the bread crumbs in another, and the flour mixed with the cayenne and nutmeg in a third. Season the chicken cutlets generously with salt and pepper.

3. Heat ⅛ inch of oil in a large skillet. While the oil heats, dip the cutlets one by one first into the flour (shake off any excess), then into the eggs (ditto), and finally into the bread crumbs, taking care not to handle the chicken more than necessary (hold the meat by the ends).

4. When the oil sizzles when a pinch of bread crumbs is thrown in, add a chicken cutlet (or two if your skillet is large; leave plenty of room around

them). Swirl the pan so the oil cascades over the top of the cutlet in waves. When the bottom is golden brown, in about 3 minutes, flip and brown the other side, swirling the pan (the swirling helps create air pockets, giving you lighter schnitzel). Transfer to a paper towel–lined baking platter or baking tray and sprinkle with more salt. Repeat with the remaining chicken.

5. Toss the salad greens and herbs with just enough of the lemon dressing to coat them lightly. Divide the salad among serving plates and top with the schnitzel. Drizzle with more dressing and garnish with the scallion.

NOTE: If the cutlets aren't thin enough, you can easily pound them with the side of a knife, a rolling pin, or a wine bottle.

SPICY CHICKEN BARLEY SOUP WITH SWEET POTATO AND SPINACH

I've made barley salads, barley stuffings, barley cakes, and barley pilafs, and all are reasonably good. But my favorite way to eat barley is ladled from the soup pot, thick as oatmeal, slippery as tapioca, and cloaked in savory broth.

I grew up with mushroom barley soup, both bobbing with meat and vegetables, eaten in my grandma Ella's cozy kitchen on her red Formica-topped table. And I make it at home with some regularity. It's a soup that Grandma would recognize: homey, scented with garlic and herbs, and loaded with carrots and celery. Nothing daring, nothing outlandish, and not at all what I was in the mood for on a particularly gray, rainy autumn day.

Oh, I wanted the barley and I wanted the soup. But I didn't want the same old barley soup. I wanted something to transport me somewhere else, somewhere sunny and hot where flannel-lined raincoats are unheard of and sweet-smelling spices are used with an open hand.

I thought back to another soup I once made, with chicken and chickpeas and North African–inspired aromatics. It had a deep, ruddy broth filled with ginger, chili powder, and paprika, along with chunks of soft sweet potato and pieces of moist chicken, brightened at the end with lemon and cilantro.

I could use this basic recipe as a template, swapping out barley for the chickpeas and spinach for the turnips to add a fresh, contrasting color to the orange liquid.

Once I had my game plan, it was a cinch to execute. Or so I thought. But then there was the barley issue.

Usually, the brand of barley I buy cooks in about forty-five minutes. But this time I had bought some pearled barley in bulk at the health food store. An hour later, it was just starting to soften, and took a full hour and a half to cook through.

By that time, I'd added almost a quart of extra water to the pot to keep the soup from gumming up into a solid mass. And my poor sweet potatoes had fallen to mush. But the flavor was intense and luscious, so I filed the recipe in my head with the mental note to add the sweet potatoes later in the cooking process and up the broth quotient.

A few weeks later in the throes of winter, I tried again. This time I used more stock and added the sweet potato thirty minutes after the barley had been simmering. It took another forty minutes for both the barley and the sweet potato to cook through, but when they did, they were soft and supple and infused with spices, as were the bite-size pieces of chicken I added at the end.

It wasn't a soup my grandmother would have ever met before, and I'm sad that I can no longer introduce them. I know she would have loved it as much as I do.

Spicy Chicken Barley Soup with Sweet Potatoes and Spinach

3 tablespoons extra-virgin olive oil

1 Spanish onion, chopped

1 teaspoon kosher salt, plus more to taste

1/2 teaspoon sweet paprika

1/4 teaspoon ground cinnamon

1/4 teaspoon chili powder

1/4 teaspoon ground coriander

1/4 teaspoon freshly ground black pepper

Pinch cayenne

1 tablespoon tomato paste

3 garlic cloves, chopped

6 cups low-sodium or good homemade chicken broth (see Note)

1 cup pearled barley, rinsed well

1 sweet potato, peeled and diced

12 ounces boneless, skinless chicken breasts or thighs,
    cut into bite-size pieces

5 ounces (1 bag) baby spinach

1/2 cup chopped fresh cilantro or mint

1 tablespoon freshly squeezed lemon juice

Lemon wedges, for serving

Time: 20 minutes,
plus 1 1/2 hours
simmering

Serves 6 to 8

1. Heat the oil in a large soup pot over high heat. Add the onion and salt and sauté until limp, about 3 minutes. Add all the spices and sauté until fragrant, about 2 minutes. Add the tomato paste and sauté for another minute, until darkened but not burned. (If the tomato paste looks too dark too quickly, lower the heat.)

2. Add the garlic and continue to sauté for 1 minute longer.

3. Return the heat to high if you lowered it, then add the broth, 2 cups water, and the barley to the pot. Bring to a boil and let simmer for 30 minutes. Add the sweet potato and continue to cook until the barley and sweet

potato are soft, about 30 minutes to an hour more, adding more water to the pot if necessary (it should not get too thick; this is soup, not stew). Add the chicken, partially cover the pot, lower the heat to medium-low, and simmer for 10 minutes.

4. Add the spinach and cilantro or mint to the pot and continue simmering until the spinach is wilted, about 5 minutes longer. Stir in the lemon juice and more salt if desired. Serve garnished with cilantro or mint and lemon wedges.

NOTE: If your chicken broth is on the salty side, reduce the salt to $\frac{1}{2}$ teaspoon to start. You can always add more salt later.

REALLY EASY DUCK CONFIT (REALLY!)

Homemade duck confit sounds like the kind of recipe you'd only make if, say, you were co-authoring a cookbook with a classically trained chef.

In my case, it was a pair of chefs, the brothers Eric and Bruce Bromberg, and it's a signature dish at their Blue Ribbon restaurants in New York City.

I wasn't looking forward to spending the day making it, and saved testing the recipe until almost the end of the project. Not that it was a challenging or persnickety procedure, but it did call for six cups of rendered melted duck fat to be poured over duck that had cured for a day or two in a salt and spice mixture, and then the whole thing would be slowly roasted in a low oven for hours. Getting close and personal with that much duck fat was not usually my idea of a good time, not to mention that I can't exactly find six cups of rendered duck fat at my local supermarket.

I could, however, get six cups of rendered duck fat from the restaurant, so I went ahead and made the dish. In the end it was marvelous—glistening, dense chunks of rich duck meat beneath crisp and salty skin as addictive as potato chips.

I saved the extra duck fat in the freezer and am still using it up in matzoh balls, to fry latkes and potatoes, and to sauté seafood, especially shrimp and scallops (a little trick the Brombergs passed on).

This said, I never planned to make duck confit again, and probably wouldn't have until Eric Bromberg accidentally let me in on a little secret.

"You know, you can confit the duck in its own fat, you don't need to add extra," he said as I was complaining about how much it would cost to buy six cups of duck fat online if you didn't happen to have friends in the restaurant business (about $40 plus shipping).

You don't?

"No, you can render out enough fat in the pan to make it work, though it's not the classic technique," he said.

At the restaurant, working in high volume, he went on to explain, it's easier and more consistent to add the fat, and they have it on hand anyway. But not so for the home cook. We decided to try the alternative, less slippery recipe to see how it compared.

So I went home and made duck confit again, this time in its own fat. I bought Moulard duck legs and didn't trim them. Then I salted them overnight. The next day, I seared the legs until there was a quarter inch of rendered fat in the pan, then covered it and baked it in the oven for three hours, the last hour uncovered to allow the duck skin to crisp.

That was it. When the duck cooled enough to handle it, I served it over a dandelion salad, letting the clinging drips of duck fat dress the bitter greens. The flavor and texture of the meat was just as good as the legs that were fully submerged in fat. And there was about two cups of extra fat in the pan, enough for a whole year of potato frying.

But the best part was how easy it was for such an impressive, company-worthy dish. It was easier than braising short ribs (no chopping, less browning and measuring!), but had the same window-steaming, cozy effect on the house and its occupants, filling the rooms with a savory scent—and me with the anticipation of a warming, hearty, and far less unctuous dinner.

Really Easy Duck Confit (Really!)

Time: 3¼ hours, plus 24 hours' refrigeration

Serves 4

1½ teaspoons kosher salt

1 teaspoon freshly ground black pepper

½ teaspoon dried thyme

8 Moulard duck legs (about 4 pounds), rinsed and patted dry but not trimmed

1. In a small bowl, combine the salt, pepper, and thyme. Sprinkle the duck generously with the seasoning. Place the duck legs in a pan in one layer. Cover tightly with plastic wrap and refrigerate for 24 hours.
2. The next day, preheat the oven to 325°F.
3. Place the duck legs, fat side down, in a large ovenproof skillet, with the legs fitting snugly in a single layer (you may have to use two skillets or sear

them in batches). Heat the duck legs over medium-high heat until the fat starts to render. When there is about ¼ inch of rendered fat in the pan, about 20 minutes, flip the duck legs, cover the pan with foil, and place it in the oven. If you've used two pans, transfer the duck and fat to a roasting pan, cover with foil, and place it in the oven. Let roast for 2 hours, then remove the foil and continue roasting until the duck is golden brown, about 1 hour more.

4. Serve the duck hot or warm. Or let the duck cool in the fat and store the duck and the fat in the refrigerator for up to a week (or freeze for months). To serve, reheat in a 400°F oven until crisped, about 15 minutes. Save the duck fat for sautéing potatoes, shrimp and fish, or latkes. You can also store the duck shredded (it takes up less space this way). Simply shred the cooled duck meat, place it in a container, and cover with duck fat. The shredded duck confit is terrific on pasta, mixed into salad greens, or piled onto crusty bread or toasts and served as an hors d'oeuvre or lunch (small bread slices, such as from a baguette=hors d'oeuvres; big slices of country bread=lunch).

5 I Never Was a Vegetarian

When I was a kid, being a vegetarian seemed cool. I was in awe of my teenage cousins, who eschewed meat. They had glasses and braces and long, unkempt hair. They wore suede jackets and clogs and, I imagined, went on dates. With boys. I desperately wanted to be just like them, albeit in a miniature, seven-year-old way.

Given my youth, the only aspects I could emulate were the unkempt hair and the vegetarianism, so I tried hard to embrace both.

The obstacles were stymieing.

We had a live-in babysitter from Germany named Gerta, whose obsessions included collecting the cotton from the tops of aspirin bottles to stuff in between her toes, and braiding my and my sister's hair into loops so tight that blue veins bulged at our temples.

Every morning, I'd vainly try to elude Gerta and her comb, but she was bigger, stronger, and smarter than I. When sheer physical force didn't prevail (I could climb a tree and she couldn't), she'd cajole: Did I want her to bake butter cookies with multicolored sugar on top? Then she'd threaten: Did I want her to call Dr. Ruby and have him come over and give me an antinaughty shot?

Giving up meat was no easier. For one, I liked it. There was rare London broil with salt and pepper eaten with my fingers in front of the TV. Sucking on the crispy tail of a roasted chicken, a part that we called the pope's nose, in all its fleshy, savory, golden glory. Gnawing the lamb chop bones to scrape away every last shred of meat, fat, and sinew.

But the notion of being a vegetarian stuck fast. Thus I insisted one Thanksgiving that like my older cousins, I would not be partaking of the turkey ever again. Could I have grilled cheese, please, instead?

My mother narrowed her eyes and asked me why. Did I suddenly not like turkey anymore?

"No," I said. "It's just that now I'm a vegetarian."

"I see," she said, taking this information in stride.

"You know," she said after a pause, "there are vegetarians who also eat fish and chicken and turkey. Maybe you could be one of those and not have to give up the turkey wings and gravy that you love."

I had forgotten about the wings.

"Besides," she added, "you need to eat some meat to get enough protein because you're still growing. Why not become a fish- and poultry-eating vegetarian until you're a teenager? Then you can go vegan if you like."

I didn't know what vegan was, and my mother explained that they were people who didn't eat any animal products, including eggs, honey, and cheese.

This made an impression. Giving up turkey and steak was one thing, but grilled cheese was quite another, not to mention mac and cheese.

I wavered and she knew it. And then my mother administered the final coup de grâce on any vegetarian resolve still intact.

"If you decide to be a chicken- and fish-eating vegetarian, I'll save the turkey neck for you after I make gravy," she said.

Need I tell you I ate turkey that Thanksgiving and those ever after? I never did become a vegetarian.

And as for my cousins, they've expanded their diets to include chicken and fish and even the occasional slice of bacon. But according to my mother, they're vegetarians still.

CRISPY TOFU WITH CHORIZO AND SHIITAKES

The closest I ever really got to becoming a vegetarian was living with one in college. My boyfriend Seth was an inspired cook. He could whip up a satisfying meatless meal from canned beans and iceberg lettuce bought at the bodega on our deserted corner in Williamsburg.

When he did procure prime ingredients—his favorite fresh tofu from Chinatown, for example—the variations were legion and sublime. Poached, stewed, braised, wok-fried, or baked, in Seth's hands tofu was good enough to make me forget I hadn't eaten bacon in months.

Then one day, a carnivorous friend came to dinner. Seth made crispy tofu, so golden and crunchy on the exterior and meltingly savory within that it reminded me of pork belly.

But as good as Seth's tofu was, it wasn't bacon.

"Just imagine what he could do with meat," my friend whispered as she left.

When the relationship ran its course, I left without asking for recipes. I didn't think that after crossing back into the land of burgers and steak, I might crave crispy tofu, too.

I spent the next decade attempting crispy tofu, always with the same sad results: The tofu cubes stuck to the bottom of the pan while the flabby centers overcooked and fell apart.

Eventually I gave up and ate my crispy tofu at restaurants when the urge struck.

But recently I decided to give home-cooked crispy tofu another go. Surely somewhere in one of my cookbooks or in cyberspace, I'd be able to find the crispy tofu key.

After a brief survey, one thing became clear. Most crispy tofu recipes assume you are dexterous with a well-seasoned wok. I am not.

Nor did I want to deep-fry the tofu. To me, deep-frying is a once-in-a-while, company-food technique. The crispy tofu that I had in mind would have to be an everyday meal that I could speedily whip up.

Eventually, I flipped to the tofu section of Deborah Madison's *Vegetarian Cooking for Everyone*. There, embedded in her recipe for Golden Tofu, was the secret: a nonstick pan and the strict instructions not to touch the tofu as it seared.

"Let it cook undisturbed while you do something else," Ms. Madison's text read.

I knew immediately that all my disastrous crispy tofu trials were the result of a stainless steel pan and too much anxious poking and prodding.

Resolved to follow Ms. Madison's technique to the letter, I set about figuring what else should go into my tofu dish.

While ambling to the grocery store, I thought through my options, remembering all the other amazing tofu dishes I'd had in my life besides Seth's. There was spicy mapo tofu, Cantonese stuffed tofu with shrimp and pork, braised tofu and pork belly.

That's when it dawned on me that other than tofu, the unifying ingredient in all those dishes was pork.

Maybe it was Seth's specter lurking in my kitchen, but in all my years of tofu cooking, it never occurred to me to add pork. And it was high time to give it a try.

I cast around the store for the appropriate pork product to add. There was no ground pork, but bacon was a possibility. So was sausage, which I chose when I remembered a gorgeous dish of tofu with Chinese sausage in my past.

There was no Chinese sausage at my supermarket. But there was dried chorizo with a similar texture.

I also picked up some shiitake mushrooms to heighten the umami meatiness of the dish.

At home, I heeded Ms. Madison and sliced the chorizo as the tofu crisped, unpoked, in the pan. When it was crusty, I improvised a little pan sauce of the sausage and mushrooms moistened with chicken broth, and seasoned with soy sauce for salty depth and a splash of mirin for sweetness.

The tofu was as perfect as Seth's, with a burnished exterior both crisp and delicate, and a supple center imbued with its pork- and mushroom-scented sauce.

Marvelous as it was, I can't say my tofu dish would have converted Seth to come over to the meat-eating side. But then again, if anything could, it just might be this.

Crispy Tofu with Chorizo and Shiitakes

1 pound extra-firm tofu, drained and cut into ¾-inch-thick slabs

2 tablespoons peanut oil

1½ cups (4 ounces) thinly sliced shiitake mushroom caps

3 ounces cured chorizo (1½ small links), diced
    (or substitute cured Chinese sausage)

2 scallions, thinly sliced, dark green parts reserved for garnish

¼ cup chicken broth

3 to 4 teaspoons soy sauce to taste

2 teaspoons mirin

Time: 30 minutes

Serves 2

1. Using paper towels, pat the tofu dry. Heat the oil in a large nonstick skillet over medium-high heat.

2. Place the tofu slabs in the pan and cook without moving until golden, about 3 minutes. Turn and cook the other side, 2 to 3 minutes more. Transfer the slabs to a paper towel–lined plate to drain.

3. Increase the heat to high. Add the mushrooms, chorizo, and the white and light green parts of the scallions. Cook, tossing occasionally, until the mushrooms are softened and light golden, about 3 minutes. Stir in the broth, soy sauce, and mirin. Cook until the sauce reduces and thickens slightly, about 1 minute more.

4. If the tofu is no longer hot, push the vegetables in the pan to one side; add the tofu and cook until heated through. Transfer the hot tofu to serving plates and top with the mushroom mixture and pan sauce. Sprinkle with the dark green scallions.

SAUSAGES WITH SWEET PEPPER AND ONION STEW AND FRIED CROUTONS

Ask any cook about their culinary emergency fund for a rainy day/citywide blackout/severe illness/case of laziness, and you'll probably get answers like boxes of pasta and jars of tomato sauce, cans of black beans, a freezer full of organic samosa wraps, or a stack of well-worn take-out menus. For me, it's sausages.

A variety of sausages tucked away in the freezer means that no matter how long past the supermarket's closing time I get home, I'll still be able to make something good to eat.

Unlike big frozen steaks or packages of chicken thighs, sausages defrost quickly, so I don't have to plan ahead. They are preseasoned and self-sufficient, so I won't have to worry about garnishes or sauces. Just fried up in a pan with an onion, or perhaps plopped down on some bagged baby spinach, and I've got as tasty a meal as a body could want.

If I remember that I'm hungry on the walk home from the subway, I can stop at the twenty-four-hour deli and pick up some bell peppers. A dish of porky, herb-spiked Italian sausage and peppers deserves far more esteem than it gets on the street fair circuit.

Such was my seemingly flawless dinner plan one recent, very late evening, when I walked in the door with a sack full of red and green peppers and some onions. Except that, no matter how deep into the freezer I rummaged, I couldn't find any Italian sausages. There was no shortage of other kinds, of course—weisswurst and knockwurst, andouille and bangers, and two kinds of chorizo, both sweet and hot.

Since I often combine sweet and hot Italian sausages when I make sausage and peppers, I figured a mix of the chorizos would work just as well, especially if I gave the dish a vaguely Spanish makeover. So instead of crushed oregano, I dug out that dusty tin of smoked paprika that doesn't get used nearly enough. And to cut the sweetness of all those onions and peppers that condense into something sublimely jamlike, I decided on sherry vinegar in place of the red wine vinegar. Then I got out my heaviest skillet and started cooking.

To make a proper pan of sausage and peppers, it's essential to first brown the sausages. It not only deepens the flavors, but provides an hors d'oeuvre for the sausage fryer, standing over the spitting pan, dipping little pieces of bread into the sausage-flavored fat. And so it occurred to me as I munched that a garnish of sausage-fat fried bread might make the perfect topping for my Spanish sausage and peppers riff. It's along the lines of what the street fair folks do when they toast the hero rolls on the same grill used for sausages. But, I reasoned, by using thinner slices of bread I could get them crisp all over, like pork-scented croutons. They would also make a nice textural contrast to all those soft, floppy peppers.

As the peppers and onions melted in the pan, I busied myself scavenging the fridge for anything salad-worthy. There were two cucumbers and some cherry tomatoes, though the tomatoes, shriveled and a little sad, were long past their salad days. Hating waste, I tossed them into the pan of stewing sausages and peppers.

I also salvaged some cilantro from a weekend guacamole fling. There was just enough to chop up as a garnish.

Finally, my concoction was ready. The tomatoes had broken down into a scarlet sauce, the color heightened by the paprika. The onions had turned caramelized and golden; the peppers, velvety and lush. In fact, the dish was almost too honeyed and lush. Unlike the Italian sausages I'm partial to, the chorizo, combined with all those peppers, tasted slightly cloying. Even the supposedly hot ones lacked a spine. Thus, so did my dish. It needed a little something, some *oomph*, some pizzazz, some teeth.

I sprinkled in more vinegar, which helped with the tang but not with the *oomph.*

Then I thought about osso buco, another meaty, sweet dish that, to my mind, always needed the sharp complexity of the gremolata served alongside. I didn't have any parsley or lemon zest to make gremolata, but I did have garlic. So I chopped some up and stirred it into the pot off the heat so it would keep its pungency. It was exactly what the dish needed. Which just goes to show, no matter what you keep in your emergency rainy day fund, garlic always adds a little interest.

Sausages with Sweet Pepper and Onion Stew and Fried Croutons

Time: 1¼ hours

Serves 4

5 garlic cloves

3 tablespoons sherry vinegar

3 tablespoons olive oil, plus additional as needed for frying the bread

2 pounds spicy fresh (uncured) chorizo or other sausage, pricked
    all over with a fork

8-inch-long baguette, sliced about ¼ inch thick

Kosher salt to taste

¼ teaspoon sweet paprika

¼ teaspoon smoked or hot paprika

2 large red onions, halved lengthwise and sliced

2 Spanish onions, halved lengthwise and sliced

2 green bell peppers, sliced

2 red bell peppers, sliced

2 pints grape or cherry tomatoes, halved if large

1 cup chicken broth

½ teaspoon freshly ground black pepper

1 bay leaf

1 bunch fresh cilantro or parsley, leaves chopped

1. Mince 4 garlic cloves and reserve. Mince the remaining garlic clove, put it in a small bowl, and cover with 1 tablespoon of sherry vinegar.

2. Heat 1 tablespoon of oil over medium-high heat in a very large skillet or Dutch oven. Add the chorizo and cook until browned all over, about 7 minutes. Transfer the chorizo to a plate.

3. Add as many of the bread slices as will fit in one layer to the pan. Cook until golden on both sides, about 2 minutes. Transfer to a plate and sprinkle

with salt. Heat a little more oil in the bottom of the pan and repeat with the remaining bread slices, frying them in batches, if necessary.

4. Heat the remaining 2 tablespoons oil in the pan. Add both paprikas and let cook for 20 seconds. Add the onions and reserved 4 minced garlic cloves and cook until limp, about 3 minutes. Add the bell peppers and sauté until the onions are golden and the peppers soft, about 7 minutes. Add the cherry tomatoes, chicken broth, black pepper, and bay leaf to the pan and bring to a simmer. Cut the chorizo in chunks and add it to the pan along with any drippings from the plate. Reduce the heat to low, cover the pan, and let cook at a low simmer for 25 minutes. Add the remaining 2 tablespoons sherry vinegar to the pan and simmer, uncovered, until the stew thickens slightly, 5 to 10 minutes longer.

5. Remove the bay leaf and stir in the reserved garlic-vinegar mixture and the cilantro or parsley. Serve the stew topped with fried bread.

OVEN-ROASTED PORK BUTT WITH ROSEMARY, GARLIC, AND BLACK PEPPER

Of all the pork roast recipes a person can prepare, few have the Paleolithic appeal of a roasted whole pig. Be it an infantine suckling or a man-size hog, roasting an entire animal in its recognizable form reduces the art of cooking to its earthiest incarnation, and unites the cook with her hunter-gatherer ancestors—even if hunting means placing an order with the butcher.

There was a time when I was obsessed with pit-roasting a whole pig. I wanted to experience the ultimate in head-to-tail cookery, and planned on savoring bits from the entire beast—especially the tail. I'd had a pig's tail at a barbecue festival in Memphis, and I couldn't get the memory of that fatty, crackling-like morsel with its toothsome cartilage crunch out of my head. And of course I fully expected the ears and snout to prove just as divine.

All I needed was a whole suckling pig and a little piece of earth to dig a hole. The rest, I was sure, would be magical.

When the right set of circumstances did materialize, it was a down-and-dirty affair involving my then-husband Joe, my hairdresser Mary, and a pale, pink, twenty-pound porker with wide staring eyes and nimble-looking little hooves.

"Piggy, Piggy, hi Piggy!" cried my hairdresser's three-year-old twins as we unloaded our dinner from the car. Joe and I were spending the weekend with Mary, her husband, Michael, and their twins at their country house, and they were easily persuaded that pit-roasting a whole pig was a marvelous idea, even though none of us had ever done it before.

The first order of business: Dig a hole.

Joe and Michael headed out to the back, shovels in hand. After several hours scratching at the hard, packed soil, they managed to excavate a section of car fender, two burlap sacks, countless rocks, and a trench just deep enough to bury our small, now garlic-slicked pig.

"Are you sure this is a good idea? We could put Piggy in the oven," Mary suggested.

"*Oink, oink!*" said the twins.

We persevered, building a fire and gently laying a foil-wrapped Piggy into the hole before covering it with a sheet of metal.

Then we waited and waited. It got dark. Mary made macaroni and cheese for the boys and she and I picked the leftovers off their plates. We all drank beer and ate chips. Joe fell asleep on the couch.

Eventually we pulled a half-baked Piggy out of the ground and stuck him in the oven. When we carved the meat near 10:00 P.M., soil clung to the fat.

Mary gave up after two bites. "I've had enough of that nasty little pig to last me a lifetime," she said, pulling pints of ice cream out of the freezer.

I stuck with it a bit longer, gnawing on the gritty, leathery tail.

But my romance with pit-roasted whole pig was decidedly over.

Now, when I crave an extreme pork experience, I roast a tail-less hunk of pork butt in the comfort of my own kitchen.

Here's the thing about pork butt (which, by the way, is cut from the shoulder of a pig, not the tush): You have to try really hard to mess it up. Season with salt, pepper, garlic, and herbs, stick it in the oven for three or so hours, and you will pull out a burnished, brawny, melting roast dripping with savory juices and nary a trace of topsoil.

You can buy a piece of butt with the skin still attached, which will blister and crackle in the oven and make a tasty nibble for the cook as she carves (eat it fast before anyone realizes what you've got). Or you can have it trimmed for a more restrained and elegant presentation.

You can buy it boneless and tied in a bundle, or bone-in in a Flintstonian chunk that will scratch any caveman itch one might have.

Any which way, it will be cheap and tasty, without evoking *Charlotte's Web*—or *Lord of the Flies*.

Oven-Roasted Pork Butt with Rosemary, Garlic, and Black Pepper

Time: 15 minutes,
plus at least 2 hours'
marinating and about
3 hours' roasting

Serves 12 to 16

1 (5- to 7-pound) boneless pork shoulder
4 fat garlic cloves, minced
4 teaspoons kosher salt
¼ cup extra-virgin olive oil
2 tablespoons finely chopped fresh rosemary
1½ tablespoons Dijon mustard
1 tablespoon freshly ground black pepper

1. Carefully cut away the skin from the pork shoulder, leaving a ⅛-inch layer of fat.

2. Using a mortar and pestle or the flat side of a knife, mash together the garlic and salt to form a paste. Stir in the olive oil, rosemary, mustard, and black pepper. Rub the mixture all over the pork and transfer to a large roasting pan. Cover tightly with plastic wrap and refrigerate for at least 2 hours or overnight.

3. Preheat the oven to 325°F and let the pork come to room temperature. Place the pork on a roasting rack fitted inside a roasting pan, skin side up. Roast, uncovered, until the meat is fork-tender (and reaches 180°F on a meat thermometer), 3 to 4 hours. Let rest at least 10 minutes before slicing and serving.

SEARED PORK CHOPS
WITH KIMCHI

Some people collect stamps, others vintage bartender guides or mounted rare butterflies. Me, I'm cultivating a prodigious collection of condiments that's slowly taking over the entirety of the fridge, much to my husband's dismay.

"But why do we need nine kinds of mustard and three types of prune spread? And when was the last time you used brine-packed green peppercorns?" he occasionally demands.

Usually, I change the subject. But recently, while unsuccessfully attempting to wedge in a quart of milk, I had to admit he had a point.

Still, the idea of just throwing out this carefully built-up inventory (certain to keep us in jalapeño jelly and salted capers for the better part of a nuclear winter) was devastating.

Plus, for someone who cooks a lot, an arsenal of strongly flavored condiments is a powerful secret weapon. Even when there is nothing in the house to eat, I can whip up a meal from the contents of many jars mixed with pasta or meat excavated from the freezer. Some of my best culinary feats have come out of such condiment alchemy.

"Fine, don't throw anything out," my husband conceded, "but how about using things up?"

It was during this campaign that I rediscovered the kimchi. A potent, mouth-searing Korean condiment made from fermented cabbage, garlic, and chiles, I originally bought it to garnish grilled steaks. But grilling season being long over, the kimchi migrated to the back of the fridge, where it languished behind the lime pickle.

It was high time to put it back in our dinner rotation, but what to do with it?

At Korean restaurants, kimchi is most often served in little bowls to accompany the meal. But I wanted it to be more integrated into the main dish, imbuing the whole thing with its peppery pungency, a little like spreading chipotles in adobo sauce on a piece of chicken before cooking.

So what if I simply rubbed the kimchi all over the pork chops that were defrosting on the counter, then panfried them?

The idea of kimchi-slathered pork sounded mighty appealing, so I gave it a go, chopping up the kimchi to release the maximum amount of flavor before coating the chops.

The thing about kimchi, as opposed to a thicker and more clinging condiment like, say, tamarind paste, is that after being patted onto a piece of meat, it can easily fall off. This meant that once I took my golden brown chops out of the skillet, most of the kimchi—along with its vibrant flavor—remained behind.

I suppose I could have mounded it back on top of the pork for serving. But without any pan liquid, the kimchi would be a distinct accompaniment rather than suffusing every porky bite.

The easiest solution was to make a little kimchi pan sauce.

My preferred pan-sauce method is beyond minimal: Just deglaze with wine and simmer until thick. But the wine we had already opened for dinner was red, and the notion of red wine and kimchi was not at all harmonious.

I did, however, have some dry vermouth on hand, and added a splash to the skillet. When it all but evaporated, I dipped in a spoon to taste. Somehow the alcohol had intensified the kimchi, making it even more assertive and biting than before—maybe a little too biting, I thought as I squinted through the sourness.

Thinking that butter would smooth out the rough edges, I tossed in a big lump. But the sauce remained stubbornly sharp.

In desperate need of a quick fix, I scavenged my condiment stash for some magical dash to make everything better. Preserved sardines? Pomegranate molasses? Quince-saffron marmalade?

I was about to give up when I spotted my teacup and the honey bear sitting next to it.

Indeed, a squirt of honey tamed the aggressive flavors, mellowing the harshness while allowing the racy garlic and chile notes to enliven the meaty pork. The dish was so good that my husband, noticing the empty kimchi container, told me later that he even contemplated suggesting we stock up.

But then, unable to fit the leftovers into the fridge, he didn't.

Seared Pork Chops with Kimchi

4 bone-in pork chops, 1 inch thick
6 tablespoons chopped kimchi (sold in Asian markets)
1 tablespoon olive oil
½ cup white wine or vermouth
1 to 2 teaspoons honey, or to taste
1 tablespoon butter
Chopped scallions, for garnish

Time: 30 minutes,
plus 30 minutes' to
24 hours' refrigeration

Serves 2

1. Smear the pork chops with 2 tablespoons kimchi and refrigerate for at least 30 minutes and up to 24 hours (the longer, the better).
2. Wipe off the pork to remove the pieces of clinging kimchi, and add those pieces to the remaining 4 tablespoons kimchi. Heat the oil in a large skillet over high heat. Sear the pork until golden brown on both sides, about 3 minutes a side. Reduce the heat to low and continue cooking the pork until done to taste, about 7 minutes longer, turning once. Transfer the pork to a plate and cover with foil to keep warm.
3. Add the wine or vermouth, 1 teaspoon honey, and the kimchi to the skillet. Raise the heat to high and simmer, scraping up the browned bits, until almost all the liquid has evaporated, about 3 minutes. Whisk in the butter. Taste and add more honey, if needed; the sauce should be tart but not puckery.
4. Serve the pork chops coated with the sauce and garnished with scallions.

BRAISED PORK CHOPS WITH TOMATOES, ANCHOVIES, AND ROSEMARY

When I think about braising, I think of carnivorous, all-day affairs. I think of browning a gargantuan slab of flesh, adding just enough liquid to partially cover it, and letting it stew for hours, steaming up the windows in a perfumed cloud of melting meat fat and oozing, succulent juices.

Braised meat is cold-weather fare, and on the first nippy day of autumn, I wanted some, badly.

The thought occurred to me early enough to make a braise, too, had I been in the possession of, say, brisket or lamb shanks.

But the freezer yielded up only its perennial hodgepodge of sausages, a smoked pheasant, and chicken breasts, none of which was right. And by the time I made it to the market, it was late. That five-pound pork shoulder wouldn't be tender until 10:00 P.M., too late for the likes of me.

I hemmed and hawed in front of the meat case, then spotted two fat, bone-in pork chops.

Technically I've braised pork chops before. But because they cook in under thirty minutes (not enough time to steam up the windows), I don't ever think of them as a proper braise in the short ribs way.

Plus the braised pork chops I've made don't seem to take on the same depth of flavor as long-simmered chunks of meat, which become deeply imbued with the aromatics in the pot as they slowly soften.

But, I thought, maybe if I aggressively season the braising liquid, would that perk them up? And if so, what flavorings should I add to the pan?

Pork, garlic, and rosemary are classic together, especially when paired with tomato. It needed a salty, pungent element, too, and I considered capers and olives before settling on anchovies.

At home, I seared the chops until they were mahogany colored, then made a quick sauce with tomatoes, garlic, rosemary, and anchovies, and popped it all in the oven to braise.

Fifteen minutes later, when the kitchen smelled rich with garlic and meat, it was ready. The anchovies had melted into the savory sauce, adding a complex saline funkiness, and the pork chops were juicy and tender and suffused with garlic and herbs.

My inner carnivore was sated, as the work of a day had been compressed into an hour. If only the rest of my work could follow suit.

Braised Pork Chops with Tomatoes, Anchovies, and Rosemary

2 (1½-inch-thick) bone-in pork loin chops (about 1½ pounds total)
¾ teaspoon kosher salt, additional for seasoning
½ teaspoon freshly ground black pepper, additional for seasoning
2 tablespoons extra-virgin olive oil
1 red onion, halved and thinly sliced
3 large rosemary sprigs
2 garlic cloves, minced
2 pounds plum tomatoes (preferably a mix of red and yellow),
    roughly chopped
6 anchovy fillets
Polenta, noodles, or rice, for serving (optional)

Time: 35 minutes

Serves 2

1. Preheat the oven to 350°F. Rinse the pork chops and pat dry with a paper towel. Season generously with salt and pepper. In a large ovenproof skillet over medium-high heat, place 1 tablespoon of oil. Sear the chops until well browned, 3 to 4 minutes per side. Transfer to a plate.
2. Add the remaining tablespoon oil to the skillet and sauté the onion and rosemary until golden, about 5 minutes. Add the garlic and cook for another minute.
3. Add the tomatoes, anchovies, and remaining salt and pepper, and cook, stirring occasionally, until the tomatoes begin to break down, about 8 minutes.

186

4. Add the pork chops to the skillet, spooning the sauce over the chops. Cover the skillet and transfer to the oven to bake until a thermometer inserted into the center of the meat reads 145°F, about 15 minutes. Allow the chops to rest for 5 minutes in the pan, then serve with polenta, noodles, or rice, if desired, to soak up the sauce.

BACON AND PECAN PRALINES

I was a Jenny-come-lately to the whole sugared bacon phenomenon. Sure, I'd dipped my share of crisp strips into drips of maple syrup sliding down my pancake stack. And I'd been to the kind of fancy restaurant that garnished their sweet egg custards with caramelized bacon shards (get it, breakfast for dessert?).

But I didn't realize it was a veritable movement until the sugared bacon my friend Shawn Kelley brought to my wedding threatened to eclipse the happy couple as the star of the event.

I didn't get to taste any that night. As the bride, I had weightier matters to focus on than sampling every hors d'oeuvre. But after listening to wistful descriptions of the caramelized, porky strips that stood tall in a glass until they crunched in the mouth, I knew that sugared bacon and I were yet another match made in heaven.

Once back from the honeymoon, I e-mailed Shawn for the recipe, which entails nothing more than sprinkling bacon strips with brown sugar and baking at 350°F for twenty-five minutes. What emerged from my oven were burnished sticks of sweet and salty meat candy. They were good for breakfast, for snacking, crumbled over salads, and even for dessert, satisfying the same urge as chocolate-covered pretzels and Crunch 'n Munch.

It turns out I wasn't the only one reveling in this porcine discovery. A culinary movement was afoot. Sugared bacon in a myriad of divine forms was showing up all over the country. There was bacon brittle, bacon brownies, bacon cupcakes, and bacon bread pudding—even bacon ice cream and chocolate bars. It seemed like once pastry cooks were given permission to put fatty pork belly in their desserts, there was just no holding them back.

And I'm no exception. Now that I've joined the fray, I've got a long mental list of sweet bacon plans, culminating in a bacon pecan pie for next year's Thanksgiving. But in the meantime, I wanted to start with something simpler.

The combination of bacon, pecans, and dark brown sugar in my dream pie made me think of pralines, which are easier than pie and seemed like perfect little vehicles to bring the triad to my mouth. Plus, since both pralines and pork are treasured in the South, I figured merging them was a natural and inevitable evolution.

Adapting a praline recipe was easy. I just stirred cooked bacon into the one that I stole from Bill Yosses, the White House pastry chef with whom I wrote a cookbook. Then I spooned the mixture on parchment and waited for it to cool.

They were exactly as I'd imagined them: caramel-y, chewy patties with a deep nutty crunch and salty, brawny tang. Addictive and compelling, I nearly polished off the entire batch all by myself. But then I remembered the sugared bacon from my wedding, which reminded me that I had a husband who might like some bacon pralines, too. So I set some aside. After all, though rarely written into the vows, there's an implicit rule in every happy omnivorous union: Don't hog the bacon, and married life will be sweet.

Bacon and Pecan Pralines

Time: 15 minutes

Makes 30

1 cup packed dark brown sugar
½ cup sour cream
¼ cup (½ stick) unsalted butter
1 cup pecan halves, toasted
⅔ cup crumbled bacon (about 5 strips, 5 to 6 ounces uncooked)
1 teaspoon vanilla extract

1. In a heavy saucepan with a candy thermometer attached to the side, melt together the brown sugar, sour cream, and butter, stirring occasionally, over medium heat. Once the butter has melted, raise the heat and bring the mixture to a boil. Boil the mixture, without stirring, until the thermometer registers 235°F, about 5 minutes. Take the pan off the heat and let cool for 2 minutes.

2. Stir in the pecans, bacon pieces, and vanilla, taking care not to splash the molten mixture. Continue to stir until the pecan mixture is thick and creamy, 1 to 2 minutes. Immediately use two tablespoons to drop 1½-inch pralines onto wax or parchment paper. Let them cool and set. Store in an airtight container.

LAMB TAGINE WITH APRICOTS, OLIVES, AND BUTTERED ALMONDS

At a recent dinner in a swanky restaurant, my braised lamb shanks were served pulled off the bone and molded into a neat little brick. The silken shreds of meat were so soft and succulent that neither knife nor teeth were required. Technically correct and perfectly executed, it held my interest for all of three bites, and then I got bored. Those supple, homogeneous morsels slid too easily across my tongue with nary a struggle. There were no elastic bits of gristle, no chewy tidbits of fat, no bones to nibble and gnaw.

My husband, however, was in his own private carnivore's heaven. Spooning up the tender remains from my plate, he sighed with pleasure: no gristle, no fat, no bones!

Remembering this scene the next time I made my way to the kitchen to braise some lamb, I decided I wanted a dish that was flexible enough to delight both the bone pickers and leavers at the table.

I started with the cut. I needed a piece of meat that had some but not too many bones. Shanks and legs are too big-boned. Stew meat and loin, too spineless. After a chat with my butcher, I settled on shoulder chops. Each chop contained a few small, gnawable bones, and plenty of velvety meat that would slip right off them after a long, gentle braise. (You could substitute entirely boneless stew meat if you and all your guests share the same bone-free ideal.)

Next, I needed to puzzle out the seasonings. Winter's persistence made me envious of other people's exotic vacations, so I focused on places I'd rather be, like Morocco. It's warmer there, and they braise their lamb with fragrant, blood-heating spices. A lamb tagine, infused with aromatics and dried sweet fruit, began to take shape in my mind.

Out came the cookbooks, starting with Paula Wolfert's classic *Couscous and Other Good Food from Morocco*. As I skimmed the thirty recipes for tagine—the name for both a traditional slow-cooked stew and the conical-covered pot it stews in—I noticed that while elements of each recipe intrigued, there was none in particular that contained them all. So I cherry-picked, stealing ground ginger and cinnamon sticks from a vegetable tagine, mixing in green olives, cumin, and paprika from lamb tagine with lemons and olives, and adding saffron because nearly all the recipes called for either that or turmeric, of which I had none. I settled on dried apricots as the fruit because their sunny hue had warmer connotations than would, say, prunes.

In terms of tagine technique, recipes varied widely, though all were cooked in their eponymous pot. I even briefly considered feeding my kitchenware addiction and running out to buy a tagine (several manufacturers, including All-Clad, make them). But common sense and my sturdy Dutch oven prevailed.

Following Ms. Wolfert's directions, I heated the lamb and spices in the pot on the stove just long enough to release the aromas but not long enough to brown the meat. Having been schooled in the belief that properly browned meat was an essential building block for any sauce, I was a little dubious. But skipping the browning also saved me twenty stove-splattering minutes, so I decided to give it a try.

After everything came to a simmer, I popped the pot into the oven and continued reading about tagines. Some were cooked in enough butter to keep for a month, preserved beneath a coating of honey, spices, and fat, somewhat like a confit. Riffing on the butter theme, I decided to garnish the tagine with butter-fried almonds.

When the meat was soft enough to fall away from the bones, the tagine was ready, and I served it over mounds of fluffy couscous, heaping the fleshy lamb chunks on my husband's plate and the bony bits on mine. Then I drizzled buttered almonds over all. Both the butter and almonds turned golden brown, taking on a nutty, roasted, caramelized flavor, almost like what browned meat would have contributed to the sauce, but gentler and sweeter. The spices had mellowed, the onions softened, the olives and apricots melted into the sauce. As Ms. Wolfert likes to write, it was really very good.

But best of all, we each got to eat our meat exactly the way we like it, and all from one pot.

Lamb Tagine with Apricots, Olives, and Buttered Almonds

Time: 2 hours

Serves 6

4 pounds bone-in lamb shoulder or neck, or 2¼ pounds boneless
  lamb stew meat, cut into 2-inch chunks
4 garlic cloves, minced
1½ teaspoons kosher salt
1 teaspoon freshly ground black pepper
1 teaspoon sweet paprika
1 teaspoon ground ginger
¾ teaspoon ground cumin
2 large Spanish onions, peeled and quartered
2 cinnamon sticks, each 2 inches long
Large pinch crumbled saffron
1¼ cups dried apricots, sliced
1 cup cracked green olives, pitted and sliced if desired
2 to 4 tablespoons butter
⅓ cup sliced almonds
Cooked couscous, for serving
Chopped parsley or cilantro, for garnish

1. Preheat the oven to 325°F. Trim the excess fat off the lamb if your butcher hasn't. Put the meat in a deep Dutch oven or cast-iron pot with the garlic, salt, black pepper, paprika, ginger, and cumin and rub the spices and garlic evenly all over the meat.

2. Thinly slice the onions. Finely mince enough of the onion slices to yield ½ cup. Add the minced onion to the pot with the lamb (reserve the onion slices).

3. Place the pot over high heat and let cook, turning the meat on all sides, until the spices release their scent, about 3 minutes. You needn't brown the meat. Add 3 cups of water to the pot (it should come three quarters of the way up the lamb), along with the cinnamon and saffron. Bring to a simmer, then cover the pot and transfer to the oven. Let braise for 45 minutes.

4. Turn the meat, then top with the onion slices. Cover the pot and let braise for another 45 minutes to an hour, or until the lamb is very tender. Use a slotted spoon to transfer the meat to a bowl, leaving the lamb broth and onions in the pot.

5. Place the pot on the stove over high heat and add ¾ cup each of the apricots and the olives. Simmer the lamb broth until it reduces by a third and thickens slightly, about 10 minutes. Return the lamb to the pot and keep warm until serving. (The tagine can be prepared 4 days ahead; chill, then remove the fat and reheat before serving.)

6. To serve, coarsely chop the remaining ½ cup apricot slices. In a small skillet, melt the butter. Add the almonds and cook until they are well browned and toasted, about 2 minutes. Put the couscous in a serving bowl and top with the almonds, butter, and chopped apricots. Pile the tagine in the center of the couscous and garnish with the herbs.

LAMB AND BULGUR KIBBE
WITH GARLIC YOGURT SAUCE

Most of the time, my husband Daniel is an eager accomplice when it comes to my more outré culinary cravings. He's gamely sampled braised chicken feet in Chinatown, crispy tripe tacos in Hell's Kitchen, and even the deep-fried gummi octopuses I made one afternoon in an oil-ridden frenzy. But when it came to raw lamb kibbe for dinner, he put on the kibbe kibosh.

"I was actually hoping for something cooked," he said.

Having already purchased the necessary freshly ground lamb, bulgur, onions, and spices, I'll admit that I wasn't prepared for the veto. But isn't marriage often about compromise?

The easiest thing, of course, would be to simply fry up the mixture. According to my prime kibbe source, *The Arab Table* by May S. Bsisu, kibbe, the national dish of both Lebanon and Syria, is as malleable as Silly Putty. It can be served raw or cooked, hot or cold. It can be formed into sheets, patties, balls, or mini-footballs and broiled, grilled, baked, fried, or poached. You can stuff it with pine nuts and fried onions, and/or drizzle it with yogurt sauce or hummus.

Since I didn't have any pine nuts, I decided to skip the stuffing entirely. Besides, once I had come to terms with the idea of cooking the lamb mixture, my heart was set on forming them into cute mini-footballs. Stuffing said footballs seemed like way too much to undertake on a weeknight. Ditto the hummus, though a yogurt sauce was doable.

Finally I chose broiling as a cooking method since it was the easiest and least messy way to attain a crisp golden crust. If I couldn't have soft, supple, and raw lamb, crunchy seemed like the next best way to go.

After reading through myriad recipes, both from Ms. Bsisu's book and online, I realized that if raw kibbe is the steak tartare of the Middle East, cooked kibbe is the meatball. Except that bulgur replaces the bread crumbs.

But here's where the recipes diverged. Some called for soaking the bulgur in water for hours before smashing it together with the meat, some called for a quick soak, and others for rinsing in several changes of water. I opted for a quick soak. All that rinsing seemed fussy.

So I soaked the bulgur while I chopped the onion and stirred up the yogurt sauce. Then I drained it in a fine-mesh sieve and mixed it into the meat.

The last addition was the salt and spices. This was the fun part. Usually, when you're working with ground meat, you don't taste it raw, especially when pork and beef are involved. But since I had planned to eat the kibbe uncooked in the first place, I figured tasting was not only perfectly fine, but a well-deserved hors d'oeuvre. So I nibbled away, tweaking the balance of salt, sweetness from the cinnamon and allspice, muskiness from the cumin, and heat from the chili powder. Once the meat was seasoned to perfection, I kept tasting because I couldn't quite make myself stop.

But remembering that my husband wanted dinner, too, I squashed what was left of the pink meat into footballs and ran them under the broiler. They emerged mahogany brown with crackling crusts. We devoured what precious few I hadn't already eaten, rolling them in the garlicky, herb-flecked yogurt sauce. Much as I loved the raw kibbe, the broiled were even better—rich, brawny, and deeply fragrant from the warmed spices.

"These are amazing," Daniel said, licking his fork. "But how come you made such a small batch?"

Lamb and Bulgur Kibbe with Garlic Yogurt Sauce

Time: 40 minutes

Serves 4 to 6

1 cup bulgur

2 cups plain Greek yogurt

2 tablespoons chopped fresh dill, basil, or cilantro, plus additional for garnish

1 fat garlic clove, minced

1¾ teaspoons kosher salt, plus additional

2 pounds ground lamb or beef

1 onion, chopped

1 teaspoon ground cumin

¾ teaspoon ground allspice

¾ teaspoon ground cinnamon

½ teaspoon freshly ground black pepper

⅛ teaspoon Aleppo pepper or pinch cayenne

4 tablespoons olive oil

Rice, pita, or other bread, for serving

Sliced tomatoes and cucumbers (optional)

1. Put the bulgur in a bowl and cover with plenty of cold water. Let soak for 20 minutes.

2. Meanwhile, in a bowl, stir together the yogurt, herbs, garlic, and ¼ teaspoon salt; chill.

3. Position a broiler rack about 3 inches from the heat source and preheat the broiler.

4. In a large bowl, combine the lamb, onion, and spices and remaining 1½ teaspoons salt. Drain the bulgur in a fine sieve, pressing down hard and squeezing to eliminate as much of the water as possible. Add to the lamb mixture and mix very well with your hands.

5. Pour the oil onto a large jelly roll pan or rimmed baking sheet. Using your hands, form the lamb mixture into 2-inch-long footballs and rest each one on the baking sheet. When all the footballs are formed, roll them in the oil, coating them all around.

6. Broil the kibbe until well browned on one side, about 8 minutes. Roll them over and broil until browned on the other side, 4 to 6 minutes longer.

7. Taste the yogurt sauce and add more salt if needed. Serve the kibbe with the sauce and rice or bread, and tomatoes and cucumbers, if desired. Garnish with more herbs.

PASTA WITH TURKISH-STYLE LAMB, EGGPLANT, AND YOGURT SAUCE

When Turkish culinary historian Engin Akin taught me how to make manti—hand-formed lamb dumplings—on a trip to Istanbul last year, every step was exquisitely wrought.

She kneaded the dough on her floured kitchen table, gently rocking it back and forth beneath manicured hands. Then she rolled it over and over with a thin wooden stick, periodically lifting the dough to check whether it was translucent and pliable enough to envelop but not overwhelm the delicately spiced ground lamb filling.

With the help of two assistants, she molded each dumpling, filling it with lamb. Once cooked, the manti was coated with thick yogurt and plenty of melted brown butter seasoned with ground chile. I devoured heaping bowlfuls, rivulets of spicy butter slipping down the sides.

Ever since, I've dreamed of making platters of buttery manti at home. But something always holds me back, such as the lack of time and two assistants with Turkish-dumpling-making skills.

What I needed was a way to shorten the process without compromising that savory, near-sacred combination of butter, lamb, garlic, yogurt, and more butter.

Figuring that other lazy manti lovers must have had the same urge, I did some online research, typing "manti" and "shortcut" into the search engine.

Entries like "fake manti" and "mock manti" came up, detailing recipes that deconstructed manti making, reducing it down to its essence. After begging forgiveness for monkeying with such an esteemed Turkish (and Armenian) classic, bloggers routinely substituted pasta shells for handmade dough, topping them with sautéed ground lamb and yogurt. It seemed like as good a place as any to start.

Instead of shells, though, I picked up bowtie pasta because I like the way their crinkled nooks and folds capture chunky, ground meat–filled sauces.

While at the market, I also grabbed a nice, plump purple eggplant. After all, what Turkish meal would be complete without one? I figured I'd make a dip or something to go alongside my rogue little entrée.

Remembering a tasty roasted eggplant salad I made last year, I tossed egg-plant cubes in oil and put them in the oven while I prepared the rest of the meal.

While the pasta boiled, I sautéed the lamb with garlic and shallots, seasoning it with mint. In Turkey, a particularly fragrant and intense dried mint would likely be used here. But I had lots of the fresh stuff in the garden, so I threw that in.

I drained the pasta and loaded it in a bowl, tossing it with the lamb, and was about to dollop the yogurt on top when I reconsidered. The pasta looked a little white and naked. It really could have taken twice as much lamb as what I bought, but it was too late for that.

To compensate, I folded in the roasted eggplant (which had yet to become salad), tossing it together. Then I added thick Greek yogurt spiked with pungent fresh garlic, and, as per my memory of Ms. Akin's feast, much more of the red pepper–spiced browned butter than I knew was good for me.

As I remembered, the butter ran down the snowy yogurt in thin golden streams, pooling delectably around the pasta. As with the manti, butter and yogurt melded into a rich sauce, generously gilding the lamb, pasta, and, in this case, eggplant with garlicky abandon.

My cheater's dish may have lacked the refined velvety character of hand-made dumplings, but the flavors I was craving were all there, enticing me to finish mouthful after mouthful until my husband and I licked clean a bowl that should have fed four. So much for leftovers the next day. But at least my mock manti was easy enough to make again very soon.

Pasta with Turkish-Style Lamb, Eggplant, and Yogurt Sauce

Time: 45 minutes

Serves 2 to 3

1 large eggplant (about 1 pound), diced into 1/2-inch cubes

5 tablespoons extra-virgin olive oil

1/2 teaspoon kosher or coarse sea salt, plus additional

3 fat garlic cloves, minced

1 large shallot, minced

1 pound ground lamb

1/4 teaspoon red pepper flakes, preferably Turkish or Aleppo (see Note), plus additional

Freshly ground black pepper

1 1/2 tablespoons chopped fresh mint or dill, plus additional

1/2 pound bowtie or other pasta

6 tablespoons unsalted butter

2/3 cup plain Greek yogurt

1. Preheat the oven to 450°F. Bring a pot of water to a boil for the pasta.
2. Toss the eggplant with 4 tablespoons of oil and a large pinch of salt. Spread on a baking sheet, making sure there is room between the pieces, and roast until crisp and brown, 15 to 20 minutes. Check often to prevent burning.
3. In a large skillet, heat the remaining tablespoon oil. Add 2 minced garlic cloves and the shallot and sauté until fragrant, 1 to 2 minutes. Add the lamb, 1/2 teaspoon salt, the red pepper flakes, and black pepper to taste, and sauté until the lamb is no longer pink, about 5 minutes. Stir in the mint or dill and cook for another 2 minutes. Stir the eggplant into the lamb. Taste and adjust the seasonings.
4. Cook the pasta according to the package directions. Meanwhile, in a small saucepan, melt the butter. Let cook until it turns golden brown and smells nutty, about 5 minutes. In a small bowl, stir together the yogurt, remaining minced garlic clove, and a pinch of salt.
5. Drain the pasta and spread on a serving platter. Top with the lamb-eggplant mixture, then with the yogurt sauce. Pour the melted butter over the top

and sprinkle on additional red pepper and the mint or dill. Serve immediately.

NOTE: You can buy Turkish or Aleppo (Syrian) red pepper flakes at specialty markets or online at www.kalustyans.com. Or substitute ground chili powder. Do not use crushed red pepper flakes; they will be too hot for this dish.

NICK'S SHORT RIBS CHILI WITH MANY CHILES

Chili without ground meat and beans is a hard habit to break.

As a documented food geek, I know perfectly well that authentic Texas chili is a slowly simmered dish of hunks of beef and a mountain of dried capsicum, which meld into a deep red ambrosia, preferably over a wood-burning campfire after a cattle roundup on the plains.

Extraneous ingredients—beans, chopped vegetables, god forbid sour cream and grated cheese, and even tomatoes and onions to some chili purists—are anathema. Rib-sticking and traditional, chili should be a meaty and minimalist endeavor.

In principle, I can imagine the beauty of such a pungent pot of meat.

But the truth of it is, I like all those frivolous additions.

I like the soft soupy texture, the indistinct, supermarket–chili powder spiciness that's sparked by sour cream, mellowed by avocado, and brightened by chopped tomatoes, scallions, hominy, ad nauseam. I like being able to spoon up my chili or use it as a dip for tortilla chips. I even like turkey chili and vegetarian chili, albeit not as much.

I've tried to embrace the classic recipe, steadfastly concocting pots of stew with hand-cut chuck beef and sacks full of New Mexican chiles. Dry and chewy, it could never measure up to my comfort-food ideal. It might be real cowboy food, but for a tenderfoot like myself, nothing beats the ruddy richness of a bubbling pot of ground, fatty meat.

Then I had Nick Noyes's brilliant, lusty chili and instantly changed my mind.

This isn't to say that Nick's chili is strictly—or even remotely—traditional. While Texans may embrace its lack of beans and veggies, they'd cringe at the provenance of the cook, who not only is not American (he grew up in London), he's never even been to Texas (changing planes in DFW excepted).

Perhaps this lack of a childhood chili association made him freer to muck with the recipe, keeping the good (the potent combination of dried chiles and chili powders) and dispense with the bad (the chewy cubes of beef).

To whit, he invented a heady, aromatic stew with a vibrant, deeply spiced mahogany sauce coating velvety shreds of tender meat.

His secret, I discovered when I peeked into the pot, is short ribs.

Now, every chef worth his toque knows that short ribs make an astonishing braise. The combination of the marrow seeping out from the bones and melding with the slippery collagen dissolving from the sinew in the flesh imbues the meat with a profound flavor and silky texture unmatched in other parts of the animal. Slow, moist cooking and a pot full of aromatics is all you need to set this cut off to its best advantage.

Nick's genius move was to use chile peppers as the aromatics. His is a diverse, mostly mail-orderable blend of robust dried anchos and pasilla negras seasoned with chipotle, guajillo, and New Mexican chili powders, and brightened with green, fresh serranos and jalapeños.

To this, he adds cumin for its earthy flavor, onions and garlic for bite, and tomato paste for sweetness and color.

Then he stirs in enough beer and water to reduce down to a thick sauce as the beef cooks, and lets the whole thing simmer in the oven for hours and hours, until the meat, he likes to say, is falling off the bones, but still has some integrity and is not cooked down to rags.

As a final refinement, Nick likes to remove the rib bones before serving, which makes the cut of the meat—and the key to the chili's superb, supple texture—a mystery. Until now.

Nick's Short Ribs Chili with Many Chiles

Time: 25 minutes,
plus 4 hours' braising
and at least 1 hour
marinating

Serves 6 to 8

FOR THE SPICE PASTE

2 dried ancho chiles

2 dried pasilla negro chiles

1 dried guajillo chile

1 tablespoon cumin seed

1 teaspoon coriander seed

½ cup mild New Mexican chili powder

1 tablespoon chipotle powder

1 teaspoon dried oregano

1¼ teaspoons kosher salt

1 cup chopped fresh cilantro

4 garlic cloves, roughly chopped

2 fresh jalapeño chiles, stemmed, seeded, and roughly chopped

1 fresh serrano chile, stemmed, seeded, and roughly chopped

1 medium onion, cut into chunks

FOR THE BEEF

5 pounds beef short ribs (bone-in), rinsed and patted dry

1 teaspoon kosher salt, more to taste

1 teaspoon freshly ground black pepper

1 cup beer

1 cup chicken broth

1 tablespoon tomato paste

Sliced scallions or onions and chopped fresh cilantro, for serving (optional)

1. To make the pepper paste, place the dried ancho chiles, pasilla negro chiles, and guajillo chile in a large bowl with boiling water to cover. Let stand until the peppers are supple, about 15 minutes. Drain the liquid; stem and seed the chiles.

2. In a small skillet over medium-high heat, lightly toast the cumin and coriander until fragrant, about 1 minute. Transfer to a food processor or blender;

add the New Mexican chili powder, chipotle powder, oregano, and salt, and pulse or process to combine.

3. Add the reconstituted dried chiles, cilantro, garlic, jalapeños, serrano, and onion to the blender or food processor. Add 1½ cups water and puree.

4. Season the short ribs with salt and pepper. Transfer to a 6½-quart Dutch oven or large casserole dish with a lid. Pour the chile-spice mixture over the ribs and turn to coat well. Cover and refrigerate for at least 1 hour or overnight.

5. When you are ready to cook the chili, preheat the oven to 300°F and let the meat come to room temperature. Place the Dutch oven over medium-high heat and stir in the beer, broth, and tomato paste. Bring to a simmer.

6. Cover the pot and transfer to the oven. Cook for 1 hour; uncover and continue cooking, stirring the meat into the sauce every once in a while, until the meat is falling apart and the chili is thickened, 2½ to 3 hours longer. Serve with the scallions or onions and cilantro, if desired.

VARIATION: BEEF, BEAN, AND HOMINY CHILI WITH CILANTRO SOUR CREAM

There's no doubt that Nick's short rib chili recipe has eclipsed mine as the favorite of our chili-loving household. But there are times my husband and I crave a steaming pot of the bean-laden, soupy stuff that we both grew up on. Mine is a fairly classic recipe with the addition of a can of hominy and a topping of cilantro-laden sour cream. But you can omit both of these and the recipe will be just as good, and maybe more like the chili that you and yours grew up on—unless you're from Texas. But then you'd probably have stopped reading this far anyway.

Beef, Bean, and Hominy Chili with Cilantro Sour Cream

Time: 30 minutes,
plus 1½ hours'
simmering

Serves 6 to 8

3 tablespoons olive oil

2 pounds ground beef

3 teaspoons salt

1 teaspoon freshly ground black pepper

1 large Spanish onion, chopped

1 red bell pepper, chopped

1 poblano pepper or green bell pepper, seeded, if desired, and finely chopped

1 jalapeño pepper, seeded, if desired, and finely chopped

4 garlic cloves, finely chopped

¼ cup chili powder (see Note)

1 (28-ounce) can diced tomatoes

2 cups chicken stock

1 (12-ounce) bottle dark beer

2 (15-ounce) cans hominy, drained

1 (15-ounce) can pinto beans, rinsed and drained

1 (15-ounce) can black beans, rinsed and drained

1 teaspoon dried oregano, preferably Mexican

1 bay leaf

1 cup sour cream

3 tablespoons chopped fresh cilantro or chives

1. Heat 1 tablespoon of oil in a large pot over high heat. Brown half the beef, breaking it up with a fork, until cooked through and golden in spots, about 7 minutes. Transfer with a slotted spoon to a plate. Season the meat with ½ teaspoon salt and ¼ teaspoon black pepper. Repeat with the remaining beef and another tablespoon oil, seasoning with more salt and pepper.

2. Return the pot to the stove and add the remaining tablespoon oil. Stir in the onion and peppers and cook, stirring, until softened, about 5 minutes. Stir in the garlic and chili powder and sauté for 2 minutes. Add the tomatoes,

stock, beer, hominy, beans, oregano, bay leaf, and remaining 2 teaspoons salt and ½ teaspoon black pepper. Reduce the heat to medium-low and simmer until thickened, about 1½ hours.

3. Just before serving, stir together the sour cream and cilantro or chives. Ladle the chili into bowls, top with a dollop of sour cream, and serve.

NOTE: You can use regular old chili powder from the supermarket for this and it will come out marvelously. But if you have fancy chili powders from different kinds of chiles, such as chipotle and guajillo and New Mexican, for example, use a mix of them here. It will add a nice complexity to the pot.

QUICK GRILLED FLANKEN WITH CHILI, SESAME, AND GINGER

We are fair-weather grillers. Unlike my parents, who've been known to grill lamb chops under a golf umbrella during a hailstorm in January, my husband and I wait for sunny days and clear nights before lugging the old kettle drum up from the basement.

This past dreary summer, it was a very long wait. But it gave me lots of time to fantasize about what we would finally grill if the rain ever stopped. Burgers, sausages, and steaks were quickly considered and then dismissed. They seemed too ordinary to satisfy such anticipation.

As I envisioned flames lapping the sizzling fat on a hunk of meat, thunderstorms rattled my drafty windows, sending in a chill. Really, what I was in the mood for was a nice, bone-warming braise.

And that got me thinking about flanken.

Flanken, a flavorsome, inexpensive slab of beef cut from the same part of the cow as short ribs, makes the silkiest and most tender pot roast. I've had it simmered into stews and soups, where moist morsels of meat fall off the bone into spoonable chunks.

How would it be grilled?

There are plenty of cuts of meat that cook up nicely both quickly grilled and slowly braised. But to a pot roast–oriented flanken eater like myself, I wouldn't have thought it could go either way.

Then I remembered something I read in Arthur Schwartz's *Jewish Home Cooking*, where Mr. Schwartz confessed to snacking on browned bits of flanken he was searing for a braise.

Flanken, he opined, also has an unbeatable beefy flavor when broiled very rare, if you don't mind that it is somewhat tough.

In fact, not only don't I mind tough, flavorful cuts of meat, I relish the chewing. I find soft, buttery cuts like filet mignon as appealing as pap.

A little more online research revealed that in Korean cuisine, flanken, called kalbi, is often grilled and served rare.

That's it; I was sold. As soon as there was a break in the rain, I ran to pick up some flanken and hauled up the grill.

For a marinade, I decided to go the way of Korea and use the ever-bracing combination of soy sauce, garlic, and chiles as my base. To this, I added brown sugar to deeply caramelize the meat crust, gingerroot, and vinegar for perkiness, and sesame oil for its rich nuttiness. I whirled it all in the blender and slathered it on the meat, saving some of the gutsy mixture to use as a sauce.

When the coals were glowing, it started to drizzle. But no matter; beneath my golf umbrella, I grilled the meat until the insides turned from dark purple to juicy ruby, and the exterior browned and seared. The meat cooked so quickly that we were already snug in the house, happily gnawing on the bones and lapping up the sauce, when the real downpour began.

Quick Grilled Flanken with Chili, Sesame, and Ginger

6 garlic cloves, minced

1-inch piece fresh gingerroot, peeled and chopped

2 tablespoons soy sauce

2 tablespoons rice vinegar, more to taste

2 tablespoons brown sugar

1 teaspoon kosher salt, more to taste

3 tablespoons toasted (Asian) sesame oil, more to taste

1 tablespoon Asian chili sauce, such as sriracha

3 pounds flanken (see Note)

Arugula or sunflower sprouts, for serving

2 tablespoons toasted sesame seeds

Time 20 minutes, plus 30 minutes' marinating to 24 hours' refrigeration

Serves 3 to 4

1. Put the garlic, ginger, soy sauce, vinegar, sugar, and salt into the blender and blend until smooth. Add the sesame oil and chili sauce and blend well.

2. Coat the flanken with just enough of the sesame mixture to cover it all over. Let it marinate for at least 30 minutes at room temperature or up to 24 hours in the refrigerator (the longer, the better).
3. Preheat the grill or broiler. Grill or broil the meat until done to taste, about 4 minutes per side for rare.
4. Toss the greens with a drizzle of sesame oil and rice vinegar and a pinch of salt.
5. Slice the meat (you can slice it off the bones or leave the bones in) and serve over the greens. Sprinkle everything with sesame seeds and more salt if desired, and drizzle with the remaining sesame sauce.

NOTE: If you can't find flanken, feel free to substitute any other cut of steak, adjusting the cooking time with the thickness of the meat. A thin flank or skirt steak will cook in 2 minutes per side for rare. A 2-inch-thick ribeye will take about 3 to 4 minutes per side.

6 Things with Cheese

Of all the unwelcome confessions a person can make on a second date—the federal indictments, unwanted love children, propensity for cross-dressing or partner swapping—abstaining from dairy products ranks pretty low. But it was almost enough for me never to want to see Daniel ever again.

Up until that soul-baring moment, it had been a perfectly delightful date. There was an art exhibit, cocktails, a long walk, all peppered with that kind of sparkling getting-to-know-you repartee that you have with a person you're madly attracted to. Eventually, our stomachs growling, the conversation turned to culinary matters, like where to stop for dinner.

We were on Lexington Avenue in the 30s, a neighborhood nicknamed Curry Hill for its plethora of Indian restaurants, and I was in the mood for fried paneer, a fresh Indian cheese that was deep-fried until the center turned molten while the exterior became brittle and crisp, served in a chili-spiked curry sauce. I told Daniel all about it, giddy with excitement.

"That sounds great," Daniel said. "But I don't eat dairy."

What?

"It makes me congested and aggravates my asthma."

Ugh, I thought, can I be serious about a man with whom I cannot share a pizza or a cheese plate, or feed runny spoonfuls of ripe vacherin?

I imagined us as a couple far into the future, with me having to take full responsibility for the contents of the entire pint of vanilla fudge swirl. Did I really want to do that? (Perhaps more to the point, could my skinny jeans handle that?)

I decided I didn't, and was about to get an excruciating, date-ending headache.

But then, for some reason—perhaps my two prior divorces with cheese-eating men had something to do with it—I stayed.

We ended up at a dive bar, eating burgers (mine with cheese, his with bacon—whew, I thought, at least he eats meat) and talking all night.

Five years and one daughter later, we're still together, and my cooking style has changed dramatically. I still use plenty of butter (which for some unknown reason Daniel can eat), but think twice before adding cream to soup or cheese to pasta. Daniel wouldn't mind if I did; he just wouldn't partake.

"I'm very tolerant of cheese; I just choose not to eat it," he always says.

But if there's one thing this marriage has taught me, it's that I like eating out of one pot more than I like eating dairy products. So in the interest of sharing, when we're supping together, I abstain, too. But I still consume plenty of milk, cream, and cheese—for my solitary breakfasts and lunches, or at restaurants with friends.

Moreover, since I'm a food writer, there are times when I'll just have to whip up a Cheddar-gooey dish of mac and cheese, or a vat of creamy New England clam chowder to develop a recipe for work. You might even say that this entire chapter was one big, long excuse to indulge in all my favorite, cheese-a-licious dishes.

And you'd be right.

HOMEMADE SPAETZLE WITH BROWNED ONIONS, SWISS CHARD, AND EMMENTALER

My ex-husband Joe was of Italian and Irish descent, not a smidgen of German blood in him. But that didn't stop him from celebrating Oktoberfest like a Bavarian every year. That meant stocking the bathtub of our fifth-floor walk-up with bottles and mini-kegs of imported beer, buying mounds of sausages and smoked pork chops from the German butcher uptown, and inviting all our friends over for an all-night feast.

At the beginning of our relationship, when we still lived in a cramped apartment in the East Village, we kept it copious but simple. We broiled the sausages and served them with sweet German mustard, black bread, pretzels, and coleslaw; that was as ambitious as we got. But the food was almost beside the point. Our friends at the time came for the beer, which Joe lovingly and carefully selected and lugged up the stairs—and, one year, even home brewed using a kit I had bought him for Christmas the preceding year.

When we moved to Brooklyn and could spread out in a kitchen the size of an actual room instead of a closet, we expanded the buffet. The sausages were still the centerpiece, surrounded by smoked pork chops and several types of German ham. We also started serving liverwurst, which we bought at the German butcher and spread on rye toasts that I painted with anchovy-garlic–hot paprika butter.

One year, it occurred to us that the coleslaw needed company. So I started braising red cabbage and apples in wine and lingonberry jam. And as a hearty vegetarian dish to offer our ever-widening circle of friends, Joe and I began making our own spaetzle, tiny egg-rich dumplings topped with browned onions and cheese.

Actually, to say Joe and I made the spaetzle by ourselves would be misleading. The recipe we were using called for three pairs of hands—one pair to hold the colander over the boiling water, one pair to pour the batter into the colander, and one pair to constantly stir the water receiving the spaetzle drips. Fueled by pilsner and mulled wine, we highly anticipated this part of the early stages of the party, and whoever showed up first was enlisted to help.

Once the spaetzle were made, we layered them in a gratin dish with grated Emmentaler cheese and soft, caramelized onions that I had sautéed earlier in the day. Then we baked everything until the cheese was bubbling and browned on top. It was gone within minutes of being served, which I always thought was a shame since leftover spaetzle, fried up for breakfast, sounds divine. Every year I promised to hold some aside for the next day, and every year I ended up eating it before the night was done. Spaetzle is just that kind of food; it lures you to the bottom of the dish, and then you're sorry it's gone.

When Joe and I broke up and the Oktoberfest parties ceased, I stopped making spaetzle for several years straight. It was too much work, I thought, whenever I craved the tiny little dumplings, requiring too many hands.

Then one day my cousins sent me a gift from their travels in Germany: a shiny stainless steel spaetzle maker, the kind that sits on top of the pot of boiling water, and obviates the need at least for one of the extra pair of hands.

But being that I was living alone at the time of the gift, and that I still thought I needed someone to stir the water, it took me months to unpack the box. When I did I read the instructions, thankfully translated into English, which didn't mention anything about stirring the water. In fact, it seemed like I could make the spaetzle all by myself, which meant there'd surely be enough left over for breakfast the next day—and several days following (barring unforeseen gluttony).

So I set about making myself a batch.

First I caramelized the onions. While they were browning, I rifled through the fridge, looking for something to make into a salad. A dish this rich needs something green to eat alongside. Even at the Oktoberfest party, I'd nibble my cheesy spaetzle with a serving of dilled cucumber salad.

There were no salad greens or cucumbers, but there was a bushy bunch of dark green Swiss chard. I could throw that into the pan with the onions and get my green and my gooey cheese in the same bite. And Swiss chard would surely go well with the Swiss Emmentaler cheese I was using.

I tried it, adding the chard to the pan with the onions and letting them wilt, then stirring the mixture into the homemade spaetzle.

While it was baking, a friend from the neighborhood called and asked what I was doing for dinner. I invited her over, and she brought another friend as well. The three of us devoured the spaetzle hot from the oven, washed down with crisp white wine instead of beer.

By the time my friends left, there wasn't a spaetzle crumb left and I resigned myself to oatmeal for breakfast. But it was easy enough to make again. Perhaps next time I'll try a double batch.

Homemade Spaetzle with Browned Onions, Swiss Chard, and Emmentaler

1½ tablespoons unsalted butter

1 large Spanish onion, halved and thinly sliced

1 large thyme sprig

1 teaspoon and pinch kosher salt, plus additional for cooking water

1 small bunch Swiss chard or beet greens, stems discarded,
    leaves cut into pieces

2¼ cups all-purpose flour

¼ teaspoon freshly grated nutmeg

2 large eggs, lightly beaten

¾ cup milk

2 cups (about 8 ounces) grated Emmentaler or Gruyère cheese

Time: 1 hour, plus
30 minutes' baking

Serves 6 to 8
as a side dish,
4 as an entrée

1. In a large skillet over medium-high heat, melt the butter and add the onion and thyme, stirring briefly to coat with the butter. Allow the onion to cook, without stirring, until it starts to get dark brown, then add a pinch of salt and stir occasionally until the onion is tender and caramelized, about 30 minutes total.

2. Stir in the Swiss chard or beet greens and cook until tender, 3 to 5 minutes, then transfer the mixture to a large bowl.

3. To make the spaetzle, combine the flour, nutmeg, and teaspoon of salt in a large bowl. In a separate bowl, whisk together the eggs and milk. Make a well in the dry ingredients and pour in the egg mixture. Mix well with a wooden spoon.

4. Fill a large bowl with ice water and keep it nearby. Place the dough in a spaetzle maker over a large pot of boiling salted water. Shave the dough into the water (alternatively, push the dough through a colander into the water). When the dumplings rise to the surface, use a slotted spoon to transfer them to the bowl of ice water.

5. Preheat the oven to 375°F. Drain the spaetzle well and transfer to the bowl with the onions and greens. Sprinkle in three-quarters of the cheese and mix to combine.

6. Scrape the spaetzle mixture into a 2-quart gratin dish, sprinkle on the remaining cheese, and bake for 25 to 30 minutes, until the top is golden brown and bubbling. Serve immediately. If there is any left over, save it for breakfast and serve it fried. Then write and tell me all about it.

CHIC QUICHE

I almost missed the boat on quiche.

I was born too late to enjoy its luscious '70s revival, and by the time the '80s staggered in, New York City cafes were overrun with unappetizing, broccoli-laden cheesy pies. Bumpy-topped and greasy, they were zapped in the microwave before being served forth, unappetizing and leaden.

I was so turned off that when I spent a college semester in Paris, it didn't even occur to me to eat quiche with the French. After all, when lunching in a cute Paris restaurant overlooking the Seine, why risk the quiche when the omelets are so ethereally fluffy and the artisanal bread sandwiches are spread with sweet butter and strewn with gossamer slices of pink *jambon*?

Eventually, the quiche craze in New York died down, and the stuff virtually vanished from my life for years.

Then one day, around the time the Julie/Julia movie came out, I flipped through my old Julia Child cookbook on a crisp autumn afternoon and ran right into the quiche chapter.

"A quiche hot out of the oven, a salad, and a cool bottle of white wine— there's the perfect light meal," Julia wrote.

It is? I was intrigued.

Her recipe for quiche Lorraine was as plain and chic as a little black dress—a homemade all-butter crust filled with heavy cream, eggs, bacon, and a dainty pinch of nutmeg.

There was no cheese, no broccoli, no overcooked asparagus or soggy mushrooms to interfere with its innate elegance. Just pork, dairy, and salt, served hot from the oven. What could be bad about that? After all, there must have been a reason that quiche became so popular in the first place.

As soon as I could manage it, I finagled a quiche-making excuse by inviting a friend over for lunch, and whipped up Julia's recipe.

Well, sort of. What I did was merge two of her recipes, the cheeseless quiche Lorraine studded with bits of bacon with her dainty quiche au from-

220

age, imbued with Swiss cheese. As much as I wanted to embrace the ideal of culinary purity by using one recipe or the other, I simply could not choose between the bacon and the cheese. I wanted them both, in one crust, at the same time.

But while it was baking I started to worry. Although combining bacon and cheese wasn't even close to the broccoli-mushroom-olive horrors of my youth, it also wasn't as minimalist as what Julia suggested, and I feared my custard would be heavy and overcrowded instead of buoyant, jiggly, and silky as Julia described.

Nonetheless, my quiche certainly smelled pretty good while in the oven. Once the center was just set, I pulled it out, cut two thick slices, and my friend and I dug in.

The custard was suffused with cheese flavor but was still light and satiny and not at all weighed down. And the nuggets of bacon added just the right salty-meaty note against the sweet, milky mellowness of the cream. It was still highly sophisticated, maybe not to the plain little black dress degree but maybe to one spruced up, let's say, with a nice Hermès scarf.

Chic Quiche

Time: 1¼ hours

Serves 8

1 recipe Perfect Piecrust (see page 391)

QUICHE FILLING
1 large egg white
3 tablespoons grated Gruyère cheese (about ¾ ounce)
5 strips bacon (about 6 ounces), cut into ½-inch strips
3 large eggs
1½ cups heavy cream
¼ teaspoon freshly grated nutmeg
¼ teaspoon kosher salt
¼ teaspoon freshly ground black pepper
1 tablespoon unsalted butter, cubed

1. Preheat the oven to 375°F. On a lightly floured surface, roll the dough to a ⅜-inch thickness and press into a 9-inch pie pan. Line the dough with foil and fill with pie weights, rice, or dried beans. Bake for 20 minutes, then remove the weights and foil and bake for an additional 5 to 7 minutes, until lightly golden.

2. Take the crust out of the oven and brush the bottom of the crust with the egg white, then sprinkle on the Gruyère in an even layer. Return the crust to the oven and bake for 10 to 13 minutes, until the cheese is lightly browned.

3. Meanwhile, in a large pan over medium heat, cook the bacon for 7 to 10 minutes, or until lightly browned but not yet crispy. Drain the bacon on a paper towel–lined plate.

4. In a medium bowl, whisk together the eggs, cream, nutmeg, salt, and pepper.

5. When the crust is lightly browned and the cheese is melted, sprinkle in the bacon pieces and carefully pour in the custard. Dot the top with the butter pieces and return to the oven. Bake for 25 to 35 minutes, until the top of the quiche is puffed up and golden and the middle is almost set. Allow to cool slightly, about 15 minutes, before serving.

VARIATION: CARAMELIZED ONION AND RADICCHIO QUICHE

I'll admit that this vegetarian quiche variation treads perilously close to the hated broccoli quiches of yore. But I wanted to create a meatless version that was as restrained yet savory as the original, only without the pork. I chose a filling of caramelized onions for their sweet earthiness paired with shredded radicchio, which adds a bitter, complex, and umami-ish flavor to the mix without overloading it with vegetable matter. Plus, instead of stirring all of the radicchio and onions into the custard, I only use a small amount, enough to flavor the delicate custard without overwhelming it. The rest of the soft, jammy mixture makes a pungent, honeyed garnish on the side.

Caramelized Onion and Radicchio Quiche

Time: 1 hour
and 25 minutes

Serves 8

1 recipe Perfect Piecrust (see page 391)

1 large egg white
3 tablespoons grated Gruyère cheese (about ¾ ounce)
3 tablespoons extra-virgin olive oil
1 large red onion, halved and thinly sliced
1¼ teaspoons kosher salt
¼ teaspoon sugar
1 medium radicchio, halved and thinly sliced (about 8 ounces)
1 teaspoon balsamic vinegar
3 large eggs
1½ cups heavy cream
¼ teaspoon freshly grated nutmeg
½ teaspoon freshly ground black pepper
1 tablespoon unsalted butter, cubed
Pinch fleur de sel

1. Preheat the oven to 375°F. On a lightly floured surface, roll the dough to a ⅜-inch thickness and press into a 9-inch pie pan. Line the dough with foil and fill with pie weights, rice, or dried beans. Bake for 20 minutes, then remove the weights and foil and bake for an additional 5 to 7 minutes, until lightly golden.
2. Take the crust out of the oven and brush the bottom of the crust with the egg white and sprinkle on the Gruyère in an even layer. Return the crust to the oven and bake for 10 to 13 minutes, until lightly browned.
3. Meanwhile, in a large pan, heat 2 tablespoons of oil over medium heat. Add the onion, ½ teaspoon salt, and sugar, and cook, stirring occasionally, until the onion is soft and browned, about 15 minutes.
4. Stir in the radicchio and the remaining tablespoon oil and ¼ teaspoon salt and cook, stirring constantly, until the radicchio is very wilted and jammy, about 10 minutes. Stir in the balsamic vinegar and cook 1 minute more.

5. In a medium bowl, whisk together the eggs, cream, nutmeg, the remaining ¾ teaspoon salt, and pepper.

6. When the crust is lightly browned and the cheese is melted, sprinkle on ½ cup of the radicchio-onion mixture and carefully pour in the custard. Dot the top with the butter pieces, sprinkle on the fleur de sel, and return to the oven. Bake for 25 to 35 minutes, until the top of the quiche is puffed up and golden and the middle is almost set. Allow the quiche to cool slightly, about 10 minutes, before serving with the remaining radicchio-onion mixture sprinkled on top.

CHEESY BAKED PUMPKIN
WITH GRUYÈRE FONDUE

"Want to hear about the latest sick thing my sister Susan made?"

It was my friend Karen on the phone. Her sister Susan is a pastry chef known for her decadent cooking. Susan is the kind of person who slathers her toast with so much butter you can see it rise up in white waves from the side view. She's been known to poach her eggs in bacon fat, and always has pints of ice cream, frozen homemade fudge sauce, nuts, sprinkles, and heavy cream on hand, just in case an afternoon ice cream sundae emergency should strike.

So I was prepared for something with a high butterfat content. But even so, the cheesy pumpkin took me by surprise.

Based on a Ruth Reichl recipe for pumpkin soup, cheesy pumpkin consists of filling the hollowed-out vegetable with layers of grated cheese and slices of French bread, and pouring in enough heavy cream to cover it all. It is then baked until the cheese melts into the cream, creating a glossy fondue that coats the softened pumpkin like cheese sauce, but richer.

Naturally, I had to make it. But as I found myself confronted with the necessary ingredients—the pound of cheese, loaf of bread, and quart of heavy cream—I got cold feet. After all, even if I did share it with my friends and neighbors, I knew I'd still eat the majority of it. And seeing the amount of cream and cheese laid out in front of me was, as Karen said, a little sick.

I wanted to cut the cream by adding another liquid, so I considered my options. Milk would make it lighter, but wouldn't add anything to the taste, so it seemed like a wasted opportunity. Chicken broth would add a meaty complexity, and I was about to defrost some when another thought hit me. White wine would not only lighten the cheese sauce, it would add brightness and make the filling even more fondue-like.

I also threw some sage into the filling because I like how the piney-ness of sage offsets the sweet denseness of winter squashes and cream.

As a final touch, I oiled the skin of the pumpkin and sprinkled it with salt in the hope that it would crisp up in the oven, and the salty, crunchy pumpkin skin would make a textured, savory contrast to all the richness contained in its belly.

While it baked, I pondered what to do with the massive amounts of leftovers I was sure I'd have, considering I'd invited only one friend over for dinner and my husband doesn't eat cream or cheese. Would the baby eat it? Would it freeze well? Just how much could I foist onto my health-conscious neighbors?

But once it emerged from the oven, steaming and runny and aromatic, I knew I didn't have to worry. My friend and I polished off half of it for dinner right then and there, and the rest I nibbled my way through in the course of a few days. It might have been sick, but in the best possible way.

Cheesy Baked Pumpkin with Gruyère Fondue

6 (1-inch) slices baguette
½ cup heavy cream
½ cup dry white wine
¼ cup milk
1 large garlic clove, peeled and smashed
3 fresh sage leaves
½ teaspoon kosher salt, plus additional for rub
½ teaspoon freshly grated nutmeg
¼ teaspoon freshly ground black pepper
1 (3- to 4-pound) sugar pumpkin, well scrubbed
5 ounces grated Gruyère cheese (1¼ cups)
1 tablespoon extra-virgin olive oil

Time: 1½ hours

Serves 4 to 6

1. Preheat the oven to 425°F. Cut the baguette slices in half lengthwise and place on a baking sheet. Bake until golden brown, 5 to 7 minutes.
2. In a medium saucepan, bring the cream, wine, milk, garlic, and sage to a boil over medium heat. Reduce the heat to low and allow to simmer for

5 minutes. Take the mixture off the heat and discard the garlic and sage. Stir in ½ teaspoon of salt, the nutmeg, and the pepper.

3. Cut the top off the pumpkin and scoop out the pulp and seeds (if you want to toast your own pumpkin seeds, and I always do, see Note). Set the pumpkin in a baking dish. Place a layer of bread in the bottom, followed by a layer of the cheese. Pour in a third of the cream mixture. Repeat for 2 more layers and replace the pumpkin lid. Using your fingers, rub the oil all over the outside of the pumpkin and sprinkle on additional salt.

4. Bake the pumpkin until the skin blisters and the flesh is fork-tender, about 1¼ hours. Allow to cool in the pan slightly, then quarter to serve.

NOTE: **TOASTED PUMPKIN SEEDS**

Preheat the oven to 325°F. Separate the seeds from the pulp, rinsing if necessary, and place on a rimmed baking sheet. Coat the seeds with ½ tablespoon extra-virgin olive oil and a generous pinch of kosher salt. Bake until the seeds are crisp and golden brown, 12 to 15 minutes.

EASY STOVETOP MACARONI, PEAS, BACON, AND CHEESE À LA JAMIE OLIVER

There comes a point for every homemade organic baby food–producing mom when she's confronted with the crack of kids' food: boxed macaroni and cheese. No matter how many butternut squashes she lovingly bakes and purees, no matter how many marble-size meatballs she rolls and sets atop whole wheat fusilli, the lure of soggy elbows slathered in cheesy sauce is too much for most any child to resist.

Dahlia has yet to reach the age of the playdate mac and cheese onslaught, but I know it's coming. Other, wiser mothers have warned me, and I'm not planning to resist the boxes of Annie's lining the shelves at stroller height of every convenience store in brownstone Brooklyn.

It's just that I also feel as if I should have one simple but terrific recipe for a quick, homemade stovetop mac and cheese manqué in my repertoire. It should be something tasty enough for grown-ups to eat, too, preferably with a different flavor profile than the Cheddar-y sauce in the box so that Dahlia wouldn't compare them—once she got old enough to speak grown-up, that is.

All this was percolating in my brain when I read a *New York Times* magazine story on chef Jamie Oliver. In it was a recipe for his tiny shell pasta with peas, cream, cheese, and mint. The article said he makes it for his kids, and it sounded incredibly yummy—reason enough to go ahead and try it to see if it filled the bill.

But honestly, the clincher that made me clip out Oliver's recipe was that his daughters and mine all have flower names, and it amused me to imagine Daisy, Poppy, Petal, and my Dahlia eating the same pasta and herb-strewn dish.

His recipe was definitely on the decadent side, containing bacon, butter, olive oil, Parmesan, *and* crème fraîche. But fat equals flavor, and I loved that Oliver mixed in mint and lemon to brighten the taste and frozen green peas to pep up the color. Plus, even if Dahlia ended up spitting it all out, she'd at least enjoy using her newly perfected pincer grip to move noodles and peas to her mouth.

I made only a few adjustments to Oliver's original, substituting basil for the mint because I had somehow managed to murder the mint plant on my deck while the basil was still flourishing (I know, mint is virtually impossible to kill, but not entirely impossible).

I also drastically reduced the amount of bacon from ten slices to two, and upped the crème fraîche. There were only two slices of bacon left in the package, and since I had purchased an entire tub of crème fraîche to make the dish, I figured I might as well use more of it (it would also compensate for the dearth of bacon fat).

I mixed it up while Dahlia was still out with her babysitter and summoned every ounce of willpower in my body not to devour the entire pot. The bacon flavor was subtle, adding more of a smoky than meaty note. And not surprising to anyone who loves pasta carbonara, it melded perfectly with the pasta, cream, and cheese.

Dahlia daintily ate her portion, lifting the pasta and peas to her lips piece by piece while I looked on, hoping she'd feed me some. She didn't, but I made up for it later when she was in bed. And while I munched, I mentally thanked Jamie Oliver for cooking such good food for his three precious flowers—and sharing the recipe so I could feed it to mine.

Easy Stovetop Macaroni, Peas, Bacon, and Cheese à la Jamie Oliver

Kosher salt

8 ounces elbow or tiny shells pasta

1 tablespoon unsalted butter

1 teaspoon extra-virgin olive oil

2 strips bacon (2 ounces), cut into thin strips (optional)

Pinch freshly ground black pepper

1½ cups frozen peas

3 tablespoons crème fraîche or heavy cream

2 tablespoons chopped fresh basil or mint

2 teaspoons freshly squeezed lemon juice, or to taste
(if using cream, use a little more)

½ cup grated Parmesan cheese, plus additional for garnishing

Time: 15 minutes

Serves 2 to 3

1. In a large pot of salted water, cook the pasta according to the package directions. Drain well.

2. In a large skillet over medium heat, melt the butter with the oil. Add the bacon, if using, and the pepper and cook until the bacon is golden brown and crispy, 5 to 7 minutes.

3. Stir in the peas and cook for a minute to defrost. Add the crème fraîche and the basil or mint and cook, stirring constantly, until bubbling, 2 to 3 minutes. Carefully add the pasta and drizzle with the lemon juice. Stir in the cheese until the pasta is completely coated and the mixture is creamy. Serve garnished with additional cheese, if desired.

VARIATION: EVEN EASIER ONE-HANDED MACARONI WITH CREAMY PEAS AND CHEESE

This is a streamlined version of Jamie Oliver's recipe that substitutes pungent sage for salty bacon. I know, it's not the same, but it makes for happier vegetarians, and is so easy that you can stir it together with one hand while holding your toddler on your hip with the other. I've done it!

Even Easier One-Handed Macaroni with Creamy Peas and Cheese

Time: 10 minutes

Serves 2 adults
or numerous
small children

Kosher salt

8 ounces macaroni or tiny shells pasta (2 cups)

$2/3$ cup frozen peas

$2/3$ cup heavy cream

2 large sage sprigs

1 fat garlic clove, minced

$1/2$ teaspoon freshly grated lemon zest (optional)

$1/2$ cup grated Parmesan cheese, more to taste

$1/4$ teaspoon freshly grated nutmeg

Pinch freshly ground black pepper

1. In a large pot of salted water, cook the pasta according to the package directions. About 30 seconds before the pasta is done to taste, stir in the frozen peas. Drain well.

2. While the pasta is cooking, in a medium saucepan, bring the cream, sage, garlic, and lemon zest (if using) to a simmer for about 3 minutes. Stir in the cheese, nutmeg, pepper, pasta, and peas. Stir well until the pasta is coated with the sauce and season with salt to taste. Serve hot, discarding the sage.

SONIA'S PHYLLO AND FETA CHEESE TORTE WITH DILL AND NUTMEG

A few years ago, when my then-boyfriend, now-husband brought me to a dinner party, I expected to be intimidated. The host, Roger, is an esteemed professor of French literature, and I'd heard that his parties were multilingual, highly intellectual affairs.

Memories of graduate school still throbbing, I worried that I couldn't keep up. But, I figured, if the conversation got entrenched in the minutia of postmodern theory, I could simply go hang out in the kitchen, where I'm always comfortable.

I had it all wrong. Roger and his friends were warm and chatty and barely even mentioned Derrida.

The intimidation came in the kitchen. That's where I caught Roger's wife, Sonia, unmolding a magnificent, domed pastry creation with a gilded crust.

I *ooh*ed and *aah*ed.

"It's a feta cheese torte, my mother's recipe from Athens," she said, slicing it into pieces. The pale, soft center was nubby textured and flecked with herbs, and the phyllo shattered into glistening shards when it met the knife. I snatched a still-warm morsel from the pan. It was savory from the cheese, sweet from spice, and crunchy from the brittle, buttery phyllo layers.

The torte, Sonia said, was a specialty for Greek Orthodox Easter. She mentioned something about its being easy, but I didn't believe her. Sonia spent her early childhood in Greece. Phyllo wrangling is in her blood.

It isn't in mine. So assuming the torte would be too labor intensive, I didn't ask for the recipe.

Since then, it has haunted me every spring when I remember its rich, tangy filling fragrant with pungent sheep's milk feta, nutmeg, and dill.

Maybe it was coming off a month of doctor-enforced dairy deprivation, but this year, I craved that torte so fiercely that nothing short of having to make my own phyllo would stop me from making it. I called Sonia for the recipe.

"Do you have to make your own phyllo?" I asked tentatively.

"Absolutely not," Sonia said. "You don't even have to butter the layers. You just pour melted butter over the top."

That did seem easy. The only hard part was finding a Greek (not domestic) feta to meet Sonia's exacting standards.

"Make sure to taste it first. It shouldn't be too salty," she counseled.

Not being a connoisseur of feta cheese, I bought the only Greek one in the store.

When I got home, though, I realized it was on the salty side, even when mixed with the cottage cheese and seasonings in the recipe. So I added a little more cottage cheese to balance things out. Then I spooned it into the phyllo-lined Bundt pan, poked some holes into the pastry, and poured a river of butter on top. An hour and change later, I pulled the torte from the oven. It had puffed and browned gloriously.

I immediately exited the kitchen; it was all I could do not to tear into the torte before it cooled enough to unmold.

Finally, I sliced myself a small piece. It was melting, luscious, and just salty enough—just as I remembered, minus the intimidation factor. And all the sweeter for that.

Sonia's Phyllo and Feta Cheese Torte with Dill and Nutmeg

1 pound Greek feta cheese

3 cups cottage cheese

3 eggs

1/3 cup chopped fresh dill

1/4 cup grated Romano cheese

1/2 teaspoon freshly grated nutmeg

1/2 teaspoon freshly ground black pepper

1 (1-pound) box phyllo dough, defrosted

1½ cups (3 sticks) unsalted butter, melted

Honey, for drizzling (optional)

Time: 1 hour and 25 minutes, plus cooling time

Makes 1 (9-inch) torte
Serves 10 to 12

1. Preheat the oven to 375°F.
2. Into the bowl of a food processor, place the feta, cottage cheese, eggs, dill, 2 tablespoons of Romano, the nutmeg, and pepper, and pulse just to combine. The mixture should still be chunky.
3. Sprinkle the remaining 2 tablespoons Romano into a Bundt pan. Taking the sheets of phyllo two at a time, drape them over the pan, poking the center through the sheets and pushing them down to line the pan. The edges of the sheets should hang over the edges of the pan.
4. Scrape the cheese filling into the phyllo-lined pan, and fold the edges of the dough over the filling, sealing the bottom of the torte. Using a sharp knife, poke at least 20 holes in the dough that reach all the way from the bottom to the top of the torte. Slowly pour the melted butter over the torte; some of the butter will seep through the holes and some will remain on top of the dough.
5. Place the Bundt pan on a baking sheet and bake for about 1¼ hours, or until the torte is puffy and golden brown. Allow the torte to cool in the pan for 1 to 2 hours before inverting onto a plate and slicing. Serve drizzled with honey, if desired. This torte can be served as an appetizer, a light lunch, a cheese course, or even a savory dessert if drizzled with enough honey.

VARIATION: SWEET PHYLLO AND RICOTTA CHEESE TORTE WITH HONEY AND WALNUTS

Making a sweet version of Sonia's feta torte was my mother's idea. Executing it, though, took several tries. Without the feta cheese to help bind the filling, the cottage cheese was too runny and made the phyllo woefully soggy.

Ricotta cheese, however, worked quite well, no matter if you use the thick, fluffy stuff you get at specialty markets or the softer and grainier cheese from the supermarket. I made it both ways out of curiosity (and hunger). The supermarket ricotta gives the torte a lighter, looser texture while the gourmet cheese is denser and more cheesecake-like. But they are both wonderful. Drizzle this with your best Greek honey.

Sweet Phyllo and Ricotta Cheese Torte with Honey and Walnuts

Time: 1 hour
and 25 minutes,
plus cooling time

Serves 10 to 12

3 eggs, lightly beaten

1/4 cup sugar

1/2 teaspoon freshly grated nutmeg

1/2 teaspoon ground cinnamon

4 cups ricotta

1 (1-pound) box phyllo dough, defrosted

1/2 cup chopped walnuts, toasted

1 1/2 cups (3 sticks) unsalted butter, melted

1/4 cup your best honey

1. Preheat the oven to 375°F.
2. Into the bowl of a food processor, combine the eggs, sugar, nutmeg, and cinnamon, and pulse to mix well. Pulse in the ricotta just enough to incorporate it; the mixture should still be chunky.
3. Taking the sheets of phyllo two at a time, drape them over the pan, poking the center through the sheets and pushing them down to line the pan. The

edges of the sheets should hang over the edges of the pan. Sprinkle ¼ cup of the walnuts into the phyllo-lined pan.

4. Scrape the cheese filling into the phyllo-lined pan, and fold the edges of the dough over the filling, sealing the bottom of the torte. Using a sharp knife, poke at least 20 holes in the dough that reach all the way from the bottom to the top of the torte. Slowly pour the melted butter over the torte; some of the butter will seep through the holes and some will remain on top of the dough.

5. Place the Bundt pan on a baking sheet and bake for about 1¼ hours, or until the torte is puffy and golden brown. Allow the torte to cool in the pan for 1 to 2 hours before inverting onto a plate. Drizzle the honey all over the top and sprinkle with the remaining ¼ cup walnuts.

BAKED CAMEMBERT WITH WALNUT CRUMBLE AND GINGER MARMALADE

I love everything about baked Brie—the oozing, creamy texture, the flaky, buttery pastry, even the too-sweet raspberry jam some people dollop on top. I love it all, except, perhaps, the Brie itself.

Supermarket Brie is bland and boring stuff. Waxy, flavorless, and altogether unappealing in its natural, unmelted state, it morphs into something voluptuous and wonderfully gooey when wrapped in puff pastry and baked. I don't usually eat solid Brie, but warm and runny and scooped up onto a cracker at a cocktail party? It puts a sway in my hips as I stand over the platter, eating as many molten globs as I can without embarrassing myself.

It turns out, however, that not everyone is as enamored of baked Brie as I am. Or so I learned at a party at my house a few years ago when I overheard a snarky, unrepeatable remark. While my group of stinky-cheese–loving friends gobbled it up, they took its inclusion on the buffet table to be ironic, baked Brie with a wink. I went along, playing up its kitsch factor without ever admitting my true feelings.

Recently, in planning the menu for another party, I thought about serving baked Brie again, mostly because I was craving it. But this was a serious, elegant, fancy party, the first I'd thrown since the baby was born. The menu also included the likes of cornmeal blinis with salmon roe, a foie gras terrine I'd gotten as a gift, and imported Iberico ham, the kind from acorn-eating, oak forest–cavorting pigs with dainty black feet. Somehow baked Brie just wouldn't fit in.

Still, I wanted it, and figured there must be some way to gussy it up enough to make it food snob–worthy.

My first thought was to use real, noble, imported Brie de Meaux from France. With its straw-colored center redolent of wild mushrooms, fresh cream, and a little funk, it's the magnificent original that all inferior American

Bries are based upon. Made from raw milk and aged for less than the requisite sixty days, it's an illegal rarity in this country. Even if I could find it, I wouldn't desecrate it by putting it in the oven.

But, I thought, I could use another intensely flavored, washed-rind cheese with a similar texture. Camembert jumped to mind. It has the same gooey interior as Brie, but with a more pungent personality.

I had pretty much sold myself on the idea, but just to make sure it would live up to the hype in my brain, I wanted to do a test run before the party.

I gathered my ingredients, including some ginger marmalade (a raspberry jam stand-in that would add a sweet and spicy contrast to the cheese without being cloying) and some walnuts for crunch.

Then I toasted the walnuts to deepen their flavor. The house quickly filled with the scent of browning nuts. It was an autumnal, rich, cold-weather scent that reminded me of apple pie, preferably the kind with a crumble on top. It made me wonder how a nut-filled crumble would taste on top of baked Camembert, especially if I cut the sugar down to the barest minimum.

Now was the time to try it since this baked Camembert experimentation would be seen only by me (and maybe my neighbor, if it wasn't awful). And if it was awful, I could toss the evidence and no one would be the wiser.

When the walnuts had cooled, I rubbed them between my hands with butter, flour, and a sprinkling of sugar until crumbs formed, then dotted them all over the cheese, wrapped it in pastry, and set it to bake (first putting it into a gratin dish to catch any ooze).

Half an hour later, when the pastry was golden and the cheese bubbling up around the edges, I pulled it from the oven and sat on my hands until it cooled just enough not to burn my tongue. Then I cut myself a delicate wedge.

The first taste to hit my tongue was butter from the pastry, followed by crunchy, crumbly nuts and a zippy sweetness from the ginger jam that dissolved into a pleasingly strong, tangy flavor from the cheese. As I chewed, I analyzed. Was there too much crumble? Not enough jam? Was the slightly musky flavor of the cheese a good match for the ginger, or would orange marmalade be better?

I wasn't sure, so I took another little slice.

Everything seemed just right as it was. But just to be ultra certain, I hacked off a sliver. And then another one, this time to even everything out.

Then I sat on my hands again and thought about whether my baked cheese was elegant enough for the big party.

Camembert was definitely a more assertive base for the marmalade and pastry than Brie, and the crumble added an unusual and delectable textural contrast. I wouldn't go so far as to call it sophisticated. Maybe *classy* is a better word. But I'll be serving it at that party. No matter what the snarks say, I bet they finish every crumb.

Baked Camembert with Walnut Crumble and Ginger Marmalade

Time: 35 minutes

Serves 8 to 10

⅔ cup chopped toasted walnuts

3 tablespoons all-purpose flour

2 tablespoons unsalted butter

1 tablespoon dark brown sugar

Pinch kosher salt

1 recipe Perfect Piecrust (see page 391), or 12 ounces prepared puff pastry (optional, see Notes)

2 (5-inch-round) Camembert cheese wheels

¼ cup ginger or bitter orange marmalade

1 large egg, lightly beaten

1. Preheat the oven to 350°F and line a baking sheet with foil. In a medium bowl, use your fingers to combine the walnuts, flour, butter, brown sugar, and salt. Gently rub the mixture together until it forms large crumbs.

2. Divide the pie dough and, on a floured surface, roll out into 2 rounds about ¼ inch thick (or unfold the puff pastry and cut into 2 pieces). Place the Camembert cheese rounds in the center of each of the dough rounds. Spread the tops of both cheeses with the marmalade, then cover with the walnut streusel. Fold the dough over the cheeses to make 2 packets. Brush each packet with the egg.

3. Set the packets into one large or two small gratin dish(es) and place on the prepared sheet pans. Bake the packets for 25 to 30 minutes for the pie pastry and 30 to 40 for the puff pastry, or until the crust is golden brown (some of the cheese may bubble out, especially from the pie pastry; puff pastry is sturdier). Serve warm.

NOTES:

You can halve this recipe if you're feeding a smaller or less greedy bunch.

If you would rather skip wrapping the cheese in a pastry crust, you can. Instead, cut the tops off the cheese rounds and place the cheeses into gratin dishes. Spread with the marmalade and sprinkle with the streusel, then bake for about 20 minutes, until the cheese is bubbling and the streusel is toasted. It's easier and very nearly as good, though I'm a sucker for the pastry. Also, the puff pastry, while easier and neater than the pie dough, isn't really quite as good. If you can make your own pie dough here, I think it's worth it.

PORT-GLAZED STILTON WITH HOMEMADE OAT BISCUITS

Back at the early stages of my career, when I was trying to make a name for myself writing cookbooks with chefs, *Food & Wine* magazine did a multipage feature on one of my effortless and enticing holiday cocktail parties, the kind with a dozen different hors d'oeuvres and six different libations. You know, the kind of party I throw every year.

Or so it seemed in print.

In reality, I had developed some hors d'oeuvre recipes for their December issue, and at the last minute, a story they had in the works fell through. So they called to see if I'd be willing to be the substitute and stage a faux holiday party in August using all the recipes I'd already developed.

Now, the fact was that I had created the dozen recipes as a kind of fantasy party wish list, not as an actual menu. That would be far too ambitious for most normal hostesses to undertake.

But that's the beauty of a photo shoot. It did not have to reflect what I actually might be capable of, but what, in the wildest, most decadent vision of the art director, he and the food stylist and photographer were capable of.

All I had to do was show up. So I did, on a sweltering Tuesday afternoon, dragging as many of my freelancing friends as were available to come dressed in their wintry velvet and woolen best.

The food stylist and her team re-created my recipes, magically transforming them into something glossy and photogenic while a makeup artist and hairstylist did the same to me.

I don't remember the names of the people who loaned us their swanky apartment for the shoot (wealthy friends of the art director), or most of the hors d'oeuvres "I" served, or even all the friends who showed up. But I still remember exactly what I wore: a full-length purple tweed skirt with a corset laceup at the waist, a Vivienne Westwood number I picked up at a sample sale. I didn't own the right top to go with it, so I stopped at Bergdorf Goodman on the way to the shoot, buying a luxurious mink-blend wrap sweater for more money than any sane person should spend on a piece of knitwear. It is the most expensive item of clothing I have bought to date, and I fully expected to return it directly after the shoot. But I fell in love with its soft, kitty-cat texture and it lives in my dresser even as I write.

Other than the details of my outfit, the only thing I vividly recall was the one super-simple hors d'oeuvre that I still make for parties: Port-glazed Stilton.

It's beyond easy: You just boil down cheap ruby Port wine with sugar, bay leaf, and black pepper until it's syrupy, then drizzle the syrup over a wedge of the best Stilton cheese you can procure. The syrup takes on a musky, spicy, herbal taste from the seasonings and adds a welcome touch of sweetness to the salty, rich cheese. It requires absolutely no real work but is highly impressive, elevating the usual cheese platter into something epicurean and mink sweater–worthy.

Usually I serve this with purchased oat crackers, the kind imported from England. But a few years ago, feeling sick and tired of paying $5 for a package of sixteen crackers, I decided to try making my own.

They were simpler than I imagined. You just mix the ingredients with your fingers until it comes together, then pat or roll it out and cut into squares.

I've made this recipe into thicker, heartier crackers and thinner, more delicate crackers and I prefer the thinner ones, though they'll crumble if you're too aggressive with the Stilton smearing. The crackers are also excellent served with soft butter and sea salt for sprinkling, and small children will nibble them right up if you leave them on a low coffee table where they can crawl or toddle up and snatch a fistful.

Of course, you can also serve the syrup-gilded cheese with purchased crackers or bread. It's what the food stylist at the shoot did, and no one could fault her for not going all out. And the results will be picture perfect, with or without the couture.

Port-Glazed Stilton with Homemade Oat Biscuits

Time: 10 minutes

Serves 8

½ cup sugar

½ cup ruby Port

½ teaspoon freshly ground black pepper

1 bay leaf

1 (1-pound) wedge Stilton cheese

Grapes

Oat Biscuits (recipe follows), for serving

1. In a large saucepan, combine the sugar, Port, pepper, and bay leaf, and bring to a boil. Cook over moderate heat, stirring occasionally, until thickened enough to coat the back of a spoon, about 5 minutes. Discard the bay leaf and let cool. (The syrup can be made 1 week ahead and refrigerated; bring to room temperature before serving.)

2. To serve, set the Stilton on a serving platter and drizzle the Port syrup over the cheese. Serve with grapes and oat biscuits or other crackers and/or bread.

Oat Biscuits

Time: 25 minutes

Makes 20 oat biscuits

1 cup whole wheat or white flour

1½ tablespoons sugar

½ teaspoon baking soda

½ teaspoon kosher salt, plus more for sprinkling

1½ cups rolled oats

½ cup unsalted butter

¼ cup plain whole milk yogurt

1. Preheat the oven to 350°F. Lightly grease a baking sheet or line with parchment paper. In a large bowl, mix together the flour, sugar, baking soda, and

salt. Stir in the oats and, using your fingers, rub in the butter to form a coarse meal. Fold in the yogurt.

2. On a lightly floured surface, roll the dough into a rectangle $3/16$ inch thick. Cut the dough into 20 rectangles and transfer to the prepared baking sheet.

3. Sprinkle the oat biscuits with additional kosher salt, if desired, and bake for about 15 minutes, or until the edges are dark golden brown. Place the baking sheet on a wire rack and allow the oat biscuits to cool for 5 minutes, then transfer to the wire rack to finish cooling. Store in an airtight container.

HEALTHY HOMEMADE CHEDDAR CRISPS

Once I realized how easy it was to make my own crackers (even easier than certain finicky chocolate chip cookie recipes I know and love), I decided to branch out from the oat biscuits I had been serving with cheese. My goal was to make a self-sufficient cracker snack that had the cheese already mixed into it, something suitable for adult- and baby-munching alike.

I based my recipe on cheese pennies—those savory, cheese-filled shortbread-like crackers with a thick crumbly texture.

Usually, I like cheese pennies only when they are hot. For some unknown quirk of physics, once they cool, their flavor mysteriously disappears. To compensate, I increased the amount of cheese stirred into the dough, and then topped the crackers with even more cheese while they were baking. The cheese topping turned golden brown and crunchy, adding a salty, tangy kick that stayed with the cracker at any temperature (an asset on the playground and buffet table both).

I also substituted whole wheat flour for the white flour, hence the recipe title. At least, they are more healthful (and tastier, says I) than Goldfish if not quite as cute (though if you've got lots of time, see the variation below).

Healthy Homemade Cheddar Crisps

Time: 30 minutes

Makes about 48 crackers

1 cup whole wheat flour

¼ teaspoon baking powder

4 tablespoons (½ stick) unsalted butter, room temperature

½ teaspoon kosher salt

Pinch cayenne (optional)

1½ cups (6 ounces) shredded Cheddar cheese

1. In a small bowl, combine the flour and baking powder. In a food processor or electric mixer with the paddle attachment, mix the butter, salt, and cayenne until creamy. Add 1 cup (4 ounces) of the cheese and mix until thoroughly combined. Gradually add the flour mixture and run the food processor or beat with the paddle until the dough pulls away from the sides of the bowl and starts to form a ball, about 7 minutes. Wrap the dough in plastic, and roll into a log about 1½ inches in diameter. Chill in the refrigerator for 1 hour or up to overnight.

2. Preheat the oven to 350°F and line two sheet pans with parchment. Unwrap the log of dough and slice into rounds 3/16 inch thick. Arrange the rounds on the prepared baking sheets and place a generous pinch of the remaining ½ cup cheese on each cracker. Bake until the crackers are golden brown, about 12 minutes. Turn off the oven and leave the crackers to crisp for an additional 5 minutes. Transfer the crackers to a wire rack to cool.

VARIATION: **CHEDDAR HEARTS OR FISHES**

Place the dough between 2 sheets of plastic and roll into a rectangle ⅛ inch thick. Using a small (1½- to 2-inch) heart- or fish-shaped cookie cutter, cut out the crackers and place them on the prepared sheet pans. Press the remaining scraps of dough together, reroll, and cut out additional crackers, then bake as directed.

7

My Mother's
Sandwich Theory of Life

In my mother's kitchen, everything is potential sandwich fodder. As long as it's small enough to be squashed in between two slices of bread, chances are that it will be, much to my parent's delight.

Brought up on my grandmother's tuna salad with chopped egg and sweet pickle relish, my mother now insists on more exotic fare. Her favorite fillings involve resuscitating doggie bags carried home from fancy restaurants. Growing up, I lunched on the likes of leftover roasted sea bass on a bagel, lamb stew in a pita, soft-shell crabs and last night's salad on toasted English muffins.

For my mother, tuna salad now means a mélange of homemade olive oil–poached tuna with capers and scallions. I've never seen my mother eat a PB&J. Nor did she serve them to my sister and me when we were kids—which naturally meant that I craved those hydrogenated fat–filled peanut butter and purple grape jelly sandwiches on white bread as if they were candy.

In addition to being an extraordinarily creative sandwich maker, my mother has a theory about sandwiches and the people who eat them.

"Good sandwiches are like interesting people, unpredictable and filled with surprises," she once told me over grilled cheese and tomato at a diner.

"Each bite should be a little different, otherwise it gets boring," she continued, rearranging the tomatoes just so and shaking on a little hot sauce from the tiny bottle she always carried in her purse.

"It's like a conversation. If you can anticipate the next sentence, why bother? If you know exactly what the next bite of a sandwich will taste like, why eat it?"

I was mystified by this at the time (I was twelve), but now that I know her better, it makes perfect sense. While the act of eating, like conversation, is a comfort, the content should be an adventure—transporting and exciting, not dull and predictable.

This philosophy extends to her cooking as well, and prevents her from ever making the same thing twice, even when she tries. What would lamb chops taste like if I added cumin? she'd wonder. Or used mushrooms instead of bacon in that frittata? Her curiosity and intrepidity inevitably win out over the tried-and-true.

Out of all the things my mother taught me about cooking, this might be the most defining, and explains why I am incapable of making something over again, even when I try. It's just one of the ways I'm my mother's child. And why I love sandwiches.

PAN BAGNAT

There are plenty of ways to flatten a *pan bagnat*, the traditional tuna and vegetable sandwich from Nice. You could weight it with some heavy books or one nice fat brick. You could squeeze it under a cast-iron skillet piled with cans or press it beneath a stack of plates. Or you could find a child of about seven and simply have her sit on it.

This was my parents' preferred method when my sister and I were of sandwich-sitting ages. Mimicking the cafes on the Côte d'Azur, which sold the sandwiches along with carafes of rosé and pastis, my mother would slice a round crusty loaf in half, anoint it with oil, vinegar, and garlic, and stuff it with tuna and tomatoes. Then my sister and I would alternate sandwich-squashing shifts, bouncing our bathing suit–clad bottoms on the well-wrapped loaf until the oil and vinegar inundated and "bathed" the bread (*pan bagnat* translates to "bathed bread"). What was once a Dagwood-fat sandwich was then compacted enough to fit in the mouth. We gobbled garlicky, tomato-and-oil-moist wedges on the beach, seasoned with sand.

I thought about my old *pan bagnat* cushions while contemplating how to turn a can of tuna into lunch. I had briefly considered a classic tuna salad sandwich. But this tuna was the fancy, olive oil–packed kind from Italy, which to my taste clashes with mayonnaise. Then I remembered my Mediterranean sandwich-sitting days, and hungered for a *pan bagnat*.

The thing about a bathed sandwich is that it works nearly as well with day-old bread, which is never in short supply *chez moi*. I had half a country loaf that would suit my needs, once I dug out some of the fluffy white crumb (regular baguettes, ciabattas, and other crusty loaves also work well).

Pan bagnat is also adaptable, and you can make one with pretty much any ingredients you have on hand—just as long as there's an anchor of garlic, oil, and tomatoes sprinkled with salty bits such as tuna or anchovies, or even lots of capers and olives for a fishless version.

Since it was summer, the tomatoes were easy. I had a pile of heirloom beauties just waiting to be called lunch. Something crunchy, vegetable-wise, was also in order. Niçoise sandwich makers use local peppers, crisp lettuce, and sometimes tiny, crunchy fava beans. Lacking those, I substituted cucumber.

In France, *pan bagnats* are generally made from either tuna or anchovies, but being a lily painter I used both, and then added mustard vinaigrette and olives just to make sure every bite was suffused with intensity. Then for richness I sliced up a hard-cooked egg, which I think is indispensable in tuna sandwiches of every ilk.

Once the sandwich was assembled, all I needed was a seven-year-old child. But there was only the cat, who isn't heavy enough and never sits where I want her to anyway. So I filled the kettle and placed it on top of a baking pan to weight down the sandwich. Then I waited as long as I could stand it. Some recipes will tell you to leave the sandwich in the fridge overnight, but I know that's not what they do in Nice, where they are made in the morning to be served for lunch. I answered twenty minutes' worth of e-mails and then gave in.

I cut a slice and bit down. The bread was still crusty on the outside, but perfumed with garlic, good olive oil, and the juice of sweet August tomatoes. The saline flavors of anchovy, tuna, mustard, and olives had unified into a delectably pungent whole, softened by the cucumber, egg, and some fresh basil leaves that I laid on top. Even without the sun, sand, and Mediterranean Sea, even without my parents and sister and cold bottles of Orangina, it still tasted just like I remembered, maybe even better.

Pan Bagnat

1 very small garlic clove, minced

1 teaspoon red wine vinegar

½ teaspoon Dijon mustard

Pinch salt and freshly ground black pepper

2 anchovy fillets, minced (optional)

2 tablespoons extra-virgin olive oil

1 (8-inch) round very crusty country loaf or small ciabatta, halved

½ Kirby cucumber or ¼ regular cucumber (see Note)

1 medium-size ripe tomato, sliced

½ small red onion, sliced

1 jar (5 to 6 ounces) olive oil–packed tuna, drained

8 large basil leaves

2 tablespoons sliced pitted olives (preferably a mix of black and green)

1 hard-cooked egg, peeled and thinly sliced

Time: 15 minutes,
plus 20 minutes'
weighting

Serves 2 to 3

1. In a small bowl, whisk together the garlic, vinegar, mustard, salt, pepper, and anchovies (if desired). Slowly drizzle in the oil, whisking constantly.

2. If using a country loaf, pull out some of the soft interior crumb to form a cavity. (If using a ciabatta, you won't need to eliminate anything.)

3. If using a Kirby cucumber, slice thinly. If using a regular cucumber, peel, halve lengthwise, and scoop out the seeds from one half. Thinly slice half of the seedless half to give you a quarter of the original whole. Add the sliced cucumber to the vinaigrette and toss well.

4. Spread half the tomato slices out on the bottom of the bread loaf. Top with half the cucumbers and some vinaigrette, then with the onion slices, tuna, basil leaves, olives, and egg slices. Top the egg with the remaining cucumbers, vinaigrette, and tomato slices. Cover with the second bread half and firmly press the sandwich together.

5. Wrap the sandwich tightly in foil, wax paper, or plastic wrap, then place in a plastic bag. Put the sandwich under a weight such as a cast-iron frying pan topped with a filled kettle, or have a small child about seven years old

sit on the sandwich. Weight the sandwich for 7 to 10 minutes, then flip and weight it for another 7 to 10 minutes (or as long as you can get the child to sit still). Unwrap, slice, and serve immediately, or keep it wrapped for up to 8 hours before serving.

NOTE: You can substitute seeded sliced green bell pepper for the cucumber.

DEVILED EGG SALAD WITH ANCHOVIES, HOT SMOKED PAPRIKA, AND TOMATO

There was a brief period when, as a kid about nine years old, I decided I wanted a signature sandwich: a brown bag lunch to call my own. It wouldn't have been anything I invented. I wasn't a cook yet, just a girl who fell hard for Harriet the Spy and her tomato sandwiches. She ate one for lunch every day, come rain or shine, through winter and summer, tomato season be damned. A spy doesn't have time to worry about seasonal ingredients.

The way I saw it, having a special sandwich I could unwrap at school every day would give me the serenity my lunchtime lacked. I detested the brisk trade in comestibles, with its complex system of sandwich value interwoven with social status. In that socioeconomic context, my salami on ryes were worth less than Lyssie Diamond's orange, and I never had much by way of cookies or potato chips to compensate for the lack.

But a tasty sandwich that I would never trade, that I'd be content to eat day in and day out, would put me above the fray.

The question was, what kind of sandwich. I wanted to pick tomato in honor of Harriet, but I didn't like tomato sandwiches. The tomato bleeds through the bread and then things fall apart.

The gustatory merits of ham and mustard, tuna salad, and Swiss cheese were compared and contrasted in my spy log before I finally settled on classic egg salad. It seemed gushy and mayonnaise-y enough to soften the bread but was not tomato-slice wet.

My egg salad plan went well for a few weeks before things started to sour—or, more specifically, to stink.

Usually my mother froze tiny cans of apple juice to pack into my lunch. It kept my sandwich cool and defrosted slowly, yielding an icy apple slush by lunchtime.

But one day, the freezer bare, I was dispatched to school with money for chocolate milk. Without that iced can to keep my egg salad cold, it baked and sweated in my locker.

I could smell it from five paces away, and so could my friends when I neared the lunch table. As I peeled off the plastic bag, a sulfurous, funky scent wafted over the room, like a silent fart, the kind we called SBDs (silent but deadly) in fourth grade. All eyes turned to me.

That was the end of egg salad and me for years to come.

I've recovered from that mortification, and now eat egg salad whenever the craving strikes. And it did one hungry afternoon.

Egg salad makes a convenient lunch if you are not transporting it anywhere in the summer. There are always eggs and mayonnaise in the fridge, and that's all you strictly need as long as you add copious grindings of black pepper to break up the eggy monotony.

But on this day, I was in the mood to zip up my sandwich with various seasonings and condiments. My idea was to approach egg salad like deviled eggs, adding pungent dashes of this and that as I would to the yolk mixture before stuffing it back into its wobbly egg white boat.

I opened the fridge. There were the anchovies singing their little fishy siren song from their cylindrical glass jar. How could I resist?

I chopped them up and mixed them into the mayo, adding cider vinegar for brightness, garlic for *oomph*, and a little smoked paprika for heat and color (and because no deviled egg is complete without paprika). Then I layered the egg salad onto toasted bread because as an adult I no longer prized soggy white bread.

Pleased with my little lunch, I was about to take a bite when I remembered Harriet. There were ripe tomatoes on the counter, and I sliced one up and nestled it over the eggs. It added the perfect juiciness—and a certain spy-like *je ne sais quoi*.

Deviled Egg Salad with Anchovies, Hot Smoked Paprika, and Tomato

3 tablespoons mayonnaise

2 anchovies, minced

½ teaspoon apple cider vinegar

Pinch smoked paprika

1 garlic clove, minced

Pinch kosher salt

2 large eggs, hard-cooked and chopped

4 slices bread, toasted

1 tomato, sliced

Time: 5 minutes

Serves 2

1. In a large bowl, mix together the mayonnaise, anchovies, vinegar, and paprika. On a cutting board, use the flat side of a knife to mash together the garlic and salt until a paste forms (or use a mortar and pestle). Add the paste to the bowl and toss to combine. Mix in the eggs.

2. Divide the salad between 2 slices of bread, top with tomato, and sandwich with the remaining 2 bread slices. Serve immediately.

TOFU SALAD WITH SWEET PICKLES AND SPICY MUSTARD

My grandma Lilly wasn't much of a cook, but she could make a mean tuna salad. Slathered with mayonnaise, shot through with chopped, hard-cooked eggs and sweet pickle relish, it seemed daring and exotic compared to the diner tuna sandwiches from the place around my corner.

We didn't get Grandma's tuna sandwiches often. Grandma usually came to our house for meals, where most tuna was grilled rare. But during the summer, Grandma took my sister and me to her beach club in Brighton Beach, where she shared a cabana with a group of bridge-playing cronies. Grandma always won, gathering her cards with a satisfied air of inevitability. At a break in the game, we ate lunch: damp tuna sandwiches on seedless rye, pulled apart into bits and speedily gobbled, then slowly digested. Grandma's rule: Wait at least thirty minutes post-sandwich before swimming in the grown-up pool, the one with the deep end. Otherwise, we'd get a cramp and drown. Swimming made Grandma nervous.

It had been decades since I've had one of Grandma Lilly's tuna sandwiches, but I craved them steadily when I was pregnant. Sadly tuna, with its high mercury content, was not on the approved preggo-noshing list.

As the cravings hit, I'd fend them off with the likes of anchovies on toast, scrambled eggs with smoked salmon, panfried trout. But nothing hit my cravings' sweet spot.

When I thought about what made Grandma's tuna sandwich so appealing to an expectant me, I realized that it wasn't actually the fish. It was the sweet-salty-pungent combination of pickle relish and mayonnaise. As far as my pregnant appetite was concerned, the tuna was merely filler to keep the other ingredients in check.

And substituting was just a matter of finding a healthful binder. Canned salmon would have worked. But I can't stand the stuff, with its cat food–like aroma that was even more intense during pregnancy.

Really, what I should have been eating more of during my pregnancy was salubrious, mineral-rich tofu.

So I chopped up some of the extra-firm that was sitting, untouched but with good intentions, in the back of my fridge, and mixed it gently with minced bread-and-butter pickles, scallions, mayo, and spicy Dijon mustard. Then I spread it on whole wheat with arugula and avocado.

It tasted nothing like tuna, nor anything like what my grandmother would have recognized as lunch. But mild and almost juicy, my tofu salad had a creamy mouthfeel and sweet pickle kick that hit the spot. And I'm still eating tofu salad, even now that my pregnancy has long given way to a baby girl— who, it turns out, adores tofu.

Tofu Salad with Sweet Pickles and Spicy Mustard

8 ounces tofu, chopped (about 1½ cups)
2 scallions, chopped
¼ cup mayonnaise
2 tablespoons minced sweet pickle
4 teaspoons Dijon mustard
Freshly ground black pepper to taste
4 slices whole wheat bread, toasted
Sliced avocado, for serving
Dark leafy greens, such as arugula or spinach, for serving

Time: 5 minutes

Serves 2

In a medium bowl, combine the tofu, scallions, mayonnaise, pickle, mustard, and pepper. Divide the salad onto 2 slices of toast and top with the avocado and greens. Sandwich with the remaining slices of toast and serve immediately.

COMTE GRILLED CHEESE
WITH CORNICHON SPREAD

Of all the reasons to visit my friends with toddling children, grilled cheese sandwiches may be the best.

Sure, I treasure the youngster rituals of dumping everything out of Aunty Melissa's purse, watching out the window for passing construction vehicles ("Look, Elliot! Cement mixer!"), and playing dress-up and hide-and-seek. But just as much, I love lunchtime, when almost every mother I know asks: "Who wants grilled cheese?" The loudest "yes" is unfailingly mine.

Most childless grown-ups I know don't bother making grilled cheese at home. (I count myself in these ranks; my infant baby, Dahlia, is still almost entirely supping on mushed vegetables and fruit and tofu.) We tend not to have the requisite ingredients (American singles, white bread) hanging around the fridge. And isn't grilled cheese, along with tuna melts, turkey clubs, and breakfast specials, the very reason they invented diners in the first place?

Such was my attitude up until recently. But after a fun-filled but grilled-cheese-less visit to a friend's house, during which her exceptional 2½-year-olds happily consumed vast amounts of garlic-sautéed broccoli, I realized I felt deprived—even after my big girl's bowl of ice cream with rainbow sprinkles.

It occurred to me that I didn't necessarily have to make playdates as an excuse to eat grilled cheese. Why not just make it at home for myself? Since the only finicky palate to appease is my own, I wouldn't be tied to yellow cheese and white bread. And really, wouldn't grilled cheese be just as good or even better when made with slightly more sophisticated, grown-up ingredients, like stinky cheese and grainy bread?

So I started experimenting, keeping the basic technique of frying the sandwich in copious quantities of butter so the surface of the bread gets crisp and lacy and brittle, while inside the cheese melts into lava, cementing the two slices.

I dug out the very best cheese I had, a nutty and intense aged raw milk

Comte from the Essex Street Cheese Company. It was certainly flavorful enough to use on its own between slices of whole wheat bread. But since I was aiming for something super-grown-up, I decided to add pungent condiments. Before frying, I painted the bread with a light smear of a mustard-cornichon dressing. It was enough to cut the richness of the butter but not obscure the earthy nuances of the cheese (though if you are using a less noble Comte or a Gruyère, feel free to slather).

The result—crunchy, buttery, tangy, and tantalizingly complex—immediately made up for that broccoli-laden lunch.

A few days later I perfected a variation on that very adult sandwich, using goat's milk Gouda and mango chutney. The sandwich had a layer of spicy-sweetness that made it completely different from the Comte version, and equally delightful.

When the grilled cheese craving struck again, I was passing by my local bagel shop. The thought of a bagel and cream cheese made me wonder if I could somehow fry it like grilled cheese. But no, cream cheese doesn't have the gooeyness factor of aged cheese, and would simply ooze out in the pan. But bagels and cream cheese made me think about lox, and lox brought to mind Barney Greengrass, where they have the most amazing horseradish Cheddar spread ever. How would that be on a toasted bagel, I wondered?

The bagel shop didn't have any horseradish Cheddar spread on offer, but they did have the actual horseradish Cheddar. So I bought some along with my poppy seed bagel. Back at home, waiting for the bagel to toast, I noshed on salami from the fridge, remembering an old friend who'd fry her salami before making it into a sandwich. I fried up a few slices and added them to my cheesy bagel along with rounds of red onion for crunch. Spicy, rich, and fatty, with a meaty edge from the salami, it was definitely as good as regular grilled cheese, and nearly as good as bagels and lox.

The next time I thought about grilled cheese, it was again because of an upcoming visit with friends with kids. But this time, they were coming over and I was cooking. Was there a grilled cheese variation that would not only please both the kids and adults but (unlike the regular kind) also pair well with cocktails?

The answer, I realized, was quesadillas: soft tortillas filled with mild cheese, then broiled until crispy and molten-centered. The kids gobbled them up. On the side I served a bracing papaya and avocado salsa for grown-up dunking. Everyone was delighted. And now there's a grilled cheese sandwich that gives kids a reason to want to visit me.

Comte Grilled Cheese with Cornichon Spread

Time: 10 minutes

Serves 2

2 tablespoons whole grain mustard

2 tablespoons mayonnaise

2 tablespoons finely chopped cornichons or other pickles

4 slices whole grain bread

¼ pound Comte cheese, sliced

2 tablespoons unsalted butter

1. Whisk together the mustard, mayonnaise, and cornichons. Spread the topping over the 4 slices of bread. Divide the cheese among the bread slices, making 2 sandwiches.
2. Melt the butter in a medium skillet over moderate heat. Cook the sandwiches until golden on both sides, 1 to 2 minutes per side, pressing down on the sandwiches with a spatula. Reduce the heat to low and cover; cook until the cheese melts completely, about 2 minutes more. Serve hot.

Goat Gouda and Mango Chutney on Rye

Time: 5 minutes

Serves 2

4 slices rye bread

4 tablespoons unsalted butter, softened

2 tablespoons Dijon mustard

4 tablespoons mango chutney

2 ounces goat Gouda, thinly sliced (or use regular Gouda)

1. Spread both sides of all 4 slices of bread with the butter. Spread the mustard on the inside of 2 slices, then spread the chutney on the inside of all 4 slices. Lay the cheese on the bread slices with the mustard, then sandwich with the slices without the mustard.
2. Place the sandwiches in a large skillet over medium-high heat. Fry for 1 to 2 minutes, then flip the sandwiches and fry for an additional minute, until the sandwiches are golden brown. Serve hot.

Salami and Horseradish Cheddar Bagel Sandwich

2 bagels, halved
3 ounces horseradish Cheddar cheese, sliced
(or substitute horseradish Cheddar spread)
¼ pound salami, thinly sliced
½ small red onion, thinly sliced

Time: 10 minutes

Serves 2

1. In a toaster oven or in an oven preheated to 500°F, toast the bagel halves until pale golden. Top each with some of the cheese and continue toasting until the cheese begins to melt.
2. Meanwhile, fry the salami slices in a skillet over moderate heat until golden, about 3 minutes. Place the salami and red onion on the bottom bagel halves. Cover with the bagel tops and serve.

Queso Fresco Quesadillas with Papaya-Avocado Salsa

Time: 15 minutes

Serves 2

SALSA

1 cup cubed fresh papaya

½ avocado, peeled and cubed

¼ cup cubed seeded cucumber

3 tablespoons chopped fresh cilantro

2 tablespoons finely chopped red onion

2 tablespoons freshly squeezed orange juice

2 tablespoons freshly squeezed lime juice

1 tablespoon extra-virgin olive oil

½ teaspoon honey, or to taste

½ teaspoon kosher salt

Freshly ground black pepper

4 (6-inch) corn tortillas

¼ pound queso fresco

1. Preheat the broiler and place an oven rack 4 inches from the heat. In a bowl, stir together the salsa ingredients. Taste and adjust the seasoning, if necessary.
2. Place 2 tortillas on a baking sheet. Crumble the cheese over the tortillas. Top with the remaining tortillas. Broil, flipping once halfway through, until the cheese is melted and the tortillas are golden, 1 to 2 minutes per side.
3. Quarter the quesadillas and top each section with 1 tablespoon salsa. Serve immediately.

WATERCRESS SALAD
SANDWICH FOR MOM

God forbid you should throw out the last wilted branches of watercress languishing in the bowl after dinner at my parents' house.

"Leave the salad," my mother will say. "I'll eat it for breakfast." And she does, piled onto toast or an English muffin.

For years, I found this habit of hers unappetizing, to say the least. A wilted salad sandwich for breakfast had absolutely no appeal, especially for the sweet-toothed, toast and jam–eating teenager that I was during her peak watercress phase.

But then one day last year, I reconsidered. It was lunchtime, and the fridge revealed a large bunch of watercress, a cucumber, an avocado, a tiny wedge of extra-sharp Cheddar cheese, and not much else beyond the prodigious collection of condiments I'm cultivating, much to my husband's dismay.

I could have easily made a salad, but I wanted a sandwich. The available ingredients made me remember my mother and her weedy breakfasts, so I figured I'd give it a try.

Since I was working from fresh ingredients and not leftovers, I decided to keep the watercress crisp and not let it wilt like my mother did. The limp texture of her greens was a major part of the turnoff.

I then turned to the cheese, which would give the sandwich its richness and heft. My parents would occasionally grate or crumble some kind of sharp cheese over their salad as a garnish, so I took that cue and did the same, grating the cheese and mixing it with the greens and cucumber. Finally I sliced up the avocado and laid it atop some bread I pulled from the freezer and toasted.

I took a bite.

Now, one of the reasons for my mother's salad obsession is her perpetual diet. So although she wouldn't stint on the salad dressing, she also didn't drown her salads with oil or cheese either.

But to my taste, the watercress sandwich was a bit too lean and healthful tasting, even with the avocado.

So I did something she never would have. I slathered the bread with mayonnaise. Its creaminess and savory flavor helped bring all the other elements together and turned mere watercress on toast into a coherent and delectable lunch.

My mother may not approve of my adaptation, but I know she'd love it nonetheless.

Watercress Salad Sandwich for Mom

Time: 15 minutes

Serves 4

1 bunch watercress, cleaned and trimmed (about 6 cups)
4 ounces aged Cheddar cheese, grated (1 cup)
1 Kirby cucumber, peeled, halved lengthwise, and thinly sliced crosswise
2 tablespoons extra-virgin olive oil
2 teaspoons freshly squeezed lemon juice, plus additional for drizzling
1/4 teaspoon kosher salt, plus additional
Freshly ground black pepper to taste
8 slices good-quality whole grain bread
3 tablespoons mayonnaise, more or less
1/2 avocado, thinly sliced

1. In a large bowl, toss together the watercress, cheese, cucumber, oil, lemon juice, salt, and pepper.
2. Spread each slice of bread with mayonnaise. Divide the avocado slices among 4 slices of bread. Drizzle the avocado with lemon juice and sprinkle lightly with salt. Mound the watercress salad over the avocado. Top with the remaining 4 slices of bread. Cut in half and serve.

CRISP AND JUICY SOFT-SHELL CRAB SANDWICHES WITH CAPERBERRY TARTAR SAUCE

Like my mother, I'm all for doing as little work as possible when it comes to ingredients preparation. She taught me to leave the veins in my shrimp, the tips on my chicken wings, the pits in my cherries, and the peels on my fava beans. But when it comes to cleaning soft-shell crabs, I go my own way.

That is, I like them cleaned, and she does not.

If you've ever cleaned a soft-shell crab, you know it's not pretty work. Step one involves cutting the face off the front of the crab, often while it's alive. Step two, pull up the top part of the flap where the shell would be and scoop out the gushy yellow innards.

Luckily, most fishmongers will do that grisly work for you. The only obstacle with this is that once the crabs are cleaned, they need to be kept very cold and cooked within a few hours, or they could spoil.

My mother obviates this problem entirely by keeping her crabs intact.

"They stay juicier if you don't cut them," she'd say as she plopped a blue critter into hot oil.

She does have a point. Her crabs are juicy and sweet, with claws that crisp and brown, turning brittle and crunchy. To me, they taste about the same as the cleaned ones, with a lot less trouble.

Still, I have a mental barrier against the crab guts—surprising since I consider most innards to be delicacies in their own right, and happily gobble kidneys, tongue, lung, and stomach of pigs, cows, and lambs. So why not crabs?

If there's another thing I learned from my mother, it's that people are inconsistent. So when I bought a couple of crabs last time they were in season, I asked the fishmonger to clean them for me.

When my mother cooks crabs, she portions out two per person (or more if they are small), dips them in flour, fries them up until they're coral-hued and crisp, and serves them with lemon wedges and fresh herbs.

But I had my mind set on something different—fried crab sandwiches. I wanted a docile starch to soak up all the saline crab juices, and toasted bread is an ideal vehicle.

My mental recipe was simple: Fry the crabs like my mother does, then slip them onto toast blanketed with homemade tartar sauce.

I had planned to use regular capers, which are traditional in tartar sauce, but while I was searching for them amidst the forest of condiment bottles in the fridge, I came upon the caperberries. These are the plump, podlike fruit of the caper plant (capers are the buds). But unlike the buds, which are soft in the mouth, caperberries are juicy and riddled with crunchy seeds. I chopped them up and mixed them into the sauce.

Then I fried up the crabs, their bellies puffing and edges crisping, and made them into sandwiches with lots of the tartar sauce, and some arugula for freshness.

I sat down and took a bite. The first thing that hit me was a layered complexity of crunches—from crab bits, toasted bread, and caperberry seeds jumbling in my mouth.

Then the crab liquor started to flow. The bread sopped up most of it, but some errant drops escaped down my chin, though I licked them up as fast as I could.

Even gutless, my crabs had juice. And with the fishmonger doing all the work, I'm still following my mother's example.

Crisp and Juicy Soft-Shell Crab Sandwiches with Caperberry Tartar Sauce

TARTAR SAUCE

1 garlic clove, finely minced

Pinch kosher salt, plus additional to taste

2 teaspoons freshly squeezed lemon juice

2 tablespoons mayonnaise

2 tablespoons chopped onion

2 teaspoons chopped soft fresh herbs such as basil, parsley, chives, tarragon, or fennel fronds

Freshly ground black pepper to taste

1 to 2 teaspoons chopped caperberries, more if desired (see Note)

2 soft-shell crabs, cleaned if desired

Flour

Kosher salt and freshly ground black pepper to taste

2 to 3 tablespoons olive oil (enough to coat the bottom of the pan)

4 slices freshly toasted crusty country bread or 2 ciabatta rolls, halved

Lettuce or arugula, for serving

Lemon wedges, for serving

1. Make the tartar sauce: On a cutting board using the flat side of a knife, mash and chop together the garlic and salt to make a paste (or use a mortar and pestle). Scrape the paste into a small bowl and stir in the lemon juice. Stir well to help dissolve the salt. Stir in the remaining ingredients and season with more salt and pepper if you like.

2. Dip the crabs into the flour seasoned with salt and pepper, shaking off any excess. Heat the olive oil in a skillet, then add the crabs and cook until they turn brown and crisp, about 2 minutes per side.

3. Slather 2 pieces of the bread with the tartar sauce and add the crabs and lettuce or arugula. Top with the remaining bread (you can slather this one with tartar sauce, too, if you like). Serve with lemon wedges.

NOTE: You can buy caperberries pickled in brine at specialty food shops. Or substitute regular capers, which you can leave whole.

8 Better Fried

E verything is better fried," the wise chef Larry Forgione once told me, "but nothing is better than fried cheese."

We were standing around at a cocktail party to celebrate something or other, nibbling divine little fried corn fritters that were being passed around on silver trays.

I was young enough not to immediately embrace the wisdom of his statement, and challenged him.

"Everything?" I asked.

"Yup," he said.

"What about pickles?"

"Yup."

"Hot dogs?"

"Yup."

"Apple pie? Eggs? Olives?"

He yupped three times, rolled his eyes, and moved away to talk to someone else, tired of this game.

But I wasn't done. I kept thinking of more things that couldn't possibly be better fried. Pasta? Bacon? Cake? Salad?

I cornered him near the bar a few hours later and continued my litany.

He yupped everything *except* the salad, and I felt somehow that I had won. But it was an empty victory.

The fact is, though I'm not sure I agree with him about cheese being the ultimate fried food, in principle, the great chef was right.

Coming into close and personal contact with a bath of blazing oil is good for most foods, searing their surface until crisp and golden and cooking their interiors quickly and evenly, making them more intense, creamier, and all-around yummier than most other cooking methods.

As much as a roasted potato is food fit for royalty, a French fry is veritable ambrosia. A crunchy fried calamari beats a floppy sautéed one, and though

I love raw clams, naked but for a squeeze of lemon, are not fried ones, topped with tartar sauce, just a wee bit better?

Of course the downsides of frying are numerous and unavoidable. I'm not going to gloss over any of them and tell you, magazine style, that frying is "Quick 'n Easy!" The fact is that while the actual act of frying is pretty fast and not at all hard, the cleanup is a bitch. That's just the way it is.

You need to heat up vast quantities of oil to scarily high temperatures (be careful when you lower the food in). No matter what you do, spitting driblets of oil will skitter everywhere—your stove, the floor, the ceiling.

Then there is disposing of the used oil. Most expert-type people will tell you to let it cool, strain it through a very fine-mesh sieve, and use it again (store it in a dark, cool place but not the fridge and use it only once more). And this is the right advice for sensible cooks who fry on a monthly basis.

But if you are like me, and fry only maybe two or three times a year, I say let the oil cool, find a large jar to pour it into, and throw it away. Old, used cooking oil can go rancid and impart off flavors to what should be edible nirvana.

Another problem with used oil: It will have a lower smoke point temperature than new oil, since heating it once has already started to break down those nasty little molecules responsible for the billowing black clouds that sometimes invade the kitchen.

In terms of both smoke point and the crispiness factor, the best of the frying fats is pure lard (don't use the partially hydrogenated stuff from the supermarket). Of course it's hard to find and taboo for many people, but if you see it, pounce, because it heats cleanly without smoke and cooks things evenly and beautifully, gilding ingredients in a crunchy, greaseless, and tasteless crust (no strange piggy flavors) that shatters when you bite down. You can get pure rendered lard from some butchers, or render it yourself if you happen to have a connection to a giant hunk of pork fat.

Another exotic though expensive frying possibility is pure, raw (virgin) coconut oil—if you don't mind a subtle coconut taste to your fried goods (excellent with fried pies and doughnuts, less so with corn dogs).

Vegetable, pure olive, and soybean oils will work well, too. But avoid canola, which is less stable when heated to very high temperatures.

Now that we've got the kinds of fats straightened out, I'll bet you're tired of thinking about fat. Maybe you're even saying to yourself, fried foods are too fatty for me to bother with anyway.

I'm not going to try to tell you that fried foods aren't on the richer side of, say, steamed broccoli. But they are also not as oily as you probably think they are.

In fact, the last time I fried up a batch of crunchy onion fritters, I tipped an entire quart of oil into the pot. When the frying was done and the oil cool, I poured it back into the same bottle to throw out. It almost filled it to the top, maybe three or four tablespoons shy of where I started, meaning the onions didn't absorb much oil at all, so neither did I. I wouldn't call it low-fat cooking, but a few fried tidbits every now and again are not a one-way ticket to obesity either.

Furthermore, the one friend I have who thinks nothing of deep-frying a few parsnips for an autumn meal is the svelte and lovely Karen.

Karen is the biggest deep-frying advocate in my close circle of friends, a partygiver whose self-described motto is: "If you go to someone's house and the hostess is deep-frying, you know you're in for a good time."

It was she who reminded me that you really don't need to heat up so much oil when you're deep-frying for an intimate dinner for two or three. She does it all the time, using her small cast-iron saucepan and only a couple of cups rather than quarts of oil.

Karen doesn't use a deep-fat thermometer (though I do). She throws a piece of bread or a sprinkling of flour into the oil and when it sizzles, it's ready. Minutes later, your fried food will be, too, and no matter what you make, you and your guests will be as happy as a chef with a piece of fried cheese.

PANFRIED CHEESE WITH ANCHOVY-DATE SALAD

There are few quips made in passing that have affected my culinary development to the degree as the one chef Larry Forgione made about fried cheese. He said there was nothing better, and I took him at his word.

Now, the great chef said this off-the-cuff at a party and probably did not expect any sensible person to cling to his utterance so tenaciously. But clinging I am, and thus I have spent a disproportionate amount of my life debating the question.

Is there, in fact, anything better than fried cheese? What about doughnuts or fried chorizo? What kind of cheese is best for frying, and what should one serve to accompany said cheese?

These are the kinds of things I ponder late at night when normal people are reviewing their day in their head or worrying about global warming.

Maybe this obsession springs from the lack of fried cheese in my childhood. The closest I came was my mother's cottage cheese pancakes, which she fried up for brunch on the occasional weekend when we weren't having bagels and lox.

But cottage cheese pancakes are not the stuff of my or the chef's dreams. No, Larry Forgione was talking about cheese fried so that it would have a gushing, runny center and crisp crust. Pancakes don't compare.

Of course when I see fried cheese on any menu, I am compelled to order it. Sadly, with the glaring exception of fried mozzarella in sports bar–type places I don't frequent, fried cheese is not a common restaurant offering. So unless I make it myself, I don't get enough.

Which leads me to my favorite fried-cheese-at-home dish of the moment: panfried mozzarella served with a sprightly salad of bitter greens and a citrusy, anchovy-date vinaigrette. The dressing and greens cut the richness of the cheese, which is marvelously milky and melty, with a flaky, flavorful crust that contrasts with the molten center.

It's the perfect thing to serve at a party—and you don't even need to leave the game on.

Panfried Cheese with Anchovy-Date Salad

1 medium orange
1 large lemon
4 large diced dates (about ¼ cup)
6 anchovy fillets, minced
2 large garlic cloves, minced
¼ cup plus 1 tablespoon extra-virgin olive oil
½ cup all-purpose flour
1 egg, lightly beaten
½ cup plain bread crumbs
8 ounces fresh mozzarella, sliced into ¼-inch-thick rounds
Extra-virgin olive oil or safflower oil, for frying (about ¾ cup)
Bitter leafy greens, such as arugula, watercress, and/or radicchio, for serving

Time: 25 minutes

Serves 4 to 6

1. To make the anchovy-date dressing, zest and juice the orange and lemon, reserving 1 tablespoon of the lemon juice and 2 teaspoons of the orange juice. Place the zest and reserved juice in a medium bowl and stir in the dates, anchovies, and garlic. Slowly drizzle in the olive oil while whisking until the dressing comes together.
2. To make the cheese, place the flour on a plate, the egg in a bowl, and the bread crumbs on a separate plate. Coat each slice of cheese in the flour, dip in the egg, and then coat in the bread crumbs.
3. Heat about ½ inch oil in a large skillet over medium-high heat. Using tongs, dip 1 cheese slice into the oil. If the oil sizzles slightly, it is ready. Working with 2 to 3 cheese slices at a time, fry the cheese until golden brown, 15 to 20 seconds per side. Transfer the slices to a plate and dab off the excess oil with a paper towel. Repeat with the remaining cheese slices.
4. Serve the fried cheese hot on a bed of greens topped with the anchovy-date dressing.

KAREN'S CHORIZO
CORN DOG BITES

My friend Karen is an egalitarian cook. She is just as likely to commence a chichi dinner party main course of *blanquette de veau* or a grilled *côte de boeuf* with pretty little bowls of Chex Mix as she is to break out the smoked salmon. When cooking for her family, Karen tries to skew healthy, along the lines of poached chicken breasts with snow peas and Asian vinaigrette. But that didn't stop her from serving Cheetos-topped pasta to her eleven-year-old daughter and a friend one memorable evening. (The friend asked if she could move in.)

And then there are her cocktail parties, of which she and her husband, Dave, a cocktail historian, have many. Somewhat perversely, the more elegant the group, the more Betty Crocker and less Julia Child Karen becomes when feeding them.

"I just love to see all those fancy people go nuts for my sausage balls," she once said proudly, displaying an empty tray that moments before held irresistible, spicy nuggets of breakfast sausage meat and grated cheese bound together with Bisquick. Then there was that bag of hot-from-the-microwave pork rinds she passed around to acclaim, and the baked olives wrapped in cheese dough that were devoured before any had a chance to leave the kitchen. Karen has an instinct for the delectable that defies food snobbery.

It's because of all this that when Karen tells me about a comestible of note, I listen keenly. And so it was with the chorizo corn dogs.

The story goes likes this: While shopping in a gourmet cheese shop, ogling the washed-rind stinkies and grainy-textured aged Goudas, Karen noticed a little plastic bag bulging with bite-size chorizos.

"They were the same size as the mini hot dogs you make into pigs in blankets, so of course I thought of turning them into corn dogs," she told me on the phone.

So she did, making a simple cornmeal batter and frying them up for a small group of friends. They were gobbled in minutes, which is typical at Karen's house.

"They were amazing," she said.

Since I wasn't at that party, I needed to make a batch myself just as soon as I could get my hands on those baby chorizos.

But weeks passed, and I never did end up in the neighborhood of that cheese shop where Karen bought them, and I never saw them anywhere else.

Finally, I decided I was hungry enough for chorizo corn dogs to compromise and use slices of regular cured chorizo.

As per Karen's instructions, I made a simple cornmeal batter and used it to coat the sausage slices before frying them until crisp all over.

They were salty, a little sweet from the cornmeal, and very spicy from the chorizo, and I could not stop eating them until all the sausage was gone.

I was so excited that I called Karen right up to tell her about it.

But her mind was on other things.

"Can I tell you about the baked cheesy pumpkin with heavy cream and Gruyère?" she asked.

The answer, of course, was yes.

Karen's Chorizo Corn Dog Bites

1 cup cornmeal
¾ cup all-purpose flour
2 tablespoons sugar
1 teaspoon kosher salt
½ teaspoon baking powder
1 egg
1 cup whole milk
Canola or vegetable oil, for frying
8 ounces dried Spanish chorizo, cut into ½-inch chunks

Time: 30 minutes

Makes about
30 pieces

1. In a bowl, whisk together the cornmeal, flour, sugar, salt, and baking powder. Whisk in the egg and milk until just combined.

2. Fill a large pot halfway with oil and heat until the temperature reaches 375°F on a deep-fat thermometer.

3. Working in batches, dip chunks of chorizo in the batter, then use a slotted spoon to lower the battered chorizo into the oil. Fry until the corn dogs are golden, about 2 minutes. Transfer to a paper towel–lined plate to drain.

VARIATION: CORNY SHRIMP FRITTERS

After frying up all the chorizo in the house, there was still some leftover corn dog batter, and hot oil in the pot. It would be a shame to waste it, so I looked around for what to dip and fry. In the fridge was a pound of shrimp that I was planning to roast with some broccoli. But surely I could spare a handful to make a nice little hors d'oeuvre.

Before dipping, I seasoned the shrimp aggressively with cayenne, salt, and pepper, trying to mimic the spiciness if not the porkiness of the chorizo. Then I battered the shrimp and fried them until golden.

They were juicier and sweeter than the sausage, but still had a kick, thanks to the chile. If you're thinking of serving the chorizo corn dogs for a crowd, you might double the batter recipe and make a batch of these puffy shrimp fritters as well. Then mix them together on one large platter and, as Karen would say, let the hungry hordes descend.

Corny Shrimp Fritters

1 cup cornmeal

¾ cup all-purpose flour

2 tablespoons sugar

1¾ teaspoons kosher salt

½ teaspoon baking powder

1 egg

1 cup whole milk

Canola or vegetable oil, for frying

½ pound large shrimp, shelled and halved crosswise

½ teaspoon chili powder

Pinch cayenne

Time: 30 minutes

Makes about
18 pieces

1. In a bowl, whisk together the cornmeal, flour, sugar, 1 teaspoon salt, and baking powder. Whisk in the egg and milk until just combined.

2. Fill a large pot halfway with oil and heat until the temperature reaches 375°F on a deep-fat thermometer.

3. Season the shrimp with the remaining ¾ teaspoon salt, the chili powder, and cayenne. Working in batches, dip the shrimp into the batter, then use a slotted spoon to lower the battered shrimp into the oil. Fry until golden, 1 to 2 minutes. Transfer to a paper towel–lined plate to drain.

SPICY, CRISPY CHICKPEAS

There comes a time for every cook in charge of a deep fryer when the combination of boredom and access leads to experimentation. It's inevitable—the oil is hot, the batter is foamy, and the cook has time on his or her hands. What's more natural than to batter and fry everything that's not tacked down?

This creative urge has spawned some of the greatest dishes of our time. If it wasn't for a long-standing tradition of intrepid Scottish fish-and-chips-mongers, we might never have had the deep-fried Mars bar, the deep-fried Kit-Kat, or, still more sublime, the deep-fried Twinkie.

And it's what I imagine happened somewhere in Spain at a tapas bar to create the deep-fried chickpea snack. After all, deep-frying a tiny, roly-poly legume that is usually cooked for hours into some soupy, stewy-type fare is just not intuitive. Have you ever seen a deep-fried lentil?

However they came into existence, deep-fried chickpeas—cooked until the outsides are glistening mahogany and the insides still creamy, then salted and spiced with smoked paprika—rival potato chips as the world's most fantastically addictive snack.

I came upon spicy, deep-fried chickpeas at Tia Pol, a tapas bar in Chelsea. The crispy orbs were so compelling that I ate bowls and bowls and bowls of them, so many that eventually I became too embarrassed to ask for more, though I couldn't stop myself from gesturing. When the chickpea munching finally ceased, I was beyond stuffed, and my fingers smelled like paprika for days.

I knew that if I didn't want to end up a Tia Pol barfly, I'd have to learn how to make those chickpeas myself.

Alexandra Raij, the former chef, was happy to give me the recipe. It consisted of nothing more than dumping a can of drained, cooked chickpeas into hot oil, then salting and spicing them with a little smoked hot paprika. The only trick, she said, was to make sure to pat the chickpeas dry before adding them to the oil. This keeps the oil from cooling down too much, and also helps stop it from splattering.

I've made the chickpeas her way many times, decimating the dented, rusty tin of smoked paprika that I carried back from Spain.

I've also made them with other seasonings, just to change things up. A combination of cumin, chili powder, and cayenne adds an earthy kick while garam masala gives more of a fragrant Indian nuance.

If you have any sage leaves around, you can drop them into the oil, too (add them three minutes after you add the chickpeas, since they cook more quickly). They will imbue your chickpeas with a vaguely Italian flavor, so you might want to skip the spices and just salt and pepper everything very well.

But no matter how you season them, be sure to make plenty of fried chickpeas. And give a nod to the ingenious and possibly bored tapas fryer who came up with these divine crunchy goodies in the first place.

Spicy, Crispy Chickpeas

Lard or oil, for frying
2 (15.5-ounce) cans chickpeas, drained, rinsed, and patted dry
1½ teaspoons coarse sea salt, preferably Maldon, for serving (or to taste)

Time: 20 minutes

Makes about 3 cups
Serves 6 to 8

FOR THE SPICE MIX
¾ teaspoon hot chili powder, more to taste
½ teaspoon ground cumin
⅛ teaspoon cayenne

or

¼ teaspoon smoked hot paprika, more to taste

or

Garam masala, to taste

or

Handful tiny fresh sage leaves

1. In a large skillet or pot, heat 2 inches of oil or lard to 375°F.
2. Add the chickpeas and fry until crisp and dark golden on the outside and creamy on the inside, about 5 minutes. (If using sage leaves, add them 3 minutes after you've added the chickpeas.)
3. With a slotted spoon, transfer to a paper towel–lined plate to drain, patting them gently with another paper towel to help remove the excess oil. Sprinkle immediately with salt and spice mix or paprika or garam masala, and toss well. Serve hot, warm, or at room temperature.

CRISPY ONION FRITTERS WITH WHOLE SPICES AND HOT SAUCE

Onion fritters are exactly the kind of thing to make when there is nothing in the house for dinner.

This is what I was thinking recently, when I was so entrenched on the couch, bone tired after a long day of doing who knows what, that I groaned to my husband Daniel that there was nothing in the house to eat.

So what if the fridge is stocked with eggs, milk, yogurt, arugula, onions, and an alarming number of condiments. In the pantry are bags of pasta and cornmeal, cans of beans and chipotle chiles in adobo sauce, not to mention the smoked mussels and corn fungus someone brought as a gift that I haven't figured out what to do with. And then there's the freezer, crammed full of sausages and chicken thighs and smoked squabs and things of that nature.

Daniel knows to translate "there's nothing to eat" into "let's order in," and, on cue, retrieved the take-out menu of our favorite local Indian restaurant.

While I was perusing it, I spotted the spiced onion fritters called pakoras and wished we could order them. At the restaurant, they are golden brown perfection, with a brittle crust containing a slew of slithery, cumin-scented onions. They don't work for takeout, though, turning limp and sad during the five-block trek.

We placed the order sans pakoras, and while we waited for the doorbell to ring, I thought about shaking off at least some of my mealtime lethargy and actually getting off the couch to make some.

I knew that once I got the image of those golden, salty, and oily fritters in my head, nothing short of whipping up a batch would rid me of it.

The only potential flaw in this plan, I discovered when I Googled "onion pakoras," was that all the recipes use chickpea flour as the base. This is probably the one thing I don't keep in my overstuffed cupboard.

No matter, I'd just use regular flour instead, and an egg to make up for the binding qualities of the legume flour.

While the oil heated, I mixed up a simple batter of flour, egg, milk, and lightly crushed cumin and coriander, and added thinly sliced onions. When I fried them, they burst into exuberant spiders with long, crunchy legs.

We ate them while they were hot, squirted with sriracha and lime juice, and they were meaty, sweet, and fiery without being so filling that they ruined our appetite for chana shag when it finally arrived.

And the best thing about onion fritters, I thought as I munched, is that I could even fry up a batch if, one day, there really wasn't much in the house to eat. Or, that being unlikely, I'll just make them again the next time I crave them. At least I know I'll have all the ingredients on hand.

Crispy Onion Fritters with Whole Spices and Hot Sauce

Time: 30 minutes, plus 30 minutes' resting time

Makes 24 fritters

½ teaspoon whole cumin seed

½ teaspoon whole coriander seed

1 cup all-purpose flour

1 teaspoon baking powder

½ teaspoon kosher salt, plus additional for serving

1 cup whole milk or water

1 large egg

¼ teaspoon freshly squeezed lime juice (optional)

¼ teaspoon Tabasco sauce

1 large onion, peeled and sliced lengthwise (top to bottom) into ¼-inch-thick slices

Canola or vegetable oil, for frying

Lime wedges, for serving (optional)

Hot sauce, such as sriracha or harissa, for serving (optional)

1. With a mortar and pestle, lightly crush the cumin and coriander seeds (the aim is to break them up, not to grind them to a powder; you want texture

and crunch). In a large bowl, whisk together the flour, baking powder, salt, and spices. In a separate bowl, whisk together the milk, egg, lime juice (if desired), and Tabasco.

2. Whisk the flour mixture into the milk mixture until just blended (do not overmix). The batter should be slightly thicker in texture than cream; if it's too thick, thin with a little bit of milk, or if it's too thin, sprinkle with additional flour. Stir in the onions. Let the mixture rest 10 to 30 minutes.

3. Meanwhile, fill a large pot halfway with oil and heat until the temperature registers 375°F on a deep-fat thermometer.

4. Working in batches, drop the battered onions by the tablespoon into the oil. Fry, turning occasionally, until golden all over, 2 to 3 minutes total. Use a slotted spoon to transfer the onions to a paper towel–lined plate to drain. Sprinkle with salt and serve, if desired, with lime wedges and hot sauce.

DEEP-FRIED BOURBON
PEACH PIES

If it weren't for a certain ten-year-old friend of mine, I might never have contemplated a fling with an electric deep-fryer. But when I heard that Madeleine Dulchin got a cute little portable one for her birthday, I begged her mother to let her bring it away with all of us for our annual Memorial Day weekend in the country.

"I'll supply the candy bars," I promised, channeling my inner fish-and-chips wrangler.

We spent three grease-splattered days testing out the relative merits of deep-fried Peppermint Patties and Tootsie Rolls versus the classic Mars bars and Snickers. (The peppermint patties, which ballooned into intense, fudgy orbs, easily won.)

Back in my own kitchen, the urge to deep-fry lived on. I didn't have an electric deep-fryer, but I did have a big pot, which is much quicker to clean than the gadget anyway.

Having overdosed on fried candy early during my weekend away, at home, I focused on more adult fodder, like olives, salami, and Camembert. But soon enough, my pesky sweet tooth got the better of me. I was craving a fried dessert that was classier than candy but more summery than doughnuts and beignets.

During our unctuous weekend, I had impulsively fried slices of tempura-battered, leftover rhubarb-strawberry pie, which were a big hit with both the under- and over-ten sets. It was while daydreaming about those crisp, fruit-filled delights that an idea glittered in my mind.

Individual deep-fried fruit pies, of course.

A Southern specialty also known as hand pies, deep-fried pies are basically fried turnovers that can be stuffed with anything either savory or sweet, though peaches are a favorite. They're what Hostess based its own cloying, fruit-scarce version on.

I delved into my cookbook collection, but even in Southern cookbooks, recipes were few and far between (I found exactly two). As always, the Internet delivered thousands. But most, it seemed, relied on plumped-up dried peaches rather than fresh fruit. According to Ronni Lundy, in *Butter Beans to Blackberries*, fresh fruit wasn't appropriate in a Southern fried pie because not only doesn't it taste right, it will also make the pie "too runny to eat out of hand."

But with fragrant, ripe peaches overflowing their greenmarket bins (not to mention my fruit bowl), I really wanted to figure out a way to use them. If runniness could be a problem, I could just briefly simmer the fruit, along with brown sugar, bourbon, and cinnamon for flavor, to condense the juices and reduce the ooze factor.

If the vast majority of recipes called for dried fruit, there was absolutely no consensus when it came to the crust. Shortenings varied from lard to vegetable shortening to occasionally butter. I chose butter because I thought the flavor would be the nicest with fresh peaches, almost like peaches and cream. I also took the advice of Ken Haedrich, in his masterful pastry tome *Pie*, to strengthen the dough with a little egg.

Finally, as a last-minute concession to the deep-fry-phobes in my life, I decided to bake half the pies as if they were turnovers.

I heated up the oil, preheated the oven, cranked up the air conditioner, and set to work. About forty minutes later, I had one each fried and baked pie on plates, awaiting my fork.

The baked ones looked glossy and golden compared to the unevenly browned fried specimens, and seemed like ideal pies for picnics. Because of the egg in the crust, they weren't quite as flaky as a regular peach pie, but the filling was juicy and succulent and just sweet enough. Delightful, I thought as I licked up the crumbs.

Then I tried a fried pie. If the baked turnovers were delicate and refined, the fried ones were over-the-top luscious. The oily bath caused the pastry to puff up and crisp on the outside but remain tender and pillowy within. And the filling held the line between liquid and solid, so eating them out of hand was a pleasure, not a hazard.

Best of all, although most deep-fried foods turn from divine to detestable when they cool down, the fried pies lost only a modicum of charm when I ate another for breakfast the next day.

Deep-Fried Bourbon Peach Pies

FOR THE CRUST

2¾ cups all-purpose flour

1 tablespoon granulated sugar

1 teaspoon kosher salt

1 cup (2 sticks) unsalted butter, chilled and cubed

1 large egg, whisked with enough ice-cold water to make ½ cup

FOR THE FILLING

1¼ pounds ripe peaches

2½ tablespoons light brown sugar

1 tablespoon Minute tapioca

2 teaspoons bourbon (or substitute orange juice)

¾ teaspoon freshly squeezed lemon juice

¼ teaspoon ground cinnamon

Vegetable oil, for frying

Cinnamon sugar (see Note), for sprinkling

1. In a food processor, pulse together the flour, granulated sugar, and salt. Add the butter and pulse until the mixture forms pea-size crumbs. Pulse in the egg mixture, a tablespoon at a time, until the dough just comes together (it should be moist but not wet, and it's okay if you don't use all of it). Divide the dough into 10 equal pieces. Flatten into discs with your palm, wrap in plastic, and chill for at least 45 minutes.

2. Meanwhile, make the filling: Using a paring knife, peel the peaches if desired (if they are ripe, the peels slip right off) and pit them; slice ¼ inch thick. Transfer the peaches to a large skillet. Stir in the brown sugar, tapioca, bourbon or orange juice, lemon juice, and cinnamon. Let sit for 10 minutes, then bring to a simmer over medium-high heat. Cook until the sugar dissolves, 2 to 3 minutes. Transfer the mixture to a bowl, preferably metal, and freeze for at least 20 minutes to cool, stirring once or twice.

3. Fill a medium pot with 4 inches of oil and heat to 375°F.
4. On a floured surface, roll out the dough into 6-inch rounds. Place 1 heaping tablespoon of filling in the center of each round. Using a pastry brush, lightly moisten the edges of each circle with water. Fold the dough over the filling and pinch the edges to seal.
5. Fry the pies, in batches, until dark golden, 3 to 4 minutes. Use a slotted spoon to transfer to a paper towel–lined plate. Sprinkle immediately with cinnamon sugar.

VARIATION: **BAKED BOURBON PEACH TURNOVERS**

For baked peach turnovers, prepare the dough without the egg, using all water instead. Shape and fill the pies as instructed. Arrange on two greased baking sheets. Prick each pie with a fork; brush the tops lightly with milk or cream and dust with cinnamon sugar. Bake in a 375°F oven until dark golden and bubbling, 30 to 40 minutes.

NOTE: To make your own cinnamon sugar, combine ¼ cup granulated sugar with 2 teaspoons ground cinnamon.

VARIATION: GINGERY DOUGHNUT FINGERS

After the unctuous weekend of the deep-fryer was nearing to a close, and all the candy, cookies, and pies had been swished in hot oil and consumed, my friend Josh realized that there had been a complete and lamentable dearth of doughnuts.

What's a deep-frying party all about without the doughnuts, Josh pointed out. Aren't doughnuts the ultimate expression of deep-fried satisfaction?

Josh, it turns out, loves doughnuts.

But the electric fryer had already been cooled down and laboriously emptied, and the principal deep-fryers, Madeleine, Marina (daughter of our friends Karen and Dave, who own the house we were staying in), and I were so grease-steeped that we could not be convinced to fire up the machine no matter what.

The following year, Josh's wife, Bryony, set about correcting this terrible doughnut lapse. She came armed with all the necessary ingredients, including yeast, flour, butter, and a jar of raspberry preserves just in case anyone in the group yearned for jelly doughnuts.

All of this doughnut to-do was no trouble because Bryony is an accomplished pastry maker. When my friend Josh was just starting to date her, he'd marvel at her cookies and cakes.

"I'm dating a baker," he'd say proudly over and over again for more than a year until he finally married her. Now he says with a satisfied nod, "My wife is an amazing baker."

And it's true. Her almond butter cookies are addictive, her butter cakes ethereal, and her pie pastry flaky and light.

So when she mentioned the word *doughnut*, I jumped in and agreed to help facilitate this worthy endeavor.

Bryony used a simple but rich yeast dough recipe, and when it had risen, she rolled it out with a wine bottle (the country house had no rolling pin). Then she cut out circles with an overturned glass, dabbed on some raspberry jelly, and sealed the doughnuts up with another dough circle. When they had risen a second time, we fried them up and ate them warm and rolled in sugar, crimson jelly dribbling out the sides.

We all agreed that doughnuts should become a Memorial Day weekend tradition up in the country, and when we packed up the fryer, I was already anticipating next year's batch.

But the next year, Madeleine didn't bring her deep-fryer. At twelve, she and Marina were already past that stage; instead, they brought a tent. Camping outside became the kid focus of the weekend. Karen picked up some pies from the Rileyville general store for our sweet-tooth satisfaction, and the doughnuts were forgotten by everyone but me.

Of course I knew that I could fry my own batch of doughnuts back in Brooklyn. All the way home in the car, I daydreamed about the texture of the warm, fluffy fried morsels enveloped in sweet, sandy sugar that crunched mildly under the tooth.

The next time I make doughnuts, I thought, I'll play up that sugariness even more by using cinnamon sugar instead of plain granulated. And maybe

I'll skip the jelly entirely, focusing on the contrast between the soft cake and crunchy sugar. Plus, they'd be a lot less work.

A few weeks later, I was doughnut-hungry enough to put my plan into action. While I was rifling through the spice shelf for the cinnamon to make the cinnamon sugar, I spotted the ground ginger.

Why doesn't anyone ever make ginger sugar, I wondered, and how would it be on a doughnut? I decided to find out.

First I made the doughnut dough, adding grated fresh gingerroot and some ground ginger for an extra kick. After it rose, I formed it into fingers so the doughnuts would look like miniature sugared crullers.

Then I fried them up, watching the slim twigs puff golden brown in the oil. As soon as they were cool enough to touch, I rolled them in ginger sugar and took a bite.

They were crisp and supremely gingery, in a fresh, lively, almost citrusy way from the gingerroot, with a sweet, sugary jolt from the ginger sugar.

I'll definitely make them again come Memorial Day, and we'll see if they're tempting enough to Marina and Madeleine to lure them out of their tent.

Gingery Doughnut Fingers

Time: 30 minutes,
plus 4 hours'
rising time

Makes
36 doughnuts

FOR THE GINGER SUGAR

¼ cup sugar

1 teaspoon ground ginger

FOR THE DOUGHNUTS

⅔ cup milk

1 teaspoon active dry yeast

2¾ cups all-purpose flour, plus additional

1 large egg

2 tablespoons sugar

1 tablespoon grated fresh gingerroot

1 teaspoon ground ginger

½ teaspoon kosher salt

½ teaspoon ground cinnamon

2 tablespoons unsalted butter, melted

Lard or vegetable oil, for frying

1. In a small bowl, combine the sugar and ginger and set aside.
2. To make the doughnuts, place the milk and yeast in the bowl of an electric mixer fitted with the paddle attachment. Cover the mixture with the flour and let sit for 10 minutes. Add the egg, sugar, fresh ginger, ground ginger, salt, and cinnamon, and mix on medium-low speed until the dough pulls away from the sides of the bowl, about 10 minutes.
3. Pour in the melted butter and continue to mix until completely incorporated, about 5 minutes more. Cover the bowl with plastic wrap and leave at room temperature for 20 minutes. Transfer the dough to the refrigerator to chill for 2 hours. It will be denser than bread dough, yet slightly springy.
4. Cut the dough into 1-ounce blobs and roll into logs (they will be about 1½ inches long), dusting the dough with flour if it is too sticky to handle. Place the logs on a greased cookie sheet 3 inches apart. Cover the sheet with a

kitchen towel and let sit in a warm place until they have doubled in size, about 2 hours.

5. To fry the doughnuts, have ready a couple of paper towel–lined plates or a large paper bag–lined platter and the bowl of ginger sugar. Fill a large saucepan halfway with fat and heat to 350°F. (You can use a deep-fry thermometer to measure the temperature.) Plunge 3 doughnuts at a time into the oil, turning frequently until golden brown, 2 to 3 minutes. Transfer the doughnuts with a slotted spoon to the lined plate or platter. Roll the doughnuts in the ginger sugar while they are still warm. Serve immediately or within a few hours. They'll be stale in 12 hours, so eat them while fresh.

VARIATION: FRIED SEMOLINA SPICE CAKES WITH ORANGE BLOSSOM WATER

You'd think after my ginger doughnuts I'd be sated for at least a few months. But no. Weeks later I was craving something sweet and crisp, sugar-coated and fried.

Instead of doughnuts, I made a yeast-free semolina cake doused in orange blossom water. The recipe is based on one from pastry chef Jehangir Mehta's cookbook *Mantra: The Rules of Indulgence,* though I added spices and the topping to make it even more perfumed. Unlike doughnuts, which grow stale in a matter of hours, these dense cakes are still good the next morning. With a cup of tea and a few tangerines, they make a fine breakfast.

Fried Semolina Spice Cakes with Orange Blossom Water

Time: 30 minutes,
plus 3 hours'
standing time

Makes 30 cakes

1 cup semolina or farina (Cream of Wheat works)

2/3 cup all-purpose flour

1/2 cup bread flour

3/4 teaspoon baking powder

1/2 teaspoon ground cinnamon

1/4 teaspoon freshly grated nutmeg

Pinch cloves

1 tablespoon unsalted butter, melted

1/2 cup sugar

3 large eggs

1 tablespoon plain yogurt

1 teaspoon freshly grated orange zest

Lard or vegetable oil, for frying

Orange blossom water, for drizzling

Confectioners' sugar, for sprinkling

1. Sift the semolina, all-purpose flour, bread flour, baking powder, cinnamon, nutmeg, and cloves into a medium bowl. In the bowl of an electric mixer, beat the melted butter and sugar on high speed for 3 minutes. Reduce the speed to low and beat in the eggs, one at a time, scraping down the sides of the bowl between additions. Add the yogurt and orange zest and beat on high speed for another 30 seconds. Cover the bowl loosely with plastic wrap, and let sit at room temperature for 3 hours. It will thicken up considerably.

2. Fill a large saucepan halfway with fat and heat to 325°F. (You can use a deep-fry thermometer to measure the temperature.) Have ready a couple of paper towel–lined plates or a large paper bag–lined platter.

3. Using a teaspoon, carefully drop dollops of the dough, 3 or 4 at a time, into the oil. Fry the dough, turning occasionally, until light brown, about

5 minutes. Using a slotted spoon, transfer the fried cakes to the paper towel–lined plate to drain. Drizzle each cake with the orange blossom water and sprinkle generously with the confectioners' sugar. Serve warm or at room temperature. These will last for several hours or even overnight.

9 Holiday Food

C lever food is not appreciated at Christmas," the great British food writer Jane Grigson once wrote. "It makes the little ones cry and the old ones nervous."

It took me years to accept this statement as truth, and admit that even the intrepid eaters in my foodie family want comfort during the holiday season.

Sure, in the weeks before a holiday, we flirt with the notion of making dramatic changes. We fantasize about whole roasted pigs in place of turkeys, fried doughnuts instead of latkes, osso buco in lieu of pot roast. And every holiday we gravitate back to the family's old favorites, serving the same menu, year in and year out.

Of course when I say that we serve the same menu, I mean *approximately*. While last year's Thanksgiving bird was brined for two days, next year's might be rubbed with salt and spices the night before. The mashed sweet potatoes, usually seasoned with some combination of butter, spices, and booze (brandy, rum, bourbon), could slurp up coconut milk and chile instead. But the roasted turkey and the mashed sweet potatoes stand, no matter how loud the siren's song of pork and buttered spaetzle. Ditto the crisp and salty latkes, the tender pot roast, and the velvety sweet-and-sour fish that punctuate our calendars as a year of good eating unfolds.

I suppose this desire to fiddle with recipes is a little like our family's culture of storytelling. It's not that we ever change the plotline, exactly. It's just that the specifics are negotiable; we pick and choose (and, okay, sometimes make up) the details depending upon our moods, our audience, or how loud the person talking over us is.

The one about the Passover when my sister and I spiked Elijah's Manischewitz with hot sauce—just to see which adult played the prophet and gulped down the wine while we children answered the door—can be poignant, cynical, or hilarious depending on the telling. And the fact that my uncle Danny turned even redder in the face than usual and downed three glasses of water afterward answered the question.

But in the larger scheme of things, the family dishes and stories stay more or less the same, getting trotted out at the appropriate time of year, then packed up with the mothballs until needed. Potato pancakes must wait for Hanukkah, lemon pot roast for Rosh Hashana, and the story of Elijah's cup for Passover. By abstaining the rest of the year, we've had a chance to yearn for them, and are willing to forget that we know them all by heart.

CRUNCHY NOODLE KUGEL
À LA AUNT MARTHA

Every family tells the same stories over and over, and one of ours is about kugel. It gets dusted off and retold on Rosh Hashana when, over my mother's experimental kugel du jour (noodle-roasted red pepper–scallion or potato-rosemary-shallot), someone inevitably spins the tale of how Great-Aunt Martha's famous noodle kugel recipe came to be.

It goes something like this: When Uncle Alan was a kid, he liked only the crunchy kugel top, and so would pick the crisp, golden noodle shards off the surface while the kugel cooled in the kitchen. He did this for a few years until his mother, my very practical great-aunt Martha, came up with her legendary solution. She began baking the kugel in individual muffin tins so it would be crunchy through and through. And, thinking realistically, if Alan did deface the tops, she could serve the kugel muffins turned upside down.

Being of the crunchy-loving, burned noodle–picking ilk myself, I always listened with interest, wondering what such a marvelous-sounding kugel would taste like and why we didn't make it like that.

"It was kind of dry and hard and salty," said my mother when I got around to asking last year. "Aunt Martha wasn't a great cook. But it's a good story."

Of course a better story would end in a prized family heirloom recipe for a noodle kugel that was crunchy and burnished on top, but still creamy and moist underneath. Made with luscious dairy products, melted butter, and many eggs, this noodle-rich legacy would be sweetened with cinnamon, sugar, and plenty of soft, chewy raisins. Maybe I could tweak Great-Aunt Martha's basic mixture something closer to my kugel ideal.

"Aunt Martha never used raisins or sugar or cinnamon. Her kugel was savory," said my mother when I related my fantasy.

So much for rehabilitating Great-Aunt Martha's recipe. Instead, I'd steal her form (baking in muffin tins for maximum crunch) and create my own kugel content.

Freed from the ancestral binds, I could go off in any number of directions, just as long as I kept the kugel's essential spirit intact. But what, exactly, was that? Given the outré kugels of my childhood—the lasagna-esque mixes of onions, tomatoes, and noodles; the herb-layered potato and mushroom gratins—what exactly could you get away with and still call kugel?

I asked my mother.

"Oh, I don't know," she replied. "I guess as long as it has potatoes or noodles or matzoh and you serve it on a Jewish holiday, it counts."

This actually wasn't far from what slightly more responsible research bore out. Rabbi Gil Marks, in his thorough book *The World of Jewish Cooking*, writes that a kugel (which comes from the German word for *ball*) was originally a dumpling made from flour or stale bread that was cooked in the cholent, a Sabbath stew of beans and beef.

The great Jewish food writer Joan Nathan defined kugels as casseroles traditionally made from noodles or potatoes. But, she added, more modern interpretations could include anything from rhubarb and blueberries to panko, goat cheese, and broccoli.

Frankly, compared to what my mother had been whipping up for decades, those variations sounded pretty run-of-the-mill. What I really craved was a classic noodle kugel made the way Great-Aunt Martha should have done (says me).

Recipes for that kind of eggy, raisin-laden noodle kugel were almost too easy to find. Since we aren't kosher, and separating meat and dairy isn't an issue, I immediately dismissed anything calling for tofu cream cheese. I also nixed recipes with bread crumb or nut or cornflake toppings. Like Uncle Alan, what I love about kugel is the crunchy noodles.

After skimming dozens of recipes, I eventually chose cottage over farmer cheese because I wanted organic, and my supermarket doesn't stock organic farmer cheese. I decided to add sour cream for a velvety texture, and use one more egg than most recipes call for, for lightness. Then I doubled the amount of cinnamon because I like it.

I also decided to soak the raisins before mixing them in. Not only would the soaking liquid add flavor, soaking the raisins would keep them from burning in the extra-hot oven needed for a very dark brown kugel top. For the soaking liquid, I could have used dark rum, Manischewitz, or kirsch, but I settled on sherry since I had an open bottle of fino I wanted to use up.

I mixed everything together and filled my muffin tins. There was still a lot of kugel mix left, so I buttered a jelly roll pan (as opposed to a deeper casserole dish) and filled that, too, figuring that the greater amount of exposed surface area would yield a higher crisp-to-soft ratio, mimicking the muffin tins. Then I baked everything at a slightly higher temperature than usual so the top would get extra crisp before the bottom had a chance to dry out.

The kugels emerged from the oven gorgeously golden, with the tips of the noodles singed to a chocolate hue.

Then I sampled both versions. As good as the muffin kugels were, the kugel baked in the jelly roll pan turned out even better—just as crème brûlée toothsome on top, but much softer and more custardy underneath, and studded with sweet pockets of plump raisins. Finally, an heirloom-worthy recipe that I could pass on.

And as an added bonus, baking the kugel in a jelly roll pan meant I wouldn't have to scrub out individual muffin cups when the party was over. Now, that would be something ever-practical Great-Aunt Martha would have definitely appreciated.

Crunchy Noodle Kugel à la Aunt Martha

1 cup raisins
Sherry or orange juice
6 tablespoons unsalted butter, cut into pieces, plus additional for the pan
1 pound wide egg noodles
4 large eggs
3 cups cottage cheese
1 cup sour cream
⅓ cup sugar
1 teaspoon ground cinnamon
Grated zest of 1 lemon
Pinch salt

Time: 1 hour

Serves 8 to 12

1. Put the raisins in a microwave-safe bowl or small saucepan and cover with sherry or orange juice. Heat on the stove or in the microwave until the liquid is steaming hot (about 3 minutes on the stove or 1½ minutes in the microwave). Let cool while you prepare the kugel mixture.

2. Preheat the oven to 400°F. Butter an 11×17-inch jelly roll pan. Cook the noodles according to the package directions and drain well. Immediately return the noodles to the pot and add the butter. Toss until the butter melts.

3. In a large bowl, whisk together the eggs, cottage cheese, sour cream, sugar, cinnamon, lemon zest, and salt. Drain the raisins and add to the bowl along with the buttered noodles. Mix well.

4. Spread the mixture in the prepared pan and smooth the top. Bake until the top is crusty and golden, 25 to 35 minutes. Serve warm or at room temperature.

VARIATION: MY MOTHER'S CRISPY POTATO KUGEL WITH ROSEMARY AND FRIED SHALLOTS

Crisp on top, meltingly soft in the center, and imbued with herbs, garlic, and shallots, this is my favorite of my mother's kugels du jour. She cooks it rösti potato–style in a skillet, searing the bottom on the stove before running the whole thing under the broiler for maximum crunch. It reminds me of a giant latke, but thicker and more aromatic.

My Mother's Crispy Potato Kugel with Rosemary and Fried Shallots

6 large russet potatoes, peeled and quartered

2 yellow onions, peeled and quartered

5 large eggs

¼ cup all-purpose flour

½ cup extra-virgin olive oil

2½ teaspoons kosher salt, plus additional for seasoning

2 teaspoons freshly ground black pepper

2 teaspoons finely chopped fresh rosemary

2 garlic cloves, finely chopped

3 shallots, peeled and thinly sliced crosswise

Time: 1½ hours

Serves 6

1. Preheat the oven to 400°F.

2. Fit a food processor with a medium grating blade. With the motor running, alternate pushing the potato and onion chunks through the feed tube. Transfer the mixture to a dish towel–lined colander. Wrap the mixture in the towel and squeeze out as much excess liquid as possible.

3. In a large bowl, whisk together the eggs, flour, ¼ cup oil, salt, pepper, rosemary, and garlic.

4. Heat 1 tablespoon of the remaining oil in a 9-inch, slope-sided skillet. Add the shallots in a single layer over high heat. Let sit several minutes before stirring. Continue to cook, stirring occasionally, until the shallots are crispy and dark brown, about 7 minutes total.

5. Fold the potato mixture and shallots in the egg mixture. Return the skillet to high heat and add the remaining 3 tablespoons oil. Tilt the skillet to grease the bottom and sides of the pan. Carefully press the potato mixture into the pan. Cook over high heat for 3 minutes (this will help sear the bottom crust of the kugel). Transfer the pan to the oven and bake until the

potatoes are tender and the top of the kugel is golden brown, 1 to 1¼ hours.

6. Place the kugel under the broiler for 1 to 2 minutes to form a crisp crust on top (watch carefully to see that it does not burn). Run an offset spatula around the edges and bottom of the kugel and carefully invert it onto a large plate or platter. Sprinkle with salt and serve.

ALMOST AUNT SANDY'S SWEET-AND-SOUR SALMON

All the other relatives in the family served gefilte fish at holiday meals, but not Aunt Sandy.

Famous in Flatbush for her flamboyant parties (think Middle Eastern meze garnished with belly dancers), Aunt Sandy liked to do things with a flourish. Instead of breaking the fast on Yom Kippur with gefilte fish, kugel, and bagels and lox, she made potage Parmentier, pesto pasta salad—and, her masterpiece, sweet-and-sour fish in a shimmering aspic.

It was a knockout of a dish. Aunt Sandy used two kinds of fish—cod and salmon—to create a pink-and-ecru mosaic. Rounds of orange carrot tangled with slivers of onion and dots of peppercorns in the pale, wobbly jelly. The adults gobbled it down to the very last tidbit of fish skin, then talked about Sandy's fish for the rest of the year, until it was time to atone, then gorge once again.

When I was a kid, I imagined being able to appreciate Aunt Sandy's sweet-and-sour fish as a passage into adulthood, similar to acquiring a taste for capers. So every year I swallowed a piece of the salmon, trying to discern its finer points. But as much as I wanted to adore it, the sharp flavors were too intense for my underage palate.

Then, suddenly, my uncle Danny died, and Aunt Sandy stopped hosting the break fast. I never had the chance to grow into sweet-and-sour fish, even now that I'm old and wise enough to start piling capers on top of my lox.

Eventually, the break-fast baton was passed to me. And one year, I decided it was time to resurrect Aunt Sandy's sweet-and-sour fish, which I became determined to love, no matter what I might have to do to the recipe to get there.

But first I wanted to do a test run to see how Sandy's recipe would hold up after all these years.

I followed it to the letter, boiling the fish bones along with onion and garlic, then seasoning the liquid with vinegar and sugar before using it to oven poach the salmon. I put it in the fridge and waited for it to gel.

Hours later, it had not. I don't know if it was the absence of a fish head in my broth, but my pretty fish remained submerged in a splashing puddle.

Still, I took a bite, and immediately remembered why I never liked Aunt Sandy's fish. Even to grown-up me, the vinegar was too tart and the sugar cloying, though I liked the idea of serving the fish with broth instead of jelly. As for the salmon itself, that was divine—cooked to velvety perfection. Salmon in sweet-and-sour broth had potential.

So I made it again, reducing the sugar and substituting balsamic for the sharper wine vinegar. I also added raisins and sliced lemons, an idea stolen from a similar recipe I found online. I eliminated the peppercorns, which were unpleasant to crunch, adding aromatic fresh thyme instead.

Finally, because I didn't want aspic, I substituted prepared fish broth for the mess of boiling bones.

As the fish baked, a rich, caramelized scent wafted through the kitchen and made me so hungry that I couldn't wait for the dish to chill before digging in my spoon.

The broth was light and refreshing with a gentle acidity that was balanced by the sweetness of the raisins. And the fish was succulent and rich and suffused with flavor. At last, I had developed a taste for sweet-and-sour fish—or rather, had developed a sweet-and-sour fish exactly to my taste.

Almost Aunt Sandy's Sweet-and-Sour Salmon

6 cups fish broth

3 garlic cloves, smashed and peeled

1 bay leaf

Kosher salt to taste

1 small red onion, thinly sliced

½ bunch thyme

8 center-cut, skin-on wild salmon fillets, 3 ounces each

Freshly ground black pepper to taste

½ cup golden raisins

1 small lemon, thinly sliced

¼ cup balsamic vinegar

2 tablespoons light brown sugar

Challah, for serving

Time: 30 minutes,
plus chilling if desired

Serves 8
as an appetizer

1. Preheat the oven to 350°F. In a large pot, simmer the fish broth with the garlic, bay leaf, and salt for 15 minutes.

2. In the bottom of a 9×13-inch baking dish, scatter the red onion and half of the thyme. Place the salmon on top, skin side down, and season with salt and pepper. Scatter the remaining thyme, raisins, and lemon on top.

3. Stir the vinegar and sugar into the broth and let simmer for 1 minute to dissolve the sugar. Remove the garlic and bay leaf from the broth, and carefully pour over the fish. Bake for 8 to 10 minutes, until the fish is just cooked through to taste. Serve hot, warm, or cold, with challah for dipping into the broth.

BRAND-NEW HEIRLOOM
POTATO LATKES

There are fat latkes and there are thin latkes, chunky latkes and smooth latkes, even latkes made with sweet potato or celery root or zucchini (my mother's favorite). But as long as they are fried until crisp and golden, then eaten hot from the pan sometime near Hanukkah, all latkes are lovable, and love them we do.

This is a good thing, because for years in my family, we were latke dilettantes, flitting from recipe to recipe without ever committing to the one perfect combination of potato, onion, salt, and egg that would define a latke for us.

As December approached, we'd clip recipes, pitting a newfound technique or ingredient combination against last year's batch. We tried every variety of potato, including purple fingerings (makes ugly latkes); experimented with parboiling (not worth the time), baking powder (yes!), beaten egg whites (no!), food processors (another yes!). All resulting latkes were delightful for a season, but none quite perfect enough to be invited back next year. And this was just fine. We were happy to continue playing the latke field without the need to settle down.

But then one Hanukkah—the year of the blender latkes where a whole potato was pulverized, then fried into flat, breakfast-like pancakes, to be exact—I'd had enough.

I was finally ready to give up the latke chase and cozy up to one eligible recipe, one that I could become so intimate with that as the years went by, I'd no longer have to fish out the measuring spoons. My pinch of this and a pinch of that would become ingrained and precise; when I was old and gray, my grandchildren would beg me to write down the proportions that by then I'd only know by feel.

But first, I'd have to start by figuring out what I wanted in a latke.

My favorite thing about them, I realized when I started analyzing, are those crisp long shards of the grated potato that gain a potato chip snap after sizzling in the hot oil. To encourage this, I decided my latkes recipe should be on the thin and lacy side rather than thick and hash brown–like.

Furthermore, I wanted an unfussy process, something that wouldn't require doing things like separating the potato starch from the drained potato liquid, then adding it back into the batter. Lastly, the ingredients should be fundamental and easy to find (no purchased potato starch, for example) if I happened to be spending Hanukkah outside of New York City, perhaps in a lovely rented beach shack in the Caribbean.

Once I had my goal in mind, I started reading recipes, looking for one that combined all these attributes, and I came close in Mitchell Davis's *The Mensch Chef*. His mother's recipe seemed right in terms of technique. She grates the potatoes and onions in a food processor, squeezes them dry, and adds egg and matzoh meal to hold everything together. Then she fries the cakes up, flattening them with a spatula until they are thin and crisp.

This sounded about right, though I wasn't crazy about matzoh meal, since it didn't fulfill my Caribbean Island criteria.

But if I stirred in flour instead and added a touch of baking powder to help lighten the earthy potatoes, well, that might just be the latke recipe I'd been looking for.

When Hanukkah came around, I put my plan into action, grating, squeezing, and stirring up the latkes just as I had sketched out in my head. Then I fried them into small, two-bite patties as my family looked on, amused and excited. As soon as they were cool enough to touch, everyone snatched one off the paper bag they were draining on.

They were compact and very brown, with a deep crunch that yielded to a tender, soft potato interior. Keeping them small helped maximize the crunch while making them all too easy to devour before they ever hit a plate (we piled the sour cream and either applesauce or salmon roe on top). They were just what we were all looking for in a latke. And we've been off the market, recipe-wise, ever since.

Brand-New Heirloom Potato Latkes

Time: 30 minutes

Makes 16 to
20 latkes

2 large russet potatoes (about 1 pound), scrubbed and
   cut lengthwise into quarters
1 large onion (8 ounces), peeled and cut into quarters
1/2 cup all-purpose flour
2 large eggs
2 1/2 teaspoons kosher salt
1 teaspoon baking powder
1/2 teaspoon freshly ground black pepper
Chicken fat, duck fat, or vegetable oil, for frying

1. Using a food processor with a coarse grating disc, grate the potatoes and onion. Transfer the mixture to a clean dish towel and squeeze and wring out as much of the liquid as possible.
2. Working quickly, transfer the mixture to a large bowl. Add the flour, eggs, salt, baking powder, and pepper and mix until the flour is absorbed.
3. In a medium heavy-bottomed pan over medium-high heat, pour in about 1/4 inch of the oil. Once the oil is hot (a drop of batter placed in the pan should sizzle), use a heaping tablespoon to drop the batter into the hot pan, cooking 3 to 4 latkes at one time. Use a spatula to flatten and shape the drops into discs. When the edges of the latkes are brown and crispy, about 5 minutes, flip. Cook until the second side is deeply browned, about another 5 minutes. Transfer the latkes to a paper towel–lined plate to drain. Repeat with the remaining batter.

NOTE: This recipe can be doubled, tripled, and so on, ad infinitum.

VARIATION: MY MOTHER'S ZUCCHINI LATKES

Decades ago, when my sister and I were young and my parents in the throes of one of their short-lived healthful-eating phases, my mother made zucchini latkes.

Thinking of it as a way to get more vegetables into the family diet, she shredded a zucchini, mixed it with potato, and fried the resulting mess up in a nonstick pan with virtually no oil. The latkes were flabby and mushy and needed globs of (nonfat) sour cream to make them vaguely palatable. My sister and I pushed them around on our plates for a while before feeding it all to the dog. Then we gorged ourselves on the milk chocolate Hanukkah gelt.

Needless to say, this was not a successful experiment in familial salubriousness. But it was mercifully short-lived. A few Hanukkahs later, we were back to shredded potatoes fried in olive oil, or, better, duck fat, until crackling brown and savory.

Even though she abandoned the idea of replacing potato latkes, my mother never gave up on the zucchini kind, which she sincerely liked. So every year, she'd try some new iteration, altering the proportions of vegetable and tuber and seasonings until she finally hit on the exact right formula. It turned out to be all zucchini, no potato, with a smidgeon of rosemary. They fry up golden and very crisp, with a lighter and more brittle texture than the potato ones, and a nice herbal flavor.

Now that my sister and I have grown into vegetable-loving adults, we've come on board with the program; zucchini latkes are as much a part of Hanukkah dinner at my folks' house as the applesauce and (full-fat) sour cream that accompany them. They're so tasty, one could even make them when it wasn't Hanukkah. Just rename them zucchini-rosemary fritters, serve them with roast chicken or a nice beef stew, and no one will suspect their Jewish—or health-conscious—roots.

My Mother's Zucchini Latkes

Time: 30 minutes,
plus 20 minutes'
standing time

Makes about
10 (3-inch) latkes

2 pounds zucchini (about 4 medium)

1½ teaspoons kosher salt

½ cup all-purpose flour

2 large eggs

2 teaspoons finely chopped fresh rosemary

1 teaspoon baking powder

½ teaspoon freshly ground black pepper

Duck fat, chicken fat, or olive oil, for frying

1. Using a food processor with a coarse grating disc, grate the zucchini. Place in a bowl and toss with 1 teaspoon salt. Let stand 20 minutes. Transfer the zucchini to a colander and squeeze out as much liquid as possible.

2. Transfer the mixture to a large bowl. Add the flour, eggs, rosemary, baking powder, remaining ½ teaspoon salt, and the pepper, and mix until the flour is absorbed.

3. In a medium, heavy-bottomed pan over medium heat, melt enough fat to fill about ⅛ inch of the pan. Once hot (a drop of batter placed in the pan should sizzle), drop 2 tablespoons batter into the hot pan for each latke, cooking 3 to 4 latkes at a time. Use the back of the spoon to flatten into ¼-inch-thick discs. When the edges of the latkes are brown and crispy, 2 to 3 minutes, flip and cook until the second side is browned, about 2 minutes longer. Transfer the latkes to a paper towel–lined plate to drain. Repeat with the remaining batter.

BRAISED FLANKEN WITH POMEGRANATE

For most of the people I know, pot roast is synonymous with brisket. And this is why I spent most of my life avoiding pot roast. At its worst, brisket cooks up dry and bland, with stringy meat that begs for nearby dental floss. But even when pot roasted to perfection (of course my mother's moist, lemony version comes to mind), it's still not as succulent as lamb shanks and oxtail.

So I was happily flummoxed when, at a friend's house, I ate pot roast that was meltingly tender and profoundly beefy. It still had that characteristic ropelike texture, but the pieces of meat were supple, not tough.

"What's your secret?" I begged my friend.

She demurred.

"Secret? What secret? It's just pot roast," she said, going on to describe a typical braised meat recipe with wine, broth, and aromatic vegetables. It was a recipe like every other pot roast I've ever seen. So why did it taste so much better?

What she didn't bother to mention was the cut of meat. It took two phone calls to get it out of her. Instead of brisket, she used flanken.

"Doesn't everyone use flanken for pot roast?" she asked innocently.

I'd always thought that flanken was specific to boiled beef or soup. But a little research divulged that the brawny cut is hugely popular in braises (and pot roasting is arguably the same as braising), especially in Germany, Austria, and Hungary. It's also frequently used in Asian cuisines, particularly Korean, where it's often seared and served rare.

Arthur Schwartz, in *Jewish Home Cooking*, extols the virtues of flanken. He points out that it's from the same part of the cow as short ribs, cut across rather than along the bones.

But while short ribs, made popular by chichi restaurants like Daniel, have achieved culinary stardom and high prices at the butcher, flanken remains cheap and obscure. And just as tasty.

Naturally, the next time I wanted to make pot roast for Rosh Hashana, I bought flanken.

At first I thought of adapting my mother's lemon pot roast recipe; I really like the way the tart lemon juice cuts the richness and heaviness of the meat. But with my sister's new citrus-free diet, it seemed like the time to try something different.

I thought of other zingy flavorings—cranberry, ginger, balsamic vinegar, Granny Smith apples. Alice, my meat-eschewing friend, suggested pineapple juice, which her mother Ethel always added to flanken when she wasn't using Coca-Cola.

"It was delicious, one of the only meat dishes I actually liked back when I ate that stuff," she said.

It was high praise. But in the end, I settled on pomegranate. The vegetable market near my house sells the seeds, and they made a festive and unusual garnish sprinkled on top of the dark brown braise. To flavor the meat with pomegranate, I used bottled pomegranate juice along with wine and broth for the braising liquid

And as a last, marvelously sweet-tart touch, I stirred pomegranate molasses into the sauce.

It was the best pot roast I'd ever made—so good, I'd even be willing to try it with brisket.

Braised Flanken with Pomegranate

4 pounds flanken ribs

½ teaspoon salt, plus additional to taste

½ teaspoon freshly ground black pepper, plus additional to taste

2 tablespoons extra-virgin olive oil

3 medium carrots, peeled and diced

3 medium celery stalks, diced

2 leeks, white and light green parts, cleaned,
    quartered lengthwise, and chopped

2 garlic cloves, finely chopped

1 shallot, chopped

½ cup pomegranate juice

⅓ cup dry red wine

2 cups chicken stock, or as needed

3 thyme branches

1 rosemary branch

1 bay leaf

3 whole cloves (see Note)

1½ tablespoons pomegranate molasses (optional)

⅓ cup pomegranate seeds

2 tablespoons chopped fresh basil

Time: 40 minutes,
plus 2 hours' braising

Serves 4 to 6

1. Preheat the oven to 325°F. Season the meat generously all over with salt and pepper. Heat a large Dutch oven over medium-high heat. Sear the meat in batches until dark golden, 3 to 4 minutes per side. Transfer the seared meat to a platter.

2. Add the oil to the pan and sauté the carrots, celery, leeks, garlic, and shallot until the vegetables are softened and slightly caramelized, about 5 minutes; season lightly with salt and pepper. Add the pomegranate juice and wine and cook, scraping the browned bits from the bottom of the pan, until most of the liquid is evaporated, about 2 minutes. Stir in the stock,

thyme, rosemary, bay leaf, cloves, ½ teaspoon salt, and ½ teaspoon pepper. Return the meat to the pot. The liquid should reach halfway up the sides of the meat. If not, add a little more stock or water until it does.

3. Partially cover the pot and transfer to the oven. Cook, turning the meat every 30 minutes until fork-tender, about 2 hours.

4. If you have time, let the meat cool, then chill overnight or up to 5 days. Then remove the fat from the surface and reheat over low heat. Stir in the pomegranate molasses, if using, and sprinkle with the pomegranate seeds and basil just before serving.

NOTE: If you like, you can wrap the herbs and cloves in cheesecloth before adding to the pot.

VARIATION: MY MOTHER'S LEMON POT ROAST

My mother's recipe comes from Edda Servi Machlin's *The Classic Cuisine of the Italian Jews*, which she adapted by using brisket instead of eye of round and marinating the meat overnight in garlic. I went one step further, adding a handful of chopped garlic to the pot with the meat as it braises. It's fresh and lemony tasting, much zestier than the usual brisket, and far more tender, too, thanks to the acid in the lemon juice. It lasts for days in the fridge, and makes excellent sandwiches. Best of all, it's about the easiest brisket recipe I've ever made.

My Mother's Lemon Pot Roast

Time: 30 minutes,
plus 3 hours' cooking

Serves 10 to 12

6 garlic cloves

1½ tablespoons plus a pinch kosher salt, more to taste

1 (4½-pound) beef brisket

1 teaspoon freshly ground black pepper

3 lemons

½ cup extra-virgin olive oil

1. Mince 1 garlic clove. Using a mortar and pestle or the flat side of a heavy knife, pound or mash the garlic with a pinch of salt until it turns to a paste.

2. Season the brisket all over with salt and pepper and rub the garlic paste into the meat. Place the brisket in a large bowl or pan, cover tightly with plastic wrap, and refrigerate for at least 2 hours or overnight.

3. When you are ready to cook the brisket, preheat the oven to 325°F.

4. Finely grate the zest of 2 lemons and reserve; juice all 3 lemons.

5. Heat the oil in a 6½-quart Dutch oven until almost smoking. Sear the brisket in the oil until browned on all sides, about 10 minutes. Pour the lemon juice over the brisket and add enough water to come halfway up the sides of the meat (about 2 cups). Bring the liquid to a boil over high heat.

6. Cover the pot, transfer to the oven, and cook for 1¼ hours. Meanwhile, mince the remaining 5 garlic cloves. Turn the meat over in the pot and add the garlic. Continue to cook until the meat shreds easily with a fork, about 1 to 1¼ hours longer. Stir in the reserved lemon zest and continue to cook, uncovered, 15 minutes more.

7. Slice and serve, with the pan juices spooned over the meat. Or let cool and refrigerate for up to 5 days before reheating and serving.

STUFFINGS FOR EVERYONE

The chestnut bread stuffing, thick with mushrooms and celery, has been such a fixture at my family's Thanksgiving table that, like the great fowl itself, it never occurred to me to question it.

Still, I'd hear whisperings about stuffing with other ingredients, like wild rice or ground meat (called *farce* in French). And let's not forget the famous turducken, turkey stuffed with duck stuffed with chicken and so on. There was a whole other turkey cavity universe out there and this year, I felt ready to meet it.

But whenever I'd bring up making a change, I'd get shot down. My foodie family, adventuresome eaters on 364 days of the year, went traditional on Thanksgiving.

My mother explained it like this: "Everyone loves that chestnut stuffing, so I put my creative energy into the side dishes."

Coming from a woman who pouts when two people at the table order the same restaurant dish, it's kind of astonishing. But that's the sort of thing that happens on turkey day.

With Thanksgiving quickly approaching, I decided to pitch one last-ditch campaign. I begged my parents to let me make a different stuffing. It worked.

In order to forestall comparisons with my mother's stuffing, I decided not to use either chestnuts or bread.

The chestnuts, which my father painstakingly peeled by hand, were a relief to be rid of. Substituting for the bread would be a fun challenge, and friendly to any wheat-avoiding guests who happened by (not impossible in my house, where last-minute guests are common).

But before I'd risk serving anything to my family on a holiday, I'd need to do a test run. So I cooked up three possibilities to see how they fared.

The first was a highly seasoned, ground pork mixture—like sausage meat stuffed into fowl instead of casings. Since I had come up with the idea after reading in my *Larousse Gastronomique* about traditional French forcemeat stuffing that dates back at least to the Middle Ages (and probably to the Romans), I decided to go for a medieval flavor profile. I liberally sprinkled the pork with spices and brandy, adding apples and dried cranberries for sweetness.

I based the second recipe on a shrimp hash. A long set of associations got me there, starting with Laura Ingalls Wilder and her family's oyster stuffing for the Christmas turkey. From there I got to oyster hash, which naturally led me to shrimp hash. But instead of using regular white potatoes, I'd make it with sweet potatoes for an autumnal cast.

And finally, in the grainy vein of wild rice, I made stuffing out of barley tossed with roasted shiitake mushrooms, chive butter, hazelnuts, and plenty of lemon to zip it all up.

Then I stuffed three chickens and invited my family over for a taste.

The stuffings were all wildly and marvelously different.

The sweet potato shrimp hash was succulent, with a spicy edge from a jalapeño and a dash of chili powder. We all agreed this could also make a quirky, substantial side dish that turkey haters and pescatarians could call dinner.

The forcemeat was the most compelling, with a deeply porky, perfumed flavor that was just sweet enough.

And the barley was as supple and addictive as mashed potatoes—the kind with loads of butter and garlic mixed in.

We debated their merits but couldn't decide on only one.

Then my mother suggested using all three, stuffing them in layers into the bird.

"Your grandma used to do that with matzoh-egg stuffing and chestnut stuffing," she said. I almost didn't believe her, but then Grandma Ella was the kind of *bubbe* who made three kinds of matzoh balls every Friday night—soft, hard, and in between, so everyone would be happy.

Of course, if I wanted to make my mother happy, I'd let her make chestnut bread stuffing.

Would it be crazy to stuff the turkey with all four?

VARIATION: LEMON BARLEY STUFFING WITH SHIITAKES, HAZELNUTS, AND CHIVE BUTTER

This makes a satisfying, autumnal side dish that's a little like mushroom and barley soup, but more solid and brighter tasting. Serve it on a bed of arugula and you've got a colorful, tangy main course.

Lemon Barley Stuffing with Shiitakes, Hazelnuts, and Chive Butter

Time: 1½ hours

Makes about 9 cups, enough to stuff a 10- to 12-pound turkey

FOR THE BARLEY-MUSHROOM MIXTURE

2 tablespoons unsalted butter

2 leeks, finely chopped

2 cups pearled barley

1 rosemary branch

1½ cups chicken or vegetable stock

1½ teaspoons kosher salt, more to taste

1¼ pounds shiitake mushroom caps, sliced ¼ inch thick

3 tablespoons extra-virgin olive oil

¾ teaspoon freshly ground black pepper

1 cup coarsely chopped toasted peeled hazelnuts

½ cup chopped fresh parsley

FOR THE CHIVE BUTTER

2 large garlic cloves, finely chopped

¾ teaspoon kosher salt

Finely grated zest of 1 small lemon

1 teaspoon freshly squeezed lemon juice, more to taste

½ cup chopped chives (about 1 bunch)

4 tablespoons unsalted butter, softened

1. Preheat the oven to 400°F.

2. Melt the butter in a large pot over medium-high heat. Add the leeks and cook, stirring, until softened, about 5 minutes. Add the barley and the rosemary branch; cook 1 minute more. Pour in the stock, 1½ cups water, and ¾ teaspoon salt. Bring to a boil over high heat; reduce the heat, cover, and simmer until the barley is tender and most of the liquid has evaporated, about 1¼ hours. Check it after an hour. If it's tender but the liquid isn't absorbed, drain the barley in a strainer. Or if the liquid has evaporated and the barley is still not tender, add a little more water. It could take up to 1½ hours.

3. Meanwhile, toss the mushrooms with the oil, ¾ teaspoon salt, and the pepper. Spread in a single layer on two large baking sheets. Roast, tossing occasionally, until tender and beginning to crisp around the edges, 20 to 25 minutes.

4. Make the chive butter: With a mortar and pestle or in a mini food processor, mash together the garlic and salt until it forms a paste. Stir in the lemon zest and juice until the salt dissolves. Pound or pulse in the chives, then stir in the butter until incorporated.

5. Spoon the hot barley into a large bowl. Stir in the mushrooms, hazelnuts, parsley, and chive butter until well combined. Taste and add more salt and lemon if necessary.

VARIATION: SPICED APPLE-SAUSAGE STUFFING WITH CRANBERRIES AND BRANDY

Unless you're gluten-free or eating low-carb, I don't know that this fragrant, lightly sweet and meaty stuffing will replace the typical bread mixture in your Thanksgiving bird. As good as it is, it might be a touch too quirky for turkey day. But please don't let that stop you from making it any other night of the year, stuffing it into a nice fat chicken.

One recipe will fill a 4- to 5-pound bird with enough left over to turn into pasta sauce the next day. Just simmer the leftover stuffing with a can or two of plum tomatoes, a few sprigs of rosemary, a large pinch of crushed red pepper flakes, a dash of red wine vinegar, and a vat of chopped garlic, then serve it over pasta with plenty of grated Romano cheese. It's marvelous and easy, and tastes entirely different than the stuffing did the night before, which is exactly what you want out of holiday leftovers.

Spiced Apple-Sausage Stuffing with Cranberries and Brandy

Time: about 1 hour

Makes about 12 cups, enough to stuff a 12- to 14-pound turkey

1 cup dried cranberries or golden raisins

¼ cup brandy

4 pounds ground pork (or substitute ground turkey)

5½ teaspoons kosher salt, more to taste

5½ teaspoons freshly ground black pepper

1 tablespoon ground cinnamon

¼ teaspoon ground cloves

3 garlic cloves, finely chopped

2½ teaspoons grated fresh gingerroot

6 tablespoons extra-virgin olive oil

4 medium leeks, finely chopped

2 celery stalks

2 bay leaves

2½ teaspoons whole coriander seed

4 medium apples, peeled, cored, and cut into ½-inch chunks (Galas work well)

2 tablespoons cider vinegar

1. In a small pot, bring the cranberries, brandy, and 3 tablespoons water to a simmer. Turn off the heat and let stand until ready to use.
2. In a large bowl, using your hands, mash and squeeze together the pork, 5 teaspoons each of salt and pepper, the cinnamon, and the cloves. Make sure the spices are evenly distributed. In a small bowl, mix together the garlic and ginger.
3. Heat 3 tablespoons oil in a very large skillet over medium-high heat. Add the leeks, celery, bay leaves, and coriander; cook, stirring, until the vegetables are almost softened, about 4 minutes. Stir in the apples and remaining

½ teaspoon each salt and pepper. Cook 2 minutes, reduce the heat to medium, cover, and cook until just tender, about 3 minutes more. Transfer the mixture to a bowl.

4. Add the vinegar to the cranberry mixture.

5. Add another tablespoon oil to the skillet over medium-high heat. Add a third of the garlic-ginger mixture and cook, stirring, for 30 seconds. Add a third of the pork and brown, breaking up with a fork, until cooked through, about 5 minutes. Add a third of the cranberries and their liquid; cook, scraping up any browned bits from the bottom of the pan, until most of the liquid has evaporated. Spoon the pork into the bowl with the apple mixture; repeat two more times with the remaining ingredients. Toss everything together; taste and add more salt if necessary.

VARIATION: SHRIMP AND ROASTED SWEET POTATO HASH STUFFING

If you can find sugary garnet or jewel yams, use them here. They'll make the contrast between the sweet, starchy potato and spicy, savory jalapeño and onion even more stark and compelling.

Shrimp and Roasted Sweet Potato Hash Stuffing

Time: 1¼ hours

Makes about 12 cups, enough to stuff a 12- to 14-pound turkey

6 pounds sweet potatoes, peeled and cut into ¾-inch chunks

7 tablespoons extra-virgin olive oil

3½ teaspoons kosher salt, more to taste

1 teaspoon freshly ground black pepper

2 medium onions, diced

2 medium green bell peppers, diced

2 large garlic cloves, finely chopped

2 jalapeños, seeded and finely chopped

2 teaspoons chili powder

2 pounds jumbo shrimp, peeled and cut into ½-inch pieces

1½ tablespoons freshly squeezed lime juice, more to taste

6 tablespoons chopped fresh cilantro or basil

1. Preheat the oven to 425°F. Toss the potatoes with 4 tablespoons oil, 2 teaspoons salt, and ½ teaspoon black pepper. Spread the potatoes on two or three large baking sheets, leaving space between the chunks so they can brown. Roast, tossing occasionally and changing the position of the baking pans so the potatoes cook evenly, until the potatoes are golden, crisp around the edges, and tender, about 35 minutes.

2. Heat the remaining 3 tablespoons oil in a large skillet over medium-high heat. Add the onions and bell peppers. Cook, stirring, until softened, about 10 minutes. Add the garlic, jalapeños, and chili powder, and cook 2 minutes more. Add the shrimp and remaining 1½ teaspoons salt. Cook, tossing occasionally, until the shrimp is just opaque, about 5 minutes.

3. Pour in the lime juice and scrape up any browned bits from the bottom of the skillet. Combine the shrimp mixture with the sweet potatoes in a large bowl and stir in the cilantro or basil. Taste and add more lime juice and salt, if necessary.

VARIATION: THE CLARK FAMILY'S TRADITIONAL CHESTNUT STUFFING

Ask my sister and she'll tell you, Thanksgiving would be just another Thursday night without this savory, mushroomy stuffing tucked into the bird—no matter how many other stuffing variations I may care to prepare. You can make it with any kind of bread you've got around. My mother usually saves bread scraps in the freezer in the weeks leading up to Thanksgiving and uses that assortment; she's even been known to use bagels. But I prefer corn bread, brioche, and challah for their richness and sweetness.

The Clark Family's Traditional Chestnut Stuffing

6 tablespoons unsalted butter, more if needed

1 large onion (about 10 ounces), diced

2 celery stalks, trimmed and sliced

1 teaspoon plus pinch kosher salt

½ teaspoon plus pinch freshly ground black pepper

¼ teaspoon freshly grated nutmeg

10 ounces mushrooms (1 box), sliced

2 garlic cloves, minced

1 pound chestnuts (see Note), roasted, peeled, and coarsely chopped

10 ounces bread, preferably stale, cubed (6 to 7 cups)

4 large eggs

2 cups chicken or vegetable stock, plus additional if needed

2 tablespoons chopped fresh parsley

1 tablespoon chopped fresh sage

Time: 20 to 40 minutes, depending on whether you roast your own chestnuts

Makes 10 cups stuffing, enough to stuff a 12-pound turkey

1. In a skillet over medium-high heat, heat 4 tablespoons butter. Cook the onion, celery, ½ teaspoon salt, the pepper, and nutmeg until the onion is

golden and soft, about 10 minutes. Scrape the mixture into a large mixing bowl.

2. Add another 2 tablespoons butter to the skillet and heat. Cook the mushrooms and garlic with $\frac{1}{2}$ teaspoon salt until the mushrooms are golden brown, 7 to 10 minutes. Scrape the mixture into the mixing bowl.

3. Add the chestnuts and bread to the bowl with the vegetables and toss to combine.

4. In a separate bowl, whisk the eggs with the chicken or vegetable stock, parsley, sage, and remaining pinch of salt and pepper. Pour the egg mixture into the chestnut-bread mixture and stir well to combine.

5. Stuff the stuffing into the turkey, or place in a 9×12-inch baking pan. Dot the top of the stuffing with more butter if baking in a pan. If using a baking pan, bake at 375°F until the top is light golden brown and the middle is almost set, 30 to 35 minutes.

NOTE: You can use a 14-ounce jar of peeled roasted chestnuts for this, or roast and peel your own chestnuts.

My father uses the microwave. Working with about 5 chestnuts at a time, he slits each chestnut almost all the way around its circumference, leaving the shell connected in one spot (there is a black dot on the chestnut that he uses as the hinge). Then he lays the nuts on a plate and microwaves them on high power for 40 seconds. The shells pop open like clams. He wets his fingers in cold water and pulls off the shells before the chestnuts cool. Repeat until all the chestnuts are peeled. The fresh ones really are better than the jarred, and he says it takes him only 15 minutes to do a pound.

CHRISTMAS COOKIE EXTRAVAGANZA

I could blame my cookie-baking obsession on the holidays. You know, claim that I'm simply riding the current of sugarplum visions, and adding to the general atmosphere of high-calorie joy to the world.

I could tell you that baking holiday cookies is a way for me to express my seasonal glee, and share the sweet-toothed sympathy for humankind that builds within my breast all year long, just waiting to burst forth in the form of diamond-shaped butter cookies and spritzed almond wreaths.

But in fact, for me, the holidays are merely a way to legitimize a baking frenzy that in April might be seen as the butter-slicked ravings of a cookie maniac. In December, it passes for normal.

This is to say, come the holidays, I like to bake cookies.

I don't mean to imply that the rest of the year is cookieless. I nibble cookies at any excuse, as in, it's raining or there's tea. Whenever a friend's birthday rolls around, I bake up a batch of their favorites, pinching a few for myself before wrapping up the rest. Every party giver in my neighborhood knows that when I ask what I can bring, I want the answer to be cookies.

Still, the holidays are different. That's when I allow myself free rein to bake as many cookies as I like.

I should probably mention here that although I do my fair share of tasting, I don't actually eat *all* those cookies. Giving them away to the *oohs* and *aahs* of family and friends is part of the pleasure. I keep mental lists of who loves which variety, and remember to give Alice extra Meyer lemon rugelach and overdose the UPS guy with chocolate chippers.

Everyone, however, gets gingerbread, because gingerbread is where I let my wackier creative urges fly. I've collected a great number of cookie cutters over the years, and along with the usual flowers, birds, hearts, and glittery snowy angels, I'll bake up gingerbread salamanders, octopuses, footprints, teapots, cacti, and even the state of Texas. And with the help of a rainbow of food colors, the palette is as varied as the shapes.

Although the baking extravaganza doesn't commence until after Thanksgiving, the planning continues all year long. In August, when everyone else is trying to decide between hot butterscotch or fudge on their ice cream sundaes, I'm ruminating over how the wet walnuts might be translated into a cookie (see the Salted Maple Walnut Thumbprints on page 335). Almost anything can be fodder for cookie inspiration.

When it comes to packing up all my holiday cookie tins, I like to mix traditional cookies with more off-the-wall flavors, combining the expected—brownies, gingerbread, and lemon squares—with the more outré, like Sesame Halvah Toffee (page 332) and Whole Wheat Demerara Shortbread (page 331). I aim for a dozen varieties, but usually end up with fifteen, just because once I get going, it gets hard to stop.

In fact, once I enter my holiday cookie paradise of softened butter, vanilla sugar, candied nuts, and chopped chocolate, it's nearly impossible to leave. Case in point: Years ago, before I was married even for the first time, and when my obsession was still waxing, the phone rang one chilly December evening. It was a guy I had gone on a few dates with, who happened to be near my apartment.

"What are you doing now?" he asked seductively.

"Making cookies," I answered, perhaps coyly.

He asked me to come join him for a drink, but I declined. I was having too much fun painting green royal icing onto Gingerbread Frogs (page 330).

Of course my husband Daniel, a cookie lover himself, knows that when you can't beat 'em, join 'em. I mix the batters, he helps roll, cut, and decorate.

And then we both eat, savoring the sweet morsels as long as they last.

GINGERBREAD FROGS

Fresh gingerroot and orange zest sets these crisp and highly spiced cookies above all other gingerbread. You can cut them into any shapes you like. I'm fond of frogs.

Gingerbread Frogs

4 cups all-purpose flour, plus additional for dusting

¼ cup finely ground nuts, such as almonds or hazelnuts

1 tablespoon ground ginger

1¼ teaspoons ground cinnamon

1 teaspoon baking soda

¾ teaspoon kosher salt

½ teaspoon freshly grated nutmeg

¼ teaspoon ground cloves

¼ teaspoon freshly ground black pepper

¼ teaspoon ground cardamom

1 cup (2 sticks) unsalted butter, at room temperature

1 cup dark brown sugar

⅔ cup molasses

1 large egg

2 teaspoons vanilla extract

¾ teaspoon freshly grated orange zest

1 teaspoon finely grated fresh gingerroot

Royal Icing (see page 343), colored sugar, dragées, or what have you,
   for decorating, if desired

**Time: 30 minutes,
plus chilling time**

Makes about
72 cookies

1. In a medium bowl, combine the flour, ground nuts, ground ginger, cinnamon, baking soda, salt, nutmeg, cloves, pepper, and cardamom.

2. In the bowl of an electric mixer, cream together the butter and sugar. Scrape down the sides of the bowl and add the molasses, egg, vanilla, orange zest, and fresh ginger. Mix until thoroughly combined, about 2 minutes. Add the flour mixture and mix on slow speed until incorporated.

3. Divide the dough into 4 discs. Wrap the dough in plastic and chill in the refrigerator for 1 hour or up to 3 days.

4. When ready to bake, preheat the oven to 350°F and line several baking sheets with parchment. Place the dough on a lightly floured surface and roll out 3/16 inch thick. Dipping the cutter in flour as needed, cut out the

cookies and transfer to the prepared baking sheets. Reroll out the scraps of dough one time only, and cut more cookies. Bake until the cookies are firm and the edges are golden, about 15 minutes. Transfer the cookies to a wire rack to cool. If you like, decorate to your heart's content.

WHOLE WHEAT DEMERARA SHORTBREAD

Using half whole wheat flour gives this shortbread a sandier texture than those made with all-white flour, and a toasted, nutty flavor. The added fiber content makes eating them by the handful seem downright good for you, too. Or at least, that's what I tell myself.

Whole Wheat Demerara Shortbread

Time: 35 minutes

Makes 1
(8-inch) round
Serves 8

½ cup all-purpose flour
½ cup whole wheat flour
½ cup (1 stick) unsalted butter
3 tablespoons Demerara sugar, plus additional for sprinkling
¼ teaspoon kosher salt

1. Preheat the oven to 325°F.
2. In the bowl of a food processor, combine the flours, butter, sugar, and salt. Pulse until a crumbly dough forms. Press the dough into an 8-inch cake pan and sprinkle with more Demerara sugar. Bake until the shortbread is golden around the edges, 25 to 30 minutes. Allow the shortbread to cool to room temperature in the pan before cutting.

SESAME HALVAH TOFFEE

At the end of every bagels and lox brunch in my family was a chunk of seven-layer halvah just waiting to be nibbled. Made from finely ground sesame seeds mixed with pleasingly gritty bits of sugar and layered with chocolate, seven-layer halvah is an old-fashioned candy that might be hard to find outside the borough of Brooklyn. This is my homemade version, composed of a sesame shortbread crust topped with bittersweet chocolate and dappled with halvah crumbles. If you don't like halvah but still love sesame, the shortbread crust is terrific on its own, especially when sprinkled with crunchy raw sugar and more sesame seeds.

Sesame Halvah Toffee

1½ cups all-purpose flour

½ teaspoon kosher salt

10 tablespoons unsalted butter, cubed

2 tablespoons tahini

2 tablespoons sesame seeds, plus additional for sprinkling

1 tablespoon vanilla extract

Demerara sugar, for sprinkling (optional)

4 ounces dark chocolate, chopped (optional)

3 ounces halvah, crumbled (optional)

Time: 30 minutes

Makes about
24 pieces

1. Preheat the oven to 325°F. In the bowl of a food processor, pulse together the flour and salt just to combine. Add the butter, tahini, sesame seeds, and vanilla. Pulse together until a crumbly dough forms.

2. Press the dough into an 8×8-inch baking dish and smooth the top with a spatula. Use a fork to pierce the top of the dough. (If not using the chocolate, sprinkle the dough generously with the Demerara sugar and additional sesame seeds.) Bake until the top is light golden brown, 20 to 25 minutes.

3. If not using the chocolate, transfer the pan to a wire rack to cool. Otherwise, scatter the chocolate pieces on top of the shortbread. Turn off the heat and return the pan to the oven for 1 to 2 minutes to soften the chocolate. Using an offset spatula, spread the softened chocolate into an even layer over the shortbread. Sprinkle with the crumbled halvah, if using, and allow to cool to room temperature in the pan before cutting.

LEMON CURD SQUARES WITH ROSEMARY

Lucy's lemon squares from the *Peanuts Cook Book* was far and away my mother's favorite cookie to make when my sister and I were kids. She'd whip up a batch for birthday parties and bake sales, whenever a homemade sweet was called for, and everyone in the family loved them—even Mocha, our old chocolate Labrador. Once he polished off an entire batch that my mother had stashed out of sight to bring to some event or other. When she saw the empty plate, she scolded my sister and me—then discovered the guilty pup licking his confectioners' sugar–dusted nose. I might still be holding a grudge.

This has not, however, diminished my fondness for lemon squares, which I've made every which way since I was old enough to bake.

This recipe is the culmination of all my trials. It's based on Lucy's in citrusy spirit, though I've monkeyed with the technique and ingredients. Instead of a thin, brittle crust with a lemonade-sweet filling, I've made a thick and buttery shortbread laced with piney fresh rosemary, topped with a bracing lemon curd that's just sweet enough.

It's definitely more sophisticated than either my mother or Lucy would have made back in the day. But I'm sure Mocha would have liked it just as well.

Lemon Curd Squares with Rosemary

Time: 1 hour and
10 minutes

Makes 24 squares

FOR THE SHORTBREAD
3 cups all-purpose flour
1½ cups (3 sticks) unsalted butter
½ cup granulated sugar
⅓ cup confectioners' sugar, plus additional for sprinkling
1 tablespoon chopped fresh rosemary
1 teaspoon finely grated lemon zest

FOR THE LEMON CURD
6 large eggs, lightly beaten
1½ cups granulated sugar
⅔ cup freshly squeezed lemon juice (3 to 4 lemons)
¼ cup all-purpose flour
1 tablespoon finely grated lemon zest
Pinch kosher salt

1. Preheat the oven to 325°F and lightly grease a 9 × 13-inch baking pan.
2. To make the shortbread base, combine the flour, butter, granulated sugar, confectioners' sugar, rosemary, and lemon zest in a food processor. Pulse until a crumbly dough forms. Press the dough into the prepared pan and bake until the shortbread is golden around the edges, about 40 minutes.
3. While the shortbread is baking, prepare the lemon curd. In a large bowl, whisk together the eggs, sugar, lemon juice, flour, lemon zest, and salt.
4. When the shortbread is ready, take it out of the oven and increase the oven temperature to 350°F. Carefully pour the lemon curd onto the shortbread base and return the pan to the oven. Bake until the topping is just set, about 20 minutes more. Allow to cool to room temperature before cutting into squares. Cover and refrigerate the bars up to 3 days. Sprinkle with confectioners' sugar before serving.

SALTED MAPLE WALNUT THUMBPRINTS

These maple-scented thumbprints look like any other Christmas cookie, but don't let that fool you. The niche of each morsel holds a walnut half covered by a thick maple glaze that's been sprinkled with crunchy sea salt. The salt adds a surprising savory note that will jolt you out of your overfed holiday complacency. It also makes these thumbprints a better match for an after-dinner digestif (anejo rum, Cognac, good whiskey, you name it) than others of its sugary ilk. If you want something more traditional, skip the salt and sprinkle with nutmeg instead.

Salted Maple Walnut Thumbprints

Time: 25 minutes, plus cooling time

Makes 42 cookies

3 cups all-purpose flour

1 teaspoon kosher salt

1 cup (2 sticks) unsalted butter, room temperature

1 cup sugar

1 cup pure maple syrup

2 large egg yolks

12 ounces walnut halves

Fleur de sel or other coarse sea salt, for sprinkling (or use freshly grated nutmeg)

1. Preheat the oven to 350°F. In a medium bowl, whisk together the flour and 1 teaspoon kosher salt. In the bowl of an electric mixer fitted with the paddle attachment, cream together the butter and sugar until light and fluffy. Scrape down the sides of the bowl, add ½ cup of maple syrup and the egg yolks, and beat until fully incorporated. Add the flour mixture and mix until just combined.

2. Using a tablespoon, drop the dough, 3 inches apart, onto two baking sheets. Using your thumb, make an indentation in the center of each round of dough. Bake until the edges are just golden, 12 to 15 minutes. Transfer to a wire rack to cool.

3. While the cookies are cooling, prepare the maple glaze. Place the remaining ½ cup maple syrup in a small saucepan over medium heat. Simmer the syrup until reduced to about ⅓ cup, 7 to 10 minutes. Carefully spoon the glaze into the thumbprint of each cooled cookie, then place a walnut and a sprinkle of salt (or nutmeg) on top. Allow the glaze to set, at least 10 minutes, before serving.

FUDGY BOURBON BALLS

My big idea with this fairly classic recipe was to substitute chocolate cookies for the usual vanilla wafers. Naturally, I originally did this because that's what I happened to have on hand when I was making a batch once, and I really liked the deeper fudgy flavor they had. I've never gone back to vanilla cookies, though if that's what you happen to have in the cupboard, go ahead and use them.

These get better after sitting for a few days, so if you can plan ahead to let them ripen for 3 or 4 days, they'll be all the better for it.

Fudgy Bourbon Balls

2½ cups chocolate cookie crumbs (Nabisco Famous wafers are the best if you can find them; you can also use chocolate graham cracker crumbs)
1¼ cups pecans
½ cup good bourbon or rum
1 cup confectioners' sugar, plus additional for rolling
3 tablespoons unsweetened cocoa powder
1½ tablespoons honey

Time: 15 minutes, plus overnight resting time

Makes about 48 cookies

1. In the bowl of a food processor, pulse together the cookie crumbs and pecans until the nuts are finely ground.
2. In a separate bowl, stir together the bourbon or rum, 1 cup confectioners' sugar, the cocoa powder, and honey. Add the mixture to the food processor and pulse until just combined. Let the dough rest, uncovered, at

room temperature for 4 hours or overnight. This will dry it out a little (it will seem quite moist, and that's okay).

3. Use your fingers to roll the dough into balls about 1 inch in diameter. Roll the balls in confectioners' sugar. Store the balls airtight if you like them moist, or uncovered if you like them to develop a crunchy sugar crust on the outside (I like the crust, but it's a matter of taste). Sprinkle with (or roll the balls in) additional confectioners' sugar just before serving.

MOIST AND BOOZY FRUITCAKE WITH RUM AND PORT (AKA DARK BROWN CAKE)

Although I spent my childhood in Flatbush, Brooklyn, a neighborhood bustling with immigrants from the West Indies, I never tasted a black cake until I made it myself.

Black cake, a dense and heady fruitcake with a near pudding-like texture and a warm, rummy flavor, is *the* fruitcake of the Caribbean. Though the recipe varies from island to island, all consist of pounds of dried fruit and candied citrus peel that have been steeped in booze, ground to a paste, mixed with copious quantities of eggs, butter, and sugar, and then tinted coal black with a bittersweet syrup called burnt sugar essence.

I read about black cake as a teenager in Laurie Colwin's *Home Cooking*, where she describes it thus: "There is fruitcake, and there is black cake, which is to fruitcake what the Brahms piano quartets are to Muzak. Its closest relatives are plum pudding and black bun, and it leaves them both in the dust. Black cake, like truffles and vintage Burgundy, is deep, complicated, and intense."

I never liked fruitcake. But since I did fancy myself the kind of person who *would* like truffles and vintage Burgundy if ever I managed to get my hands on some (I was nineteen at the time), I decided I'd give black cake a try.

I mentioned it to my childhood babysitter Germaine, from Grenada, who wrinkled her nose.

"Black cake, now that's too much work, and it's expensive because you need a lot of candied fruit and a good bottle of rum to make it right," she warned me.

But I was undeterred, and Germaine reluctantly agreed to procure the burnt sugar essence from a West Indian grocery near her home in exchange for some cake. (Lacking access to a West Indian grocery, you can boil brown sugar with a little water until it turns as dark as tar and starts to smell burned.)

Then I ran around town with my credit card, charging the dark rum and

338

Manischewitz wine I got someone to sell me illegally, along with mountains of candied citrus peel, glacé cherries, and nearly every variety of dried fruit I could think of.

I layered everything into my largest soup pot, dousing it all with booze. Then I let it sit, as instructed, for the minimum of two weeks. (At this Germaine shook her head. "On Grenada we start soaking our fruit in summer to get it ready for Christmas," she told me. But I needed my soup pot back.)

Every day, I stirred the fruit, which helped it absorb all the liquid and also broke it down and mashed it up, making it easier to grind when it finished soaking.

Before baking, I stirred in the burnt sugar essence, which turned my batter from speckled tan to night-black. Then I baked it, and when the cake cooled, I showered it in yet more rum and Manischewitz (I don't know why Manischewitz is traditional for this cake, but it is, so I used it).

I let the black cake ripen for a few days before frosting it, as Colwin commands, with swags and garlands of pink royal icing. It was very festive looking, almost a pity to cut, had I not been dying to try it. But first I set aside a slice to bring to Germaine.

The rest I served to friends who, after deriding the swampy color, managed to devour the entire inky pink thing, first eating the pieces I cut for them, then commandeering the knife and trimming off slivers until only the crumbs remained. Even those were dispatched by one of my friends and her well-licked index finger.

Black cake was a success.

A few days later I made my way back to Brooklyn and handed Germaine her portion. Even she had nothing but good things to say, in her way, about my black cake: "And next time, it will be even better when you soak the fruit longer," she insisted, daintily finishing her wedge.

Almost every year since then, I think about making black cake. But I always remember it when the holidays are creeping up in November, which I know would not pass muster with Germaine, who had become my black cake voice of authority. Plus, Germaine has since moved back to Grenada, derailing my easy route to burnt sugar essence.

Eventually my desire for black cake trumped Germaine's voice in my head. I set about making it, regardless that Thanksgiving was around the corner.

This time, I didn't have to cajole the booze. I just went to the liquor store and picked up the darkest rum they had, along with a bottle of inexpensive ruby Port to stand in for the Manischewitz, which they didn't have. But I knew the fruity, grapy character of ruby Port would work just as well, and maybe even better than the kosher wine. I've since heard that Nigella Lawson uses Madeira in her black cake, and I imagine that would be fine, too.

I also couldn't find candied cherries. To be honest, I didn't look very hard. Like most sensible people, I abhor them, and it always astonishes me when I meet someone who actually likes fruitcake littered with those red and green gummy gobs (it must remind them of an otherwise happy childhood). Instead, I bought dried cherries.

I mounded all the fruit into an ornate, Chinese-patterned porcelain jar with a lid, which felt very adult compared to my old college soup pot. Then I poured in the rum and Port and stirred it daily for two weeks.

While the fruit macerated, I could have hunted through Brooklyn in search of burnt sugar essence. It's probably not even that hard to find in my neck of the woods.

Or I could have simmered up a batch myself. But I had decided when I embarked on black cake, part II, to leave it out. Although the color was striking, it was not, in my opinion, black cake's raison d'être. That would be the vibrant, robust flavor that tasted like sunbaked sugar plums heightened by a winey complexity and bittersweet, butterscotch nuance.

I mixed up the cake using Colwin's basic recipe, tweaking the proportions of eggs and butter to match what I had in the house, and adding almonds for a gentle crunch and a little unsweetened cocoa powder to mimic the bitterness of the burnt sugar essence, if not the color. When the cake had cooled, I brushed it with more rum (I had used up all the Port in the fruit), and hid it in a closet, hoping to forget about it until Christmas.

I lasted until Hanukkah, which fell the week before, and brought it along to my parents' house as a post-latkes nosh.

Before serving the cake, I covered it with a thick snowdrift of confectioners' sugar in lieu of pink royal icing. Then I cut the cake into slices. The color was a ruddy dark chocolate brown, and the flavor just as compelling as I remembered it, with a slight chocolate undertone from the cocoa powder.

Now that I've tasted both truffles and vintage Burgundy, I can vouch for Colwin; black cake (or dark brown cake, in this case) is just as complicated, deep, and intense. And nearly as elusive.

Moist and Boozy Fruitcake with Rum and Port (aka Dark Brown Cake)

Time: 3½ hours, plus at least 2 weeks' macerating time

Makes 3 (9-inch) cakes, or two 9-inch cakes and two 8-inch loaf cakes, which are nice to give away

1 pound pitted prunes (2¼ cups)

1 pound dark raisins (2¾ cups)

1 pound dried currants (3½ cups)

1 pound dried cherries (2⅓ cups)

3 ounces candied citrus peel (orange and lemon) (½ cup)

3 ounces candied ginger (½ cup)

1 bottle (750 ml) dark rum, plus additional for brushing the cakes

1 bottle (750 ml) ruby Port or Manischewitz wine

4 ounces blanched almonds (⅔ cup)

⅓ cup boiling water

¼ cup unsweetened cocoa powder

2 cups (4 sticks) unsalted butter, at room temperature

2½ cups dark brown sugar

1 tablespoon vanilla extract

10 large eggs, at room temperature

4 cups all-purpose flour

4 teaspoons baking powder

1 teaspoon ground cinnamon

½ teaspoon freshly grated nutmeg

¼ teaspoon baking soda

¼ cup molasses or cane syrup

Confectioners' sugar, for serving (or Royal Icing, see Note)

1. At least 2 weeks before you intend to bake the cakes, place the prunes, raisins, currants, cherries, citrus peel, candied ginger, rum, and Port or wine in a large glass jar, plastic container, soup pot, or lidded vase. Stir the fruit once a day.

2. The day you intend to bake the cakes, preheat the oven to 250°F. Butter and flour 3 (9×2-inch) cake pans, or 2 (9×2-inch) pans and 2 (8-inch) loaf pans (or some other combination of pans as you see fit). Line the bottom of the pans with parchment and butter the parchment.

3. In the bowl of a food processor or using a heavy-duty blender, grind the almonds to a coarse meal. Stir the ground almonds into the fruit mixture to distribute it evenly. Transfer the fruit-almond mixture to the food processor or blender in batches and pulse until a chunky paste forms. Place the fruit paste as you grind it into the second largest bowl you have in the house. Or pile it on a rimmed baking sheet to hold it.

4. In a small bowl, whisk together the boiling water and cocoa powder until smooth.

5. In the bowl of an electric mixer, cream together the butter and brown sugar. Scrape down the sides of the bowl, add the vanilla, and beat in the eggs one at a time. Transfer the butter mixture to the largest bowl you have in the house—or use a soup pot. You need a lot of room to mix this much batter. I use a giant wooden salad bowl.

6. In a separate bowl, mix together the flour, baking powder, cinnamon, nutmeg, and baking soda. Using a spatula, fold the flour mixture into the butter-sugar mixture. Add the cocoa powder mixture and molasses or cane syrup to the giant bowl and fold together to combine. Stir in the fruit.

7. Transfer the batter to the pans and bake until the cakes are firm on top and a cake tester inserted into the center comes out clean, about 2½ hours (this time will vary if you vary the pan size; just keep checking it). While the cakes are still hot, brush them with additional rum. Allow the cakes to cool in the pans before unmolding. Brush with more rum and wrap in cheesecloth (or clean dish towels or even sturdy paper towels) and foil. Let ripen for at least 3 days and up to a month before serving.

8. When ready to serve, sift confectioners' sugar all over the cakes. Or ice with Royal Icing (see Note).

NOTE: To make Royal Icing, beat 4 egg whites with a tablespoon of lemon juice or water until frothy. Slowly beat in 6 cups confectioners' sugar and beat until smooth. Beat in food coloring and almond extract, if desired. Use immediately, before it hardens.

10 My Sweet Tooth and Me

Ever since I can remember, I've had a sweet tooth as big as my head.

As a child, I'd eat sugar straight from the sugar bowl and lap up honey from the jar. My first word, naturally, was *cookie*. My parents were so delighted they even gave me one, something that didn't happen often in our house, where the cupboards were stocked with rice cakes and joyless, high-bran cereals.

To get my sugar fix, I'd scoot over to my best friend Abby's house, a tween's paradise of Cocoa Puffs and Entenmann's. At Abby's, lunch was just as likely to be blueberry blintzes as it was macaroni and cheese, and no one noticed if you just ate the blueberry filling and nothing else.

As I got older, I realized that the key to being able to eat the sweet things I craved was to bake them myself. Cooking and baking were looked up to with respect by my parents, who saw my efforts as industrious. Plus, by baking the cookies myself, I also got to nibble the dough, which every adolescent and even some adults know is the best part.

By the time I got to high school, not only had I learned how to bake, I had learned how to parlay those cookies and brownies into friendships and dates. Almost everyone, it turns out, is happy to save you a seat in the cafeteria if you habitually arrive packing cheesecake.

I'd bake tart and gooey lemon squares for my girlfriends, and chocolate whiskey cakes for the boys I had crushes on. Underage as I was, I could take the booze from my parents' liquor cabinet if it was in the name of making something good to eat. And some of it did make it into the baked goods, too.

This social strategy worked in a professional milieu as well. Plying my boss with muffins was the ticket to success at my very first summer job in college. I had made the mistake of taking a position I was entirely unqualified for— working as a news assistant at a highly respected business journal. At eighteen, I didn't know the difference between a stock and a commodity, and worse, I couldn't care less. But as long as I kept up with a steady supply of baked goods, my job was secure.

Of course when I left home and was earning my own money, I could also buy whatever sugary confections I wanted. Once, when I was dining out with my friend Bernard in a darling French provençal café in Soho, we pored over the dessert menu, unable to choose just two. Then it hit me. I was an adult with my very own credit card, and if Bernard and I wanted to order four desserts for the two of us, there was no one who could stop us.

It was with Bernard and his parents at another celebrated downtown restaurant, Chanterelle, where I learned that some fancy chefs don't just serve desserts and petits fours after a meal. At Chanterelle, your dessert came with trays and trays of little pastries, cakes, and bonbons, and then when you think you can't possibly eat another bite, the owner, Karen Waltuck, comes around with a plate of mocha éclairs or miniature blueberry tarts. The night we dined there, I was so stuffed from the extravagant meal it nearly broke my heart when I couldn't finish all the sweets before me. So, perhaps greedily, I asked to have everything uneaten wrapped up. Bernard's parents were a little aghast, but Karen Waltuck was delighted by my enthusiasm, and sent me home with a fat foil package.

It was late enough that I felt compelled to cab it back to my college apartment on 123rd Street. As the taxi meter ticked away on the long drive uptown, I soon realized that I'd have just enough money for the fare but not for a tip (oh, those terrible days before cabs took credit cards).

But the cabbie, who turned out to be a foodie who hoped to dine at Chanterelle one day, was thrilled to take my package of treats instead of cash.

So I handed it over, happy in the knowledge that once again, my sweet tooth had saved the day.

NOT-SO-IRISH SODA BREAD

When I was in college, I somehow acquired a recipe for what I've always considered to be the ultimate Irish soda bread. Made with buttermilk plus butter, eggs, raisins, and sugar, it's baked in a heavy iron skillet so the top and bottom crusts become crunchy and browned, while the center stays tender and pale, studded with treacly bits of black raisin.

Over the years I've played with the basic formula, adding a little more butter, removing some sugar, and sprinkling the top with caraway seeds. Everyone I've ever served it to—in warm little slices with chunks of tart apple and some good Cheddar cheese—has immediately declared it to be the best Irish soda bread they've ever had. Until recently.

My friend Vivian Ryle looked at the plate of moist, even slices I plunked down in front of her, arched an eyebrow, and sipped her tea.

"This doesn't look like Irish soda bread," she said, nibbling a corner. "And it doesn't taste like Irish soda bread either," she insisted, adding quickly that of course it was nonetheless delightful. Ever so rich and lovely.

But why did I call it soda bread?

After marrying an Irishman and living in Tramore in Waterford County for a year, Vivian has considerably more authority on the subject than I. In fact, the only time I ever visited the Emerald Isle (in 1996 to attend their wedding), I didn't even come across any loaves of soda bread. There was brown bread and scones and crusty yeasted bread. There were baguettes and Pullman loaves, even pumpernickel and rye. Any soda bread I've tasted has been from within these five boroughs, except for that one time I found some crumbly stuff in an Irish pub in Paris.

I told Vivian all this and she nodded. "I'm not surprised. Nobody in Ireland serves real soda bread anymore. It's something people make at home, but you wouldn't find it in shops and restaurants. If you had it, you'd see how different yours is."

My curiosity was piqued. Did she have a recipe? She did not, but gave me the phone number of her Tramore neighbor and friend, Mary Morrissey, an accomplished baker.

A few days later I reached Mrs. Morrissey, caught in the middle of icing a cake as she picked up the phone. After the requisite pleasantries, I asked for her recipe.

"I swear by Darina Allen," Mrs. Morrissey said, referring to the Irish television cooking celebrity and owner of the Ballymaloe Cookery School. She found one of Darina's cookbooks and read me the soda bread formula, which consisted of nothing but flour, buttermilk or sour milk, salt, and baking soda.

"What?" I said, aghast. "No raisins? No caraway seeds? No butter or eggs?"

"Oh, there wouldn't ever be those things in a true soda bread," Mrs. Morrissey said solemnly.

If it had "sultanas and maybe a dessert spoon of sugar," she explained, it would be called spotted dog or spotted dick. Soda bread with caraway seeds was called seedy bread. But once you start adding eggs and sugar and butter, she continued, "Well, now you've got yourself a cake."

"So why," I asked, "does American Irish soda bread often seem to have raisins and/or caraway?"

"Oh, I couldn't tell you that," she chuckled. After giving me a few more tips for making a light bread (use your hands like a "large claw" to bring the ingredients together, use a wide basin to mix in so there's plenty of air surrounding the flour), we hung up and I set to work.

The recipe was easy. An hour later, I had a bumpy-crusted golden bread marked with a cross ("for religious reasons," said Mrs. Morrissey) cooling on the counter.

I cut myself a small, warm slice. It was crumbly and tender, with a clean, pleasantly sour taste from the buttermilk. Thanks to Mrs. Morrissey's tips, it possessed a featherlight crumb. I slathered it with softened butter, poured myself a cuppa, as they say, and enjoyed a tasty snack.

But a few hours later, when I went back for another piece, the loaf had cooled and compacted into something hard, dry, and bland. I tried to cut slices to toast, but it instantly broke apart under the knife.

I called Vivian and complained; did I do something wrong?

"It sounds right to me," she said with a laugh. "You see? I told you your recipe was nothing like a real soda bread."

Not-So-Irish Soda Bread

3 cups all-purpose flour

2/3 cup sugar

1 tablespoon baking powder

1½ teaspoons salt

1 teaspoon baking soda

1¾ cups buttermilk

2 eggs, well beaten

4 tablespoons unsalted butter, melted

1½ cups raisins or currants

1 tablespoon caraway seeds

Good aged Cheddar cheese, for serving

Tart apples, cut into slices, for serving

Time: 1½ hours

Makes 1 (10-inch) loaf
Serves 8 to 10

1. Preheat the oven to 350°F. Grease a 10-inch skillet and line with parchment or wax paper.

2. In a bowl, whisk together the flour, sugar, baking powder, salt, and baking soda. In a separate bowl, combine the buttermilk, eggs, and 2 tablespoons melted butter. Add the wet ingredients to the dry and stir until just combined. Do not overmix. Stir in the raisins or currants and caraway seeds.

3. Pour the batter into the skillet. Brush the top of the bread with the remaining 2 tablespoons melted butter. Bake until golden and firm to the touch, about 1 hour. Cool 10 minutes before slicing and serving with Cheddar and apples.

VARIATION: TRADITIONAL IRISH SODA BREAD
[ADAPTED FROM DARINA ALLEN]

Try to time this to eat right out of the oven when it's warm, crumbly, and comforting. I prefer the whole wheat version, which is called brown soda

350

bread in Ireland. It has a nuttier, richer flavor, and lasts a lot longer than the white flour version.

Traditional Irish Soda Bread

Time: 45 minutes

Serves 6 to 8

3¼ cups all-purpose flour, or use 2¼ cups whole wheat flour
  and 1 cup all-purpose flour
¾ teaspoon salt
½ teaspoon baking soda
1½ cups buttermilk or yogurt mixed with a little milk,
  or additional as needed
Softened butter, for serving

1. Preheat the oven to 450°F. In a large bowl, sift together the flour, salt, and baking soda. Make a well in the center and pour in the buttermilk or yogurt. Using your hand, mix in the flour from the sides of the bowl. The dough should be soft but not wet and sticky. If it's dry, add a little more buttermilk or yogurt.

2. Turn the dough out onto a well-floured work surface. Wash and dry your hands. Knead the dough lightly for a few seconds, then pat the dough into a round about 1½ inches thick. Place it on a buttered baking sheet and, using a sharp knife, cut a deep cross in the center of the dough, reaching out all the way to the sides.

3. Bake for 15 minutes, then reduce the oven temperature to 400°F and continue to bake until the top is golden brown and the bottom of the bread sounds hollow when tapped, 25 to 30 minutes longer. Serve warm with butter.

RHUBARB "BIG CRUMB" COFFEE CAKE

Rhubarb is an alarmingly sour vegetable passed off as a fruit but requiring a huge mound of sugar to effect the transformation.

Crumb cake is a huge mound of sugar disguised as a cake but demanding a bracing counterpoint—say, a swallow of coffee or tea—to allay its cloying sweetness. These two truths coexisted in my mind without overlapping until I bit into a piece of crumb cake so texturally perfect (soft sliver of cake topped by a deep layer of grape-size crumbs), yet so toothachingly sweet that the only antidote was sucking on the lemon in my seltzer.

The sourness of the lemon immediately made me think about the rhubarb I had in the fridge. It occurred to me that instead of cutting its tartness with a mountain of sugar, why not mix the rhubarb into a crumb cake to cut the cake's sweetness?

It was an "Aha!" moment, as when some forebear first paired caviar with Champagne. Or when peanut butter met jelly.

A little crumb cake background is in order. I've spent a good part of my adult life actively pursuing the perfect crumb cake recipe: a high ratio of melt-ingly tender crumbs to buttery, velvety cake. But that requires a lot of sugar, and I was determined to find a formula that had the crumb without the cloy. Did the rhubarb epiphany mean that perfection was within my grasp?

I added cubed rhubarb to the cake batter, and covered it all with giant crumbs using a technique lifted from *Cook's Illustrated* magazine. It calls for making a homogeneous brown sugar dough, then pinching off marbles to form crumbs. It's slightly more time-consuming than the usual streusel-making method of pulsing the ingredients in a food processor and dumping them on the batter, but when it comes to a magnificent crumb cake, I'm happy to put in ten extra minutes.

But the cake was still cloying. The rhubarb had melted into acidic puddles of pulp: no peanut-butter-and-jelly harmony here.

So I contemplated all the successful rhubarb desserts I'd ever had until I hit upon a rhubarb crisp made by Claudia Fleming when she was at Gramercy Tavern (full disclosure: I wrote a cookbook with her).

I remembered her saying that tossing the rhubarb in just a bit of sugar encourages the sturdy stems to absorb the syrup that forms. It was exactly what I needed my rhubarb to do. Though I was loath to add more sugar to a recipe that was already overloaded, I did it anyway.

When rhubarb crumb cake No. 2 cooled, I dug in. The rhubarb was mellow and gently sweet, with still enough zesty bite to offset the sugary cake. At last I had crumb cake fulfillment. Which just goes to show: When less isn't more, try adding more.

Rhubarb "Big Crumb" Coffee Cake

Time: 1½ hours,
plus cooling

Serves 8

FOR THE RHUBARB FILLING

½ pound rhubarb, trimmed

¼ cup granulated sugar

2 teaspoons cornstarch

½ teaspoon ground ginger

FOR THE BIG CRUMBS

⅓ cup dark brown sugar

⅓ cup granulated sugar

1 teaspoon ground cinnamon

½ teaspoon ground ginger

⅛ teaspoon salt

½ cup butter, melted

1¾ cups cake flour

FOR THE CAKE

⅓ cup sour cream

1 large egg

1 large egg yolk

2 teaspoons vanilla extract

1 cup cake flour

½ cup granulated sugar

½ teaspoon baking soda

½ teaspoon baking powder

¼ teaspoon salt

6 tablespoons softened butter, cut into 8 pieces

1. Preheat the oven to 325°F. Grease an 8-inch-square baking pan.
2. For the filling, slice the rhubarb ½ inch thick and toss with the sugar, cornstarch, and ginger. Let macerate while you prepare the crumbs and cake.
3. To make the crumbs, in a large bowl, whisk together the sugars, spices,

salt, and butter until smooth. Stir in the flour with a spatula. It will look like a solid dough.

4. To prepare the cake, in a small bowl, stir together the sour cream, egg, egg yolk, and vanilla. Using a mixer fitted with the paddle attachment, mix together the flour, sugar, baking soda, baking powder, and salt. Add the butter and a spoonful of the sour cream mixture and mix on medium speed until all the flour is moistened. Increase the speed and beat for 30 seconds. Add the remaining sour cream mixture in two batches, beating for 20 seconds after each addition, and scraping down the sides of the bowl with a spatula. Scoop out about ½ cup of the batter and set aside.

5. Scrape the remaining batter into the prepared pan. Spoon the rhubarb over the batter. Dollop the remaining batter over the rhubarb (it doesn't have to be even).

6. Using your fingers, break the topping mixture into big crumbs, about ½ inch to ¾ inch in size. They don't have to be uniform; just make sure the majority are around that size. Sprinkle the crumbs over the cake. Bake the cake until a toothpick inserted into the center comes out clean of batter (it might be moist from the rhubarb), 45 to 55 minutes. Cool completely before serving.

BLOOD ORANGE
OLIVE OIL CAKE

One of my favorite wedding gifts is a whimsical, undulating porcelain cake stand with a domed glass cover. Presiding over the counter like an elegant dowager, its presence cajoles: "Isn't it time to make some lovely cake?"

For a cake enthusiast like myself, the answer is always yes, and I've been building up a small repertoire of quick, easy cakes that I can whip up without turning on (and later cleaning) the food processor or electric mixer.

The key is using liquid fat (melted butter or oil) that doesn't require creaming, and chemical leavening (baking powder and/or soda) to eliminate the vigorous beating of eggs.

Usually I rely on melted butter for the fat. Although the results aren't as light textured as oil-based cakes, I like butter's richer, more complex flavor.

These sweets have kept my cake stand occupied for the better part of my marriage. But now that baby makes three, there's been a hitch. Our infant's diagnosis of gastroesophageal reflux disease led to the suggestion that I, her breast-feeding mama, give up cow's milk dairy. And this meant butter.

Of course I could have just put my cake baking on hold during my abstinence. But that empty cake stand just made me sad. Besides, I could still eat sugar and eggs and flour, so as long as I substituted oil for butter, my confectionary intake need not be affected.

As I read through recipes calling for vegetable oil, it occurred to me that my favorite oil is olive. So why not use that?

Plus, unlike the blander oils, good olive oil has character. I've had olive oil cakes in the past and liked their pronounced flavor. I even baked one once, though it required beating yolks and whites separately with an electric mixer, which disqualified it from the quick and easy category.

Could I bake a similar cake without all the egg beating? I turned to the Internet to see if I could find a recipe. A few clicks brought me to Dorie Greenspan's extra-virgin olive oil cake, which seemed like a cinch. The only catch was that Ms. Greenspan called for yogurt. But a quick substitution of sheep's milk yogurt fixed that.

Her recipe also called for lime zest, which I didn't have. But I did have some nice blood oranges, and grated the peel from those instead.

That left me with two denuded oranges, which, I feared, would fossilize before I had a chance to eat them. A small wave of anticipatory guilt that I'd have to throw out fruit that cost $1.50 each made me decide to use them immediately. I juiced one and chopped up segments from the other, adding it all to the cake batter and reducing the yogurt to compensate for the extra liquid.

While the cake was baking, every corner of the house pulsed with the scents of citrus and olive. I could barely wait for my cake to cool before cutting a sliver. It was every bit as good as my more buttery confections, but with a distinct herbal flavor from the oil and juicy bits of orange strewn throughout the very fine crumb.

Although the recipe also works perfectly with regular oranges, the cut loaf, dappled with ruby dots of blood orange, is much prettier. And it looks better in the cake stand, too.

Blood Orange Olive Oil Cake

Time: 1 hour and 20 minutes, plus cooling

Serves 8 to 10

3 blood oranges

1 cup sugar

Buttermilk or plain yogurt

3 large eggs

1¾ cups all-purpose flour

1½ teaspoons baking powder

¼ teaspoon baking soda

¼ teaspoon salt

⅔ cup extra-virgin olive oil

Whipped cream, for serving (optional)

Honey–Blood Orange Compote, for serving (see Note), optional

1. Preheat the oven to 350°F. Grease a 9×5-inch loaf pan. Grate the zest from 2 oranges and place in a bowl with the sugar. Using your fingers, rub the ingredients together until the orange zest is evenly distributed in the sugar.

2. Supreme an orange: Cut off the bottom and top so the fruit is exposed and the orange can stand upright on a cutting board. Cut away the peel and pith, following the curve of the fruit with your knife. Cut the orange segments out of their connective membranes and let them fall into a bowl. Repeat with another orange. Break up the segments with your fingers.

3. Halve the remaining orange and squeeze the juice into a measuring cup. You'll have about 1/4 cup or so. Add buttermilk or yogurt to the juice until you have 2/3 cup liquid altogether. Pour the mixture into the bowl with the sugar and whisk well. Whisk in the eggs.

4. In another bowl, whisk together the flour, baking powder, baking soda, and salt. Gently whisk the dry ingredients into the wet ones. Switch to a spatula and fold in the oil a little at a time. Fold in the orange segments. Scrape the batter into the pan and smooth the top.

5. Bake the cake for about 55 minutes, or until it is golden and a knife inserted into the center comes out clean. Cool on a rack for 5 minutes, then unmold and cool to room temperature right side up. Serve with whipped cream and Honey–Blood Orange Compote, if desired.

NOTE: To make the Honey–Blood Orange Compote, supreme 3 more blood oranges according to the directions above. Drizzle in 1 to 2 teaspoons honey. Let sit for 5 minutes, then stir gently.

CHOCOLATE CHIP PECAN LOAF CAKE

Once I was back on butter (it turns out my abstinence didn't help poor Dahlia's digestion), I put my butter-rich loaf cakes back into the cake stand rotation. This recipe is similar to a pound cake, with a sweet, buttery crumb that melds well with the pecans and chocolate—almost like a big, soft chocolate chip cookie in sliceable form.

Chocolate Chip Pecan Loaf Cake

Time: 1¼ hours, plus cooling

Makes 1 (9-inch) loaf cake
Serves 8 to 10

1 cup sugar
⅔ cup plain yogurt
3 large eggs
1¾ cups all-purpose flour
1½ teaspoons baking powder
¼ teaspoon baking soda
¼ teaspoon kosher salt
⅔ cup unsalted butter, melted
½ cup chocolate chips
½ cup chopped toasted pecans

1. Preheat the oven to 350°F. Grease a 9×5-inch loaf pan.
2. Using a whisk, whisk together the sugar and yogurt. Add the eggs, one at a time, and whisk until completely combined.
3. In a separate bowl, mix together the flour, baking powder, baking soda, and salt. Add the dry mixture into the wet and mix until just combined.
4. Using a spatula, fold in the melted butter a little at a time. Fold in the chocolate chips and pecans.
5. Scrape the batter into the prepared pan and bake for 50 to 55 minutes, or until the cake is golden and a tester inserted into the center comes out

clean. Allow the cake to cool in the pan for 5 minutes before turning it out onto a wire rack to cool to room temperature, right side up.

VARIATION: WHOLE WHEAT CINNAMON SNACKING CAKE

The only problem with having a cake recipe in your repertoire as easy as the Chocolate Chip Pecan Loaf Cake is the temptation to make it all the time. Adding a little whole wheat flour gives the loaf at least some nutritive value without robbing it of its moist richness (I didn't cut the fat, after all). And the cinnamon adds richness and spice. If you like the deep, wheaty flavor of brown bread, you'll love this cake.

Whole Wheat Cinnamon Snacking Cake

1 cup light brown sugar

⅔ cup plain yogurt or buttermilk

1 tablespoon vanilla extract

1 teaspoon ground cinnamon

3 large eggs

1 cup all-purpose flour

¾ cup whole wheat flour

1½ teaspoons baking powder

¼ teaspoon baking soda

¼ teaspoon kosher salt

⅔ cup unsalted butter, melted

Time: 1¼ hours, plus cooling time

Serves 8 to 10

1. Preheat the oven to 350°F. Grease a 9×5-inch loaf pan.
2. Using a whisk, combine the sugar, yogurt or buttermilk, vanilla, and cinnamon. Add the eggs, one at a time, and whisk until completely incorporated.
3. In a separate bowl, mix together the flours, baking powder, baking soda, and salt. Whisk the flour mixture into the egg mixture until no longer lumpy.

4. Using a spatula, fold the melted butter into the batter in 3 additions.
5. Pour the batter into the prepared pan and bake until golden brown and a cake tester inserted in the center comes out clean, 50 to 55 minutes. Allow the cake to cool in the pan for 5 minutes before turning it out onto a wire rack to cool to room temperature, right side up.

Walnut Streusel Filling and Topping

Adding walnut cinnamon streusel to the Whole Wheat Cinnamon Snacking Cake makes it sweeter and a little crunchy, more like a coffee cake than pound cake, though still satisfying enough for dessert.

1⅓ cups chopped walnuts
6 tablespoons all-purpose flour
4 tablespoons (½ stick) unsalted butter, cubed
2 tablespoons dark brown sugar
¼ teaspoon kosher salt

1. To make the streusel, use your fingers to combine the walnuts, flour, butter, sugar, and salt in a small bowl.
2. Pour half of the Snacking Cake batter into the prepared pan, then crumble on half of the streusel. Pour the remaining cake batter over the streusel and crumble on the remaining streusel. Bake as directed above.

ST. MARK'S GOOEY HONEY BUTTER CAKE WITH LEMON AND CINNAMON

There was one man ahead of me at the Made by Molly stand at the Park Slope farmers' market. And there was one piece of Molly Killeen's St. Louis Gooey Butter Cake.

I had schlepped up from Prospect Heights with husband and baby in tow just for a piece of that cake, which a friend had described to me.

"It's yeasty on the bottom, like a babka, and sweet and gooey on top, like cheesecake but stickier. It melts in your mouth," she said.

I'd been putting off the twenty-minute walk, but on this day, I was determined to have that cake, no matter what.

Except that the man ahead of me ordered the last square.

"Oh no!!" I groaned loudly. The man turned around.

"Excuse me," I said, panicking. "I'll buy you anything else you want if you let me have that cake."

He looked at me with pity. My husband and baby inched away, embarrassed.

"You really want this cake," the man said, agreeing to give it to me in exchange for a brownie and two coconut bars. It seemed fair.

I took a big bite. It was exactly as my friend described, though more moist and cakey than gooey. Nonetheless I was hooked and did not want to wait for next week to get more. I'd just have to make it myself.

Getting the recipe was easy. I asked Ms. Killeen and she e-mailed it, scaling down the proportions to what would fit into a 9×13-inch baking pan.

It wasn't hard, but it did involve two steps. First, you make a yeast dough for the cake, then you top it with a treacly mix of corn syrup, butter, sugar, eggs, and vanilla. It didn't sound like it would produce anything nearly as divine as the cake I finagled on the sidewalk, but then the beauty of baking is the mysterious alchemy of butter, sugar, and eggs.

Before I broke out my mixer, though, I did a little research to compare Ms. Killeen's recipe to some others. Hers was unusual in the use of a buttery yeast dough. Most recipes I found relied on cake mixes or Crisco.

Ms. Killeen had told me that she started using the yeast dough as a way to cut down on the cloying sweetness of the cake, which she remembers from her childhood near St. Louis.

"New Yorkers like things less sweet than people in the Midwest," she told me.

I mixed together the dough, and waited impatiently for it to rise and then bake. When it emerged from the oven, the top was puffed and golden. A few minutes later, it compacted into a dense, curdlike layer, similar to the center of a pecan pie, but firmer, and with a buttery, crackling crust on top. It was still very sweet, but not toothachingly so or oozing, and it went down all too easily with a cold glass of milk.

My only complaint was the use of corn syrup, which I am trying to avoid. So the next time I made it, I substituted honey and added a lot of grated lemon zest, because ever since my first Luden's cough drop, I've always loved the combination of lemon and honey. And while I was playing with the recipe anyway, I mixed some cinnamon into the crust, hoping it would bring out the warm, toasty quality of the yeast dough.

When the cake had cooled, I sampled my efforts. With its caramelized notes and vivid citrus nuance, I liked my honey-lemon-cinnamon cake even better than the original. I rechristened it St. Mark's Gooey Cake after my cross street in Brooklyn.

Just like Molly's recipe, the cake is simple enough that anytime I get a craving for it, I can make it myself . . . without having to play *Let's Make a Deal*.

St. Mark's Gooey Honey Butter Cake with Lemon and Cinnamon

FOR THE CRUST

3 tablespoons milk, at room temperature

1¾ teaspoons active dry yeast

6 tablespoons unsalted butter, at room temperature

3 tablespoons sugar

2 teaspoons ground cinnamon (optional)

1 teaspoon kosher salt

1 large egg

1¾ cups all-purpose flour

FOR THE TOPPING

3 tablespoons plus 1 teaspoon honey (or use corn syrup)

2½ teaspoons vanilla extract

12 tablespoons (1½ sticks) unsalted butter, at room temperature

1½ cups sugar

½ teaspoon kosher salt

1 large egg

Freshly grated zest of 1 lemon (about 1 tablespoon), optional

1 cup plus 3 tablespoons all-purpose flour

Confectioners' sugar, for sprinkling, if desired

Time: 1 hour, plus
2½ to 3 hours'
rising time

Serves 8 to 12

1. In a small bowl, mix together the milk with 2 tablespoons lukewarm water. Add the yeast and whisk gently until it dissolves. The mixture should foam slightly.

2. Using an electric mixer with the paddle attachment, cream the butter, sugar, cinnamon if using, and salt. Scrape down the sides of the bowl and beat in the egg. Alternately add the flour and milk mixture, scraping down the sides of the bowl between each addition. Beat the dough on medium speed until it forms a smooth mass and pulls away from the sides of the bowl, 7 to 10 minutes.

3. Press the dough into an ungreased 9×13-inch baking dish at least 2 inches deep. Cover the dish with plastic wrap or a clean tea towel and allow to rise until doubled, 2½ to 3 hours, in a warm, dry place.

4. When the dough is almost ready, preheat the oven to 350°F and make the topping. In a small bowl, mix together the honey with 2 tablespoons water and the vanilla. Using an electric mixer with the paddle attachment, cream the butter, sugar, and salt until light and fluffy, 5 to 7 minutes. Scrape down the sides of the bowl and beat in the egg and lemon zest. Alternately add the flour and honey mixture, scraping down the sides of the bowl between each addition.

5. Spoon the topping in large dollops over the risen crust and use a spatula to gently spread it in an even layer. Bake for 35 to 45 minutes. The cake will rise and fall in waves in the dish with a golden brown top but will still be liquid inside when done. Allow to cool in the pan before sprinkling with confectioners' sugar for serving, if desired.

NOTE: If you'd rather cling to tradition, omit the lemon and use corn syrup in place of honey.

HONEY-GLAZED PEAR UPSIDE-DOWN CAKE

All good cooks steal recipes. Be it "my" special chocolate birthday cake from Rose Levy Beranbaum's *Cake Bible*, or the much-heralded green tomato basil pie I clipped from some forgotten magazine so many potlucks ago, stealing—or, let's say, borrowing—is how good cooks build their repertoires.

Of all the hundreds of recipes I've lifted over the years, none has worked its way into my dessert rotation quite like Claudia Fleming's roasted chestnut honey pears. But no matter how many times I serve the thyme-scented caramelized fruit to the accolades of family and friends, I never quite remember to give credit where credit is due.

Naturally, over the years of pear glazing, I have taken some liberties with the original formula. And then there are the mistakes I've made that stuck because they either made the pears even better, or easier.

For example, Claudia uses Italian chestnut honey, which I never seem to remember to pick up when I'm in the right kind of specialty store. So I have been substituting whatever honey I've got in the cupboards, usually orange blossom. It makes for a subtler but no less delectable pear cake.

She also calls for adding the honey and butter in two additions. The first is to simmer the pears in, and the second to create a honey butter sauce at the end. But once when I was harried and distracted, I accidentally threw everything into the pan at once. The pears came out sweeter and thoroughly candied, transformed from juicy fresh fruit into glowing amber jewels with a dense, toothsome texture. I've never gone back.

Usually when I make honey-glazed pears, I serve them with a slice of soft, homemade pound cake, which absorbs all the good, buttery, honeyed pear juices, becoming suffused with their perfume.

But one day I found myself with a load of Bosc pears, a dinner I needed a dessert for, and the itch to do something newish and a little fancier. As impressive as the honey pears and pound cake combination is in the mouth, it's not very striking on the plate. A pear tart, with glistening, shapely wedges of fruit, makes a much grander presentation.

So I contemplated baking a pear tart, maybe a mahogany pear tart tatin with a flaky puff pastry crust. But then I'd lose the supple, spongelike cake factor, since a pastry crust doesn't absorb syrupy fruit juices as well.

I started thumbing through other dessert books looking for a solution when I hit upon a photo in Dorie Greenspan's *Baking: From My Home to Yours*. Called Swedish visiting cake, it pictured an almond-topped butter cake that was baked in a skillet.

It reminded me both of tart tatin, which is also often made in a skillet, and of my—I mean Claudia's—skillet-roasted pears.

What if I simply glazed the pears as usual with honey, thyme sprigs, and butter, then poured the cake batter on top and baked the whole thing?

If I flipped it over for serving like an upside-down cake, shouldn't it emerge as golden as a pear tart tatin, but with a moist, cakey layer that would be perfectly primed to sop up all the luscious pear drippings?

I mixed up the batter, changing things slightly as I went (replacing almond extract, which I abhor, with extra vanilla, which I adore), and poured it over a pan of roasted pears. Then I popped it back into the oven and hoped for the best.

An hour later, the cake unmolded just like I had imagined, with glossy, honey-gilded pears crowning the pale cake. The *oohs* and *aahs* commenced as soon as the dessert hit the table, and continued until the very last crumb was happily devoured.

Naturally, everyone asked where I got the recipe.

"Um, I stole it twice over," I reluctantly confessed.

But no one really cared. Just as long as I promised to make it again and again, my double thievery was easily forgiven.

Honey-Glazed Pear Upside-Down Cake

¼ cup chestnut or other intense honey

4 small or 3 large Bosc pears, peeled, quartered lengthwise, and cored

3 fresh thyme sprigs (optional)

1 cup sugar

Finely grated zest of 1 lemon

2 large eggs

1 tablespoon vanilla extract

1 cup all-purpose flour

¼ teaspoon salt

½ cup plus 1 tablespoon unsalted butter (1 stick), melted and cooled

¼ cup sliced almonds

Time: 1½ hours,
plus cooling

Serves 6 to 8

1. Preheat the oven to 350°F. In a 9-inch (not nonstick) skillet, simmer the honey until it begins to reduce, caramelize, and darken in color, 6 to 10 minutes. (Do not let the honey burn. If it starts to smell burned, turn off the heat.)

2. Arrange the pears, close together and cut side down, in a circular pattern in the pan (the stem ends should point toward the center). Simmer over medium heat, turning them from one cut side to the other, until they begin to turn golden, about 10 minutes.

3. Flip the pears over to their curved side and scatter with the thyme sprigs if using. Transfer the pan to the oven and roast, uncovered, until very tender, about 25 minutes.

4. Meanwhile, in a large bowl, whisk together the sugar and lemon zest. Whisk in the eggs and vanilla. Fold in the flour and salt; stir in ½ cup melted butter.

5. When the pears are soft, remove the skillet from the oven and brush the edges with the remaining 1 tablespoon melted butter. Pour the batter on top of the roasted pears and scatter the almonds over the batter. Bake until a toothpick inserted in the center comes out clean, 25 to 30 minutes. Let the cake cool for 30 minutes in the pan. Run an offset spatula along the edges of the pan to loosen the cake; carefully invert the cake onto a serving platter. Serve warm or cooled.

WHISKEY-SOAKED DARK CHOCOLATE BUNDT CAKE

Although I learned to cook at my parents' knees, when it came to baking, I was on my own. Sure, my dad could turn out a crusty baguette. But for gooey chocolate chip cookies, peanut brittle, or strawberry pie—the kinds of things that appealed to a teenage sweet tooth—I turned to my great-aunt Maida.

Okay, Maida Heatter wasn't really my aunt. But after baking my way through her *Book of Great Chocolate Desserts*, that's how I thought of her—as a kindly presence dispensing nuggets of wisdom in every recipe like so many walnuts in a brownie. It was from her that I learned to use a chilled bowl and beaters for the fluffiest whipped cream, and room-temperature ones for billowing egg whites.

Most important, she taught me how to make the boozy, fudge-filled 86-proof chocolate cake that earned me temporary entry into my high school's cool clique.

Even back then, I was given to extravagance. I discovered that giving the cake a good douse of Wild Turkey from my parents' liquor cabinet was vastly superior to Aunt Maida's temperate little sprinkle. When combined with the topping of confectioners' sugar, it made an icing-like exterior with a sweetness that mitigated its high-alcohol burn.

Somewhere on the road to adulthood, I stopped making that cake, choosing to bake more sophisticated chocolate tortes and sip my (now legal) tipple on the side.

But my friend Dave's birthday made me unearth the recipe. Dave is a cocktail fanatic, so a bourbon-imbued cake seemed just the thing to take to his party.

I hadn't looked at the recipe in years, but there it was, the instructions splattered with chocolate smudges and my cryptic note in the margin to drizzle the cake with extra spirits.

In high school, I was comfortable enough playing with cake toppings, but I wouldn't have dared to monkey with the structure of the batter itself.

Now, however, I have no such inhibitions. I remembered Aunt Maida's cake as delectable but slightly on the sweet side, with a flavor that spoke more of butter, liquor, and sugar than intense dark chocolate. So I decided to punch up the fudge quotient a bit.

The recipe called for five ounces of unsweetened chocolate.

Back in high school, I used supermarket baking chocolate. Now my pantry was stocked with fancy-pants brands like Valrhona, which would help deepen the flavor. So would the addition of a couple of tablespoons of unsweetened cocoa powder, which would help cut the sweetness. I also increased the amount of salt because I like my chocolate with a savory undertone.

Aunt Maida had also included a goodly half-cup of bourbon in the batter. I planned to double that, replacing some of the water she called for. But right next to my bottle of Wild Turkey was a bottle of rye that I knew Dave was particularly fond of. Because he espouses rye in Manhattans in lieu of bourbon, I thought maybe he'd like it in his birthday cake, too.

And in fact, he did. The cake—rich, dense and very chocolaty, with a spicy, peppery, burned-caramel tang from the rye—was a hit. After all, who could resist raising a toast and a fork at the same time?

Whiskey-Soaked Dark Chocolate Bundt Cake

Time: 30 minutes,
plus baking
and cooling

Serves 10 to 12

5 ounces unsweetened chocolate

¼ cup instant espresso powder

2 tablespoons unsweetened cocoa powder

1 cup bourbon, rye, or other whiskey, plus additional for sprinkling

½ teaspoon kosher salt

1 cup (2 sticks) unsalted butter, softened

2 cups granulated sugar

3 large eggs

1 tablespoon vanilla extract

1 teaspoon baking soda

2 cups all-purpose flour

Confectioners' sugar, for garnish, if desired

1. Grease and flour a 10-cup-capacity Bundt cake pan (or you can use two 8- or 9-inch loaf pans). Preheat the oven to 325°F.
2. In the microwave or a double boiler over simmering water, melt the chocolate. Let cool.
3. Put the espresso and cocoa in a 2-cup (or larger) glass measuring cup. Add enough boiling water to come up to the 1-cup measuring line. Mix until the cocoa and espresso powders dissolve. Add the whiskey and salt; let cool.
4. Using an electric mixer, beat the butter until fluffy. Add the sugar and beat until well combined. Beat in the eggs, one at a time, beating well between each addition. Beat in the vanilla extract, baking soda, and melted chocolate, making sure to scrape down the sides of the bowl with a rubber spatula.
5. On low speed, beat in a third of the whiskey mixture. When the liquid is aborbed, beat in half the flour. Repeat the additions, ending with the whiskey mixture. Scrape the batter into the prepared pan and smooth the top. Bake until a cake tester inserted into the center of the cake comes out

clean, about 1 hour and 10 minutes for the Bundt pan (the loaf pans will take less time; start checking them after 55 minutes).

6. Transfer the cake to a cooling rack. Unmold after 15 minutes and sprinkle the warm cake with more whiskey. Let cool before serving, garnished with confectioners' sugar, if you like.

TRIPLE CHOCOLATE TRIFLE WITH RASPBERRIES

My parents love to tell the story of me and the bowl of *schlag* (whipped cream) at Demel Coffeehouse in Vienna. I was a toddler, the tale goes, held in my mother's arms in front of the pastry counter, when I pitched myself forward, diving into that bowl of said *schlag*. I made it up to my wrists before being caught but, after licking the white fluff from my fingers, apparently spent the rest of the day ecstatic.

I can't say I remember it. Though given my predilection for anything creamy, it seems likely. And it may explain why giant bowls of whipped cream—preferably hiding a layer of rich pudding underneath—still make me weak in the knees.

And of the multitude of whipped cream–topped pudding possibilities, the queen of them all is trifle.

With its layers of cake, sherry, custard, and whipped cream, trifle is more than just pudding. It's a grand dessert, a celebration unto itself in a cut crystal bowl. A genuine crowd pleaser, large quantities can be assembled days in advance, making it an ideal dessert for a holiday party.

I thought about all this when I was planning a little soiree. Because the menu included latkes that would have me chained to the stove frying for most of the night, I wanted dessert to be something I could plop on the table with no last-minute fussing. Yet it also needed to be festive and compelling enough to seduce my carb-filled guests, many of whom would be under twelve.

With the kids in mind, I decided that a typical boozy trifle (with good reason called a tipsy parson pudding in England) might not be the best thing. But I worried that simply leaving out the sherry would spoil the dessert's balance and character, and that the cake might be too spongy without the added booze.

But what if I substituted a moister cake that didn't need either a libation or hydration? And what if that cake contained yet another crowd pleaser, like chocolate?

The moistest chocolate cake I know how to bake is brownies. A brownie trifle would certainly appeal to the kids at the table. But the combination of brownies and custard seemed off—the fudge flavor would obscure the delicacy of the eggs and vanilla.

The antidote was simple: When in doubt, add more chocolate. Though not in the least traditional, a chocolate pudding–brownie trifle would happily fill the bill. I knew the kids would be smitten. And if I added tart, juicy raspberries and nuggets of bittersweet chocolate to rein in the sumptuous sweetness, I bet the adults would be, too.

Putting everything together was a snap. Five days before the party, I made my favorite recipe for brownies and another for chocolate pudding. Then the day before, I layered them with the berries, chopped chocolate, and plenty of whipped cream.

By the time I pulled my gorgeous creation out of the fridge, my guests were groaning with potato pancake overload. But the sight of a glass bowl filled with chocolate and billowing whipped cream revived them all. The toddlers gathered round, ready to dive right in. Certainly it was a sentiment I could relate to.

Triple Chocolate Trifle with Raspberries

Time: 1½ hours,
plus 3 hours'
chilling time

Serves 8 to 10

FOR THE BROWNIES

1 cup plus 2 tablespoons unsalted butter

3 ounces finely chopped unsweetened chocolate

½ cup cocoa powder, sifted

2½ cups granulated sugar

3 eggs, beaten

1 tablespoon vanilla extract

1½ cups all-purpose flour

½ teaspoon kosher salt

3 tablespoons Cognac, rum, or bourbon (optional)

FOR ASSEMBLY

½ cup granulated sugar

8 tablespoons unsweetened cocoa powder (½ cup), sifted

2 tablespoons cornstarch

Pinch salt

1¾ cups whole milk

3 cups heavy cream

2 large egg yolks

10 ounces finely chopped bittersweet chocolate (2 cups)

2 tablespoons unsalted butter

1 teaspoon vanilla extract

¼ cup confectioners' sugar, for whipped cream

1 to 2 pints fresh raspberries

1. To make the brownies, preheat the oven to 350°F. Grease a 9×13-inch baking pan.

2. In a large saucepan, melt the butter. Remove the pan from the heat and stir in the chopped chocolate until fully melted. Stir in the cocoa and sugar until combined. Slowly add the eggs, whisking the chocolate mixture constantly, then whisk in the vanilla. Fold in the flour and salt.

3. Pour the batter into the prepared pan. Bake until just firm, about 25 minutes (do not overbake). Transfer the pan to a rack to cool. If using the spirit, use a fork to prick holes in the hot brownies and drizzle it evenly over the pan.

4. In a large bowl, mix together the granulated sugar, 3 tablespoons cocoa powder, the cornstarch, and salt. Whisk in ¾ cup milk. In a large saucepan, bring the remaining 1 cup milk and ½ cup cream to a boil over medium heat. Whisk the hot milk mixture slowly into the cocoa mixture. Return to the saucepan. Cook over medium heat, whisking gently, until slightly thickened, about 2 minutes (you may see a simmering bubble or two; that's okay, but don't let it boil).

5. In a medium, heatproof bowl, whisk the yolks. Whisking them constantly, very slowly dribble about half of the chocolate mixture into the yolks until fully combined. Pour the yolk mixture into the saucepan, whisking constantly. Cook, whisking occasionally, over medium-low heat until thickened, about 5 minutes. (Do not let the mixture come to a simmer at this point. If the pan begins to steam thickly, remove from the heat for a few moments and stir well before continuing.) Transfer to a bowl and let cool slightly.

6. Melt 5 ounces (1 cup) chopped chocolate with the butter. Stir until smooth. Stir in the vanilla. Cool 5 minutes, then fold the mixture into the thickened egg mixture. Place plastic wrap directly against the pudding (to keep a skin from forming), and chill until set, about 3 hours. (The pudding and brownies can be made up to 2 days ahead.)

7. Just before assembling, in an electric mixer, beat the remaining 2½ cups cream with the remaining 5 tablespoons cocoa powder and confectioners' sugar until it forms soft peaks. Scrape down the sides and fold in any excess cocoa or sugar.

8. Cut the brownies into 1-inch squares. Fit a layer of brownie squares in the bottom of a 4-quart trifle, glass, or other bowl. Top with half the pudding, a third of the cream, a third of the remaining chopped chocolate, and a third of the raspberries. Repeat the layering until all the ingredients have been used, ending with a layer of brownies, whipped cream, chocolate, and raspberries. Serve immediately, or cover with plastic wrap and chill for up to 24 hours before serving.

KATE'S IMPOSSIBLY FUDGY BROWNIES WITH CHILE AND SEA SALT

In high school, while most of the other girls in my class were perfecting their sultry glances and coquettish tilts of the head, I was hiding in the kitchen, perfecting my brownies.

They went on dates to the movies and the mall; I baked up brownies with both pecans and walnuts. I tried them nutless, too, and with raisins and almonds, like a candy bar. I made raspberry brownies, butterscotch brownies, spicy brownies with black pepper and ginger. My idea was that once I hit upon the magical combination of chocolate, sugar, and butter, I'd give them to that leather-jacketed guy I admired from afar. And of course, he'd fall instantly in love with me at the very first melt-in-the-mouth bite and ask me to the prom, after which we'd get married and live happily ever after.

It all seemed so easy at fifteen.

Not surprisingly, none of this came to pass. In the end, I was never satisfied with my brownie variations and never had the nerve to offer any to Mr. Leather Jacket. I ended up going to the prom with a friend, and the whole marriage question is a three-part saga better left for another time.

But had I known Kate Krader back when I was in high school, things might have worked out differently.

This is because Kate Krader, an editor par excellence at *Food & Wine* magazine, bakes the best brownies I've ever tasted. Fudgy and very moist but not at all sticky, they have a profound, dark cocoa flavor that's heightened by the judicious sprinkle of flaky Maldon sea salt she scatters on top before baking. Kate's brownies manage to tread the line between dense and light, with the salt crunching enticingly before the bittersweet chocolate notes explode on the tongue.

Luckily for me, Kate has a generous nature and gave me the recipe just for the asking. My only change, which you can ignore, is to add a tiny pinch of cayenne to the batter. I think the chile complicates and intensifies the chocolate flavor, and the heat adds a nice zippy tingle to all that gooey richness. But either spicy or plain, these brownies will change your life, whether you're still in high school, or still getting over it.

Kate's Impossibly Fudgy Brownies with Chile and Sea Salt

2 sticks plus 2 tablespoons unsalted butter

3 ounces unsweetened chocolate, chopped

1½ cups all-purpose flour

½ teaspoon kosher salt

⅛ teaspoon cayenne, optional

½ cup plus 1 tablespoon cocoa powder

2½ cups sugar

3 large eggs, lightly beaten

1 tablespoon vanilla extract

Maldon salt, for sprinkling

Time: 45 minutes

Makes 24 (2-inch) squares

1. Preheat the oven to 350°F. Line a rimmed 9×13-inch baking sheet with parchment paper.
2. In a microwave or in the top bowl of a double boiler, melt together the butter and chopped chocolate, stirring until smooth. Meanwhile, combine the flour, kosher salt, and cayenne in a medium bowl.
3. Transfer the chocolate mixture to a large mixing bowl and whisk in the cocoa powder and sugar. Add the eggs and vanilla; whisk until smooth.
4. Fold in the dry ingredients and continue folding until no lumps remain.
5. Scrape the batter into the prepared pan and smooth the top with a spatula. Sprinkle all over with Maldon salt. Bake for 25 to 30 minutes, until the edges just begin to pull away from the sides of the pan and the top is set and shiny.
6. Allow the brownie to cool completely in the pan before cutting into 2×2-inch squares.

DECADENTLY BITTERSWEET CHOCOLATE ICE CREAM

In the summer between high school and college, when all my overachieving New York City friends were getting internships in law firms and TV studios to help further their careers, I got a job making ice cream to help further mine. Only I didn't know it at the time.

The ice cream maker at Peter's Ice Cream Café in Brooklyn Heights was the size of an industrial washing machine and looked like one, too. I'd pour the custard and any flavorings through the top and, after much mixing and freezing, watch skiable quantities of ice cream spiral out. Freshly churned and barely frozen, it had a luscious, buoyant texture like soft-serve. It was irresistible, so I didn't, lapping up bowl after bowl of the pale, barely set stuff before it compacted and solidified in the deep freezer.

The most popular ice-cream flavor at Peter's was something called Chocolate Decadence, a rich, ganache-like chocolate ice cream so thick and fudgy you practically had to use a chain saw to cut through it. It required sacks of unsweetened cocoa powder, which I needed to feed by hand into the top of the whirling, belching machine while it was running. It spit back amber clouds of cocoa dust that coated my clothes, my hair, my face. No matter how well I swabbed down in the tiny restroom of the ice-cream shop, on Decadence-making days, wasps buzzed around my head on the walk to the subway.

This is my version of Peter's recipe. I've made it a bit lighter so you can use a regular ice-cream scoop to dish it out. And I add the cocoa powder all at once to the custard, so you needn't worry about wasps—unless you eat a cone of this heady stuff outside in summer. But it's worth the risk.

Decadently Bittersweet Chocolate Ice Cream

2 cups whole milk
½ cup heavy cream
⅔ cup sugar
2 ounces chopped bittersweet chocolate
¾ cup unsweetened cocoa powder
4 large egg yolks
1 teaspoon vanilla extract
Pinch kosher salt

Time: 30 minutes,
plus freezing time

Makes 1½ pints

1. In a large saucepan over medium heat, bring the milk, cream, and ⅓ cup sugar just to a simmer, stirring until the sugar is dissolved. Take the pan off the heat and add the chopped chocolate and cocoa powder. Whisk until the mixture is smooth.

2. Have ready a large bowl of ice and water. In the bowl of an electric mixer using the whisk attachment, combine the egg yolks and the remaining ⅓ cup sugar until thick and pale. Add the chocolate mixture in a slow stream while whisking. Pour the custard back into the saucepan and place over medium-low heat, stirring constantly, until a thermometer reads 170°F. Pour the custard through a sieve into a metal bowl set in the ice and water and let cool.

3. When the custard is cold, whisk in the vanilla and salt. Pour it into an ice-cream maker and freeze according to the manufacturer's directions. Transfer the ice cream to an airtight container and store in the freezer.

VARIATION: RIDICULOUSLY EASY MAPLE WALNUT ICE CREAM

Long before I was the ice cream mistress of Peter's Café, I was churning up all sorts of frozen delights in my parents' small ice-cream machine. My dad had purchased it long before sleek, lightweight ice-cream machines became standard equipment on wedding registers, before every foodie worth her chef's knife had or at least coveted one.

Back then, ice-cream machines were big, bulky, and expensive. Ours was the self-freezing kind, meaning you didn't have to put a bowl in the freezer before pouring in the custard. It churned and froze the mixture simultaneously and quickly. Mix in some sweetened cream or sorbetworthy fruit puree, and thirty minutes later, be prepared to gorge.

My father, more interested in savory ice creams than sweet, was ahead of his time in flavor combinations. His first project was gazpacho sorbet, which morphed into a pure garlic sorbet when he realized that his favorite thing about gazpacho was not, in fact, the tomatoes.

Blue cheese, smoked salmon, and even caviar ice cream followed close on its heels, though I'll admit my preference was for the sugary stuff.

That was fine with him. As long as I cleaned up after myself, I was free to experiment with the machine as much as I wanted.

The first flavor I ever made was maple walnut. I got the recipe from the pink booklet that came with the fancy machine, and it couldn't have been easier. You simply poured maple syrup and cream into the machine's bowl, turned it on, then added toasted walnuts at the end. No custard cooking with its potential egg curdling, no cooling and straining. Just the essence of maple bound in a voluptuous frozen cream studded with crisp bits of nut.

Over the years, I've played around with other maple ice creams that use more exacting, complicated techniques. And perhaps they are slightly more refined on the tongue. But I always come back to this one, which has a purity missing from recipes that also use egg yolk. I've jiggered the proportions, decreasing the cream and adding milk for lightness. And when I can get it, I like to use grade B maple syrup, which has a more intense flavor than the lighter grade A. I also cook the syrup down before adding it, which gives the finished ice cream a dreamy, creamy texture. And finally, I add a pinch of salt to bring out the maple's savory side. Adding salt to ice cream is a trick my dad taught me, and it works no matter if your ice cream is savory or sweet.

Ridiculously Easy Maple Walnut Ice Cream

⅔ cup maple syrup, preferably grade B
2 cups heavy cream
⅔ cup whole milk
Large pinch kosher salt
¾ chopped toasted walnuts

Time: 10 minutes,
plus freezing time

Makes 1½ pints

1. In a large saucepan over medium heat, bring the maple syrup just to a boil. Reduce the heat to low and simmer to thicken for 5 minutes.
2. Take the pan off the heat and whisk in the cream, milk, and salt. Transfer the mixture to a bowl to cool to room temperature, then chill until quite cold, at least 1 hour and up to 2 days.
3. Freeze the mixture in an ice-cream maker according to the manufacturer's directions. When the ice cream is almost at the desired consistency, stir in the nuts and continue freezing another 5 minutes. Transfer the ice cream to an airtight container and store in the freezer.

VARIATION: CHOCOLATE-COCONUT SORBET FOR DANIEL

This is what I make for my husband Daniel, who doesn't eat regular ice cream (or cream at all). The coconut milk makes the sorbet velvety and smooth and brings out the fruitiness of the bittersweet chocolate. It's kind of like the frozen version of the Coconut Hot Chocolate on page 429, but with a smoother mouthfeel, thanks to all the churning the ice-cream machine does for you. If you serve this with sweetened shredded coconut and a drizzle of chocolate sauce, it tastes like a frozen Mounds bar. And there's nothing the matter with that.

Time: 10 minutes, plus freezing time

Makes 1½ pints

2 (15-ounce) cans unsweetened coconut milk (3 cups)

½ cup sugar

2 ounces chopped bittersweet chocolate

3 tablespoons unsweetened cocoa powder

2 teaspoons dark rum

¼ teaspoon kosher salt

Chocolate Sauce with Honey (recipe follows), for serving

1. In a saucepan over medium heat, stir the coconut milk and sugar until the sugar dissolves. Reduce the heat to low and add the chocolate, cocoa powder, dark rum, and salt, whisking until smooth.
2. Transfer to a bowl, let the mixture cool, then chill until very cold, at least 1 hour (and up to 2 days).
3. Freeze the mixture in an ice-cream maker according to the manufacturer's directions. Transfer to an airtight container and store in the freezer. Serve with Chocolate Sauce with Honey.

Chocolate Sauce with Honey

In a small saucepan over medium-low heat, combine ¼ cup sugar, 2 tablespoons honey, pinch salt, and ⅓ cup water. Heat, stirring constantly, until the sugar dissolves, 2 to 3 minutes. Add 4 ounces chopped bittersweet chocolate and 2 tablespoons butter, whisking until emulsified. Continue to whisk over the heat until the sauce is thickened and glossy, 4 to 6 minutes. Use immediately or cool and transfer to an airtight container and refrigerate.

Makes about 1 cup

11

There's Always Room for Pie (and Tarts)

In my senior year of high school, I got a job helping the baker at a local café make it through the Thanksgiving baking rush.

Had I thought it out before applying, I might have realized that "making it through the Thanksgiving baking rush" means, in fact, rolling out dozens and dozens and dozens of piecrusts. And as much as I was an avid amateur baker at the time, homemade piecrust just wasn't my thing. When I'd want to make pie, I'd either use a mix-in-the-pan crust, a graham cracker crust, or (and don't tell anyone) a purchased frozen piecrust that I'd sloppily recrimp so it looked homemade. To this day, I like to leave the decorative edges on my crusts loose and messy just to make sure people know I made it all by hand.

Despite my lack of piecrust experience, I was hired for the job, probably because I agreed to work overnight the Wednesday before Thanksgiving. At seventeen, I had lots of energy for all-nighters, especially pastry-fueled ones.

Prepping the dough was easy. The baker showed me how to use the giant stand mixer to gently mix chunks of butter into flour until everything was sandy; then we dribbled in just enough water to bring the dough together. I weighed out dough balls, patted them into discs, and stacked them neatly in the walk-in refrigerator. While they solidified, I mixed up vats of filling with canned pumpkin and spices, pecans, eggs, and maple syrup.

It was all going so smoothly that I don't think the baker realized just how green I was until she watched me attempt to roll out my first batch.

I unwrapped the dough and went at it vigorously with the rolling pin, sliding the wooden wand back and forth until the dough was as thin as paper. I looked down and felt proud and pleased—until the baker pointed out that I had neglected to flour the work table and therefore effectively glued the crust to it.

She showed me the proper rolling technique, and I spent the next six hours practicing it. By the time the sun came up that next morning, I was rolling out crusts as if I'd been doing it all my life.

The trick, I learned, is to add just enough flour to keep the dough moving, but not so much that the dough becomes stiff and hard to work with. I sprinkle on the flour bit by bit, dusting each side of the dough disc with some before rolling, and adding just the lightest scattering anytime the dough starts to stick. I also turn the dough of each crust over several times as I roll it to keep it from attaching itself to the table. There's a rhythm to it: Roll, roll, sprinkle, sprinkle, flip, sprinkle, roll. As long as you keep the dough moving around, it won't adhere to the table.

I've since also learned that for very sticky dough, rolling it out between two pieces of plastic wrap or wax paper can save heartbreak at the end of the day.

Now homemade pie is so much a part of my baking life that not a season goes by without my making at least one. I take advantage of the first stalks of spring rhubarb, the ripest summer peaches and berries, autumn's apples, pears, and squashes, winter's citrus. And even when the fruit bowl is bare, there's still my year-round stash of chocolate, peanut butter, nuts, and cream to play with. Pie is an adaptable creature.

Besides, no matter what's in it, a well-made pie makes everyone happy. As much as people adore brownies, clamor for cookies, and esteem fancy cakes, nothing tickles their warm, cozy inclinations like a home-baked pie. Even if you use a purchased crust.

PERFECTION IN A PIE TIN

A few years ago, I achieved perfection in a piecrust, and it smelled like pig.

Not in a muddy, barnyard way, but with a mildly meaty, nutty aroma, like the scent of caramelized bacon fat bubbling in the pan. Carefully confected with part butter and part lard, this pie pastry was everything bakers and bloggers wax poetic about: a golden-brown-around-the edges epiphany richly flavored with dairy and a slight glimmer of pork, and just salty enough to contrast with the sweet apple filling; the texture was as flaky as a croissant but crisp. It shattered when you bit it, then melted instantly on the tongue.

The only problem with my masterpiece, I told my guests as they licked the crumbs off their plates, was that I was never, ever going to make it again.

Because what they didn't see was the outsize effort that went into acquiring and preparing the not-so-secret ingredient to my success: leaf lard, the creamy white fat that surrounds a young hog's kidneys. The veritable ne plus ultra of pig fat, it's hard to track down (I special ordered it from a friendly butcher) and a headache once you get it. Step one: Pick out any bloody bits and sinews, chop the fat into bits, and render it slowly in a double boiler for eight hours. At the end of the day, be prepared for a kitchen that smells like breakfast at a highway diner, and a smoking pan full of molten fat crowned with burned cracklings.

The leaf lard may have made great crust, but like homemade cassoulet and puff pastry, it was a culinary Everest I felt no need to climb twice.

But Everest became a lot more manageable when I discovered that rendered leaf lard was now available at my farmers' market and by mail order (see Note).

With this convenience at hand, I decided to have a pre-Thanksgiving piecrust bake-off to see if, with the prep times and mess factor being equal, lard pastry really was the best when tasted side by side with my standby favorite all-butter crust—or whether my perception of the lard pie's sublimity was heightened relative to the number of hours the darn thing took to make.

And while the kitchen was a floury mess anyway, why not trot out a few more piecrust recipes and come up with something definitive, the piecrust recipe I'd turn to Thanksgiving after Thanksgiving? I wanted a recipe that was simple enough to memorize and straightforward to prepare.

Although I was open to using something as rarefied as rendered leaf lard for the fat component in the recipe, I decided that all the other ingredients in the crust should be as accessible as possible. That nixed using a mix of flours with different protein levels (like bread flour, cake flour, and Wondra). For this pie, I went with all-purpose all the way. I also ruled out adding an acid such as vinegar, lemon juice, or sour cream (which some say make for a more tender crust), simply because I wanted to avoid too many variables.

Flakiness and flavor were my priorities, and figuring out which fat would give me the best of both was the goal.

But before I started baking, I did some research, looking over the piecrust recipe canon. Most were a combination of shortening and butter, or all butter, so I started there. I made five crusts: all-butter, all-shortening, fifty-fifty butter shortening, 70 percent butter to 30 percent shortening, and vice versa. Crisp, flaky, and sweetly luscious with deep, browned flavor, the all-butter crust was the hands-down favorite. The shortening crust was a bust among tasters; all agreed that the unpleasant greasy film it left on the palate (even when combined with 70 percent butter) was not worth the vague texture improvement. Was its popularity with bakers due to cost, since shortening is much less expensive than butter?

But Rose Levy Beranbaum, author of *The Pie and Pastry Bible*, gave another explanation: aesthetics. Because shortening is manufactured for stability at extreme temperatures (both hot in the oven and cold in the fridge), it is very easy to work with, she explained. "Shortening crusts enable you to get fancier decorations that will hold up when you bake."

Once she mentioned it, I realized that even my quickly crimped borders on the shortening crusts stayed pert in the oven compared to the butter border, which melted into impressionistic Gaudi-like undulations.

Round one going to butter, I experimented with oil crusts after becoming intrigued by the Mediterranean appeal of a pie pastry scented with extra-virgin olive oil holding a caramelized pear-pomegranate filling. I tested several olive oil variations, freezing the oil before cutting it into the flour, adding egg, baking powder, and some butter as desperation measures. Then I went on to test canola oil, grapeseed oil, coconut oil, and ghee. Not one managed to even get close to a minimally acceptable flakiness level.

I had better luck using a chilled mixed nut butter combined with regular butter, which turned out a subtly flaky and cookie-like crust, with a toasted, nutty flavor that goes particularly well with pumpkin pie.

A dozen or so piecrusts down, it was finally time to pull out my hero, the rendered leaf lard. I pitted it against an array of animal fats: suet, duck fat, plus processed supermarket lard.

The processed lard was not, in fact, available at my local Park Slope supermarket, but I easily found it in a nearby bodega. I ordered rendered duck fat online, and picked up suet from my local butcher, who charged me a token dollar, and told me he usually threw it away.

Then I baked and baked. The whole house took on a rich pastry scent with undertones of roasted meat and butter, tinged with ginger, nutmeg, thyme, and honeyed apples from the fillings.

Not wanting to give up the flavor of butter entirely, I tested all the recipes using half butter, half other animal fat, and also at a ratio of 70 percent butter to 30 percent other fat. I also made a few crusts using 100 percent high-fat European-style butter.

Firmly in the land of animal fat, the crusts were spectacular, each in its own way. The high-fat butter produced a markedly flakier, more tender, and puff pastry–like crust than those made with regular butter. It also shrank a bit less when I prebaked it.

In terms of mixed fat crusts, tasters (that is, my parents, my husband, my neighbor, and myself) preferred those made with 70 percent butter. The higher proportion of animal fat pushed the meatiness factor too far onto the savory side of the pie spectrum, better for quiches than fruit and custard fillings.

Of the three animals, pig, cow, and duck, the duck fat crust had the lightest flavor and texturally struck a balance between crisp and flaky.

The leaf lard crust was as gorgeous as I remembered, puffing up in the oven and crumbling deliciously when you cut it. That characteristic faint bacon nuance was happily still there. Not so with the processed lard pastry, with a flavor veering closer to rancid than bacon.

The pie revelation, however, was the suet pastry. As easy to work with as the shortening crust, it retained its shape perfectly in the oven, baking up crisp yet marvelously tender and flaky, and tasting rich and meaty, though not identifiably beefy.

Suet is also easy to find (most butchers can get it for you), and inexpensive. One caveat: Suet is sold unrendered, but as I found out by way of my own laziness, you do not need to render it. Simply cut out the pinkish bits, chop up the white fat, and toss it in with the butter. More refined bakers might blanch at the idea; if you're one of them, go ahead and render to your heart's content.

As for me, I'll move on to the next obsessive round of piecrust testing, playing with some of the fats I've yet neglected, like goose fat, marrow, foie gras fat, browned butter, and truffle butter. And if I ever can find a source for bear fat, I'll try that, too.

Perfect Piecrust

Time: 15 minutes, plus chilling time

Makes 1 (9-inch) single piecrust; recipe can be doubled for a double crust; divide the dough into two balls to form two discs before chilling.

1¼ cups all-purpose flour
¼ teaspoon kosher salt
10 tablespoons unsalted butter, preferably a high-fat, European-style butter such as Plugra, chilled, and cut into ½-inch pieces (or use a combination of fats, see Variations)
2 to 5 tablespoons ice water

1. In a food processor, briefly pulse together the flour and salt. Add the butter and pulse until the mixture forms chickpea-size pieces (3 to 5 1-second pulses). Add the ice water, 1 tablespoon at a time, and pulse until the mixture is just moist enough to hold together.
2. Form the dough into a ball, wrap with plastic, and flatten into a disc. Refrigerate at least 1 hour before rolling out and baking.

VARIATIONS: You can experiment with different textures and flavors by substituting 3 to 4 tablespoons butter with any of the following fats: shortening, lard, beef suet, duck fat, or an unsweetened nut butter, such as hazelnut butter, almond butter, or mixed nut butter. All should be well chilled before using.

CHEDDAR CRUST: This crispy crust pairs nicely with apple pie or savory pie fillings. Pulse together 1¼ cups all-purpose flour with ¾ teaspoon salt. Add ¾ cup grated sharp Cheddar; pulse until it forms coarse crumbs. Add 8 table-spoons chilled, cubed butter and proceed according to the directions for the basic piecrust.

PREBAKED CRUST: Preheat the oven to 375°F. On a lightly floured surface, roll out the piecrust to a 12-inch circle. Transfer the crust to a 9-inch pie plate. Fold over any excess dough, then crimp the edges with your fingers. Prick the crust all over with a fork. If you have time, freeze the crust for 15 to 30 minutes; otherwise skip this step. Cover the pie with aluminum foil and fill with pie weights (you can use pennies, rice, or dried beans for this). Bake for 15 min-utes; remove the foil and weights and bake until pale golden, 5 to 7 minutes more.

NOTE: If you are in New York, rendered leaf lard can be purchased from the Flying Pigs Farm stand at the Union Square and Grand Army Plaza farmers' markets on Saturdays.

Elsewhere, you can obtain it by mail order from Dietrich's Meats, 610-756-6344, www.dietrichsmeats.com. Rendered duck fat is available online from www.dartagnan.com. Suet can be purchased from butchers.

UN-PUMPKIN PIE
(CARAMELIZED BUTTERNUT
SQUASH PIE WITH BRANDY)

For years, my family used canned pumpkin in our pumpkin pie. Taking a cue from my father, the most opinionated pumpkin pie lover in our lot, our goal was for the spiciest, most gingery pie possible. When you're spooning in heaps of ginger powder, cinnamon, clove, and grated gingerroot, we all thought, it hardly matters whether you use canned pumpkin mush or a fresh puree—it's all just a vehicle for ferrying sugar and spices to your mouth.

Besides, we'd tried fresh pumpkin, struggling to carve up a big, tough jack-o'-lantern-esque orb before steaming and pureeing it. Once all the spices were added and the pie was baked, the flavor didn't seem that different from Libby's and definitely not worth the effort. So canned won out.

At some point when I was in college while flipping through my dog-eared *Fannie Farmer Cookbook*, I noticed a recipe for winter squash pie.

It looked a lot like pumpkin pie but called for winter squash puree in place of pumpkin, heavy cream in place of evaporated milk, and a fat dose of brandy along with the usual spices. It sounded appealing on every count and even though it was March, I decided to try it.

Obtaining the winter squash puree was far easier than that jack-o'-lantern experience—I simply halved a butternut squash and roasted it until tender. Then I whirled it in the food processor before adding the other ingredients, kicking up the ginger slightly as per the Clark family custom.

As I mixed everything together, I noticed that the proportions of cream to squash were higher than pumpkin to evaporated milk in the usual recipe. I hoped this would make for a lighter pie, and I was right. It was silky and creamy without being pasty or heavy. Even with the hefty dose of ginger, the flavor was fresher and brighter than pumpkin pie, but close enough to fool people come Thanksgiving. And the brandy added a warm, sophisticated note.

When the holidays rolled around, I made another squash pie and brought it to my parents' house without revealing the secret ingredient until the last crumb was devoured. No one was really surprised. Culinary trickery is a long-standing tradition in our family and hidden butternut squash is mild compared to disguised horsemeat or surreptitious rabbit.

Since then, I've never consistently gone back to putting pumpkin in my pumpkin pies. I did occasionally waver—there were the years I tried the same gingery, brandied recipe with sugar pumpkins and cheese pumpkins, which have denser, sweeter, and more intensely flavored flesh than those jack-o'-lantern types. They worked perfectly well. But they are hard to track down, heavy to carry home from the farmers' market, and have thick rinds that are a royal pain to cut through even with my meat cleaver. Butternut squashes have the great advantage of being easy to find and small enough to carry home in my purse. And the thin skin slips right off with a vegetable peeler.

I discovered how easy they are to peel when following a recipe for roasted butternut squash salad. While I was slathering the squash cubes with olive oil and salt, I could imagine tossing them with butter cubes and sugar, and cooking the squash until almost candied, then turning it all into pie.

I was itching to try this candied squash pie so badly that I made one almost immediately, not caring that plums were still in season and it was eighty degrees out. And my friends ate it all up, declaring it the best pumpkin pie they'd ever had—even when I told them it was squash.

Un-Pumpkin Pie (Caramelized Butternut Squash Pie with Brandy)

Time: 2 hours

Serves 6 to 8

1 recipe Perfect Piecrust (see recipe, page 391)

2½ pounds butternut squash, peeled, seeded, and cut into 2-inch chunks

2 tablespoons unsalted butter, cubed

2 teaspoons granulated sugar

1 cup heavy cream

1 large egg

2 large egg yolks

¼ cup light brown sugar

3 tablespoons brandy (or rum is nice, too)

1 teaspoon vanilla extract

1½ teaspoons ground ginger

1 to 2 teaspoons freshly grated gingerroot, or more to taste

¾ teaspoon freshly grated nutmeg

½ teaspoon ground cinnamon

Pinch kosher salt

1. Place the pie dough between two sheets of plastic wrap and roll into a ⅜-inch-thick round. Line a 9-inch pie pan with the dough, use your thumb and forefinger to flute the edges, and chill in the refrigerator for 30 minutes or up to a day; lightly cover the dough with plastic if leaving for more than 2 hours.

2. Preheat the oven to 375°F. Place the squash on a baking sheet; dot with the butter and sprinkle with the granulated sugar. Bake, stirring every 10 minutes, until the squash is fork-tender, 30 to 35 minutes.

3. Line the crust with foil, fill with pie weights, and place on a baking sheet. Bake the crust until set, about 15 minutes. Remove the foil and weights and bake until pale golden, 5 to 10 minutes longer.

4. While the piecrust is baking, prepare the filling. Puree the squash in a food processor until smooth (you should have about 1¾ cups puree). Add the cream, egg, yolks, brown sugar, brandy or rum, vanilla, ground ginger, grated

fresh ginger, nutmeg, cinnamon, and salt, and puree until combined. Scrape the filling into the piecrust and smooth the top with a spatula.

5. Reduce the oven temperature to 325°F. Bake the pie until the filling is just set but still jiggles in the middle, 35 to 40 minutes. Let cool completely before serving.

VARIATION: **BRANDIED PUMPKIN PIE**

If you must have pumpkin, you can skip step 2 and substitute 1 15-ounce can pure pumpkin puree for the pureed squash. Don't use pumpkin pie filling, which is already sweetened and spiced.

You can also use fresh roasted sugar or cheese pumpkin puree in place of the squash. Halve your pumpkin, then roast cut side up (sprinkled with sugar and dotted with butter, if you like) at 375°F until very tender. Scoop the flesh out of the skin and puree. Proceed as above. The same goes for any other variety of squash that tickles your fancy. Acorn, dumpling, turban, and kabocha all work well, though because their skins are harder to peel, I find it easier to roast them in halves like pumpkins instead of peeled in cubes like the butternut squash.

NECTARINE AND BLACKBERRY PIE À LA CRUSTMASTER

Before Bill Yosses became the pastry chef of the White House, earning him the nickname "The Crustmaster" from President Obama for his flaky pies, he and I wrote a dessert cookbook together.

It was a long-drawn-out labor of (mostly) love, and by the time we were done with the first draft, we'd come up with so many new recipes and techniques that we just couldn't bear to leave out that we went ahead and basically wrote the entire book all over again. Pastry chefs, especially the most talented ones, tend to be perfectionists, and Bill is no exception. Anyway, this writing and rewriting went on until the publisher finally made us stop. The book, called *The Perfect Finish*, saw the light of day in June 2010.

Not surprisingly, one of Bill's great obsessions was pie. We made scores of them, testing different flours and fats in the crust, baking methods, and filling flavors. We eventually handed in a recipe for what we considered to be the best possible nectarine pie.

But then Bill started making pies at the White House, and they were such a hit that he continued tinkering with our heretofore "perfect" recipe. His efforts paid off when he came up with an even better technique, which we hurried into the otherwise finished book moments before it went to press.

His brilliant innovation was to prebake the bottom crust entirely for a fruit pie before adding the filling and top crust, then baking it again. The second round of oven time cooks the fruit into luscious softness while the top crust browns and the bottom crisps up even more. This means that you're never left with a soft or soggy crust, even when using the ripest, juiciest fruit.

And the raw top crust will adhere to the bottom crust, Bill assured me, so you're not compromising fruit pie aesthetics in any way. Just improving the texture.

The next time I made a fruit pie, I tried out Bill's technique, using my regular pie dough recipe and baking the bottom crust through and through, as if it were for a custard pie. Since it was early September, I chose nectarines and blackberries to mix into the filling, sweetening them with a combination of white and light brown sugar for added richness.

As it baked, I started to worry that the bottom crust would become hard and cookie-like, which is nice in a tart but not what I wanted in a fruit pie.

Plus I had other reasons for my anxiety. I was taking my pie experiment to a good-bye potluck feast for the *New York Times* food critic Frank Bruni. Frank had eaten the best pies all over New York, and he was, after all, a critic. I began to think that maybe I should have played it safe.

The pie came out of the oven a golden brown, purple-splotched beauty. As least it looked good.

Throughout the dinner the pie sat in the kitchen of our editor Trish Hall, who was hosting. We ate our way through the handiwork of the entire staff of the Dining section—Mark Bittman's watermelon and feta salad, Pete Wells's spicy fresh creamed corn, Nick Fox's fiery chili and corn bread, Trish's seared steak with chimichurri sauce, Kim Severson's raw kale salad, and a terrific white gazpacho brought by Julia Moskin but made by chef Seamus Mullen.

By the time we were ready for dessert, we were all too full of wine and food to be analytical about a pie. Everyone ate it up, but, in the midst of teary-eyed toasts and fare-thee-well sentiments, I certainly wasn't surprised that no one, myself included, paid much attention to the nuances of crust texture.

It wasn't until I got home later that night with a piece I had managed to save for my husband Daniel that I could focus on it. And just as Bill described, the bottom crust was crisp and very brown, but still flaky. Even though the fruit was supremely gushing and runny and the pie had been sitting for several hours, it still maintained a healthy crunch, which was a lovely contrast to all that ripe, sweet fruit.

Indeed, The Crustmaster had struck again, leaving only buttery crumbs in his wake.

Nectarine and Blackberry Pie à la Crustmaster

Time: 2 hours

Serves 6 to 8

2 recipes Perfect Piecrust (see recipe, page 391)

2½ pounds (about 6 cups) peaches and nectarines,
   pitted and sliced ½ inch thick
1 tablespoon freshly squeezed lemon juice
½ cup granulated sugar (or less if the fruit is very sweet)
⅓ cup light brown sugar
Pinch kosher salt
2½ tablespoons cornstarch
1 tablespoon vanilla extract
2 cups blackberries
1 large egg white, lightly beaten
Demerara sugar, for sprinkling

1. On a very lightly floured surface, roll out 1 recipe Perfect Piecrust and line a 9-inch pie pan with about 1½ inches of overhang. Using your fingertips, flute the edges of the dough around the pie pan. Chill the dough at least 30 minutes and up to overnight. Cover lightly with plastic wrap if leaving for more than 2 hours.

2. Roll out the remaining recipe of Perfect Piecrust. Using 2½-inch circle cutters or assorted cookie cutters of a similar size, cut out 10 to 15 shapes (frogs are nice). Transfer the cutouts to a wax paper–lined plate and chill. Reserve the leftover dough for another purpose (such as Sugar Pie, see page 406).

3. Preheat the oven to 375°F. In a large bowl, combine the peaches and nectarines with the lemon juice. Add the granulated sugar, brown sugar, and salt and gently toss until the sugar dissolves. Allow the fruit to macerate at room temperature for 30 minutes.

4. Meanwhile prebake the crust. Line the crust with foil and fill with pie weights. Bake for 25 minutes, or until the edges of the crust begin to crisp

but do not take on color. Remove the weights and the foil and bake for an additional 5 minutes to crisp the bottom of the crust.

5. Raise the oven temperature to 400°F. Add the cornstarch and vanilla to the fruit and stir until the cornstarch dissolves. Add the blackberries and toss gently. Scrape the fruit mixture into the prebaked pie shell. Arrange the chilled cutouts on top of the filling. They should touch each other in places but still have enough spaces in between for the fruit to be visible. Brush the cutouts and the fluted edge of the crust with the egg white and sprinkle generously with the Demerara sugar. Transfer the pie to the oven and bake for 40 minutes, or until the crust is pale gold.

6. Lower the temperature to 350°F. Continue baking the pie for an additional 35 to 40 minutes, or until the filling is bubbling and the crust is deeply golden brown.

INDIVIDUAL FRENCH HONEY-APPLE TARTS

Another stellar recipe from Bill "Crustmaster" Yosses, this one is even easier than pie if you buy the puff pastry instead of making it yourself (Bill won't mind). It's an apple tart in the French tradition—a sugary, flaky, almost cookie-like crust topped with gossamer, glistening, butter and sugar–basted apple slices. It would be like an apple palmier, if such a thing existed, and is hands down my favorite apple tart, especially for the small amount of work that gets you there.

Uncharacteristically, my changes to Bill's recipe were minimal. All I did was cut rectangles out of the puff pastry instead of circles (for less waste), and swap honey for the corn syrup Bill uses.

The only caveat is to make sure to use the best quality, all-butter puff pastry you can find. There are too few ingredients here for it to hide behind, and the pastry really needs to shine.

Although best made on the day you plan to eat them, I've served them the next day to *oohs* and *aahs*. Just store them at room temperature and reheat them for a few minutes before serving.

Individual French Honey-Apple Tarts

Time: 1¼ hours

Serves 8

1 package (14 to 16 ounces) prepared puff pastry, defrosted
    if necessary
2 tablespoons honey
1¼ pounds mixed variety apples (about 3), peeled, cored and
    sliced ⅛ inch thick
1 cup confectioners' sugar
½ cup (1 stick) unsalted butter
1 vanilla bean, seeds scraped and reserved

1. Preheat the oven to 350°F and position a rack in the center of the oven. Line an 11×17-inch baking sheet with parchment.

2. On a lightly floured surface, unfold the pastry. Using a sharp knife, cut the dough into four squares along the fold. Cut each square in half and roll into a rectangle, about 7 by 3 inches. Transfer the rectangles to the baking sheet.

3. In a small saucepan over low heat or in the microwave, warm the honey. Prick the dough all over with a fork and brush each rectangle lightly with the honey. Layer the apple slices closely together on top of each rectangle in a row. Transfer the tray to the refrigerator to rest for 10 minutes.

4. Meanwhile, in a medium saucepan, combine the confectioners' sugar, butter, and vanilla bean seeds. Simmer until the sugar and butter are melted, whisking to combine.

5. Brush the top of each tart with a third of the sugar mixture. Transfer the pan to the oven and bake, basting with the sugar mixture every 20 minutes, until the pastries are puffed and golden, about 60 minutes. Let cool 5 minutes before serving.

JAIMEE'S PEAR-ALMOND PIE

One Monday morning, my recipe tester Jaimee Young arrived at "the office" (read: my house) with a captivating description of the pie she made for friends over the weekend.

"I used almond paste in the crust to make it like a frangipane, and added cinnamon and ginger to the pear filling. It came out softer than most pies, a little cakelike and really good—no leftovers," she said with a wistful sigh.

It was one of those days where we were supposed to be testing nothing but savory grilled foods for a grilling cookbook. But the thought of tender pears and almond paste flavored with warm spices was too enticing to ignore. I begged her to make it for me in between the shrimp kebabs and skirt steaks we were getting paid to cook.

Jaimee's sweet tooth is only slightly smaller than mine, and she was all too happy to oblige.

A few hours later, as the steak sizzled out back, we dug into Jaimee's pie. We meant to eat just a few bites and share the rest with my neighbors. But as the afternoon clicked by, the pie in the pan shrank and shrank, each of us cutting tiny slivers off the ends, you know, to even it out. When we realized that we'd consumed almost half the pie ourselves, we called my neighbor and made her take it away. Then Jaimee wrote up the recipe so we wouldn't forget it.

And here it is. It's an ideal pie to make for Thanksgiving or Christmas, maybe instead of the usual apple. But trust me, you'll love it any time of the year—even in grilling season.

Jaimee's Pear-Almond Pie

Time: 1½ hours,
plus chilling time

Serves 6 to 8

FOR THE CRUST

½ cup plus 2 tablespoons almond paste

½ cup plus 1 tablespoon unsalted butter

¼ teaspoon kosher salt

1 large egg yolk

1¼ cups all-purpose flour

FOR THE FILLING

5 Bartlett pears (about 2¼ pounds), peeled, cored,
    and cut into 1½-inch chunks

Freshly squeezed juice of ½ large lemon (1½ tablespoons)

1 tablespoon cornstarch

1 tablespoon granulated sugar

½ teaspoon ground cinnamon

¼ teaspoon ground ginger

¼ teaspoon ground cloves

¼ cup sliced almonds

Heavy cream, for brushing

Demerara sugar, for sprinkling

1. First, make the crust. Using an electric mixer with the paddle attachment, cream together the almond paste, butter, and salt until smooth, 5 to 7 minutes. Add the egg yolk and beat to combine. Beat in the flour on a slow speed, in three additions, until just combined. Press the dough into a flat disc, wrap in plastic, and chill in the refrigerator for 30 minutes and up to overnight.

2. Take the dough out of the refrigerator while you make the filling; this will allow for an easier roll out. To make the filling, combine the pears, lemon juice, cornstarch, sugar, cinnamon, ginger, and cloves in a large bowl. Allow to sit at room temperature while you roll out the dough.

3. Place the dough between 2 sheets of plastic wrap and roll out to a ¼-inch-thick round. Line a 9-inch pie pan; there should be a 1-inch overhang of dough. Scrape the filling into the pie pan and sprinkle with the almonds. Fold the overhang over the filling. Chill the pie in the refrigerator while the oven heats up.

4. Preheat the oven to 375°F. Brush the top of the crust with heavy cream and sprinkle with Demerara sugar. Bake for about 45 minutes, until the edges of the pie are golden brown and the fruit is fork-tender. If, after about 25 to 30 minutes, the crust starts to get too brown before the filling is tender, tent the top of the pie with foil and continue baking.

SUGAR PIE

My grandmother never made this sticky-crisp pastry with leftover pie dough (possibly because she never made pie), but my recipe tester Jaimee's grandma LaVora Karn sure did. This is her recipe, spiced up with a touch of cinnamon. And it's a dazzler: Leftover butter pie pastry is smeared with brown sugar and more butter, then baked until gooey in the center and brown and flaky around the edges. It reminds me of a giant Pop-Tart, but oh so much better. Eat while warm, preferably by yourself. You won't want to share.

Sugar Pie

Piecrust scraps
2 to 6 tablespoons dark brown sugar
Ground cinnamon, to taste (optional)
1 to 3 tablespoons unsalted butter, chilled and diced

Time: 30 minutes

Serves 1 to 2

1. Roll the pie scraps together about $\frac{1}{8}$ inch thick. Sprinkle the sugar and cinnamon, if using, into the center of the dough and dot with the butter. Fold the edges of the dough over the filling and transfer to a pie pan or baking sheet. Using the tines of a fork, poke holes in the top of the crust to form an initial or a star. Chill in the refrigerator while the oven heats up.

2. Preheat the oven to 350°F. Bake the pie for 20 to 25 minutes, or until the crust is golden and the sugar begins to melt out.

TWENTY-INGREDIENT PIE (SPICED APPLE-PEAR-CRANBERRY CRUMB PIE)

When my sister and I were kids of about seven and eight, we earnestly decided that the very best pie in the world would be one made with twenty ingredients.

The number 20 was magical but not random. I don't remember exactly how we got there, but I think it was inspired by a book about a witches' brew, because eye of newt was one of our ingredients (my mother convinced us that raisins made a fine substitute).

Making such a pie required ransacking the cupboards, fridge, and fruit bowl to extract every variety of fruit, spice, and nut we could find until we had amassed enough volume to fill a (usually purchased) piecrust. Although twenty ingredients was the goal, it was seldom reached. We tended to give up around fifteen. But even so, the pies were amazing to our sugar-obsessed, little-girl taste buds.

This is my grown-up version. With my well-stocked pantry, hitting twenty was pretty easy. And I have to admit, this pie is a lot better than those thrown-together assemblages of my childhood (a homemade crust helps). Although the number 20 is nostalgic, it also makes sense here because the combination of apples, pears, cranberries, and rum raisins nestled beneath a nut and oat crumb topping is both harmonious and profound. The rich, autumnal flavors work really well together to make an urban-style harvest pie—perfect for Thanksgiving.

Twenty-Ingredient Pie (Spiced Apple-Pear-Cranberry Crumb Pie)

Time: 90 minutes

Serves 6 to 8

1 recipe Perfect Piecrust (see recipe, page 391)
½ cup golden raisins
½ cup dark raisins
⅓ cup dark rum
⅔ cup dark brown sugar
2 apples (about 1 pound), peeled, cored, and cut into ½-inch slices
2 large pears (about 1 pound), peeled, cored, and cut into ½-inch slices
⅔ cup fresh or frozen cranberries
3 tablespoons granulated sugar
2 tablespoons cornstarch
2 tablespoons freshly squeezed lemon juice
½ teaspoon ground cinnamon
¼ teaspoon ground ginger
¼ teaspoon freshly grated nutmeg
Pinch kosher salt

FOR THE CRUMB TOPPING
½ cup all-purpose flour
½ cup rolled oats
½ cup light brown sugar
¼ cup chopped toasted walnuts
1 teaspoon ground cinnamon
½ teaspoon freshly grated nutmeg
¼ teaspoon kosher salt
½ cup (1 stick) unsalted butter, chilled and cubed

1. On a lightly floured surface or between two sheets of plastic wrap, roll the pie dough into a ⅜-inch-thick round. Line a 9-inch pie pan with the dough, use your thumb and forefinger to flute the edges, and chill in the refrigera-

tor while you prepare the filling (or for up to 1 day; lightly cover the dough with plastic if leaving for more than 2 hours).

2. In a medium saucepan over medium-high heat, combine the raisins and rum with ⅓ cup water. Stir in the brown sugar and bring to a boil. Simmer, stirring occasionally, until the sugar is dissolved, then remove from the heat, cover, and let cool to room temperature.

3. In a large bowl, combine the apples, pears, cranberries, granulated sugar, cornstarch, lemon juice, cinnamon, ginger, nutmeg, and salt. When the raisin mixture has cooled, scrape it into the fruit mixture, tossing well to combine. Allow the fruit mixture to rest at room temperature while you bake the crust.

4. Preheat the oven to 375°F. Line the crust with foil, fill with pie weights, and place on a foil-lined baking sheet. Bake the crust until light golden brown, about 20 minutes. Take the pan out of the oven and remove the foil and weights.

5. Scrape the filling into the crust, piling the fruit into a mound in the center so it does not spill out. Return the pie to the oven and bake for 30 minutes.

6. Meanwhile, prepare the crumb topping. In a medium bowl, mix together the flour, oats, brown sugar, nuts, cinnamon, nutmeg, and salt. Using your fingers, rub the butter into the flour mixture until large crumbs form. Carefully remove the pie from the oven and sprinkle the crumb topping all over the filling. Return the pie to the oven and bake until the fruit is very tender and the juices are bubbling, another 30 to 35 minutes. Check after 20 minutes; if the crumb topping looks too brown, tent the pie with a sheet of foil. Allow the pie to cool for 25 to 30 minutes on a wire rack before serving.

KAREN'S PEANUT BUTTER PIE

Here is yet another swell recipe from my friend Karen Rush, who, until she finally decides to write her own cookbook, is a rich source for me to pilfer from (thanks, Karen!).

The long story of this amazing pie is that Karen got this recipe from Shelley Mihalik, a neighbor of hers in Pennsylvania where her husband Dave's family owns a country house. The country house used to be an old fishing lodge called Silver Lake House, and when Shelley was a teenager, she waited tables there in the summertime. Now she and her husband Greg own the Rileyville Country Market, where Shelley makes and sells a host of terrific pies, including this one.

One bite of this pie, which has a dense and luscious filling reminiscent of the center of a peanut butter bonbon and a crunchy chocolate cookie crust, and Karen knew she needed the recipe. Not wanted the recipe, but *needed* it in order to maintain her equilibrium and happiness. If she didn't get it, she'd obsessively dream about that pie all winter long until she could taste it again in the spring. And pining for pie doesn't do anybody any good.

The recipe was unbelievably simple—an uncooked mix of cream cheese, peanut butter, and cream is piled into a dark chocolate crust and topped with mini chocolate chips, which add just the right textural note to break up all the decadent whipped creaminess of the filling.

Since getting the recipe, I've made this pie almost a dozen times, tweaking it slightly along the way. Once I made it with Smucker's "natural" peanut butter instead of Jif, only because that's what we had in the fridge and I liked it even better—it had a deeper, more peanut-y flavor, even if the texture was not quite as satiny. I've also made it with almond butter, which gives it a toastier but mellower taste, and I like that, too.

Really, you cannot go wrong with this pie. It's nutty happiness in a chocolate crust.

Karen's Peanut Butter Pie

Time: 20 minutes,
plus additional
time for chilling

Serves 6 to 8

FOR THE CRUST

8 ounces chocolate wafer cookies (about 30 cookies)

6 tablespoons unsalted butter, melted

2 tablespoons sugar

FOR THE FILLING

1 cup (8 ounces) smooth peanut butter (preferably natural style),
   at room temperature

8 ounces cream cheese, at room temperature

1/3 cup sugar

1 1/2 teaspoons vanilla extract

1 cup heavy cream, cold

1/2 cup mini chocolate chips or chopped honey-roasted peanuts,
   for garnishing

1. Preheat the oven to 350°F and generously butter a 9-inch pie pan.

2. To make the crust, crush the cookies into crumbs using a food processor, or place them in a plastic bag and roll over them with a rolling pin until crumbled. Mix the cookie crumbs with the butter and sugar until thoroughly combined. Press the mixture into the prepared pie pan, going up the sides as far as possible. Bake until the crust is firm, 8 to 10 minutes. Cool on a wire rack.

3. To make the filling, using an electric mixer, cream together the peanut butter, cream cheese, sugar, and vanilla. In a separate bowl, whip the cream until soft peaks form. Using a spatula, fold the cream into the peanut butter mixture until completely combined. Scrape the filling into the cooled crust and smooth with the spatula. Sprinkle mini chocolate chips or chopped

honey-roasted peanuts or both, if desired, on top. Refrigerate for at least 20 minutes and up to overnight before serving.

VARIATION: **CHOCOLATE—ALMOND BUTTER PIE**
Substitute almond butter for the peanut butter and, if you like, chopped salted almonds for the roasted peanuts.

WHOLE LEMON TART
FOR MY MOTHER

Everyone has their favorite sweet flavor. For some it's chocolate; for others it's toasted nuts or berries or coconut. Generally, I'm a caramel person, though I'm easily swayed. But my mother is a hard-and-fast lemon lover of the extreme kind, and her favorite way to eat lemon is in lemon tart.

It probably started with my grandmother Lilly, who, although not much of a dessert maker, could manage to turn out a mean lemon meringue pie. This childhood predisposition left my mother prone to fall in love with French lemon tarts during my parents' first visit to France after they both graduated from medical school. There, in the company of my mother's aunt Martha and uncle Jack, she fell for the country's classic, puckery, curd-filled, and shiny glazed lemon tarts that were even better, she thought, without the cloying and froufrou meringue swirls on top.

Since then, every summer on vacation in France, where our family exchanged houses with unknown French families in small towns all over the country, we ate lemon tarts. It was methodical. We'd take stock of every pastry shop in striking distance, then taste through their lemon tarts for an entire month, until we decided which lemon tart was the best of the neighborhood.

This gave me a deep schooling in French lemon tarts, and by the time I was ten, I knew exactly what made them good.

First off, the glaze, if present, needs to be thin, not gloppy, and when you bite into it, the curd underneath should jolt your tongue awake with citrus zinginess. If you don't blink hard in surprise from the sourness, it is too sweet. The curd's texture should be silky, and if there are any lumps, they should be bits of grated lemon zest and nothing else. And finally, the crust should be crumbly like a shortbread but thin and delicate and a little sweet to offset the lemon's tanginess.

Tasting dozens of lemon tarts to find the best was one thing, but as soon as I started on my pie-baking binge, I decided it was high time for me to master a family recipe, one that I could whip up for my mother's birthday and/or Mother's Day for as long as she still loved lemon above all other flavors.

It's been over a decade since I happened on this sweet-tart version, which has all the necessary lemon tart qualities, and is extremely easy as well. Instead of making a separate curd on top of the stove and then baking that into the crust, as most lemon tart recipes have you do, in this one, the filling is whirled together in the food processor, then cooked in the oven directly in the almond-scented crust.

In the baking process, the filling takes on an attractive golden brown hue, which in my mind obviates the need for any glaze. But if you are the shimmering type, you can paint on some melted and strained lemon or ginger marmalade when the tart is perfectly cooled.

My mother, however, prefers a simple dusting of confectioners' sugar over the top. Its pure whiteness reminds her of her mother's lemon meringue pie. And when it comes to pie, nostalgia is almost everything.

Whole Lemon Tart for My Mother

Time: 1 hour,
plus cooling time

Makes 1 (9-inch) tart
Serves 8

FOR THE ALMOND TART SHELL

1½ cups all-purpose flour

½ cup blanched almonds

⅓ cup confectioners' sugar

Freshly grated zest of ½ lemon

Pinch salt

½ cup (1 stick) unsalted butter, cold and cubed

1 large egg, lightly beaten

FOR THE LEMON FILLING

2 large lemons

1¼ cups granulated sugar (or use 1⅓ cups if you like a slightly sweeter tart)

2 tablespoons cornstarch

Pinch kosher salt

½ cup (1 stick) unsalted butter, melted

1 large egg

2 large egg yolks

1 tablespoon vanilla extract

Confectioners' sugar, for dusting (optional)

1. To make the tart shell, place ¼ cup flour and the almonds in a food processor with the blade attachment. Run the motor until the almonds are finely ground, about 1 minute. Add the remaining 1¼ cups flour, sugar, lemon zest, and salt, and pulse to combine.

2. Add the butter and pulse until a coarse meal forms. Add the egg and pulse just until a crumbly dough comes together. Press the dough into a disc, wrap in plastic, and chill for 1 hour or overnight.

3. When ready to bake the tart, roll the dough out between two sheets of plastic to a ⅜-inch thickness. Line a 9-inch tart pan with the dough and chill for 30 minutes.

4. Preheat the oven to 325°F. Line the tart shell with foil and fill with baking weights. Bake until the tart shell is pale golden, 20 to 25 minutes. The tart shell can be baked up to 8 hours before filling.

5. To make the filling, grate the lemon zest and place it in the bowl of a food processor. Using a sharp knife, cut the tops and bottoms off the lemons. Stand each lemon up and follow the curve of the fruit with the knife to remove the white pith. Cut the fruit into segments, removing the seeds. Place the fruit in the bowl of the food processor and add the sugar, cornstarch, and salt. Run the motor until thoroughly combined. Scrape the mixture into a large mixing bowl.

6. In a separate bowl, whisk together the butter, egg, egg yolks, and vanilla. Pour the butter-egg mixture into the lemon mixture and whisk to combine. Pour the lemon filling into the tart shell and bake until the top is bubbly and lightly browned, 25 to 30 minutes. Allow the tart to cool completely in the pan before serving. Dust with confectioners' sugar just before serving, if desired.

12 Lessons in Imbibing

Like many Jewish kids, the first time I got drunk, it was from nips of Manischewitz at the Passover seder. I was probably nine, and discovered that the viscous, syrupy wine from my uncle Alan's cup was vastly tastier than the purple grape juice in mine. He let me have only a few slurps, but it was enough to set off a fit of giggles that lasted until I fell asleep on the couch. I remember being awakened for the afikomen, too dazed to bargain in my usual hard-driving manner, and sad about missing the rest of the dinner.

I learned to enjoy dry wine when I was a teenager, small amounts sipped with my parents at dinner. I liked the grown-up way it made me feel as I'd try to tease out the tastes they could identify—roses and cherries and earth.

By the time I got to be a senior in high school and my fake ID granted me access to the seediest bars in the East Village, I thought I had it all down when it came to booze. In an awkward attempt toward sophistication, I spurned honest pints of beer in favor of vermouth-cassis, a vile, chilled pink kirlike libation garnished with a twist.

College brought to my attention the usual array of blender drinks, white wine spritzers, and strange cocktails with names like Fluffy Ruffles and Piccadilly lifted from the pages of *Mr. Boston*. And with graduate school came an appreciation of brown spirits—single malt scotches, single barrel bourbon, aged rum.

I never did, and still don't, see the point to vodka, which disappears into the mixer almost without a trace. If there's one thing I've learned it's that I like to taste the alcohol in what I drink. It helps me keep track of how much I'm imbibing so I don't end up asleep on the couch, missing out on the fun. My earliest lesson in drink has proved to be the most important, ever since I started drinking out of my own glass.

HOMEMADE MARASCHINO CHERRIES

"Maraschino cherries? Why bother?"

This was not the effusive response I was looking for when I mentioned that I was going to undertake a homemade version that weekend.

"What would you use them in besides Shirley Temples, anyway?" my friend added, wrinkling her nose.

Though she forgot about Manhattans and Rob Roys, she had a point. Homemade maraschino cherries is not the most practical of recipes. Then again, being the kind who occasionally bakes her own graham crackers, I'm not always the most practical of cooks.

But making maraschino cherries wasn't about practicality. And it wasn't about trying to mimic those vinyl-textured, frighteningly neon, and once potentially poisonous (remember red dye #2?) vermilion orbs. It was about, in part, trying to recapture the glory of a faded confection.

A century ago, maraschino cherries were concocted from Croatian marasca cherries macerated in fragrant liqueur of the same fruit. When added to cocktails and desserts, they were a luxurious, elegant touch, not a complacent or ironic one. A confluence of events—the temperance movement, a glut of Oregon cherries, and a preserving process that involved oceans of lipstick red dye, corn syrup, and almond extract—conspired to give us a cocktail garnish arguably more prized for its long, tongue-tieable stem than the poor misused fruit itself.

History aside, what I really wanted was something delectable to float in my Manhattan. Thus, making my own maraschino cherries in the height of fresh cherry season seemed like a worthy pursuit.

Before I set out on that sticky path, however, I surfed online to see what might be the best substitute for the black, sour, and unavailable marasca. Opinions varied from fresh sweet cherries to jarred or frozen sour cherries, to plumped-up dried tart cherries. Toby Cecchini, who published an article on maraschinos in the *Times* magazine several years ago, used frozen dark

in IMBIBING

419

sweet cherries. Few mentioned what to me seemed the obvious substitute—fresh sour cherries. But likely that's because fresh sour cherry season is about three weeks long. And then there's all that pitting.

As for the maraschino liqueur, no problem. On the way to the greenmarket, I'd stop at my local liquor store on Flatbush Avenue and pick some up.

It turns out, finding maraschino liqueur in Brooklyn was harder than finding fresh sour cherries in January. I eventually located some in Manhattan, the fancy Luxardo brand that cocktail aficionados swear by.

I also picked up a pint of brandy to make spiced brandied sweet cherries, which are perfect for gilding things like pistachio gelato and pound cake—especially during the icy swamp of winter, when a homemade spirit-preserved cherry feels like July sunshine in your mouth.

Ingredients in hand, I set to pitting. I wish I could now write that after pitting several pints of cherries both sour and sweet, I had developed a brilliant shortcut. But alas, there is nothing to do but give in to the project, and plan on scarlet fingertips for twelve hours afterward. (And by the way, jarred pitted sour cherries work reasonably well, too, though they end up more flaccid.)

Once the cherries were pitted, I had another maraschino decision to make. Did I want to macerate the sour cherries like my brandied sweet ones, by bringing the alcohol to a gentle simmer before pouring it over the fruit? Or did I want to do like my online sources, and keep everything cold? I opted to heat the maraschino, which I knew would hasten the maceration time and further impregnate the cherries with booze.

I made a mason jar full of each—maraschino sour and brandied sweet—and hid them in the refrigerator for two days to ripen. Then I stirred a cocktail and pulled out the maraschinos. Both the liquid and cherries glowed Kool-Aid red, vaguely recalling their fluorescent commercial counterparts.

But that's where the resemblance ended. They were seductively crisp-textured, and steeped with an exotic, piney, floral flavor that was just sweet enough but balanced by the tart tang of the cherry.

Sublime in my Manhattan, they were even better over coconut sorbet, and I got giddy imagining them piled on top of an adult ice cream sundae. And I'm definitely inviting my naysayer friend over for Shirley Temples to prove that the best things are worth the bother.

Homemade Maraschino Cherries

Time: 20 minutes,
plus 2 days'
macerating

Makes about 1 pint

1 cup maraschino liqueur

1 pint sour cherries, stemmed and pitted, or substitute 1 (24-ounce) jar
    sour cherries in light syrup, drained

Bring the maraschino liqueur to a simmer in a small pot. Turn off the heat and
add the cherries. Let the mixture cool, then store in a jar in the refrigerator for
at least 2 days before using, and up to several months.

Homemade Spiced Brandied Cherries

Time: 20 minutes,
plus 2 days'
macerating

Makes about 1 quart

1 cup sugar

2 whole cloves

2-inch piece cinnamon stick

4 cardamom pods

1 quart sweet cherries, stemmed and pitted

½ cup Cognac or other aged brandy

1. In a small saucepan, combine the sugar and spices with a cup of water. Bring
   to a simmer, stirring until the sugar dissolves. Let simmer for 5 minutes.
2. Turn off the heat and add the cherries and brandy to the pot. Let cool, then
   store the mixture in a jar in the refrigerator for at least 2 days before eating,
   and up to several months. These are great over ice cream.

RYE MANHATTAN

Ask any hipster bartender worth his arm garters what's the best booze to mix into a Manhattan and the answer will be rye. Although bourbon has usurped rye as today's Manhattan foundation, rye has history. According to David Wondrich, the erudite cocktail historian (and my friend and neighbor), when the Manhattan cocktail was created in 1874, it was made with rye whiskey, the most popular spirit of the era. This was a good thing. Bourbon Manhattans, opines Dave, are so sickly sweet that no amount of fiddling with the bitters and vermouth can save them. Luckily, there are a number of excellent rye whiskies on the market, and if you can find a high proof rye, Dave recommends that above all (don't plan on operating any heavy machinery after your tipple).

This is my husband Daniel's adaptation of Dave's Manhattan, jiggered to meet our exact tastes. Daniel makes a lot of these, especially in winter when cocktails infused with brown spirits warm the soul better than white spirits (or so we think). Garnished with a homemade maraschino cherry, it redeems even the most frustrating, exhausting, harried day.

Rye Manhattan

2 ounces rye whiskey, plus a dash

1 scant ounce sweet vermouth

2 dashes angostura bitters

1 maraschino cherry, preferably homemade

Serves 1

Stir the rye, vermouth, and bitters well with plenty of cracked ice. Strain into a chilled cocktail glass and garnish with a cherry.

KUMQUAT-CLEMENTINE
CORDIAL

In a blissful and more organized alternate reality that I do not inhabit, I would have thought about the holidays in August. That's when, surrounded by ripe, seasonal fruit, I could have turned it into a delightful elixir—maybe peach and lemon verbena wine, or a sour cherry ratafia—to distribute to my nearest and dearest in December and bring joy their world.

But alas, this holiday gift inspiration bubbled up long past the prime of peaches and cherries.

Still, I liked the idea of a homemade libation. Even more than cookies, it would be a present that nearly everyone on my grown-up list would actually want (and easier to make in volume than dozens of cookies). Certainly a bottle of my homemade brew would trump everyone else's predictable Champagne single malt offerings in a far more elegant and economical manner.

Since citrus is some of the best fresh fruit available in December, I decided I'd finally try out a provençal orange wine I'd read about several years ago in Mireille Johnston's classic cookbook *The Cuisine of the Sun*. The recipe, I remembered, was easy. Just mix up fresh citrus with white wine, brandy, and sugar and let it macerate.

The problem, I discovered when I dug out the recipe, was the rather biblical forty days' maceration time.

What I needed was an abridged recipe that I could whip up in an hour and that would be ready in a week.

Sadly, Ms. Johnston's text didn't offer any shortcuts. But flipping through the book, I noticed another recipe for an orange liqueur where the fruit was steeped in brandy (without wine) with coriander seeds. The headnote advised drinking this whenever one "feels melancholy, anxious, or even merry—truly wonderful for all occasions."

It seemed too good to pass up. Except the maceration time was an even longer two months.

Still, the more I thought about it, the more I wondered whether it really needed that much resting time. After all, shouldn't a mixture of citrus juice, good-quality booze, and sugar taste good from the moment it is made? In fact, isn't that what's known in most circles as a cocktail?

I supposed the coriander or other spices would need some time to infuse, as would the citrus. And even if my homemade concoction—which I starting calling a cordial in my head because I liked the quaint sound of it—wasn't quite ready, I could always keep it for another forty days and drink it myself. It certainly wouldn't go to waste.

At the greengrocer where I went to pick up oranges, I got distracted by a profusion of more exotic citrus—pomelos, blood oranges, kumquats. With its alliterative allure, kumquat cordial sounded more intriguing than orange cordial and more euphonious than pomelo cordial, so I bought a box of those instead.

Then, at the liquor store, I bought several bottles to play around with: white rum, Cognac, and bourbon. I also got some gin, which I figured would be nice with coriander.

Once at home, I sliced the kumquats very thinly, figuring that smaller pieces of fruit would infuse more quickly and could be stuffed into the necks of the decorative bottles I picked up to house the cordial.

As I was slicing, I realized a kumquat's flavor was in its thick, fragrant skin and not in the minuscule amount of juice. If I wanted my cordials quickly, I would need to supplement with another citrus juice. A bowl of clementines on my counter was quickly dispatched.

I also decided to play around with different combinations of spices in addition to coriander. With its flowery shape, star anise would look pretty in the bottle, so I added that, along with cinnamon, the coriander, and allspice berries.

Then I capped the bottles and left them on the counter, giving them a good shake every day to encourage the infusing.

A week later, I poured myself a nip of each one. Even in that short amount of time, the flavors had metamorphosed into something deeply perfumed and rich with spice and citrus. There was just enough sugar to smooth out the alcohol, but not so much as to make it cloying. They were marvelous on their own, but I could also see using the cordials as a base for a Champagne

424

kumquat cocktail (just top with sparkling wine), or spiked with boiling water for a modern-day toddy. And how could they be bad over vanilla ice cream?

Although I didn't succeed in making the orange liqueur à la Mireille Johnston, my cordials still fit her description to a T—truly wonderful for all occasions.

Kumquat-Clementine Cordial

Time: 10 minutes, plus 1 week macerating

Makes about 2 cups
Serves 12

¼ cup sugar, preferably superfine
3 tablespoons clementine juice (from 1 to 2 clementines)
6 kumquats, thinly sliced and seeded
1 clementine, thinly sliced
1¾ cups white rum (375 ml)
3 whole allspice berries
2 whole star anise, broken in half if necessary to fit through the bottle neck

1. Have ready a glass bottle with a cork or jar with a lid for macerating. Place the sugar in a large glass measuring cup or bowl. Stir in 1 tablespoon boiling water for 1 minute. Add the clementine juice and continue stirring until the sugar dissolves, about 1 minute longer.

2. If using a bottle for storage, shove the kumquat and clementine slices through the top (you might have to curl them into cylinders first). Add the sugar syrup and remaining ingredients. Shake once a day for a week before serving.

3. Serve as is, over ice, with a splash of seltzer, topped with chilled white wine or sparkling wine, or as a hot toddy topped with boiling water.

VARIATIONS: To make a brandy cordial, substitute brandy for rum, and replace the spices with 1 cinnamon stick and 1 whole clove. For a gin version, substitute gin for the brandy, reduce the sugar to 3 tablespoons, and replace the spices with 3 peppercorns and 6 coriander seeds. For bourbon, use 3 tablespoons sugar and replace the allspice with a cinnamon stick.

CHOCOLATE EGG CREAM

Despite all the sepia-toned, misty-eyed New York City nostalgia surrounding the egg cream, all it is, really, is a cold glass of chocolate milk spiked with seltzer and stirred until the top bubbles and froths like beaten egg white. (I write, naturally, of chocolate egg cream; I am aware that vanilla ones exist, though their appeal baffles me.)

Like most sweet-toothed Brooklyn natives, I spent my childhood sucking down egg creams at newsstands and luncheonettes, often accompanied by my favorite diner lunch: bacon on a toasted, buttered bagel. Since I was not aware of the egg cream's iconic ties with Jewish cuisine, I didn't realize how thoroughly *treyf* my meal was, though I did appreciate the sweet-salty contrast of the bacon and the U-Bet's chocolate syrup.

Since egg creams were so ubiquitous in my five-borough existence, I assumed they were a staple for kids all over the country. Didn't everyone slurp them up when they were kids?

Going to college set me straight. There were people—like, lots of them—who'd never even heard of an egg cream, let alone tried one. And if they had heard of the drink, they assumed it would contain both eggs and cream. It doesn't, and never has. Egg creams are nothing if not sweetly ironic.

Given this enormous lack, I made it my personal mission to introduce my non–New Yorker Barnard classmates to the egg cream, which back then was available in diners on the stretch of Broadway below the campus before the big box stores invaded. For the most part, my new friends were grateful, though I'll admit that not everyone was as smitten with the drink as I am. But there's just no accounting for taste.

All of this was a long time ago. Now it's nearly impossible to find an egg cream, even in Brooklyn. When you do, it's inevitably at some retro-themed place and made by someone who likely isn't schooled in the proper egg cream proportions of syrup, milk, and seltzer.

Because of this sad state of affairs, I make my egg creams at home, keeping a bottle of U-Bet chocolate syrup in the door of the fridge at all times. You just never know when the egg cream urge is going to strike.

Chocolate Egg Cream

Serves 4

¾ cup U-Bet chocolate syrup (see Note), chilled
3 cups whole milk, chilled
2 to 3 cups seltzer water, as needed

Divide the chocolate syrup into the bottoms of four tall glasses (3 tablespoons per glass). Top each with ¾ cup milk, then fill with seltzer water to the top of each glass. Use a long-handled spoon to stir briskly. Serve immediately with a straw.

NOTE: If you cannot find Fox's U-Bet chocolate syrup, you can easily make your own. In a small saucepan over medium heat, bring 1 cup water and ½ cup sugar to a boil, whisking until the sugar is dissolved. Whisk in ⅔ cup unsweetened cocoa powder (preferably Dutch process) and ¼ teaspoon kosher salt. Simmer, whisking, until the mixture is slightly thickened, 5 to 10 minutes. Remove from the heat and stir in 1 teaspoon vanilla. Cool to room temperature, then transfer to the refrigerator to chill thoroughly.

VARIATION: MOCHA EGG CREAM
Add a shot of espresso to each glass along with the chocolate syrup. This is the best pick-me-up I know.

COCONUT HOT CHOCOLATE

A few years ago, I asked my husband Daniel what sweet treat he wanted me to make for him on Valentine's Day.

Anything you crave, I promised, offering homemade chocolate tortes, dense chocolate truffles, mini raspberry tarts, nut-filled, heart-shaped cookies covered in confectioners' sugar.

"What I'd really like," he said, "is hot chocolate."

Compared to my rather elaborate list of confections, this would seem like a simple request.

But Daniel doesn't eat cream. Or milk. Or soy milk, rice milk, or nut milk, for that matter. And making a really good hot chocolate without any of these wasn't, at least to me, an obvious maneuver.

My first thought was to skip the dairy and use water. After all, I'd often read that in pre-Columbian Mesoamerica, chocolate was consumed primarily as a frothy, water-based beverage thickened with grains and sweetened with honey. Milk is a relatively recent, European addition.

To find a recipe with some measure of authenticity, I turned to food historian Maricel Presilla's fascinating book *The New Taste of Chocolate: A Cultural and Natural History of Cacao with Recipes* (Ten Speed Press, 2001).

There were several dairyless hot chocolate concoctions, rich with spices like anise, dried rosebuds, and cinnamon. But all of them also called for obscure ingredients—whole cacao beans and a toasted corn flour called pinole, for example. And I didn't have time to track them down before V-Day arrived.

Then I remembered a sophisticated creamless version I learned from a French chocolatier. Milk, he sneered, murders the finer nuances of premium-quality chocolate.

I didn't necessarily agree. But since I didn't have a better idea, I followed his instructions, mixing together cocoa powder and sugar with boiling water, then stirring in chopped 70 percent cocoa mass chocolate until it melted.

This hot chocolate was dark and concentrated, with a pronounced bitter edge. It was so intense that I served it in espresso cups.

Daniel and I sipped our tiny portions. It was good, in an austere, highly adult way. But it wasn't the luscious hot chocolate of our dreams.

The following year, I tried again, adding beaten egg yolks to the water-based mixture in hopes of a hot chocolate closer to my creamy yet creamless ideal. But I added too many and ended up with pudding.

Any normal person might have given up. But with Valentine's Day rounding the corner again, I wanted to give it one more go.

Thinking back to those pre-Columbian recipes, I picked up Ms. Presilla's book. While flipping through the pages, I spotted a recipe for chocolate-coconut soup made with coconut milk.

Coconut milk! It's creamy yet dairy free, and easy to find; and, as any Mounds bar lover will attest, coconut is a fantastic match with chocolate.

I mixed up a batch that very night, using the sneering chocolatier's recipe but substituting coconut milk for some of the water. It was fudgy, decadent, slightly bitter from the cocoa, and very, very creamy.

It was a cup of hot chocolate good enough to serve to my lactose-free valentine. And that's really saying something.

Coconut Hot Chocolate

Time: 15 minutes

Serves 2

2 tablespoons cocoa powder

1 (15-ounce) can coconut milk

1/4 cup dark brown sugar

Pinch kosher salt

1 ounce bittersweet chocolate, chopped (about 1/4 cup)

1 teaspoon vanilla extract

Meringue Topping (recipe follows), optional

1. Whisk the cocoa powder into 1/3 cup boiling water.
2. In a saucepan, combine the coconut milk, sugar, and salt. Simmer, stirring, until the sugar is dissolved, about 2 minutes. Whisk in the cocoa

mixture and chocolate until smooth and hot. Stir in the vanilla. Serve with the Meringue Topping, if you like.

Meringue Topping

1 large egg white (see Note)
3 tablespoons superfine sugar

Time: 5 minutes

Makes about 1 cup

Use an electric mixer on medium speed to beat the egg white until it begins to foam, about 1 minute. Add the sugar tablespoon by tablespoon as the mixer is running. Continue to beat until the egg white stiffens to soft peaks and is shiny, about 5 minutes.

NOTE: If you started with a whole egg and you'd like an even richer hot chocolate, whisk the egg yolk into the mixture after you've taken it off the heat. Make sure to whisk vigorously so it doesn't clump. If it does, strain before serving.

VARIATION: COCONUT MERINGUE EGGNOG

Valentine's Day is not the only torturously cream-filled day of the year for Daniel. Christmas Eve, with everyone diving into the eggnog bowl, is another. With its mountainous blobs of whipped cream and milk, my traditional eggnog recipe is poison for my husband. Every year, I feel a little guilty about serving it when he can't partake—not guilty enough to abstain altogether, mind you, but bad enough to try to come up with a substitute.

After my hot chocolate success, the answer was obvious: Substitute coconut milk for the regular milk and a frothy egg white meringue for the whipped cream. The result is both rich and buoyant, with fluffy meringue pockets bobbing in the satiny custard. This recipe is rather restrained with the booze. If you like more punch, feel free to embellish.

Coconut Meringue Eggnog

3 (13.5-ounce) cans coconut milk

8 eggs

1/3 cup plus 1 tablespoon sugar, plus additional to taste

1/8 teaspoon kosher salt

4 teaspoons vanilla extract

1/2 cup rum

2 tablespoons brandy

Freshly grated nutmeg, for garnish

1. In a small saucepan over medium-low heat, bring the milk to a simmer.
2. Separate the eggs, reserving 8 yolks and 4 whites (reserve the remaining 4 whites for another use). In a large bowl, whisk together the yolks and 1/3 cup sugar. Whisking constantly, slowly pour the milk into the sugar mixture until fully incorporated. Whisk in the salt.
3. Return the mixture to the pot over medium heat. Cook, stirring constantly with a spatula or wooden spoon, scraping the bottom and sides of the pot, until the mixture is thick enough to coat the back of a spoon, 5 to 10 minutes. Strain through a fine-mesh sieve into a large bowl. Cool to lukewarm before stirring in the vanilla.
4. Using an electric mixer, beat the 4 egg whites with 1 tablespoon sugar until soft peaks form. Gently fold the whipped whites, rum, and brandy into the custard. Ladle the eggnog into cups and serve, garnished with nutmeg.

BIBLIOGRAPHY

Beranbaum, Rose Levy. *The Cake Bible*. New York: William Morrow Cookbooks, 1988.
———. *The Pie and Pastry Bible*. New York: Scribner, 1998.
Bsisu, May S. *The Arab Table: Recipes and Culinary Traditions*. New York: William Morrow Cookbooks, 2005.
Colwin, Laurie. *Home Cooking: A Writer in the Kitchen*. New York: Knopf, 1988.
Greenspan, Dorrie. *Baking: From My Home to Yours*. New York: Houghton Mifflin, 2006.
Haedrich, Ken. *Pie: 300 Tried-and-True Recipes for Delicious Homemade Pie*. Boston, MA: Harvard Common Press, 2004.
Heatter, Maida. *Maida Heatter's Book of Great Chocolate Desserts*. Kansas City, MO: Andrews McMeel Publishing, 2006.
Johnston, Mireille. *The Cuisine of the Sun: Classical French Cooking from Nice and Provence*. Newton, MA: Biscuit Books, Incorporated, 1996.
Lundy, Ronni. *Butter Beans to Blackberries: Recipes from the Southern Garden*. New York: North Point Press, 1999.
Machlin, Edda Servi. *The Classic Cuisine of the Italian Jews*. New York: Giro Press, 1993.
Madison, Deborah. *Vegetarian Cooking for Everyone*. New York: Broadway Books, 2007.
Marks, Gil. *The World of Jewish Cooking: More Than 500 Traditional Recipes from Alsace to Yemen*. New York: Simon & Schuster, 1999.
Mehta, Jehangir. *Mantra: The Rules of Indulgence*. New York: Ecco Books, 2008.
Presilla, Maricel. *The New Taste of Chocolate: A Cultural and Natural History of Cacao with Recipes*. San Francisco, CA: Ten Speed Press, 2001.
Schwartz, Arthur. *Jewish Home Cooking: Yiddish Recipes Revisited*. San Francisco, CA: Ten Speed Press, 2008.
Smith, Bill. *Seasoned in the South: Recipes from Crook's Corner and from Home*. Chapel Hill, NC: Algonquin Books of Chapel Hill, 2005.
Wechsberg, Joseph. *Blue Trout and Black Truffles*. Chicago, IL: Academy Chicago Publishers, 1985 (originally published in 1953).
Wolfert, Paula. *Couscous and Other Good Food from Morocco*. New York: William Morrow, 1987.

INDEX